INDIRA GANDHI

An Era of
CONSTITUTIONAL DICTATORSHIP

Attention Authors

'We Convert Fighters into Writers'. That's the motto of Manas Publications since more than four decades. Our message to the world is that India can win the battle not only by the bullet but also by the pen. There is no dearth of intellectuals in our country, but their knowledge is confined to them only. No sincere effort has been made by any other publisher to channelise their knowledge in national interest. That is why the talent of a large number of intellectuals remains latent. An author transforms his knowledge into a manuscript, and it is our job to spread his/her knowledge by converting it into a beautiful book. For over four decades, Manas has been motivating the intellectuals by publishing their manuscripts and would like to publish your manuscript too. If you or your colleagues have any manuscript ready for publication or are working on it, kindly contact us with detailed synopsis and list of contents. We will transform your work into a valuable publication. If you wish, we can also suggest you the suitable subjects for writing the books related to your area of expertise. Manas is known for its publishing quality and commitments. We take utmost care in production and give wide publicity to the book as well as its author through our national and international distribution network.

INDIRA GANDHI

An Era of
CONSTITUTIONAL DICTATORSHIP

Madhav Godbole, IAS (Retd)
Former Home Secretary & Secretary Justice, Govt of India

Manas Publications
(We Convert Fighters into Writers)
New Delhi - 110 002 (INDIA)

MANAS PUBLICATIONS
(We Convert Fighters into Writers)
(Publishers, Library Suppliers, Importers & Exporters)
4402/5-A, Ansari Road (Opp. HDFC Bank)
Darya Ganj, New Delhi - 110 002 (India)
Phones: Off.: 011-23260783, 23265523, Res.: 011-23842660
E-mail: manaspublications@gmail.com
manaspublications@yahoo.com
Website: www.manaspublications.in

ISBN 978-81-7049-550-5
₹ 995

Designed by
Veronica Grafic Arts

Printed in India at
R.K. Print Services, Delhi
and published by Mrs Suman Lata for
Manas Publications
4402/5-A, Ansari Road (Opp HDFC Bank),
Darya Ganj, New Delhi - 110 002 (INDIA)

For

SUJATA

Books by the Author

1. *Secularism: India at a Crossroads*, 2016
2. *The God Who Failed – An Assessment of Jawaharlal Nehru's Leadership*, 2014
3. *Good Governance: Never on India's Radar*, 2014
4. *India's Parliamentary Democracy on Trial*, 2011
5. *The Judiciary and Governance in India*, 2008
6. *The Holocaust of Indian Partition: An Inquest*, 2006
7. *Public Accountability and Transparency – The Imperatives of Good Governance*, 2003
8. *The Changing Times – A Commentary on Current Affairs*, 2000
9. *Unfinished Innings – Recollections and Reflections of a Civil Servant*, 1996
10. *Rural Employment Strategy – A Quest in the Wilderness*, 1990
11. *Public Expenditures in Maharashtra – A Case for Expenditure Strategy*, 1989
12. *Industrial Dispersal Policies*, 1978

Preface

The birth centenary year of Indira Gandhi, 2017, saw a stream of books on her. A reader may well ask: "Is this just another book on her?" Indira Gandhi's turbulent and highly controversial stewardship was a memorable period of India's post-independence history and inevitably led to large and incisive writings on her, even as compared to Mahatma Gandhi and Jawaharlal Nehru. Varied facets of her career have been explored therein. One may therefore ask, what is new in this book.

One can 'reinvent' facts in this age of reality, imagined reality, facts and alternate facts, my truth, your truth, half truth, convenient truth, inconvenient truth, truth-after-the event and so on. But I have done no such thing. My emphasis has been on analysing the events dispassionately, apolitically, and in as detached a manner as possible. During the period, I had worked with Y.B. Chavan, when he was Home and Finance Minister in Indira Gandhi Cabinet. I also worked with S.B. Chavan, when he was the Chief Minister of Maharashtra, during the Emergency. I was Joint Secretary, Department of Economic Affairs, Ministry of Finance, handling World Bank matters when bank assistance was sought for the fertiliser projects. I have known and interacted with a number of officers and public figures who worked with her. These insights find reflection in the book.

My focus is on two aspects – close look at multiple facets of Indira Gandhi's personality which often create an impression of a split personality, and analysing what remains of her highly controversial legacy. The major part of her legacy is debilitating, dreadful, and shattering. This is an ever-lasting burden India has to carry. During her life-time, she was hailed as 'Goddess Durga', 'the Empress of India', 'the most powerful woman in the world', 'woman of millennium', 'the only man in her Cabinet' and so on. Political power, howsoever exhilarating, intoxicating and maddening it may be for the person wielding it, is ephemeral. In the assessment of a person by history, it becomes just a footnote. What matters is the enduring impact of a person on the well-being of the society, its governance, political and public life, and its institutions.

Public opinion surveys conducted from time to time are often misleading and serve the purpose of satisfying the egos of the leaders, and are a result of image-building efforts by political parties, their followers and the media. But the judgment of history is harsh. History is unkind, merciless and ruthless in its assessment.

Desire to bequeath a lasting legacy is a trait of most politicians. This was evident from the time-capsules buried by Indira Gandhi and Narendra Modi. The first called *Kalapatra* was buried on 15 August 1973 inside the Red Fort. It was taken out when the Janata government came to power in 1977. Though no authentic details are available, it was reported that it contained glowing references to the accomplishments of Indira Gandhi and Jawaharlal Nehru. The second time-capsule was buried in the foundation of Mahatma Mandir in Gandhinagar. It was alleged that it was mostly about Modi and his tenure as Chief Minister.

But, public perception of a leader's legacy is often quite different than the official version contained in time-capsules.

As for the supposedly most powerful political office in the world, American presidency, Lyndon Johnson's legacy is remembered as Vietnam war; Jimmy Carter's as Iran hostage crisis; Richard Nixon's as Watergate and not the opening of American doors to China; Ronald Reagan's as 'tear down this [Berlin] wall'; George W. Bush's as Iraq war and the axis of evil; and Obama's as health care. As for India, Nehru's legacy in popular perception is the humiliating defeat by China, and the intractable Kashmir problem, and not laying the foundations of parliamentary democracy and secularism; Rajiv Gandhi's Bofors and Muslim Women's Divorce Act, V.P. Singh's as Mandal Commission, and P.V. Narasimha Rao's as the demolition of Babri Masjid and economic reforms.

Indira Gandhi was Prime Minister for sixteen years. Declaration of Internal Emergency is not her only legacy, as has been largely written about over the years. Her legacy is evident in diverse areas of public life. Her tenure saw rewriting of not just the history but also the Constitution of India. She rewrote the rules of the game for most institutions. She changed the political culture of the country. Over the years, several of these scars have become deeper and more pronounced. As I see, her enduring achievements are in areas of national security – the peaceful atomic explosion, space programme, strides in the scientific fields such as Antarctic expedition and setting up of a research station there. Her contribution to sustainable development, nature and wild life conservation, was notable at the time when these concepts had not caught the public imagination. Notably, all these were removed from politics.

Prima facie, in terms of his stature and popularity at home and abroad and grip over government and his party, Narendra Modi's style of functioning resembles that of Indira Gandhi but such a superficial comparison hides more than what it reveals. There are some basic differences in the make-up of the two leaders.

One thing which intrigued me most while studying Indira Gandhi was her dual or even multiple personality. As a person, she comes off as a highly sensitive, likable, loving, family woman. She had keen interest in poetry, music, painting, literature and other fine arts. She was well read and articulate. The other side of her personality, which came out in her political dealings, was quite the opposite. She was scheming, suspicious of everyone around, with a tremendous feeling of insecurity, devoid of any scruples and sense of values. How these totally different personas lived together and were at ease with each other is a mystery. Interestingly, she herself was aware of this phenomenon. Indira Gandhi will ever remain an enigma.

In writing this book, I have tried to look at her regime critically but not unsympathetically. Now that over three decades have elapsed since her tragic death, one can look at the events more objectively. As the time passes, inevitably, evaluation and assessment becomes more detached from political overtones, rhetoric and political philosophy. This can be seen from the chapter scheme of the book. It is designed to look at the positives and the negatives of her Prime Ministership.

Chapter 1, "The Lengthening Shadows – End of An Era", analyses the happenings in the last few weeks of her life before her assassination, and how, in a sense, the end was pre-ordained by her own actions.

Chapter 2, "Blue Star – Many Unanswered Questions", argues that the Punjab problem was neglected for long, there was gross ineptitude on the part of the Central Government, and the army action was avoidable. The white paper brought out by the government was anything but 'white'. I have also argued that not giving Chandigarh to Punjab was a crucial mistake and have suggested that even now it is not too late to correct it. Non-release of the relevant public records, even though over thirty years have elapsed since Blue Star, is a major handicap in any serious study of this period.

Chapter 3, "Amazing Journey – Empress of India", deals with the Bangladesh War, defeat of Pakistan army, and creation of Bangladesh – the crowning glory of Indira Gandhi's career. It also discusses the Simla Agreement. It is my view that it was a major failure so far as India was concerned. As it appears, P.N. Haksar was primarily responsible for wrongly advising Indira Gandhi in the matter.

Chapter 4, "The Emergency – Legalising Constitutional Dictatorship", is an in-depth analysis of this shocking chapter in India's recent history, based in part on Shah Commission Report which was withdrawn and destroyed by Indira Gandhi when she came back to power in 1980 and has since been resurrected and published by Era Sezhiyan. The chapter discusses two important case studies of the time – detention of Gayatri Devi, Maharani of Jaipur, and Income Tax raids on Baroda Rayon, which were examined by the Commission. Pranab Kumar Mukherjee, who demitted office as President of India in August 2017, was closely involved in both these cases as the then Minister of State for Revenue in Finance Ministry, a sad reflection on ethical mooring of a person occupying the highest public office. I have also discussed at length the goings-on in Indira Gandhi's farmhouse, on the outskirts of Delhi, which were exposed by Arun Shourie after in-depth research. The case was badly botched up by some of the best known officers of the time, leading to the fiasco of the inordinately-delayed raid. In analysing it, I have highlighted how the so-called 'steel frame' of the country was totally undermined and shattered by Indira Gandhi and how the concept of committed bureaucracy has hit the death-knell of this institution. One does not know how long the institution of All India Services would survive.

Chapter 5, "The Ugly Face of Majoritarianism", brings out the series of Constitutional and Statutory Amendments carried out by Indira Gandhi, some of them unashamedly and blatantly to serve her own personal interests. There must not be another case in history anywhere in the world where such legislations were sponsored by the ruler and meekly passed by a mute, deaf and dumb brute majority in Parliament. The other Constitutional Amendments destroyed even the basic structure of the Constitution. If the Supreme Court had not laid down the *Laxman Rekha* (the sacrosanct line) for the powers of Parliament to amend the Constitution, I have serious doubts if democracy and free society that we take for granted in India would have survived. In fact, with the unnerving experience of this period, I shudder at the thought of any political party getting two-thirds majority in Parliament! Finally, equally importantly, the chapter brings out how, with all the unbelievable power which Indira Gandhi enjoyed at the time, she was reluctant to act on some critical issues – electoral reforms, black money, establishment of a Lokpal, anti-defection legislation, and most importantly, separation of religion from politics, which would have made substantial difference to the public life in the country.

In Chapter 6, "Devaluing the Institutions", I have argued that the strength of democracy lies in its institutions. Indira Gandhi made deliberate efforts to weaken them, from their very roots, by seeking to establish committed judiciary and committed bureaucracy, undermine the office of Governor, establish feudal practices in the governance of the country, misuse Article 356, strain Centre-State relations, destroy internal democracy in the ruling Congress party, promote dynastic family rule, institutionalise corruption, and debase Parliament. Coming as it did on the background of her father, Jawaharlal Nehru, who made Herculean efforts to build and nurture institutions throughout his tenure, this was particularly shocking.

Chapter 7, titled "Mirage of Socialism – Lost Opportunities", discusses some of the myths surrounding Indira Gandhi's economic philosophy and argues how Indira Gandhi was not really a Leftist or a socialist. All her actions from time to time were meant to retain power and increase her hold over the party. But, this cost the country dearly in terms of mindless recourse to nationalisation and expansion of the public sector. On return to power in 1980, when her hold over the party became absolute and her reliance on Communists and Leftists declined, her radicalism was nowhere to be seen. The slogan, *Garibi Hatao* (remove poverty), which was a counter to the opposition parties' demand of *Indira Hatao* (remove Indira) was nothing but a political ploy which came handy in all her electioneering. The chapter analyses the opportunities lost because of the Leftist policies pursued by Indira Gandhi.

And finally, Chapter 8, "An Enigma", discusses the riddle that was Indira Gandhi. It sheds light on sensitive features and outstanding qualities of Indira Gandhi's personality. It brings out how Indira Gandhi saw herself, how the people close to her saw her, her entourage, her style of functioning, her sense of humour, her Press conferences, her special flair for foreign affairs, roller-coaster ride of her popular mandates, no-confidence motions she faced, and takes a look at some of her enduring achievements.

I trust that, by and large, these are the criteria on which Indira Gandhi will be judged by history. The assessment will depend on the then surviving impact of her good and bad legacy. What I have outlined is the impact as I see it now. In that sense, it may be called the first draft of the history of Indira Gandhi years.

I have italicised some portions of the text to invite the attention of the readers. The names of places, towns and cities are retained as they were at the relevant time. Reference to the source of the quoted material is given in the bracket at the end of the quotation, with the name of the author/publication followed by the year of publication and the page number.

Pune
February 2018

Madhav Godbole

Acknowledgements

Dilip Majgaonkar of Rajhans Prakashan, Pune, a reputed publisher of Marathi books, had requested me to write a book on Indira Gandhi to commemorate her birth centenary in 2017. It has been published in December 2017. This book is a larger and more comprehensive study. I am thankful to Majgaonkar for getting me interested in this important period of India's history. I must also place on record the immense help I received from the persons in charge of the libraries in Pune: N.A. Chaudhuri from the Gokhale Institute of Politics and Economics, Ms Manjiri Joshi from the Indian Law Society's Law College, and Ms Chaya Mangsulkar from the Indian School of Political Economy.

I must place on record my grateful thanks to my friend Unni Eradi for providing valuable inputs, particularly pertaining to the functioning of the Shah Commission, on whose staff he worked at the time. It was Unni who gave me his own copy of the Shah Commission Report resurrected and brought out by Era Sezhiyan, on which I have relied for writing some portions of the book.

My wife, Sujata, has been a constant source of encouragement and support. I am indebted to her for her untiring help, patience and forbearance. I have dedicated this book to her.

I am grateful to V.K. Sharma, Editor, for the attention devoted to the manuscript and giving it the valuable finishing touches. I am obliged to Manas Publications for bringing out the book so expeditiously and elegantly.

Madhav Godbole

Highlights of the Book

- Liberation of Bangladesh and the resounding defeat of Pakistan army in the ensuing war marked the pinnacle of Indira Gandhi's popularity when she came to be called empress of India. But what was gained in the war, was lost in the Simla Accord talks with Pakistan. A once-in-a-life-time opportunity was lost to solve the Kashmir problem.
- Though Justice J.C. Shah authored a comprehensive, objective and analytical report within a very short time, the author makes a point that Justice Shah, who had earlier commented adversely on the imposition of Emergency and Indira Gandhi's policies pertaining to appointment of judges, should not have been appointed to head the Commission of Inquiry.
- The book is based on the irrefutable evidence brought out in the Shah Commission Report, which was destroyed by Indira Gandhi, but was resurrected and published by Era Sezhiyan, former Member of Parliament.
- The book brings out the invidious role played by Pranab Kumar Mukherjee, the then Minister of State for Revenue (and later President of India), as brought out by Shah Commission, in the detention of Maharani Gayatri Devi and raids on certain business houses.

- In sharp contrast to the most recent case of Tony Blair, former Prime Minister of United Kingdom, in the Iraq Commission of Inquiry, Indira Gandhi refused to take any responsibility for the excesses committed during the Emergency. The court cases against her could not proceed due to her delaying tactics. The author has advocated that the only way to bring her to books was to disfranchise her from contesting elections for a period of twelve years.
- In spite of credible information, the raid on her farm house was deliberately delayed and foiled by the then senior officers due to the fear of her coming back to power and the fear psychosis which prevailed at the time. It showed what the so-called 'steel frame' had been reduced to.
- Though Indira Gandhi was the supreme national leader and her Congress party had two-thirds majority in Parliament and most State Legislatures to get the Constitution amended, she avoided taking action on five major areas – electoral reforms, anti-defection (anti *aaya rams* and *gayaa rams*) legislation, black money and demonetization, appointment of Lokpal, and separation of religion from politics, which would have made significant difference to India's public life.
- Series of Constitutional Amendments undertaken by her were a death-knell to the liberal democracy and changed even the basic structure of the Constitution. Her confrontation with the judiciary was a water-shed which eventually made the Indian judiciary the most powerful judiciary in the world, quite contrary to what she wanted it to be.
- The book brings out her strained relations with Y.B. Chavan, her Finance and Home Minister.
- Her sham pursuit of socialism and the election slogan of 'remove poverty' (*garibi hatao*) ushered in and perpetuated an era of lost opportunities.

- Her regime was marked by institutionalization of corruption.
- No other Prime Minister has done as much to weaken the institutions which constitute the strength of democracy. These included Parliament, the statutory and constitutional office-holders, the judiciary, the civil service, the media, etc.
- Operation Blue Star could have been avoided but for Indira Gandhi's indecisiveness, distrust of her colleagues, and reluctance to address the issues. The author argues that Chandigarh should have been given to Punjab. Even now, it is not too late to take such a decision.
- The author believes that Indira Gandhi wanted to die as a martyr and therefore she consciously over-ruled the advice of her senior officers to replace the Sikh security contingent.
- Indira Gandhi was a riddle, an enigma, who comprised several personalities, with split-personality traits. Perhaps, this is the first book to analyse this phenomenon in depth.
- Her legacy is not just turbulent but also deeply troubling. The book is effectively a first draft of history of what remains of her legacy.

Contents

Abbreviations

ACC	:	Appointments Committee of the Cabinet
AEC	:	Atomic Energy Commission
AICC	:	All India Congress Committee
AIR	:	All India Radio
AIR	:	All India Reporter
AP	:	Andhra Pradesh
ARC	:	Administrative Reforms Commission
BBC	:	British Broadcasting Corporation
BSF	:	Border Security Force
CBDT	:	Central Board of Direct Taxes
CBI	:	Central Bureau of Investigation
CID	:	Crime Investigation Department
CJ	:	Chief Justice
CJI	:	Chief Justice of India
CIA	:	Central Intelligence Agency [of USA]
COJA	:	Committee on Judicial Accountability
CPI	:	Communist Party of India
CPI(M)	:	Communist Party of India (Marxist)
COFEPOSA	:	Conservation of Foreign Exchange and Prevention of Smuggling Act

CRP	:	Central Reserve Police
CRPF	:	Central Reserve Police Force
DDA	:	Delhi Development Authority
DIG	:	Deputy Inspector General
DRDO	:	Defence Research and Development Organisation
FRG	:	Federal Republic of Germany
GDP	:	Gross Domestic Product
GOC-in-C	:	General Officer Commanding in Chief
GoI	:	Government of India
HP	:	Himachal Pradesh
J&K	:	Jammu and Kashmir
KKK	:	*Kissa Kursi Ka*
IAS	:	Indian Administrative Service
IB	:	Intelligence Bureau
I&B	:	Information and Broadcasting
ICS	:	Indian Civil Service
ICU	:	Intensive Care Unit
IE	:	*Indian Express*
IGP	:	Inspector General of Police
IIT	:	Indian Institute of Technology
IMF	:	International Monetary Fund
INS	:	Indian Navy Ship
IOC	:	Indian Oil Corporation
IPS	:	Indian Police Service
ISI	:	Inter-Services Intelligence [of Pakistan]
J	:	Judge
JILI	:	*Journal of Indian Law Institute*
JP	:	Jayaprakash Narayan

LIC	:	Life Insurance Corporation of India
LoC	:	Line of Control
Ltd	:	Limited
MCD	:	Municipal Corporation of Delhi
MEA	:	Ministry of External Affairs
MISA	:	Maintenance of Internal Security Act
MLA	:	Member of Legislative Assembly
MP	:	Member of Parliament
MP	:	Madhya Pradesh
NDC	:	National Development Council
NSG	:	National Security Guard
PAC	:	Public Accounts Committee
PM	:	Prime Minister
PMF	:	Para-Military Force
PMH	:	Prime Minister's House
PMO	:	Prime Minister's Office
PNB	:	Punjab National Bank
POK	:	Pakistan Occupied Kashmir
POW	:	Prisoner of War
PSU	:	Public Sector Undertaking
PSYWAR	:	Psychological warfare
PUCL	:	Peoples Union for Civil Liberties
R&AW	:	Research and Analysis Wing
RBI	:	Reserve Bank of India
RPA	:	Representation of People Act
RSS	:	Rashtriya Swayamsevak Sangh
SBI	:	State Bank of India
SC	:	Supreme Court
SGPC	:	Shiromani Gurdwara Parbandhak Committee

SPG	:	Special Protection Group
SSP	:	Samyukta Socialist Party
UN	:	United Nations
UNDP	:	United Nations Development Programme
UP	:	Uttar Pradesh
USSR	:	Union of Soviet Socialist Republics
VVIP	:	Very Very Important Person

1

The Lengthening Shadows – End of an Era

INTRODUCTION

Last few days of Indira Gandhi's life make for a disturbing reading. It was as if everyone knew what was coming, including Indira Gandhi. But, intelligence agencies charged with providing her security were not permitted, by Indira Gandhi herself, to do anything to avert the tragedy!

SPEAKING OF DESTINY

Was Indira Gandhi aware of her destiny to rule India? At least it did not seem that way. It is often stated that Nehru wanted Indira to succeed him and that the Kamraj Plan, under which several senior ministers, including Morarji Desai and Lal Bahadur Shastri who were the potential successors, were asked to resign and take to the Congress party work, was meant to clear the field for Indira Gandhi to take over as Prime Minister, after him. But, Indira Gandhi's letters to her American friend, Dorothy Norman, bring out quite a different story.

Indira Gandhi was in regular touch with Norman, to whom she wrote on 13 October 1963, just a few months before Nehru's death, to say:

> My need for privacy and anonymity has been growing steadily these last three years.... Privacy, unfortunately, is

> not possible for me even in the remotest corner of the subcontinent.... Last May in London, I lost my heart to a small house which was for sale. Such a wonderful location. Central, yet very quiet and next door to a park. If only I could have bought it. One room for myself and the rest (only two, I fear) rented out. Rents are so high and this would have solved the foreign exchange problem. But the major hurdle was the foreign exchange with which to buy it. I spent much time figuring out ways and means and finally when I learnt that an acquaintance had bought it, I was terribly depressed for months. It was as if a door had been slammed in my face. My father and sons have kept me tied to Delhi. Part of that problem is solved – Rajiv is in England and Sanjay finishes school by the end of the year. My living in London would make it easier for him to go abroad. And I would be able to see something of the boys and yet be on my own. Free to work or to rest. The only way out might be to get an adequate job – not under the government or business auspices.... I am not running away from anybody or anything. I can claim to have done my duty to my country and my family all these long years.... *But now I want another life.* It may not work out. I may not like it or be good at it. But at least it deserves a trial. *There is a compulsion within me which is driving me away from the old life.* Is this wrong? (Norman, 1985: 96-97)

Was this the same Indira Gandhi that we saw in her tumultuous term as the Prime Minister? How much a person changes over the years!

In her letter dated 8 May 1964, just a few days before Nehru's death, Indira Gandhi had written:

> *The whole question of my future is bothering me. I feel I must settle outside India at least for a year or so* and this involves earning a living and especially foreign currency. This isn't just yet (sic) but it is a nagging worry. The desire to be

> out of India and the malice, jealousies and envy, with which one is surrounded, are now overwhelming. Also the fact that there isn't one single person to whom one can talk or ask advice even on lesser matters. (Norman, 1985: 103)

But the destiny had willed something quite different for her.

The following account given by Gill, however, shows her belief that she was born to rule: On the eve of her election as the Prime Minister, Indira Gandhi wrote to her son Rajiv in London,

> How hard it is from being a king,
> When it is in you and the situation?

This impromptu recall of Robert Frost's verse when various aspirants were still fighting out their grim battle for succession shows how she perceived her position: it was in her to be the 'king'. (Gill, 1996: 225)

Nani Palkhivala, one of the most outstanding senior advocates of the Supreme Court, who was offered the post of Attorney General of India in 1968 but politely declined, has written about what he had learnt from a co-passenger on a flight to Delhi in 1975. A clairvoyant had told the co-passenger that Indira Gandhi would lose her election case and still "she would become the most powerful woman in the world". When asked by Palkhivala, "Did the soothsayer say anything else?" "Yes. He said the extraordinary power which the Prime Minister is to acquire will end in March 1977." "Did he make any other prediction?", asked Palkhivala. "Yes, he said that Jayaprakash Narayan who is today the most popular figure in India's public life would be stricken by a fatal illness which would carry him away in about two years. He also said that Mr Y.B. Chavan who aspires to be the Prime Minister of India would never attain that position." All the predictions had come true. Palkhivala called on Indira

Gandhi on 22 March 1977 when the results showed that the Janata Party had won a landslide victory and Indira Gandhi had to resign. Palkhivala had narrated to her his conversation with the total stranger on the plane in June 1975 and had said, "Indiraji, if it be any consolation, may I tell you that what has happened since the election case was filed against you … seems to have been preordained." She had tears in her eyes – the only time I saw her in such a sad mood. (Palkhivala, 1994: xviii-xix)

But, no clairvoyant was necessary to tell about the tragedy which was looming after the Operation Blue Star. Indira Gandhi herself knew that she had signed her own death warrant by ordering the army action in the Golden Temple.

INDIRA GANDHI'S PREMONITIONS

It appears that Indira Gandhi had a premonition that her end was near. I can do no better than give the long quotation below of the graphic account of the happenings of the last few days of Indira Gandhi's life, written by Adams and Whitehead in *The Dynasty: The Nehru-Gandhi Story*:

> Marie Seton was in India from March to June 1984, and observed that Indira was exhausted. She said Indira told her 'that she could no longer respond to a challenge – always her strongest point. This she could always do. She could always improvise. Now she was retreating from communication. She had always had moods like this. She would describe it as being stinking (sic). She would say, 'I am stinking now, right all the way through.' All Indira's last letters show an encircling despair: 'The situation here is a disturbing one … the terrible period we are going through here. I am truly depressed.' Death was much in her mind….

Vishnu Mathur a producer making a film about Rajiv, felt himself lucky to obtain a brief interview with Indira in the rose garden of her house. In the event, he found her voluble and relaxed, prepared to make (sic) time to talk about her family. He said, 'I was hoping for ten minutes but she spent two or two and half hours with me, as if she had to talk compulsively. She talked about Rajiv, she talked about Sanjay, about her husband Feroze – I was running out of film.'

When she last saw Pupul Jayakar, Indira said she was going to Kashmir, as she had never seen the Chinar leaves turn brilliant red and orange in autumn. It seemed for her time to return to the ancient homeland. She said, 'Papu [her father] used to love rivers, but I am the daughter of the mountains, and my heart is free of care. I have told my sons (sic) that when I die, to scatter my ashes over the Himalayas.' She had already spoken to Rajiv and Sonia about the arrangements for her funeral, and spoke to fourteen-year-old Rahul, telling him 'to be brave when the time came: she had lived her life and done all she had to do and could do; he was not to cry for her.'

On October 30, at a meeting in Bhuvaneshwar in Orissa, Indira gave her last great public pronouncement of defiance: 'It does not matter to me whether I live or die. As long as I draw breath I will carry on serving. And when I die, every drop of my blood will nourish and strengthen my free and undivided country.' That night P.C. Alexander, her Personal (sic) Secretary, found her looking all her sixty-seven years. He said, 'For the first time in my experience I found her to be very, very tired. She did not like to be told she looked tired but I told her she was, so I would just take a couple of minutes.... (Adams, 1997: 312-313)

Pranay Gupte, in his book, *India – The Challenge of Change*, has written about how everyone in Indira Gandhi's household dreaded about what the future held in store. Gupte has written:

> Among Mrs Gandhi's aides, there was, since the Amritsar event, a growing conviction that it would be only a matter of time before Sikhs took action against the Prime Minister. They feared that Indira Gandhi would be killed in vengeance. Was she herself seized by some premonition? In a half-complete hand-written note which her personal assistant, R.K. Dhavan, found after her death, she had written: 'I have never felt less like dying, and that calm and peace of mind is what prompts me to write what is in the nature of a will. *If I die a violent death, as some fear and a few are plotting,* I know the violence will be in the thought and the action of the assassin, not in my dying – for no hate is dark enough to overshadow the extent of my love for my people and my country; no force is strong enough to divert me from my purpose and my endeavour to take this country forward.
>
> A poet has written of his 'love' – 'How can I feel humble with the wealth of you beside me?'. I can say the same of India. I cannot understand how anyone can be an Indian and not be proud – the richness and infinite variety of our composite heritage, the magnificence of the people's spirit, equal to any disaster or burden, firm in their faith, gay spontaneity even in poverty and hardship.' (Gupte, 1989: 30-31)

Gupte has also written about the recollections of Professor Buultjens, who taught political economy and comparative religions at New York University and was a visiting professor at many institutions around the world. He was a close friend of the Nehru family. He recalled being in Delhi on 1 June [1984], when the Prime Minister was giving her Generals the go-ahead for Operation Blue Star ... Mrs Gandhi had said to Buultjens, 'You know, this is the most difficult decision of my political career. This is war on your own people.'

A couple of months later, Buultjens had accompanied Mrs Gandhi to Delhi's Red Fort, from whose ramparts she delivered her annual independence day speech on 15 August. He noticed that the sixty-six years old Prime Minister became breathless as she climbed the steep stairs to the rostrum, and the long-time tick in her right eyelid had become more pronounced.

"It must be very tiring to go up all those steps," Buultjens said to Mrs Gandhi.

"I may never have to do it again," she replied cryptically.

Only two days before the assassination, Buultjens had spoken with Mrs Gandhi on the telephone about the continuing controversy concerning the army action in Amritsar. Although Sikhs generally had not supported the terrorists ... there was almost universal condemnation in the Sikh community of Operation Blue Star.

"We are all besieged," Mrs Gandhi said to Buultjens. "But we will pull through this one."

A few weeks before this conversation, Buultjens had telephoned the Prime Minister to relay the news that he had been selected as a recipient of the prestigious Toynbee prize, given annually to an outstanding social scientist. Buultjens requested that Mrs Gandhi formally hand out the award.

"I would be delighted," Mrs Gandhi said to Professor Buultjens. Then she mysteriously added, "But I may not be around to give it to you." In fact, that proved to be the case.

"When I retire," she once said to Buultjens, "I will go to Cambridge as a visiting professor – if they will have me. You will have to come and help me there, because I am not much of an academic. And I have another job for you. You will have to help me with my memoirs. *I must tell my story*...." Death had snatched away Indira Gandhi's chance of explaining herself to the world, and to history. (Gupte, 2009: 71-72)

Janaki Ganju, the Washington lobbyist for India, recalls meeting Indira Gandhi on 14 August 1984. There was mounting concern among her aids about reports that assassination plots were being hatched against her. Some of her aids were insistent that she skip the traditional independence day address from the ramparts of the Red Fort on 15 August.

"Tell me, Ganju, how many of your Presidents have been killed?", Indira said to Ganju. The reference was to US Presidents, of course; even though Janaki Ganju was an Indian citizen and indeed worked on behalf of the Indian government in Washington, Indira would always tease him by calling him 'American'.

Ganju started reciting the number of American Presidents who had been killed. Indira interrupted him.

"I know my history," she said. "The point I am trying to make is that if someone wants to get you, they can always succeed." She paused, then added: "I am going to give my speech tomorrow." (Gupte, 2009: 319-320)

Pupul Jayakar has written about her last meeting with Indira Gandhi on 26 October 1984, more or less bringing out the accounts referred to earlier:

> Indira Gandhi was to visit Srinagar the next morning. She had never been there in autumn, and she was eagerly looking forward to seeing the Chinar leaves change colour. She wanted to lie in the sun and see the green of the leaf turn rust, vermilion, and gold; the brown of a falling leaf. Perhaps it was the end of life in the leaf that made her pursue the question of death. For as she mused she said, "My father

loved rivers, but I am a daughter of the Himalayas and I have told my sons" – for a moment she seemed to have forgotten that Sanjay was dead – "that my remains should be scattered on the snow-tipped Himalayas." As I was leaving, she called out to me, "Remember what I said, Pupul, remember." (Jayakar, 1986: 367)

THE LAST DAY

The day of her assassination, 31 October 1984, changed India's history decisively. No one could have imagined what was to follow that day. When the Prime Minister was in Delhi, her residence used to be very crowded in the mornings with throngs of people coming, from all over India, with their grievances, or just to get a glimpse, *darshan* of her. But that day, she had set apart the morning for an interview with legendary Peter Ustinov, the British actor, who was to produce a film on her for the BBC. The interview was to be at 9.20 AM in the rose garden in the lawns of the adjacent bungalow which was a part of her residential complex. There was only a wicket gate between the two. Indira Gandhi, wearing a bright saffron sari, stepped out of her living quarters at 9.15 AM and started walking at her usual brisk pace to go for the interview. Her Sikh bodyguard, Beant Singh, who had been on security duty at her residence for several years, saluted her and as she proceeded further fired three shots aimed at her abdomen from his pistol. As soon as the shots were heard, Beant Singh's junior, Satwant Singh emerged from the hedge and opened fire from his Thompson automatic carbine and fired 40 shots at her. Mrs Gandhi collapsed in a pool of blood. It was now 9.17 AM. She must have died instantly, though she was rushed to the All India Medical Institute where all efforts were made to save her. She wanted to die 'on her two feet'. Her wish was fulfilled. What happened thereafter has been written about extensively.

I do not therefore want to repeat it. Thus came to an end the unforgettable, stormy Indira Gandhi era.

J. Krishnamurti, well-known philosopher and thinker, said on passing away of Indira Gandhi, "Don't hold memories of Indira in your mind, that holds her to the earth. Let her go." His hand made a gesture towards space and eternity. (Jayakar, 1986: 368)

DID SHE WANT TO DIE A MARTYR'S DEATH?

It can be seen from Shekhar Gupta's essay in, *The Assassination and After*, that "the conspiracy to assassinate Indira Gandhi was under discussion for quite some time." He has written:

> Sub-Inspector Balbir Singh, the man who was first assigned the task of finishing off Mrs Gandhi, had been promised refuge in a western country of his choice.... But as far as the specific murder conspiracy is concerned it seems to be the brain-child of men around Mrs Gandhi, worked out at a series of meetings in Gurudwara Bangla Sahib.... The first conspiracy originated as early as on 26 June, barely three weeks after Operation Blue Star when an incensed sub-inspector Balbir Singh casually talked in terms of killing Mrs Gandhi at Gurudwara Bangla Sahib ... some people who offered him sanctuary in Pakistan.... While one of the men in the Gurudwara even went to the extent of offering a kamikaze or rather like the Palestinian suicide bombers in Beirut, by offering to ram Mrs Gandhi's motorcade with a car-full of explosives, there was consensus on using a safer method. The amateurs, at one stage, thought in terms of using a poison gas to quietly exterminate their quarry. The second choice was a strong plastic explosive to be set with a time-device on the path of Mrs Gandhi.... As time passed these sessions were no longer such a secret. *According to senior police officers it was a*

> *subject of common gossip in the police lines that some Sikhs in the security branch were planning to kill Mrs Gandhi. The murmurs also reached some officers and inspector Yoginder Sharma even showed the initiative of removing 12 Sikh guards from the security cordons, only to be rebuked by the Prime Minister's Secretariat for jumping the gun*.... That Beant Singh was not as much of a cold-blooded mercenary as an irrational fanatic is clear from the fact that as late as 27 October he made no effort to hide his feelings. He turned down the customary bonus of ₹100 Mrs Gandhi gave to all her securitymen on Diwali. The fact was, significantly, recorded in the daily diary by one of his immediate superiors. But it seems the senior officers who were meant to take action just went through the diary casually without understanding the import of the note. (Shourie, 1985: 28-29, 32)

This is not the correct depiction of what actually happened. In view of the disturbing reports compiled by intelligence agencies, matters pertaining to Prime Minister's security were considered by a committee presided over by Cabinet Secretary at which Principal Secretary to Prime Minister, senior security officers to Prime Minister, Home Secretary, Director, Intelligence Bureau, among others, were present and the decision was taken to change the Sikh security contingent. It was a very correct and timely decision taken at the highest level.

But, Indira Gandhi refused to change her Sikh bodyguards. She may have been worried that it will send a wrong message to the Sikh community when the need of the hour was to remove the mistrust and anger which the Sikhs had against her. *Or did she consciously want to die a martyr's death?* Unfortunately, her style of functioning was so autocratic and over-bearing that none of the senior officers had the courage to speak to her personally and to prevail upon her to go by their decision to change the security contingent. On the contrary, as V. Balachandran, former Special Secretary, Cabinet Secretariat, had pointed out in his article "Lest We Revisit 1984":

> H.D. Pillai, the only officer who took concrete action in trying to prevent the assassination by withdrawing her guards on intelligence report, was humiliated and punished. None of the higher echelons in the Indian bureaucracy who were party to this decision of withdrawal of guards stood by that outstanding officer when he was suspended and made to suffer on totally unjust grounds. (*The Asian Age*, 25 August 2005)

Earlier, Indira Gandhi had even objected to an ambulance being kept at her residence as a standard practice on 24 × 7 basis. With the setting up of the Special Protection Group (SPG) under an Act of Parliament, the situation has now improved qualitatively. But, an explicit provision needs to be made in the SPG Act that in matters of security of the protectee, the judgment of the security agency shall prevail and would not be open to question by the protectee.

Gupte has written:

> On the day that the Prime Minister was assassinated, there was no massive outpouring of grief for Mrs Gandhi in most places across this huge country. There was, of course, alarm over the brutal manner in which she had been murdered ... but about Indira Gandhi herself there was a noticeable ambivalence.... Other than her friends, her Congress party associates and the sycophants who now stood to be deprived of her patronage, most people simply did not shed tears for her. (Gupte, 1989: 86)

The next morning the body of Indira Gandhi was placed in Teen Murti House, where she had lived with her father during his term as Prime Minister. Mourners silently filed past the body to pay their last respects. Outside, the agitated crowds were shouting *'Indira Gandhi amar rahe'* (long live Indira Gandhi). But there was also a more ominous slogan, *'khoon ka badla khoon se lenge'* (blood will be avenged by blood). Was anybody listening? This was a fore-warning of the genocide of Sikhs to follow in which nearly 3,000 Sikhs were massacred and their properties destroyed in Delhi.

2

Blue Star – Many Unanswered Questions

INTRODUCTION

The Punjab State came into being after Haryana was carved out in 1966. Sikhs had a majority in it and constituted 55 per cent of the total. It comes as a surprise but Khushwant Singh had written: "The only chance of survival of the Sikhs as a separate community is to create a State in which they form a compact group, *where the teaching of Gurumukhi and the Sikh religion is compulsory*." On the other hand, the States' Reorganisation Commission was of the view that a separate Punjabi-speaking State would solve neither the language nor the communal problem. On the contrary, the Commission argued, "far from removing internal tensions, which exist between communal, and not linguistic and regional groups, it might further exacerbate the existing feelings." (Diwan, 1978: 23, footnote 27) The assertion of Khushwant Singh is difficult to accept. It is also not in keeping with the precepts of the Constitution. Inter-mixing of religion and politics in Punjab, as compared to any other State, has always been a matter of serious concern.

Kuldip Nayar has in the book *Tragedy of Punjab – Operation Blue Star and After* brought out that when the proposal for creation of Punjabi *Suba* (State) was placed before the Congress Working Committee in 1965, Prime Minister Lal Bahadur Shastri was in favour but it was opposed by three persons – Morarji Desai, Biju Patnaik, former Chief Minister of Orissa, married to a Punjabi Hindu, and Ram Subhag Singh, then a Cabinet Minister. Their argument was that it would further divide the Sikhs and Hindus and would encourage communalism. Writing in 1984, Nayar had made a pertinent observation: *Punjab's tragedy is that there are no Punjabis any more in Punjab – only Sikhs and Hindus.* (Nayar, 1984: 7) Could this have been avoided? This chapter provides some answers.

GENESIS OF PUNJAB PROBLEM

The Anandpur Sahib Resolution, which gave rise to the prolonged Punjab agitation and culminated in Operation Blue Star followed by the tragic assassination of Indira Gandhi in 1984, was adopted by the Working Committee of the Shiromani Gurdwara Parbandhak Committee (SGPC) in October 1973. It was finally adopted in the form of twelve resolutions by the general house of the Akali Dal at its session held in Ludhiana in August 1977. Arun Shourie has emphasised that apart from the specific demands listed in the resolutions, the basic political thesis of the resolutions consists of five propositions:

- The Sikhs are a separate nation.
- The Akali Dal and the SGPC are its representatives and spokesmen.
- The aim of the Akali Dal is to establish the political supremacy of the Sikhs.
- For doing so, it will use 'all possible means'.
- As a step towards this goal, there must be redistribution of territories between Punjab and the States around it, and a truly drastic redistribution of powers between the Centre and the States in general. (Shourie, 1987: 165)

The above basic philosophy raised serious questions about the very survival of India as a nation. Secondly, many of the demands mentioned in the resolutions were loosely worded and had not been thought through fully. As a result, their acceptance would have been problematic. Thirdly, it is only within the framework of the Constitution that any demands can be considered. Fourthly, where the interests of other States were concerned, such as river water distribution or merger of areas from the adjoining States into Punjab, the Centre will have to necessarily consult the concerned States and obtain their concurrence. These basic ground rules made clear by Indira Gandhi could not be faulted. However, as brought out in the following discussion, dilatory tactics were adopted by the Central Government in dealing with this explosive issue, though it was fully aware that Pakistan was actively aiding and abetting the Punjab agitation. As Lt. Gen. Brar, who led the Operation Blue Star has written in his book, *Operation Blue Star – The True Story*, "The Centre dragged its feet far too long in implementing the Anandpur Sahib resolution, even fractionally." (Brar, 1993: 157)

The enormity of the Punjab problem can be gauged from what the white paper had stated: From August 4, 1982, when the Akali Morcha was started, up to June 3, 1984 [when the Blue Star was launched], there were 1,200 violent incidents in which 410 persons were killed and more than 1,180 injured. From January 1, 1984 to June 3, 1984, there were 775 violent incidents in which 298 persons were killed and more than 525 injured. (GoI, 1984: 32) While this showed the increasing ferocity of Bhindranwale's violence, it also brought out the heavy price India had to pay for inaction by Indira Gandhi government.

Parliament took keen interest in the situation in Punjab. The subject was discussed in the Lok Sabha on 4 November

1982, and thereafter on eleven occasions in 1983. This included the discussion on the adjournment motion moved by Madhu Dandavate on 28 February 1984. In her brief intervention, Prime Minister Indira Gandhi said that the government had agreed to the transmission of *Gurbani* but they could not go ahead as the Akalis did not allow laying of transmission lines. *Dealing with the demand regarding entry of police into the Gurudwaras, the Prime Minister said that she entirely agreed with the Members that no religious place be made a sanctuary for criminals and accumulation of arms.* (Kashyap, 1998: 78)

The President's rule imposed on 6 October 1983 could not be terminated due to the disturbed law and order situation in the State though the maximum permissible one year period was about to elapse. The Constitution (Forty-eighth Amendment) Bill, 1984 was therefore passed by both houses of Parliament in August 1984 which enabled the continuance of the President's rule for a period of two years.

One point which struck me was that there were frequent changes in incumbents holding the crucial home portfolio (Zail Singh, P.C. Sethi, P.V. Narasimha Rao). As a result, there was no continuity in leadership. It appears that the Prime Minister did not have faith in any of her Cabinet colleagues and was therefore dealing with Punjab matters herself. Often, Rajiv Gandhi was involved in the discussions with the Akalis. There was no effort to build an all party consensus on the issues.

Rivalry, between Zail Singh and Darbara Singh, the two stalwarts of Punjab, was responsible in no small measure for the aggravation of the Punjab problem. The Congress party High Command in Delhi failed to bring them together. In fact, the tussle between them was used to increase the hold of the Centre over Punjab affairs. Building counter-weights in States to prominent party leaders at the Centre has been a long established policy of the Congress party.

ZAIL SINGH'S MEMOIRS

Zail Singh, who was Union Home Minister and later elevated to the position of the President of India, was often charged with having encouraged the rise of Bhindranwale, being responsible for the support extended by the SGPC to Bhindranwale, and the deteriorating law and order situation in the State. Since his role had become highly controversial and has been widely commented upon in the writings of a number of persons, I have deliberately decided to reproduce below a somewhat long quotation from Zail Singh's book, *Memoirs of Giani Zail Singh – The Seventh President of India*. This would help in better understanding of the issues. In it he has clarified his position and has refuted all these allegations. He has stated:

> It has been variously alleged that I had a hand in creating him [Jarnail Singh Bhindranwale] or propping him up from obscurity or bringing him into limelight from the sidelines for the sole purpose of using him as a pawn on the chessboard of politics or transforming him into a countervailing influence against the Akalis.... In a book entitled *Amritsar* by Mark Tully and Satish Jacob of BBC, it was insinuated that I had a hand in bringing the Sant on the centrestage. *Their main source of information in matters relating to Punjab was none other than Darbara Singh, the then Chief Minister of the State.* The allegation that I had created Dal Khalsa, whose avowed aim was to demand a sovereign Sikh State was also given currency. It was a most baffling and unrealistic statement. A man the very foundation of his (sic) life was laid on the bedrock of patriotism and unity of the country could not have thought of aiding the formation of an anti-national body.... When in April 1980, the Nirankari Baba Gurbachan Singh was murdered in Delhi, the crime was linked to Sant Jarnail Singh Bhindranwale.... I, as the Home Minister, told Parliament that Bhindranwale was not

involved in it. There was no concrete evidence to show his complicity, but my detractors seized upon this opportunity to criticise me.... In September 1981, a warrant for the arrest of Sant Bhindranwale was issued by the Punjab government.... Before the Punjab police could reach Chandu Kalan, where the Sant was adjourning on some religious mission, he had left the place. An utterly false impression was tried to be created that I had a hand in it! When Sant Bhindranwale was ultimately arrested, he was released by the Punjab government. This was again attributed to me, which was a total travesty of facts. After some time, Sant Bhindranwale came to Delhi and drove around the capital with his armed supporters. He did not break any law and the arms borne by his followers were licensed ones. Sant Bhindranwale undertook a trip to Mumbai and engaged himself in some religious ceremonies without let or hindrance by the Maharashtra government. On his return to Punjab, he was not arrested by the government headed by Darbara Singh. *He made himself comfortable in Guru Nanak Niwas and my advice to Mrs Gandhi to arrest him was not heeded.... I never had any occasion of meeting Sant Bhindranwale.* The nearest I got to him was at the *Bhog* (final prayers) ceremony of Jathedar Santokh Singh, the President of the Delhi Sikh Gurdwara Management Committee, who was shot dead.... The Sant was sitting cross-legged as everybody does in such a Sikh congregation and I had no communication with him whatsoever. There were a number of dignitaries present at the ceremony including party men and ministers. A fantastic lie was spread that I had touched the feet of the Sant. The perpetrators of this lie were not conversant with or pretended to be ignorant of the Sikh tradition that no one bows to a person in the presence of the Holy scripture, which is worshipped as living Guru. The Sant was a short distance

> away from where I was sitting and it does not indicate that I had any proximity with him. I had no contact with him whatsoever ... Mark Tully and Satish Jacob missed these points. Though they remained tenacious (sic) to their statement, they erred on facts. *They were wilfully misled by someone who did not see eye to eye with me....* It was really the responsibility of the State Government of Punjab to apprehend anyone posing a threat to law and order or creating discord between the various communities. *My advice to Mrs Indira Gandhi to take a suitable hard line in time was not accepted, which unfortunately, led to the tragic events of 1984.* (Zail Singh, 1997: 289-292)

Zail Singh has also written:

> She [Indira Gandhi] made it a point to discuss with me major events and issues facing the country [when he was the President of India], but I realized that she developed some hesitation to discuss the Punjab problem, which she had entertained (sic) even during my tenure as Home Minister. The then Chief Minister of Punjab, Darbara Singh, had tried to persuade the Prime Minister to let his government have a free hand in dealing with the Akali agitation without interference from the Union Home Ministry. Mrs Gandhi had conceded this request, after which *I had stopped tendering advice on the Punjab affairs*. This had happened towards the end of 1981. Under my directions, the Home Secretary was (sic) to submit files directly to the Prime Minister and except the Prime Minister and myself, very few persons were aware of this arrangement. I was dealing with all other issues coming in the purview of the Home Ministry. *I was totally dissatisfied with the handling of the Punjab problem by the State Government. The Prime Minister, Mrs Indira Gandhi, did not show much inclination to advise them to mend their ways.* I did

not press the issue, but did point out to her that all was not well with the functioning of the government of Punjab. The picture was quite unsavoury.

In December 1983 … Mrs Gandhi told me that the Punjab tangle had become more complicated and it would be helpful to utilize the services of someone who could bring about a rapprochement…. When the name of Swaran Singh … came up, I supported it strongly…. I noticed with interest that Rajiv Gandhi was also keenly involved in the matter, as in many other matters of national character.

I told Mrs Gandhi that Punjab affairs were being mishandled for quite some time resulting in an impasse and it was unfortunate that she had not shown much understanding of this diagnosis. Mrs Gandhi admitted that this had been my consistent opinion, the non-acceptance of which had made the matter more serious and intractable. But now she wanted my advice on how best to untangle this problem, which was becoming more and more complicated. Both of us agreed to make use of the persuasive abilities of Swaran Singh, who was the right man to hold negotiations with the Akalis. On my return from tour of the three foreign countries, *I was met by Swaran Singh, who gave me the tidings that an understanding had been reached between the government and the Akalis. It was agreed upon by the two sides that the Anandpur Sahib Resolution would be referred to a Parliamentary Committee, the contentious city of Chandigarh would be transferred to Punjab and the question of compensation to Haryana State would be referred to a judicial body. Sikhs would be allowed to wear small kirpan (which was their religious symbol) even during their aeroplane flights. I was told by Swaran Singh that the Central Government had accepted these propositions and was about to make an announcement to this effect. It was also decided that a committee would be set up to look into the question of Punjabi speaking areas left out of Punjab, to include them in the State. The Akali Party had also accepted the arrangement. But the government changed its stance and sprang a surprise. An altogether different statement was made by Home Minister, P.C. Sethi, in Parliament.* Swaran Singh felt aggrieved and thought that he was let down by the government by its somersault. He seemed shocked beyond words, but it went to his credit that he abstained from making any sour comment publicly at the turn of events caused by the Central Government for inexplicable reasons. *Though I admired Swaran Singh's forbearance and stoicism, I was struck by a feeling that he should have at least let the nation know of the debacle for which the government alone was responsible. I came to know later that it was due to the intransigent attitude of Darbara Singh ... who took the oft-repeated line, that if these solutions were accepted, things would go out of his control. He also thought that if Swaran Singh got the credit for solving the tangle, it would lower the prestige of the State Government. Obviously, the Punjab State leaders were more interested in their prestige than in finding an acceptable solution to the long-standing problem.*

Indira Gandhi called on Zail Singh and suggested imposition of President's rule in Punjab after the assassination of Lala Jagat Narain, a veteran journalist and a freedom-fighter, and murder of some Hindu passengers travelling in a bus, by the supporters of Bhindranwale. Zail Singh has stated that he was opposed to imposition of the President's Rule. He felt that it would "embroil the Central Government directly in the imbroglio". But Mrs Gandhi seemed to have made up her mind already on the issue.

Some leaders of the Akali Party (Longowal group) met Zail Singh who advised them to postpone their agitation by a month to enable negotiations to be held in a healthy atmosphere. When Indira Gandhi called on him, he had some positive suggestions to offer to end the deadlock, but

> I realized that the Prime Minister was in no mood to receive any advice. I told her that this ordinance [conferring powers on the Governor to declare any part of the State a disturbed area which would automatically authorise the Governor to call in the Army for help in restoring the law and order] would be construed as a measure of repression and would cause deeper cynicism.* And this is what actually happened.

The Akali leaders had approached Zail Singh with a suggestion that "I should resign from the Presidency. I told them that I was not inclined to do so, as I was not elected by the Akalis alone, but by a vast electoral college consisting of MPs and MLAs. People professing all religions and belonging to all castes and coming from all parts of the country had voted me into office." (Zail Singh, 1997: 164-165, 171-173)

Zail Singh must be complimented for not resigning at that critical time as that would have led to serious difficulties and would have further vitiated the atmosphere by introducing communal overtones.

I have given these long quotations as they bring out the inner workings of the State and Central Government. It also bears out the criticism of opposition leaders that Indira Gandhi was not able to assert herself in finding a lasting solution to the Punjab problem. Indira Gandhi in this term as Prime Minister was quite a contrast of what she was prior to 1977. In spite of resounding popular mandate, India was let down by Indira

---

* Since President Zail Singh had not approved this Ordinance before launching the Operation Blue Star, the government had to declare the whole state of Punjab as a disturbed area to be able to call in the Army.

Gandhi in tackling Punjab problem. More importantly, she paid for it with her own life.

The 9th Asian Games were to be held in Delhi in 1982. The Akali Dal announced that it would hold demonstrations at the inaugural ceremony and also during the games. As the agitators would have to come to Delhi through Haryana, strict security measures were taken to screen the visitors from Haryana. This led to lot of bitterness among the Sikhs. Even prominent and well-known Sikhs, including senior armed forces officers also were not spared from body searches and searches of their vehicles. Zail Singh has stated that while the Sikhs were complaining that they were being treated as second class citizens, they were at the forefront in organizing the games:

> All the five important dignitaries leading the inaugural ceremonies in the Jawaharlal Nehru Stadium were Sikhs namely, myself, the President of India, Buta Singh, the Cabinet Minister, Raja Bhalinder Singh, President of the Indian Olympics Committee, Umrao Singh, a Punjab politician, and K.S. Bains, an official. Rajiv Gandhi called them *Panj Pyaras* (five beloved ones created by the Tenth Guru at the time of baptising them and metamorphosing the Sikhs into a martial community). The calling of conventions of Sikh intellectuals and Sikh ex-servicemen by the Akali leaders added fuel to the fire of discrimination against the community.... I reminded the government that during my Chief Ministership ... they never had spoken the language of communalism. *The Punjab government kept sitting like a sphinx without taking any step*.... The Punjab government had spent huge sums to cope with the Akali *morcha*. I told Mrs Gandhi that not even a fraction of that amount had been spent on publicity to mould public opinion against communal activities. (Zail Singh, 1997: 175-176)

These lengthy extracts from Zail Singh's book bring out the nuances of not only Punjab politics but also Government of India's inability or reluctance to take a firm stand on issues. As can be seen from the discussion hereafter, there are contradictory versions of most events and happenings. I find that the following issues finally led to the tragic outcome.

CONGRESS PARTY AND BHINDRANWALE

In the 1980 Lok Sabha elections, the Congress(I) won 12 out of the 13 Lok Sabha seats from Punjab. A substantial number of Sikhs had voted against the Akali Dal.

> *Bhindranwale campaigned for Congress(I) candidates.... Bhindranwale was also on the dais when Mrs Gandhi made a campaign speech* for P.S. Bhinder's wife in Gurdaspur in December 1979.... [After the murder of Nirankari chief in Delhi] Bhindranwale was interrogated by the CBI on 5 May 1980. But it was left at that.... The fact that Bhindranwale had been allowed to choose his own time and place for his arrest [in Chowk Mehta] indicates either the helplessness or complicity of the Punjab government. *Here was a fugitive from justice who had been unnecessarily lionised*. When he was a 'wanted' man he led the procession against the use of tobacco in Amritsar. It was as if all Punjab had become Chambal, where the writ of the dacoits and the gun, not of the government and the law, runs. (Nayar, 1984: 7, 36-37, 42)

At one of her meetings with Akalis, Indira Gandhi told the Akalis that "Bhindranwale is not a good man; you have been supporting him unnecessarily." The Akalis retorted that it was the Congress(I) which had been supporting him; during the 1979 Gurudwara election he had put up 40 candidates against the Akalis and he had received assistance from the Congress(I). (Nayar, 1984: 44)

After the murders of Baba Gurbachan Singh and Lala Jagat Narain, there was a warrant for Bhindranwale's arrest. He was in Chando Kalan in Haryana at the time. However, no arrest was made. Instead, Haryana Chief Minister, Bhajan Lal, had personally ordered an official car to transport Bhindranwale 200 miles away to his own Gurudwara at Mehta Chowk near Amritsar. Bhajan Lal was telephoned by Zail Singh and told not to arrest Bhindranwale. Chief Minister Darbara Singh told Inder Malhotra that Home Minister [Zail Singh] was "protecting him still". (Gupte, 2009: 316)

DIG, A.S. Atwal's murder shook the State and New Delhi. Nayar has recalled:

> *Darbara Singh [Chief Minister] wanted the police to enter the Golden Temple to arrest the killer. New Delhi did not agree. If forcing an entry into the temple was at all an option, this was probably the most opportune time to do so because even the Sikh community was shocked* – Atwal, a Sikh, had been murdered as he came out of the Darbara Sahib after prayers. And Bhindranwale was still at the Guru Nanak Niwas. (Nayar, 1984: 76)

Marwah, another fine IPS officer, has been equally vehement in the criticism of the handling of the situation at the time. He has written about the uncertain response of the State Government after the killing of A.S. Atwal, DIG of police:

> The Punjab government dithered once again and became a prisoner of its own indecision. *Not wanting to lose ground to the scheming Union Home Minister,* the State Government decided to wait for the concurrence of the Union Government before allowing the State police to take even the most basic action as required under the law.... *The fact that the Chief Minister had to seek instructions from the Union Home Ministry for sending police officers to enter the precincts*

> *of the Golden Temple complex to investigate the murder of their own senior officer gives some idea of a situation in the State....* Caught in a siege mentality, the government became a prisoner of its own indecision! (Marwah, 2009: 260-261)

I fully agree with Marwah's assessment in his book, *India In Turmoil: Jammu & Kashmir, the Northeast and Left Extremism*, that it was a blunder to dismiss the Darbara Singh government after a bus was hijacked and six Hindu passengers were killed on 5 October 1983 ... the Central Government took the easy option of blaming the Darbara Singh government. As Marwah has written:

> *Darbara Singh's secular credentials were never in doubt, even though he was not the ablest of Chief Ministers.* With his dismissal two things happened: one, the field was left open for Bhindranwale to spread the communal virus and take terrorism to new heights, and two, no less serious, the buffer between the government at the Centre ... and the State was removed. (Marwah, 2009: 262)

Though stoutly denied by the Congress Party, one is left with a strong suspicion that Bhindranwale was the creation of the Congress Party. Marwah, who was closely associated with Punjab matters at the time, has also stated that *Bhindranwale was "a creation of the Congress party".* (Marwah, 2009: 255)

As late as 29 April 1984, *Rajiv Gandhi was asked, "Is Bhindranwale an extremist?" He evaded a reply and said, "This is for you to evaluate."* Asked, "Do you think he is a political leader?", Rajiv responded, "he is a religious leader and has not shown any political inclination so far." (Patwant Singh, 1985: 150-151) This ambivalence was shocking, to say the least, at a time when Bhindranwale's activities had created terror in Punjab.

In this context, reference must be made to the following observations of Brar:

> During the period January to May 1984, over 150 people were murdered by Bhindranwale's men, *while the administration once again, pathetic in its impotence, looked on from the side-lines.* Bhindranwale was, by then, running a parallel government from within the sacred shrine. Chief Minister Darbara Singh's statement that law and order forces would not be sent into the Golden Temple, strengthened his position further. *I often wonder what the custodians of law and order were doing during the three months prior to Operation Blue Star, while the Golden Temple was gradually being fortified and converted into an arsenal? Can one believe with any degree of seriousness that the intelligence agencies failed to bring the seriousness of the situation to the notice of the Centre?* No convincing answer is available as to why matters were allowed to go this far. (Brar, 1993: 158)

This is as severe an indictment as it can get by one of the most responsible persons who had to finally deal with a thankless and no-win situation. Marwah too says, "Masterly inactivity by the government only emboldened Bhindranwale." (Marwah, 2009: 256)

K.P.S. Gill has described how Bhindranwale had become a significant pawn in the Congress(I)-Akali political tangle.... When Bhindranwale was arrested on 20 September 1981, he was lodged, not in a jail as he should have been, but in the ample comfort of the circuit house.... Once again, the investigations were scuttled; political expediency prevailed over the exigencies of the law. October 15 [1981] saw Bhindranwale a free man. (K.P.S. Gill, 1997: 80-81)

When Indira Gandhi held a meeting with the Akalis in Chandigarh on 21 September 1981, they gave her a memorandum of 15 points. Interestingly, as Bhindranwale had been arrested only a day earlier, the first demand of the Akalis pertained to his unconditional release. As stated earlier,

Mrs Gandhi told the Akalis, 'Bhindranwale is not a good man; you have been supporting him unnecessarily.' The Akalis replied, 'You have supported him for four years, we have supported him for 20 days.' (S.S. Gill, 1996: 322)

At the *Bhog* ceremony of *Jathedar* Santokh Singh in December 1981, along with Bhindranwale, Rajiv Gandhi and two prominent Central ministers of Indira Gandhi government, Zail Singh and Buta Singh, were present. As K.P.S. Gill has rightly stated, though they knew of his presence at the *Bhog*, "yet they chose to attend". (Gill, 1997: 82) According to Nayar and Khushwant Singh, both Zail Singh and Buta Singh "touched Bhindranwale's feet". (Nayar and Khushwant Singh, 1984: 42, footnote) But, as brought out in Zail Singh's memoirs quoted earlier, he has stoutly denied it.

Bhindranwale's growing stature and pretence to divinity can be seen from the fact that:

> with breathtaking audacity he adopted the practice of carrying, at all times, a steel arrow in hand, imitating the Tenth Guru; rumours were set afloat that the *baaz*, the holy falcon, another symbol associated with Guru Gobind Singh, was sighted hovering protectively over him. It was whispered that the 'spirit' of the Tenth Guru had descended upon Bhindranwale; that he was an incarnation; even, among the more reckless, the blasphemous claimed that he was the 'Eleventh Guru' of Sikhism. This was the power of the Golden Temple, and of the symbols of the Faith. They conferred an aura of sainthood, almost of divinity, on the semi-literate evangelist of hate. (Gill, 1997: 85-86)

Over a period of time, the stature of Bhindranwale had grown. The Prime Minister of India he mocked as 'Panditain', daughter of a Brahmin, a remark redolent with the contempt that the Jat Sikh has for those who work with their minds rather than their hands. Asked whether he would meet

Mrs Gandhi he answered, 'No I don't want to, but if she wants to meet me, she can come here.' (Guha, 2007: 561)

K.P.S. Gill has written:

> The Golden Temple was defiled by horrors still unimagined ... Bhindranwale's men had already begun the process of disfiguring the Akal Takht. They smashed through the marble walls to create positions for the guns.... *A great arsenal had been built up within the Akal Takht; for months, trucks engaged for kar seva, supposedly bringing in supplies for the daily lunger, had been smuggling in guns and ammunition. The police never attempted to search these vehicles entering the Golden Temple, apparently on 'instructions from above'. But when one such truck was randomly stopped and checked, a large number of sten guns and ammunition were recovered. The terrorists, it was discovered after Blue Star, had even set up a 'granade manufacturing' facility, and a workshop for the fabrication of sten-guns within the Temple complex..... Ex-army veterans and deserters under the leadership of the cashiered Major General Shabeg Singh, provided weapon training to Bhindranwale's men in the Temple complex itself.*

This was "*a period of stupefying inaction*", as Gill calls it. (Gill, 1997: 92, 94-95)

As a former Union Home Secretary, I find it impossible to believe that State Government and the Central Government were unaware of this. Clearly, there was a political decision to turn a blind eye to it. How much short-sighted can the politics get, even at the highest level!

INDIRA GANDHI'S INDECISIVENESS

A few days after the army action, CPI(M) leader Surjeet authoritatively exposed the government's record of sheer bad faith during the negotiations with the Akali leaders. He cited three specific instances of accords concluded with the Akalis from which the government backed out. He also cited other specific instances of opportunities of accord spurned by the government. Noorani has lamented:

> In an atmosphere fouled by violence and surcharged with tension, lucky is an administration which gets such opportunities. But incompetent, if not malevolent, surely, must be the regime which spurns them. There was undoubted progress in the negotiations. Only the territorial issue remained. (Patwant Singh, 1985: 151)

Indira Gandhi held three meetings with the Akalis. There was no perceptible progress. Nayar has written:

> The Akalis recall their last meeting ... with bitterness; they believe that she had decided to break off the talks beforehand. They found her formal and intractable. While comparing the atmosphere of informality and friendliness at the first two meetings, they say that the third meeting was cold and ritualistic. They could not comprehend why she had changed her attitude. After the last meeting, they felt humiliated and they said at many religious congregations that they had not been served even a glass of water. (Nayar, 1984: 49)

The talks with Akalis which began in April 1982, continued intermittently till early 1984 but did not lead anywhere, mainly because of Indira Gandhi's indecisiveness. As stated earlier in Zail Singh's memoirs, even serious talks held by Swaran Singh with the Akalis which had arrived at an agreement on practically all points proved infructuous due to the intransigence of the government.

G.S. Chawla in his article in *The Indian Express* of 14 November 1983 had brought out the developments.

> Things appeared set for a settlement, he recalled: Four Akali leaders, Prakash Singh Badal, G.S. Tohra, J.S. Talwandi and Balwant Singh reached the capital to be available to Swaran Singh, who was shuttling between the government and the Akalis. After three prolonged meetings with Swaran Singh, the Akali leaders left for Amritsar on the morning of November 3. He had promised to inform them by 5 PM about the final outcome of the talks. He had two meetings with the Cabinet Committee members that day.... At 5 PM a brief statement was prepared and approved by the Cabinet Committee which was read out to the Akalis on phone at Amritsar from the office of the Finance Minister Pranab Mukherjee. The Akalis were satisfied with the statement and had agreed to postpone the announcement of the next phase of their agitation. The draft of the statement was circulated to the members of Cabinet Committee later in the evening. Home Minister P.C. Sethi was to make a statement in Parliament the next day. But the statement he made the next day was different from the one read out to the Akalis on phone.... After Sethi's statement, the Akalis announced their plans to agitate at the time of Asiad. Surjeet fully corroborated this version. He had also played some part in it.

Thereafter Farooq Abdullah took a hand and after talking to Indira Gandhi had said, "I think by the grace of God, there is hope of settlement and something good might come out of it."

However, nothing came of it. The talks continued.... As [I.K.] Gujral remarked as late as May 6, 1984, "*it is ironical but true that each time the final approval was denied in the name of the Prime Minister*." (Patwant Singh, 1985: 156-159)

I have quoted earlier from the memoirs of Zail Singh, who too had referred to Swaran Singh's and his own frustration at the last-minute reversal of the stand by the government.

Even when Darbara Singh government was in position, all decisions, including whether to arrest Bhindranwale or not, were being taken by the Central Government. This 'remote control' proved catastrophic. After the gruesome murder of Atwal, DIG, on the doorsteps of the Golden Temple by the followers of Bhindranwale, the State Government was prepared to permit the police to enter the temple but, again, it was the Central Government which declined the permission.

Gupte has recalled his conversation with Manmohan Singh, Chairman of Frick India, who also headed organizations such as the Delhi Chamber of Commerce, regarding Singh's conversation with P.C. Alexander:

> The PM never listens – either she demands an explanation, or she gives you a lecture,' Singh quoted Alexander as saying. In fact, Mrs Gandhi declined to meet personally with the Akalis, passing on the task instead to top aides such as Alexander. Her son and heir-apparent, Rajiv Gandhi, also occasionally met with the Sikhs. Manmohan Singh told me [Gupte] that the Akali Dal's President, the late Harchand Singh Longowal, expressed to him his dismay over Mrs Gandhi's refusal to meet with him or the rest of the Akali leadership. (Gupte, 2009: 323)

This is somewhat surprising and does not tally with the other reports according to which Indira Gandhi had at least three meetings with the Akali leaders, quoted earlier by me. I also doubt if Alexander would have spoken so irreverently about Indira Gandhi.

B. Raman, in his book, *The Kaoboys of R&AW – Down Memory Lane*, has stated that long hours of secret negotiations were held by Rajiv Gandhi and two of his close associates with the Akalis. Talks with Akali leaders based abroad were held by Kao. Raman was present in all these talks and had all these negotiations secretly recorded and [he] spent endless hours transcribing them. 'When I retired on August 31, 1994, I had handed over these records for safe custody in the archives of the organisation [R&AW]. Today, 23 years later, nobody knows where those records of historical importance are.' (Raman, 2007: 28)

According to Gupte:

> The Akalis and others familiar with the on-again off-again negotiations, suspected that Mrs Gandhi was being recalcitrant because she had an ulterior motive. She let the Punjab crisis drag on, they suspected, in order to rally State's Hindus behind her and in order to unify the Hindu majority of the north Indian States, all of whom were concerned about the growing shrillness of the Sikh's agitation. By stonewalling the Sikhs, Mrs Gandhi was consolidating her position with the Hindu majority in north India, whose support she deemed especially critical in the national elections that were to be held in January 1985. (Gupte, 2009: 324)

It may be pertinent to refer to the personal letter dated 23 March 1984 Indira Gandhi had written to A.C.N. Nambiar, based in Switzerland at the time, who was working for India from abroad during the freedom movement and had later became a close family friend of Nehru and Indira Gandhi:

> The most unfortunate part is the attitude of the opposition parties which is irresponsible, to say the least. They all encouraged the Akali Dal in their demands so that it became impossible to come to an agreement. It was mistake to involve the opposition parties in those talks. The situation now is extremely serious. Terrorism and violence is growing, and those who are not at all committed to India or to any values, seem to be gaining the upper hand. Some of our opposition is realising its folly and their staunchest

supporter, Surjeet of CPI(M) has issued a statement condemning their latest remarks. (Balachandran, 2016: 322)

This brings out the thinking of Indira Gandhi and shows that the situation had reached a dead-end and there was no hope of any negotiated settlement.

THE CHANDIGARH QUESTION

For years Chandigarh question has become linked in public mind with Fazilka-Abhor area. This has been because of Indira Gandhi's insistence that Chandigarh can be given to Punjab only if Punjab agrees to give its Fazilka-Abhor area to Haryana, as compensation. Noorani, in his article "A White Paper on a Black Record" reproduced by Patwant Singh et al in their book, *Punjab – The Fatal Miscalculation,* has brought out the following aspects which have very rarely come into public discussion, except of the few experts and knowledgeable persons who may have been closely involved:

(i) *Fazilka-Abhor is not contiguous to Haryana.*

(ii) *At least 60 of its 115 villages are Punjabi-speaking.... According to one estimate, of the total population of 4,00,000 of Fazilka tehsil, 1,50,000 were Sikhs.*

(iii) When linguistic States were created in 1956, only two States were excluded from it, namely, east Punjab and Bombay.

(iv) When Punjabi Suba was conceded a decade later after much violence, Chandigarh was denied to it.

Noorani has referred to an article in *The Indian Express* of 11 April 1983 written by Sardar Hukam Singh, former Speaker of Lok Sabha, who was the Chairman of the Parliamentary Committee on the Punjabi Suba, in which he had exposed the intrigues surrounding the creation of Punjabi Suba. "In her book *My Truth*, Mrs Gandhi reveals, "I went to Y.B. Chavan and said I heard that Sardar Hukam Singh was going to give a report in favour of the Punjabi Suba and that he should be stopped." Imagine doing this to a parliamentary body. But then, "I was very bothered and I went around seeing everybody". Why? Mrs Gandhi is candid: "To concede the Akali demands would mean abandoning a position to which the Congress was firmly committed and letting down the Hindu supporters in the projected Punjabi Suba; and not to do so would precipitate a Sikh agitation which would certainly turn violent." It is this concern for her Hindu supporters in the Punjabi Suba which explains Mrs Gandhi's policy all these years.

(v) The terms of reference of the Boundary Commission, which was appointed on 23 April 1966, were loaded against Punjab. The Commission was directed to apply the linguistic principle with due regard to the census figures of 1961 and other relevant considerations. The Commission was also asked to take into account such other factors as administrative convenience and economic well-being, geographic contiguity and facility of communication and *ordinarily ensure that the adjustments that they may recommend do not involve breaking up of existing tehsils*. Everyone knew that the census figures of 1961 were unfair to Punjab for the simple reason that in the communally charged atmosphere, to which the Akalis had also contributed, large numbers of Punjabi-speaking Hindus claimed Hindi as their mother tongue. *The concern for the preservation of tehsils was indefensible.*

(vi) Chandigarh was surrounded on three sides by the Punjabi region and on the remaining side it abutted the Hindi region. Even the highway which connected it with the Hindi region passed through the Punjabi area first.

(vii) On 22 January 1984, some 150 eminent Punjabis highlighted that '*Chandigarh was built to compensate Punjab for the loss of its capital, Lahore*. There is no reason for that decision to be altered. Surely, the nation can afford to give Haryana the funds for its own capital'.

(viii) *Other disputed areas, like Fazilka and Abhor should be settled on the basis of contiguity with village as a unit.*

Noorani has rightly underlined that "Mrs Gandhi's stand on Fazilka and Abhor alone was responsible for the deadlock: The country has been made to pay a heavy price for it." (Patwant Singh, 1985: 153-156, 160)

Dr Ambedkar was fond of saying that boundary marking is the job of a surveyor; boundary-making is the task of a statesman. Noorani has drawn a parallel between the stand taken by the Central Government in regard to Bombay and Chandigarh. But so far as Nehru's stand against Bombay being given to Maharashtra was concerned, it was based on his sincere conviction that linguistic States were not in the interest of the country, in the long term, and bilingual or multi-lingual States would be more suited to India. I fully shared Nehru's concerns. I had dilated on them in my book, *The God Who Failed: As Assessment of Jawaharlal Nehru's Leadership* (pp 157-160). The fierce, and often narrow-minded regional, linguistic and cultural ethos evident in a number of States and the intense inter-State disputes and conflicts it is giving rise to in recent years have shown how justified were the concerns of Nehru. Unfortunately, Congress party had strongly advocated the concept of linguistic States right from 1930s and it was unable to turn the tide of public opinion. Having conceded the principle of linguistic States all over the country, it was difficult to justify making an exception only in a few cases. As both Maharashtra and Gujarat were not prepared to live in a bilingual State, the only question which remained was that of the future of Bombay city. Nehru and the Congress High Command adopted a very unreasonable stand and tried to stick to its prejudiced and pre-conceived notions by resisting transfer of Bombay to Maharashtra. Finally, after much violence and agitation, including the death of a number of persons, Bombay was reluctantly given to Maharashtra.

In the case of Chandigarh, however, at no time the decision of the Centre to link it up with Fazilka and Abhor was justified. There was no justification for making Chandigarh a Union Territory. A new capital could easily have been constructed for Haryana. The latest example is that of Andhra Pradesh where Chandrababu Naidu, with his astute leadership and commendable statesmanship, decided to build a green-field capital for the State at Amravati. Even in this case, suggestions were made to declare Hyderabad as a Union Territory and, following the example of Chandigarh, to make it a capital of both Telangana and Andhra Pradesh. Fortunately, wiser counsels prevailed.

It is only due to Indira Gandhi's rigid stand that Chandigarh problem remained unresolved during her life-time. If she had taken a reasonable position on the subject, and Chandigarh had been given to Punjab, the whole Punjab agitation would have taken a different and more conciliatory turn. For all that I know, even Blue Star could have been avoided.

It is unfortunate that even after Indira Gandhi's assassination, though almost all political parties have been in power at the Centre at one time or another, this issue has remained unaddressed. I strongly believe that a new beginning should be made by announcing the transfer of Chandigarh to Punjab and a decision to build a new capital for Haryana. As for the future of other Punjabi and Hindi speaking areas in dispute, a Boundary Commission may be appointed with a clear guide-line that village should be adopted as the unit, subject to the other usual criteria such as contiguity, communications, cultural ties etc.

LAUNCHING OF OPERATION BLUE STAR

Zail Singh's recollections of his interaction with the Prime Minister before launching of the operation are highly relevant to understand the dynamics of the situation. Zail Singh has written in his memoirs:

> Towards the end of May 1984, *Mrs Indira Gandhi mentioned nonchalantly* that some people had suggested to her to send the police into the Golden Temple complex to flush out the militants entrenched therein, but she was not exactly convinced of this course, as it was likely to have an unfavourable fall out. *But, at the same time, she said, she could not see any alternative.* I seriously pondered over Mrs Gandhi's thinking. I told her that this course would not be proper, as it could have serious repercussions. The entry of police in the Complex was bound to inflame the public mind. Plausible alternatives could definitely be considered. *She positively gave me an impression that she agreed to what I said.* I tried my best to persuade her not to take any provocative step, but to adopt subtle methods to dislodge the armed men from religious places. Reflecting over this suggestion, *she said that she would certainly apply her mind to other means, but did not disclose how her mind was actually working.* (Zail Singh, 1997: 177)

In the meanwhile, pressure from all spheres, including political parties, was building up on the government to take strict action. Nayar has written:

> Though both the Prime Minister and the Home Minister had already said that they would not allow the police to enter the temple, it was reported that Zail Singh had threatened to resign if government ever changed its mind. Zail Singh did not contradict the report when it was reported in the papers because he received many congratulatory telegrams. However, when the opposition raised it in Parliament, the government insisted on his issuing a contradiction, which he did. (Nayar, 1984: 80)

MANY UNANSWERED QUESTIONS

Lt. Gen. K.S. Brar, himself a Sikh, who led the Operation Blue Star has written about the saga in his book, *Operation Blue Star – The True Story*. He has answered a number of questions which he had often been asked. But, still some important questions remain:

- Why the police did not enter the Golden Temple earlier is a troubling question. If they had done so, there would have been no need to take the extreme step of calling in the army.
- Another crucial question is why the operation could not have been entrusted to Para-Military Forces (PMFs). Marwah has written that the task of flushing out the entrenched terrorists was first entrusted to the CRPF. The Director-General of the CRPF personally went to Amritsar to take stock of the situation and plan his strategy. However, what he saw there convinced him that the task was beyond the capacity of his force, which was not equipped and trained in the use of heavy weaponry

required to confront the heavily armed terrorists. After several visits he reported to the Union Home Ministry about his inability to undertake the task. (Marwah, 2009: 266) Since no dates have been mentioned by Marwah, it is not clear if this was before the fortification of the Golden Temple by Bhindranwale, or after. If it was after the fortification, it was a realistic assessment.

Kuldip Nayar has written that the fact that the troops went into the Golden Temple had upset the Sikhs most. When asked, Chief of Army Staff, General Dyal said, 'It was not a para-military job; the terrorists were too well entrenched. Every conceivable place in the temple had been used as an emplacement. Only the army could have done the job'. Surendra Nath, a fine IPS officer, who was Advisor to Governor of Punjab, too was of the same opinion. (Nayar, 1984: 109) But, these assessments too were after Bhindranwale had taken a refuge in the Golden Temple and its fortification was done to perfection. *The question remains why the government had to wait that long.*

It is necessary to mention that in May 1988, almost four years after Operation Blue Star, the PMFs had launched "Black Thunder" to evict militants and criminals who had taken refuge in the Golden Temple. The PMFs had successfully carried out the operation. Even Brar has admitted that "the operation was well executed and was successful in clearing the Temple, literally without a shot being fired." (Brar, 1993: 153) Of course, the two situations were poles apart. In 1984, the situation had been permitted to go so much out of hand due to the Central Government's shocking mis-handling that the only option which was left was to call in the army. But, this certainly could have been avoided.

Reference must be made in this context to the contingency plan which was prepared by the Ministry of Home Affairs in 1991-92, to take pre-emptive action to take over the Babri Masjid to protect it from lakhs of 'invading' *kar sevaks*. The entire planning and preparation, up to the minutest detail, was done by the PMFs, as a joint operation. I was Union Home Secretary at the time. It was another matter that due to Prime Minister P.V. Narasimha Rao's reluctance, the operation was not executed. A huge force of 20,000 PMFs, fully trained and equipped commandos, dog squads, water cannons and a host of paraphernalia was kept idling just 10 kilometres from Ayodhya, while the Babri Masjid was being demolished. But it showed the capabilities of PMFs. (Godbole, 1996: 357-375) I am of the view that similar option could have been seriously explored, *before the fortification* of the Golden Temple began. Outstanding police officers, who were closely associated with the events, namely, Julio Rebeiro, K.P.S. Gill and Ved Marwah could have been entrusted this responsibility.

- Brar has stated that Bhindranwale's armed followers were in forcible occupation of as many as seventeen three or four storeyed houses from which, in most cases, the legitimate inmates had been evicted. Some of these houses had been occupied as early as two months ago, and in the intervening period had been fortified into well defended 'observation and early warning posts', manned with light machine guns and other automatic firing weapons with their sights directed towards open spaces along the approaches to the Temple and the narrow, labyrinthine maze of lanes running below. Surprisingly, P.S. Bhinder, IGP [who was the blue-eyed boy of Sanjay Gandhi during the Emergency and whose wife was a Congress(I) MP], had failed to order the police, including the CRP [Central Reserve Police], to evict the militants from these houses despite their visible presence along with their weapons. (Brar, 1993: 41) I have given this extensive quotation to show the state of affairs before the army was called in. The situation could have been well taken care of earlier, particularly since the State was under President's Rule. But, clearly, there was no political will.

- Brar has rightly stated that "one finds no plausible reason why the government failed to order the police to arrest Bhindranwale earlier." (Brar, 1993: 26) This was before Bhindranwale moved into the Golden Temple on 15 December 1983, and when he was staying in Guru Nanak Niwas, which was not a part of the Golden Temple complex. There were no restrictions on the police entering the place.

Reference must be made to the plan prepared by R.N. Kao, chief of R&AW, to fly in the commandos by helicopter over the building and to send them into the building to take away Bhindranwale. This was just the replica of what the American Navy SEALs did in Pakistan to eliminate Osama bin Laden in May 2011. It was highly creditable that such a daring plan was prepared by R&AW in 1983-84. Sandeep Unnithan has in his article "The Untold Story – The Secret Operation Before Blue Star" (*India Today*, 10 February 2014) brought out how extensive training of commandos had been done and the minutest details had been worked out. When Kao explained the plan to Indira Gandhi, she asked, "How many casualties were likely?" Kao said may be all commandos, and a few civilians, including the destruction of the helicopter. Indira Gandhi declined to give a go-ahead. The Operation Blue Star undertaken later resulted in many more casualties, apart from causing extensive damage to the Golden Temple and deeply hurting the Sikh psyche. There was no rational explanation for Indira Gandhi's reluctance to permit R&AW to launch the operation. The authenticity of this plan is confirmed by what one of Brar's officers, who was in the commando group, had narrated to Brar. (Brar, 1993: 39)

- Army appears to have been hustled by the government in taking action without giving it time to prepare for it fully. Since the government files and records have not still been made public, there are more than one versions of what actually happened during this crucial period of decision-making. According to Adams and Whitehead, "Indira asked General K. Sunderji, her Army Commander-in-Chief, if he could take the Golden Temple without damage. In response, *he produced aerial pictures taken the previous day showing that all windows, doors and other orifices were barricaded with bricks and sandbags. Sunderji warned her that the chances of grievous damage were very high*. (Adams, 1997: 311)

  Nayar has written that General A.S. Vaidya was summoned to Delhi on 25 May by cutting short his visit to Kashmir, and told of the mission. When General Vaidya spoke to Lt. Gen. K. Sundarji, GOC-in C, Western Command, Sundarji had said that he would need three weeks for preparations. Mrs Gandhi had turned this down and had asked him to move in by 3 June. (Nayar, 1984: 93)

  Adequate thought was also not given to the directions which were given to the army. Army was asked to use minimum force and ensure the safety of the *Harmandir Sahib*, the dome-roofed building where the reading of the Sikh holy book, *Guru Granth Sahib*, has continued without a break for more than two hundred

> years. But, the *Akal Takht*, though nearly as holy as the *Harmandir Sahib*, was clubbed with 'other buildings around the water'. The white paper issued by the government confirmed that the *Akal Takht* was not included in the order prescribing minimum use of force. (Nayar, 1984: 93)

As K.P.S. Gill has stated:

> After months of dithering, the Centre suddenly deployed the army on 3 June 1984. The operation itself commenced less than three days later *under political pressure*, *indeed in a state of political hysteria*, long before the army could dig in and make a realistic evaluation of the situation. It was this undue haste that resulted in both the unnecessary loss of life and excessive damage to various buildings within the shrine. *The army was sent in with needless haste, virtually blind, and once again, crippling restrictions on what they could and could not do within the Temple.* (Gill, 1997: 96)

Ved Marwah is also of the same view:

> *The army leadership had apparently taken a rather simplistic view of the situation* ... the army should have given itself more time to understand the complexity and the sensitivity of the problem and prepare itself for the difficult task. It should have first made an in-depth study and assessment of the determination and capability of the well-armed extremists before launching its ill-fated offensive.... *A badly planned operation had little chance of success.* Unnerved by the heavy casualties the troops suffered in the first few minutes of the offensive, the army decided to use tanks to neutralise the firing machine guns. The tanks and heavy weapons knocked down not only the military fortifications, but caused heavy damage to the sacred buildings and almost destroyed the Akal Takht. (Marwah, 2009: 266-267)

Brar has written:

> The army, no doubt, had very little time for preparation and was just about able to assemble the necessary troops and equipment in time. I am certain the Army Chief would have preferred more time, but this was not possible due to the many factors.... As soon as the final 'go-ahead' was received, the operations were to commence at the earliest and be completed expeditiously, desirably within 48 to 72 hours ... among the parameters to be kept in view was that minimum force was to be applied. (Brar, 1993: 36-37, 127)

Reference may be made in this context to the Bangladesh War. There are two diametrically opposite versions of what happened at the time. According to one version attributed to General [as he then was] Manekshaw, when asked by the Prime Minister as to how soon the army could commence the operation, he had told the Prime Minister that army was not equipped and ready to undertake the operation at that stage and that it would have to await till after the monsoon. Indira Gandhi had accepted this. According to another version, Indira Gandhi never made any such suggestion to Manekshaw and she did not want Indian forces to go into Bangladesh till the situation in that country was ripe and conducive. But, if the first version was to be believed, why did General Vaidya not insist on more time from the Prime Minister before the attack was launched? In fact, from all accounts, the army did not appreciate the gravity of the situation and was confident of finishing the job within 72 hours!

T.N. Kaul, former Foreign Secretary, has written:

> A serving General of the army had sent the Prime Minister a verbal note advising categorically against the use of the army and an alternative action plan. She agreed with this suggestion but some ambitious hot-headed military brass

> advised her to let the soldiers move in and told her that it would be a short and swift operation with minimal loss of life and damage to the temple ... the Army Chief did not oppose it, nor did he point out any adverse fall-out.... The Army Commander also assured her that no heavy weapons would be used, the operation would be over in one night and the casualties on both sides would be minimal. All three assurances proved wrong. (Kaul, 2000: 114-115)

This version is quite the opposite of what some others have written and which I have quoted. One does not know whom to believe since the relevant documents have still not been made public.

- Launching the operation on Guru Arjun Dev's martyrdom day when there was to be a large congregation of pilgrims in the Golden Temple raises serious questions. The threat given by Akalis of State-wide agitation from 3 June 1984 to start communal violence, non-payment of revenue and irrigation charges, stoppage of water and electricity to neighbouring States and movement of foodgrains from Punjab was a matter of anxiety but not such a catastrophe that Operation Blue Star had to be launched the same day. The agitation could have been contained by the large police and para-military force which was available with the government.
- Brar has asserted:

> There is no truth whatsoever in some reports, which found their way into the Press, that the army had been given detailed intelligence about the defences within the Golden Temple many weeks earlier and that, in fact, we had built a large model of the Temple somewhere in the plains of Uttar Pradesh, where rehearsals were carried out well before the actual operation.... The assessment of the number

> of weapons in the possession of the extremists was somewhere in the region of 200-250 of which, *we were told*, the majority consisted of 12 bore guns, point 303 bolt action rifles, pistols and revolvers as well as a sprinkling of automatics (light machine guns and carbines). *What we finally discovered after the Operation was a different story altogether*.... [When the Operation Blue Star was under way, it was found that] Of the fifty or so light machine guns, as many as thirty were around the Akal Takht itself. Normally, an army unit would deploy this quantum of fire power to cover an area of about eight kilometres. (Brar, 1993: 39, 44, 154)

According to Kuldip Nayar, when President Zail Singh visited the Golden Temple after Operation Blue Star:

> The President was surprised that so many arms had been brought into the Temple by the terrorists without the knowledge of the authorities. He was specially harsh to the then Governor [B.D.] Pande [former Cabinet Secretary] who accompanied him on his visit to the Temple. Pande too pleaded that he too was not aware that such a large quantity of arms had been smuggled in. (Nayar, 1984: 112)

This is simply unbelievable. As a former Union Home Secretary, I know that according to the standard mailing list, all sensitive secret and top secret intelligence reports are sent in sealed covers to President of India, Prime Minister, Home Minister and certainly to the Governor, when a State is under President's Rule, unless instructions were given to the central agencies not to send the reports to the President. It is quite likely that this was the position, in view of Zail Singh's stand on this issue. It would be recalled that later, during Rajiv Gandhi's time when the relations between Zail Singh and Rajiv Gandhi had become strained, he had complained that intelligence reports and communications from Indian embassies were being kept away from him. Even during the Sikh riots after Indira Gandhi's assassination, Zail Singh had complained that his telephone had been tampered with and the members of Sikh community could not get in touch with him. Against this background, Zail Singh's statement may be true but it does not mean that the government did not have the knowledge of the goings on in the temple.

- K.P.S. Gill has stated: "there was complete lack of information; no realistic intelligence existed on the actual strength of the terrorists, of the quantity and deployment of arms available to them, or even a sufficiently detailed layout of the devastation impact on some of the most sacred buildings. *What could well have been won by strategy and planning had to be seized by brute force.* (Gill, 1997: 96-97) While I fully agree with the concluding comment of Gill, I have doubts about the first part of the observation.

It is important to note what Tully has stated:

> *For months before operation bluestar there had been no secret about the fact that Sant Jarnail Singh Bhindranwale, with the assistance of a retired General of the Indian army, was turning the Akal Takht into a fortress. I filmed the fortification of the shrines three months before bluestar.* (Tully, 1991: 154)

Against this background, who can believe that the government or the army was taken by surprise?

As brought out elsewhere, the government had all the intelligence reports of what was happening in the Golden Temple. May be there was a communication gap and the information was not shared with the army, before the operation. The army should also have made efforts to get full briefing before planning its strategy. But, obviously, the army was not given sufficient time by the government to do so.

Brar has written: most of the information given by the intelligence agencies to the army was vague, based on conjectures and turned out to be gross under-estimation. For the first time, in this case, government had placed the police and para-military forces under the overall control of the army. Army has asserted that it was not aware of the extent of fortification in the Golden Temple, the sophisticated lethal weapons, not just stored but strategically positioned, under the command of one of their own former officers, Major General Shabeg Singh (Retd) who had joined hands with Bhindranwale. Frankly, I find this impossible to believe. How can it be that the resistance which it encountered took the army by surprise? This is totally unbelievable. It also shows the inadequate planning on the part of the army.

- In his article on the government white paper, Noorani has contested the government's claim that it did not have adequate information about the lethal weapons stored in the Golden Temple by terrorists. He has written:

> On June 13, the Prime Minister told the opposition leaders that there was a failure of the government's intelligence network. We were also told that the government and the army were taken by surprise by the nature and the quantity of weapons discovered in the Golden Temple. Soon reports began to appear in the Press which proved that the intelligence agencies had penetrated the terrorists' camp and

had fully informed the government. Two recent ones will suffice.

Prem Kumar reported in *The Statesman* of July 4: 'The arrival of light machine-guns and sophisticated self-loading rifles had been taken notice of by the various agencies. The information received was so detailed that even the make and the country of origin of the weapons was known…. The authorities had some idea of the source of these weapons, mainly smuggled from Pakistan, and obtained through thefts and robberies and leakages from Indian ordinance units…. Many may be surprised over the fact that the Central and State Governments used to receive almost hourly reports of monthly meetings of Akali leaders even when only five or six of the top leaders attended these meetings in the Temple complex. When Sant Bhindranwale discussed his plans with only one or two close confidants, the information reached the authorities. It is understood that the government got information about Sant Bhindranwale even when he was confined to the Akal Takht and till as late as June 6.

As P.S. Bhinder, former IGP, whose wife was a Congress(I) member of Parliament, told Neerja Chowdhury and Shahnaz Anklesaria of that paper, shortly before he quit, "*Intelligence information reached the places it should have. It was political failure.*"

A.S. Pooni, Home Secretary of Punjab, also confirmed that 'the government had a fair idea of the kind of weapons inside the Golden Temple.' These included light machine guns, self-loading rifles and grenades.

How did they reach there? In Kar-Seva trucks carrying food and construction material. 'They were not intercepted because there were oral instructions 'from the top' until two months ago not to check any of the Kar-Seva trucks', Bhinder told the two correspondents.

They reported (July 8) that fortifications had been made only since last February. "*All this was known to the government*", a senior police officer revealed.

Four intelligence agencies were at work – CID, IB, R&AW and military intelligence. Two thousand men of Punjab police and the CRP had been deployed round the clock around the Temple. Incidentally, much earlier on June 14, Lt. Gen. J.S. Aurora had also pointed out that it was only after February this year that defences were dug in the Temple complex. The White Paper completely glosses over these points. (Patwant Singh, 1985: 148-150)

AFTER BLUE STAR

Mark Tully was greatly shocked when he visited the Golden Temple after the Operation Blue Star:

> Heavily armed soldiers in battle fatigues had replaced the pilgrims. There was a sullen silence. The walls were pockmarked with bullet holes. Squash-head shells fired by tanks and designed to destroy by sending shock waves through their targets had pulverized the frontage of the Akal Takht, leaving hardly a pillar standing, blackening marble walls and destroying plaster, filigree and mirrorwork decoration more than 200 years old. The floors of the shrine were carpeted with cartridges. The white marble of the pavement outside was stained with blood. (Tully, 1991: 154)

According to Adams and Whitehead:

> President Zail Singh visited on 8 June, when there was still sporadic gunfire, and wept to see the destruction. 'The

> complex looked like it was bombed from an aeroplane', said one of the aids. The President and the most senior Sikh minister in Indira's Cabinet, Buta Singh, were ex-communicated by Sikh high priests. Khushwant Singh, an MP and one-time Indira supporter, told her in Parliament, 'You made a mistake for which the country will pay the price for centuries to come … *it was an enormous error of judgment*. (Adams, 1997: 312)

Visit of Zail Singh to the Golden Temple after the Operation Blue Star invited considerable attention for several reasons, the most important was that he was himself a devout Sikh. Though he was deeply moved by what he saw and was greatly disturbed by the damage done to the holiest Sikh shrine, he conducted himself with great dignity and poise and defended the action of the government, though he had opposed even the entry of the police in the Golden Temple, leave aside army action. Any adverse reaction by him would have greatly damaged Indian government's image, both domestically and internationally, apart from inflaming the Sikh public opinion. He advised the high priests that "the services offered by the government for repairs should be accepted without rancour." His advice in the public speech in the Golden Temple was not only sober, mature and timely, but required lot of political courage. He said: "The Sikh leaders and organisations in general and the SGPC in particular, had made no serious efforts to make others understand the noble principles on which the foundations of this modern faith had been laid. All that they had been able to accomplish was to give the Sikhs a political identity and to establish distinctions of flags, banners and slogans…. *To use religion for political purposes was grossly incorrect. To mix politics with religion was quite inappropriate.* It was extremely wrong to equate those who lost their lives in political agitations and armed conflicts with the Sikh martyrs, who had made supreme sacrifices serving the cause of the Gurus in defence of the weak, the poor and the victims of tyranny and injustice." It was not surprising that after Zail Singh's speech, the High Priest of Akal Takht, Jathedar Kirpal Singh, stood up to read a pungently worded memorandum, which created a piquant situation. But Zail Singh sternly told him that he could have handed over the memorandum to him earlier, or could have read it out prior to his speech, so that Zail Singh could have dealt properly with the points raised by him. (Zail Singh, 1997: 194-195)

When seen in contrast to the shocking and intemperate utterances of Farooq Abdullah, former Chief Minister of J&K, a former Central minister and now a member of Parliament who was elected with hardly 12 per cent of the valid votes cast, about the troubling situation in the Valley in early 2017, I find Zail Singh's speech particularly statesman-like and praise-worthy.

Zail Singh has noted that Rajiv Gandhi, who was General Secretary of AICC and had accompanied him, was unhappy with the visit of Zail Singh to Amritsar. "The frequency of Rajiv Gandhi's visits to me also decreased", Zail Singh has noted. Zail Singh's broadcast to the nation on AIR on 17 June 1984 too did not go down well with Indira Gandhi, though he was supportive of the action taken by the government. (Zail Singh, 1997: 195)

Lt. Gen. J.S. Aurora, a highly decorated Bangladesh War hero, in his interview to *The Illustrated Weekly of India* on 22 July 1984, was candid in his assessment: "*My reaction is the army should not have gone into the Golden Temple* ... they [army] were given an unpleasant job which they had to do. No army likes to take action against its own people." In reply to a question "But what was the alternative? The Temple had become an arsenal, Aurora said:

> This is what I don't understand. If you can accept the fact that arms were allowed to be smuggled in, that Bhindranwale was allowed to build himself up – with the help of Sanjay Gandhi and Zail Singh – that training was allowed to go on and the intelligence about the activities was, as the government says, non-existent; *If you accept this colossal failure of the government without a blink, why are you surprised when I say the army should not have gone in? The army was used to finish a problem created by the government. This is the kind of action that is going to ruin the army.*

He added:

> The government showed no sense, no sensibility in handling the crisis ... *Mrs Gandhi has not only undermined democratic institutions, she has undermined her own lieutenants.... As for the army, I think as an ex-officer, it is totally wrong for me to correct their mistakes by hindsight. But yes, mistakes were made.*

Aurora was disturbed by Sikh's erosion of faith in government. He said, Sikhs in Bombay asked him whether arms were really found in Darbara Sahib. 'They could have put them there, couldn't they?' (Patwant Singh, 1985: 133-134, 140, 144)

As for the reactions of political parties, the CPI(M) was not consistent in its stand on Blue Star. At one stage, it supported the action and later, it criticised the action. Communist Party of India (CPI) was, however, consistent in its support for the action taken by the government. Swaran Singh told *Amrit Bazar Patrika* on 17 June 1984 that Operation Blue Star was not necessary, 'especially when other solutions were available'. He went on to say that the sanctity of the Golden Temple was first defiled by the extremists and then by the government. 'Two wrongs do not make a right'. (Patwant Singh, 1985: 229)

Marwah has stated:

> *What Bhindranwale could not achieve in his lifetime, was achieved by this ill-planned operation, after his death. The Hindu-Sikh divide was complete. The Sikh community was alienated like never before*, not only in India but also in countries like Britain, Canada and the US where there was sizeable Sikh population.... Unfortunately, the army in Punjab followed Operation Blue Star with another tragic operation, '*Woodrose*' ... its aim was to flush out the armed extremists from their hideouts in the rural areas, but the manner in which the operation was conducted, further humiliated and angered the Sikhs.... *The Sikh anger against these operations was so strong that disaffection also spread to the police force.* (Marwah, 2009: 268-269)

K.P.S. Gill was forthright when he wrote:

> Irrespective of what had preceded the Operation, it is with reason that the Sikhs were offended by what was done to their holiest shrine. Indeed, *those who hastily planned and rashly precipitated this action owe an explanation* not only to the Sikh community but to the entire Indian nation, to the army, and to the families of almost a hundred officers and *jawans* who sacrificed their lives to free the Golden Temple from the malevolence of the crew of murderers who had installed themselves there, as also to the families of more than 550 innocent civilians who were killed in the cross fire. (Gill, 1997: 97)

Kuldip Nayar's assessment of casualties is different: "the figures were 554 dead and 121 injured. The actual casualties were much higher and a figure of 3,000 would be nearer the truth." (Nayar, 1984: 109) According to the government's white paper, 4,712 persons, including large number of devotees caught unawares in the temple when curfew was imposed in Amritsar, were killed in the operation.

Mark Tully, in his book, *No Full Stops in India*, has described the Operation Blue Star as "Indian army's clumsy attack … which shook the foundations of the Indian nation." (Tully, 1991: 153)

WHITE PAPER ON PUNJAB

The instrument of white paper has often been used by the governments to rewrite history for the posterity. Punjab white paper, published by the government on 10 July 1984, belonged to this genre. Interestingly, P.V. Narasimha Rao, under whose watch Babri Masjid was demolished, was also the Minister for Home Affairs at the time. He moved a motion in the Lok Sabha on 24 July 1984 for taking into consideration the white paper. Taking part in the discussion, Madhu Dandavate alleged that the white paper had tried to conceal the failure of the government to bring about the settlement of Punjab negotiations on the one hand and their total failure to check the extremist activities, to prevent induction of arms and also restrain Bhindranwale on the other. Atal Bihari Vajpayee, C.T. Dandapani and Indrajit Gupta, among others, participated in the discussion.

Intervening in the discussion, Prime Minister Indira Gandhi refuted the argument that Congress(I) had regarded only the Akalis as the representatives of the Sikhs. National unity and integrity were her party's supreme objectives and nothing could be allowed to come in its way. What had happened in Punjab, she pointed out, was not simply a story of cruelty or merciless violence against the innocent people but a concerted attempt of a combination of internal and external forces to encourage divisive forces and if possible to divide the country. Referring to the demands of Akalis, the Prime Minister said that after the second meeting, they had come forward with two demands regarding water and territory. The government's stand had been that Chandigarh could not go to Punjab unless Haryana got something in its place. Akali Dal had not given up Anandpur Sahib Resolution and *the government were not willing to accept terrorism from the Golden Temple and piling up of arms there. The government, she reiterated, did not want the police to go in and to interfere with religion.* The army action had to be taken only when the matter came to a dead end. She was deeply pained in taking the action. But it had to be done in the national interest. She assured the House that the army would not stay there permanently and would be withdrawn as soon as the *kar seva* was completed.

Replying to the debate, *P.V. Narasimha Rao admitted that though the white paper did not contain information which every one wanted to know in the country,* it did bring out the essentials of what the present generation and the posterity needed to know.... *No one, he said, had won and no one had lost. It was secularism that had triumphed.* (Kashyap, 1998: 79-81)

A.G. Noorani in his article, "A White Paper on a Black Record", referred to earlier, tore apart the white paper in shreds. He stated that the white paper 'does not answer any of the questions people are asking today. It is much too tattered a fig leaf to cover the nudity of the government's hideous record in Punjab.' He alleged that the white paper was not deliberately brought out earlier, though repeatedly demanded by opposition members in Parliament, as that would have required disclosure of truth about the negotiations with the Akalis, which the government did not want to do. *He also asserted that the government had not been able to show any foreign hand though Indira Gandhi was making such claims from time to time. The former Governor B.D. Pande had said on 15 November 1983 that he had no evidence to prove the existence of a foreign hand.* The next day, Indira Gandhi had angrily retorted in Lok Sabha, "If he does not have the information, that is his business. But mostly, officials go by very technical definitions." (Patwant Singh, 1985: 145, 147)

It is surprising that doubts were being expressed about the external support received by the extremists in Punjab and that the former Governor of Punjab had said that he was not aware of it. This is simply shocking. The weapons confiscated in the Golden Temple after the Blue Star showed that several of them had the markings of Pakistan on them. Hein G. Kiessling, a German political scientist and historian who lived in Pakistan from 1989 to 2002, in his book, *Faith, Unity, Discipline – The Inter-Services Intelligence (ISI) of Pakistan*, has stated: "At the beginning of Ayub Khan's time, a covert action division was created in ISI. During the 1960s, it was involved in the support of local militant groups in north-east India, and *from mid-1970s it also helped insurgent Sikhs in Indian Punjab.*" (Kiessling, 2016: 28)

Reference must also be made to the very pertinent observations of Marwah:

> It was only later when the Sikh extremists dominated the political scene in Punjab that the Pakistan government decided to allow free flow of weapons to the extremist groups in the State. One of the factors that emboldened the Pakistan government to come out openly in support of the Sikh extremists was the change in the attitude of the West towards the Pakistan government under General Zia-ul-Haq. The Soviet Union's intervention in Afghanistan had made the US dependent on Pakistan's ISI for channelling funds and weapons to the mujahideen in Afghanistan. The shrewd Pakistan President exercised his leverage to ensure that there would be no criticism by the international community for his support to terrorism in Punjab…. Bhindranwale's demands were confined to grievances of the Sikh community, but as Pakistan's level

> of support increased and the ISI started taking a more direct interest in the extremist movement, he started echoing the Pakistan agenda: the break-up of the Indian Union. Giving up their earlier demand for a 'Punjabi Suba' within the Indian Union, Bhindranwale's followers now demanded secession from the Indian Union, and formation of an independent State from the Indian Union and the formation of an independent Sikh State. There was another reason for Pakistan's support to the terrorists in Punjab. Smarting at its defeat in the 1971 War and separation of one half of the country, the Pakistani ruling establishment, especially the army, saw in these developments an opportunity to settle scores with India. (Marwah, 2009: 259, 265)

If Indian elite, Parliament and even the Governor of a sensitive State like Punjab were not aware of this, blame must be placed on the Indira Gandhi government for not taking the country into confidence and educating the public opinion, as she did so effectively during the Bangladesh crisis.

But the narration of Noorani regarding intelligence, given earlier, are truly disturbing. In his concluding observations, Noorani had added "...Perhaps, like many other expressions, 'the healing touch' also means something different to her [Indira Gandhi]. One recalls that on her return to power she promised on January 14, 1980 in an address to the nation, 'our country needs the healing touch'. Soon thereafter, several non-Congress(I) governments were toppled and the process continues to this day." (Patwant Singh, 1985: 145-146, 161)

NO LESSONS WERE LEARNT

Another attempt was made by the extremists to take over the Golden Temple. Marwah, who was the Director-General of National Security Guard at the time, and K.P.S. Gill of Punjab

Police were entrusted the responsibility to flush out the extremists. As stated earlier, the 'Operation Black Thunder' was a total success. But, importantly, the prelude to this operation was no different than what it was during Indira Gandhi's leadership, though now Rajiv Gandhi was the Prime Minister. Marwah has written:

> The extremists made yet another bid to take over the Golden Temple complex. They once again methodically infiltrated the temple complex and managed to smuggle large quantities of arms and explosives. The government and the security forces once again decided to look the other way while all this was going on.... *Inaction by the government emboldened the terrorists holed up inside the temple complex so much so that they confidently announced the formation of an independent 'Khalistan'*.... On 10 August 1986, General Vaidya, was killed by the Sikh extremists to avenge 'the sacrilege', committed by the army in Golden Temple, under his command in 1984. (Marwah, 2009: 272. 275)

The government was indecisive and reluctant to take action till no other alternative was left but to rid the Golden Temple of the extremists. Finally, Operation 'Black Thunder' was launched in April 1988 to flush out the extremists. I am mentioning this only to underline that India had not learnt any lessons from Blue Star disaster. The misuse of other religious places has also continued, as seen in J&K over the years. Not a happy note on which to end this turbulent and unnerving chapter.

3

Amazing Journey – Empress of India

INTRODUCTION

Handling of Bangladesh crisis in an astute and statesman-like manner was the finest achievement of Indira Gandhi. Several features were particularly noteworthy. *First*, She built a team of competent, level-headed, and mature advisors which consisted of D.P. Dhar, P.N. Haksar, P.N. Dhar, T.N. Kaul and R.N. Kao and largely went by their advice. *Second*, she kept herself available to the Bangladesh freedom fighters, intellectuals and leaders for consultations. *Third*, her timing, whether for going to war or recognition of Bangladesh was perfect. Once the direction and timing was decided, she gave a free hand to the armed forces. *Fourth*, she took the leaders of opposition parties and Parliament into confidence on a continuous basis and made this into a national cause. This was in sharp contrast to Nehru's approach during the Chinese War in 1962 when he tried to hold back information from Parliament. *Fifth*, she mobilised domestic and international public opinion assiduously and also involved Jayaprakash Narayan in visits to several countries to explain India's position. *Sixth*, she was firm with the Americans, when warranted, and showed real metal when Nixon dispatched the Seventh Fleet to the Bay of Bengal. *Seventh*, soon after the Pakistan army surrendered in Bangladesh, she ordered cease-fire in Kashmir and on the western front. This dispelled the fears in some Western countries that India wanted to destroy Pakistan completely. *Finally*, by entering into Indo-Soviet Friendship Treaty at the crucial time, she check-mated not just the Chinese but also the Americans. It was unfortunate that the gains of Bangladesh War were, in a sense, squandered by mishandling of Simla Accord.

I.G. Patel, who was Secretary, Economic Affairs, saw Indira Gandhi closely at the time. His observations are therefore pertinent to assessment of her role. Patel has written:

> *The time was for cool heads and quiet diplomacy combined with firm resolve; and Mrs Gandhi rose to the occasion superbly.* I was asked how long we could sustain a conflict if the sanctions were applied. I was able to say confidently that with 1,000 million dollars in reserves and 10 million tonnes of foodgrains in stock – a measure of revival achieved since 1966 [when she took over] – we could easily manage for three or four months. (Patel, 2002: 144)

AMERICA'S PRO-PAKISTAN POLICY

American policy during the period is commonly described as tilting towards Pakistan but I believe that it was not just a 'tilt' but a pronounced Pakistan-centric policy. In his speech in the UN, ambassador George Bush had the temerity of referring to the Indian army operations in Bangladesh as 'aggression'. External Affairs Minister Swaran Singh had to invite the American ambassador in Delhi, Keating, on 7 December 1971 to express deep regret at the above comment. America was anxious to use Pakistan as a gateway for establishing relations with China, just as now Pakistan is a gateway for handling Afghanistan. *Second*, America did not want break-up of Pakistan. *Third*, it did not want India to make any in-roads into the Pakistan Occupied Kashmir (POK). Declassified American government papers show that, on 10 December 1971, "Irwin calls in Jha [Indian ambassador in USA] and states that the US cannot countenance India's taking of any territory which would have a 'most profound and long-lasting effect on US-Indian relations.' *He then asks Jha to obtain assurances from his government that India has no intention of taking any territory, including any part of Azad Kashmir.*" (Shanker, 2010: 349) Concerns such as human rights or upholding democratic values and principles were never of any importance to the Americans.

Though the American consulate in Dacca was sending continuous feed-back to Washington on the atrocities perpetrated by Pakistan army in East Pakistan, the Nixon administration turned a deliberate blind eye to it. Gary Bass in his book, *Blood Telegram – India's Secret War in East Pakistan,* has extensively catalogued the correspondence during the period:

> On the night of March 25, 1971, the Pakistan army had begun a relentless crackdown on Bengalis … untold thousands of people were shot, bombed, or burnt to death, in Dacca alone. Archer Blood, the United States Consul General in Dacca, had spent that grim night on the roof of his official residence, watching as tracer bullets lit up the sky, listening to clattering machine guns and thumping tank guns. There were fires across the ramshackle city. Blood detailed how Pakistan was using US weapons – tanks, jet fighters, gigantic troop transport airplanes, jeeps, guns, ammunition – to crush the Bengalis. The White House did not want to be seen as doing anything that might hint at the breakup of Pakistan. The Dacca consulate stubbornly kept up its reporting. But, Blood later recalled, his cables were met with a *'deafening silence'*. He retched up his dispatches, sending in a blistering cable tagged *'selective genocide'*. The White House staff passed this up to Kissinger, who paid no heed. Then on April 6, two weeks into the slaughter, Blood and almost his entire consulate

> sent in a telegram formally declaring their 'strong dissent' – a total repudiation of the policy that they were to carry out. *That cable – perhaps the most radical rejection of US policy ever sent by its diplomats – blasted the United States for silence* in the face of atrocities, for not denouncing the quashing of democracy, for *showing 'moral bankruptcy' in the face of what they bluntly called genocide.* (Bass, 2013: xii-xiii)

Attention may be invited in this context to the high level Hamoodur Rahman Judicial Commission, under the Chairmanship of Chief Justice of Pakistan Justice Hamoodur Rahman, which was appointed by the Government of Pakistan in December 1971, with Justice S. Anwarul Haq, Judge of the Pakistan Supreme Court, and Chief Justice of Sindh and Baluchistan High Court, as members. The Commission had held the army fully responsible for several acts and had recommended action against a number of senior functionaries. Bhutto feared that if the report was made public, the people of Pakistan would rise in revolt. The report was not therefore released but it got leaked and its contents became widely known. Important thing to note is that *a high level Judicial Commission of Inquiry appointed by the Government of Pakistan* had substantiated the atrocities perpetrated by Pakistan army on hapless residents of East Pakistan.

Bass has also written, "Nixon and Henry Kissinger ... were driven not by Cold War calculations, but a starkly personal and emotional dislike of Indians and Indira." (Ray, 2014: 132)

Kalyani Shankar in her book, *Nixon, Indira and India: Politics and Beyond*, has brought out the forces which were at work in the way American policies came to be shaped at the time:

> Nixon was obsessed with his China opening and did not want any hurdles.... "Our objective should be to buoy Yahya for at least another month while Pakistan served as

> gateway to China," Kissinger told Nixon at the beginning of June [1971]. "Even apart from the Chinese things," the President replied, "I wouldn't help Indians, the Indians are no goddamn good...." Kissinger admitted in his memoirs: "There was no doubt about the strong arm measures of Pakistan military. But Pakistan was our sole channel to China; once it was closed off, it would take months to make alternative arrangements...." [But at the same time] neither British nor the Americans wished to be made scapegoats for the breakup of Pakistan. (Shanker, 2010: 214-215)

President Nixon's tilt towards Pakistan did not stop at sending the Seventh Fleet to the Bay of Bengal. America wanted to go much further, incredibly further. T.N. Kaul, the then Foreign Secretary, has in his book, *A Diplomat's Diary (1947-99), China, India and USA (The Tantalising Triangle)*, has shed light on these American initiatives:

> *Nixon wanted to draw China into an Indo-Pak conflict on Pakistan's side*, without direct American involvement on land. He also hoped to draw the USSR and thus weaken both Communist Russia and China, as well as non-aligned India and fight to the last Indian and Pakistani!.... *When China did not intervene militarily, the US beat a hasty retreat and withdrew the 'Enterprise'*. The Bangladesh War could have ended on December 9 when Pakistani forces in East Pakistan were willing and ready to surrender. *Yahya Khan, expecting military intervention by USA and China, delayed the surrender* as he felt that US pressure on India directly and through Russia would give back 5,000 square miles in West Pakistan and 400 square miles in Pakistan Occupied Kashmir (POK) to Pakistan before a cease-fire. *Nixon also directed the US delegate in the Security Council, George Bush, along with the support of China and other members, to pass a*

> *resolution* accordingly.... *The Soviet representative vetoed the US resolution.* (Kaul, 2000: 92-93)

Gupta Ray in his book, *Birth of a Nation*, has stated:

> *It was officially claimed that the task force [Seventh Fleet] was sent to evacuate US citizens, 47 of them total,* who on their own choice stayed back in Bangladesh, while all foreigners including many Americans were evacuated under the Indian safe conduct. This ridiculous explanation could never justify dispatch of such a strong armada to the war zone. Writing in *Washington Post*, Jack Anderson, who claimed to have studied the secret White House papers, gave the following reasons behind the decision to send the USS Enterprise to the Bay of Bengal:
>
> (a) to compel India to divert her ships and aircraft to shadow the task force;
>
> (b) to weaken India's blockade of East Pakistan ports;
>
> (c) to divert INS Vikrant from military missions, and
>
> (d) to force the Indian aircraft on defence alert, thus reducing offensive operations against East Pakistan.
>
> The very presence of Enterprise in the Bay of Bengal caused jubilation in the Pak army. Biharis distributed sweets.... A Russian task force consisting of nuclear submarines, destroyers, cruisers, tankers, minesweepers and other supporting ships, along with atomic missiles were already in the Indian Ocean. According to Jack Anderson, the commander of the forces was authorised to [take] action in case US or China intervened. (Gupta, 2016: 263-264)

Gupta Ray has written:

> Short of direct involvement, China did everything. It extended verbal, moral, political and material support to Pakistan liberally. It also made some troop movements

> which turned out to be merely symbolic and psychological moves to frighten India. (Gupta, 2016: 262)

This is also borne out by the account given by Kalyani Shankar:

> Dennis Kux pointed out in his book, *The US and Pakistan*, that after 22 November 1971, the Chinese passed a message through General Vernon Walters, the US defence attaché, urging Washington to 'exert influence' to prevent further deterioration of the situation. The next day Kissinger, accompanied by Ambassador Bush held his first secret meeting with the Chinese envoy Huang Hua in New York to review how the US and China could deal with the East Pakistan issue in the UN. Kissinger showed the draft of the resolution. Huang Hua assured Kissinger that China would support Pakistan in the Security Council and would follow Pakistan's lead as to whether to take the issue further or not. (Shanker, 2010: 223)

According to Shankar,

> About the same time, Kissinger received a message that Huang Hua wanted a meeting with them. Misreading his intentions, Kissinger and Nixon thought China was proposing to intervene militarily against India. Kissinger said excitedly, 'This call for a meeting is totally unprecedented. They are going to move. No question they are going to move.' While discussing the consequences of a Chinese intervention, they also anticipated a Soviet move.... But to their utter surprise, the Chinese said that independence for East Pakistan was a foregone conclusion. It was prepared to endorse UN proposal for a standstill ceasefire and forego a demand for mutual troop withdrawal. (Shanker, 2010: 235)

Deliberate propaganda was carried out by USA that India wanted to dismember West Pakistan and that it was only under the pressure of the Americans that Indira Gandhi declared a cease-fire. Kaul has forcefully refuted both these contentions.

Reference must be made to Bhutto's drama in the UN. As Dennis Kux writes:

> In a fiery forty minute speech, Bhutto castigated the British and the French as "opportunists", called the Soviet representative "Tsar Malik", and charged that Indian Foreign Minister Swaran Singh had hands "full of blood". At the same time, Bhutto thanked the United States for 'its stand on principle' and expressed appreciation of China's help. As he ended his speech, Bhutto tore up his notes and made a dramatic exit with tears rolling down his cheeks, declaring, "I will not be any party to legalising aggression." (Shanker, 2010: 236)

In a television interview on May 12, 1977, Nixon told his interviewer, David Frost, that India planned to invade West Pakistan in 1971, inviting a potential clash with China. And it was pressure from the USA and the Soviet Union that prevented Indira Gandhi to carry out the invasion. C.S. Pandit had probed into the matter and found that this was based on gossip collected by one of the staff members of American embassy in New Delhi and was totally baseless. (Pandit, 1977: xi) This once again showed Nixon's hatred of India, even though so many years had elapsed.

K.P.S. Menon, former Indian ambassador to China and USSR, has in his book, *The Indo-Soviet Treaty – Setting and Sequel*, stated that words like murder and massacre, let alone genocide, do not seem to exist in the American vocabulary. Not a word of sympathy for the people of Bangladesh has escaped President Nixon's lips. (Menon, 1971: 31)

Khasru in his book, *The Bangladesh Military Coup and the CIA Link*, has stated:

> Nixon delayed Bangladesh's recognition out of his consideration for Pakistan. Bhutto had requested America to give him a little time to see what basis remained for a future relationship with Dhaka. He hoped that we would bear this in mind in our own actions. The situation has now changed considerably with Mujib's return and the statements he has made, and, we are, of course, taking this into account in our continuing examination of the recognition question and other issues. But we will not want to complicate unduly any progress toward an understanding which they might achieve," Nixon informed the British Prime Minister, referring to Bhutto and Mujib. Kissinger had also suggested to Nixon that he should consult Chou En-lai, China's Prime Minister, to "show how much you take them into consideration". (Khasru, 2014: 9-10, 15)

K.P.S. Menon has written:

> Our armed forces fought with perfect discipline and boundless heroism.... "If you want to see how a modern war should be fought", said a commentator over the BBC, "go to India." The operations of the Indian army, said another commentator, were characterized by flexibility, ferocity and speed, and some of its feats have established a record in military history. The relations between the civilians and the armed forces were exactly as they should be. (Menon, 1971: 143)

Reference must be made to the letter written by Indira Gandhi to President Nixon on 15 December 1971. It was drafted by Haksar and, as was to be expected, it was hard-hitting. She emphasised that war could have been avoided if the power, influence and authority of all nations, and above all the United States, had got Sheikh Mujibur Rehman released. She clarified: 'we are asked what we want. We seek nothing for ourselves. We do not want any territory of what was

East Pakistan and now constitutes Bangladesh. We do want lasting peace with Pakistan.' She ended the letter by asking, 'where precisely we have gone wrong before your representatives or spokesmen deal with us with such harshness of language'. (GoI, 1975: 611-613) Nixon is reported to have been greatly upset with the letter.

I am not surprised with what Kalyani Shankar has written:

> Even now Kissinger holds the view that Nixon's South Asia policy was not a mistake. According to him, under the circumstances prevailing at that time it was the right policy. 'And we really did not have many other choices. India was not a special friend of the United States during that period and it adopted its own policy – strict neutrality with some benevolence towards the Soviet Union. And those were facts of life.' Kissinger further explained that each side did what they felt they had to do. '*Each side would probably do the same thing again*.' (Shanker, 2010: 243)

The last sentence is in keeping with the American pro-Pakistan policy even today, whatever may be the outward political rhetoric of President Donald Trump regarding the new Afghanistan policy. Pakistan going into the China orbit has added a new worrysome element for India.

INDO-SOVIET PEACE AND FRIENDSHIP TREATY

K.P.S. Menon has stated: Nixon had warned that in the event of a war between India on the one hand and Pakistan and China on the other, India should not expect any help from the USA. Is it any wonder that, in these circumstances, India should have turned to an old and tried friend, the Soviet Union, for a reaffirmation of its friendship? (Menon, 1971: 47-48)

Kaul has stated:

> He [Haksar] and I were mainly responsible for drafting the Indo-Soviet treaty ... which I had been negotiating with the Soviet Foreign Office for almost two years from 1969 to 1971.... The signing of the treaty was decided by Mrs Gandhi who had a good sense of timing. She chose this time because of our deteriorating relations with Pakistan and China. (Kaul, 2000: 107)

Kalyani Shankar has stated that Indo-Soviet treaty was Indira Gandhi's sharp response to the newly developing axis between the US, Pakistan and China. Kissinger described the agreement as a 'bombshell'. According to Robert Dallek, Nixon and Kissinger were convinced that there would be a war. (Shanker, 2010: 219)

The treaty of peace, friendship and cooperation between India and USSR signed on 9 August 1971 checkmated the moves of all the three conspiring parties, namely USA, Pakistan and China. Article IX of the treaty declared:

> Each High Contracting Party undertakes to abstain from providing any assistance to any third party that engages in armed conflict with the other Party. In the event of either Party being subjected to an attack or a threat thereof, the High Contracting Parties shall immediately enter into mutual consultations in order to remove such threat and to take appropriate effective measures to ensure peace and security of the countries.

Kaul has emphasised the significance of the role played by Indira Gandhi between 1968 and 1972, in the formulation and implementation of the foreign policy of India. She was able to safeguard the sovereignty, independence and territorial integrity of India without having any designs of acquiring extra territory either in West Pakistan or in Bangladesh. He has specifically underlined that India's signal victory over Pakistan in 1971 raised Indira Gandhi's stature in India and the world, as a strong, tough and determined leader.

Wing Commander R. Venkataraman has in *India's Higher Defence – Organisation and Management*, stated:

> The war of 1971 would be remembered as a war in which the politico-military leadership displayed great maturity in planning and timing of operations. The Prime Minister had a clear perception of national interests and understanding of defence, thus providing decisive leadership throughout.... In complete contrast to the events of 1962, free and frank discussions helped evolve a national consensus in 1971, as Parliament was kept fully informed. (Venkataraman, 2011: 121, 125)

Commodore Rai, in his book, *Warring Nuclear Nations – India and Pakistan*, is effusive in his praise of the role of Indira Gandhi during Bangladesh War and finds it comparable with that of Winston Churchill. (Rai, 2014: 54)

BUILDING INTERNATIONAL OPINION

Indira Gandhi must be given credit for making relentless efforts to create public opinion world over against Pakistan's atrocities in East Pakistan and the resultant huge refugee problem in India. She herself travelled to a number of countries and apart from meeting government heads, she interacted with the leaders of public opinion, media, intellectuals and others. Our diplomatic missions in all countries were galvanised to pursue these matters. She even persuaded Jayaprakash Narayan to go to a number of countries to explain India's position. It must be admitted that this made a powerful impact as compared with the situation India faced with the Chinese aggression in 1962. India's efforts at that time were very subdued.

I have given later the gist of her interactions with the media in a number of countries. Rai has stated:

> After Mrs Indira Gandhi's talks with President Nixon in Washington on 4 November [1971], at dinner in the White House, Mrs Gandhi graphically depicted the magnitude of the refugee problem thus: "Imagine the entire population of Michigan State suddenly converging on New York State, and imagine the strain it would cause on the administration and on services such as health and communications and on resources like food and money – this not in conditions of affluence, but in a country already battling with problems of poverty and huge population.... From those who value democratic principles, we expect understanding and a certain measure of support ... our people cannot understand how [those] who are victims and who are bearing a burden and have restrained themselves with such fortitude, should be equated with those whose actions have caused the tragedy". In a television interview in Paris on 8 November, she said that she was prepared to meet President Yahya Khan to discuss all the problems, but that East Bengal was "not a problem between India and Pakistan but between West Pakistan and the Bengalis." (Rai, 2014: 88-89)

TAKING PARLIAMENT INTO CONFIDENCE

Indira Gandhi spoke in Parliament often to create a sense of confidence that government was keen to listen to their views and to take them into account while arriving at the decisions. She made Parliament aware of the fact that government will have to act in the framework of international norms. Her close attention to what political parties had to say was evident from her speech in the Rajya Sabha on 27 March 1971 when she said, with a tongue in the cheek:

> It is good to see that the parties have expressed certain views. For instance, the Swatantra Party has expressed admiration for the socialist programme of Shri Mujibur Rahman. The Jan Sangh has supported his secular policy and have said that the people of East Bengal are their brothers. I hope they will extend the same sympathy to all the people in our own country too!.... I held a meeting this morning with the leaders of the opposition which [practice] I hope to continue. (GoI, 1975: 523)

Parliament passed a resolution on 31 March 1971 expressing "profound sympathy for and solidarity with the people of East Bengal in their struggle for a democratic way of life ... this House demands immediate cessation of the use of force and the massacre of defenceless people. This House calls upon the peoples and the governments of the world to take urgent and constructive steps to prevail upon the Government of Pakistan to put an end immediately to the systematic decimation of people which amounts to genocide." (GoI, 1975: 524-525)

Indira Gandhi made a statement in Lok Sabha on 24 May 1971 after visiting refugee camps in Assam, Tripura and West Bengal on 15 and 16 May. She told Parliament that 335 camps had been established till then. Over 60,000 refugees were coming across every day. "*So massive a migration, in so short a time, is unprecedented in recorded history. About three and half million people have come into India during the last eight weeks. They belong to every religious persuasion – Hindu, Muslim, Buddhist and Christian.* They come from every social class and age-group. They are not refugees in the sense we have understood the word since Partition. *They are victims of war who have sought refuge from the military terror across our frontier*.... The problems which confront us are not confined to Assam, Meghalaya, Tripura and West Bengal. They are national problems. Indeed the basic problem is an international one." She also emphasised that "there can be no military solution to the problem of East Bengal. A political solution must be brought about by those who have the power to do so." (GoI, 1975: 527-528)

In her speech in the Lok Sabha on 26 May 1971, Indira Gandhi minced no words when she said, "It is a problem created by calculated genocide that is resulting not only in the murder of tens of thousands of men, women and children but also of forcing many more to seek refuge and shelter in India. It is a problem that threatens the peace and security of India and indeed of South-East Asia. The world must intervene...." She made an appeal to all political parties to sink their differences and to remain united. She urged them not to give a communal colour to the situation. "I shall continue to keep in touch with the leaders of opposition and with other members of this House.... I hope the members will feel free to come to see me to express their views or whatever knowledge they have on the subject." (GoI, 1975: 530-531)

Speaking in the Rajya Sabha on 15 June 1971, replying to the observation of one member, she underlined, "I am not in the habit of begging. I have never begged. I am not begging now.... We are sending our emissaries to various countries because this is an international responsibility." (GoI, 1975: 532)

She spoke at a public meeting at India Gate in New Delhi on 9 August 1971 when she said that by then over 73 lakh people had taken shelter in India to escape massacre by the Pakistan army. She said the question of recognising Bangladesh will be considered at the appropriate time. She ridiculed the programme of some political parties to offer *satyagraha* on the Bangladesh issue. She said "even the biggest and the richest country would totter under such heavy burden." She made an appeal to remain united and face the challenge with fortitude. (GoI, 1975: 535-537)

INTERACTIONS WITH THE MEDIA

In the interview given to Mark Tully of BBC on 1 November 1971, she was forthright and brutally frank. In reply to a question whether she was "particularly worried about the attitude of American government in this matter?", she said, "I would not isolate the American government because I think that many governments are hesitating to take a positive stand on this issue." In reply to another question, "What is the remedy for this cause?" she promptly replied, "Obviously to solve the problems of East Bengal." Tully asked a question: "I think there has been universal admiration for the way that India has coped with the problem of looking after the refugees. But I think some people are confused as to why India will not accept a larger United Nations presence in the refugee camps as Pakistan has suggested. Why won't India accept this?" Indira Gandhi replied: "If I might deal with the admiration part first. It is a little bit of irritant because, it is nice to be admired, but if people think you say a few flattering words and that is enough, well it is not because we are getting the verbal admiration and it seems to us the others are getting the more (sic) material help. So far as the UN observers are concerned we already have ten people.... Apart from that what we resent is the two countries being put on par."

In another interview to Michael Charlton of BBC on 1 November 1971, Indira Gandhi was strident, at times. In reply to one question, she said, "Other things may have remained the same, but India has not. We are not dependent upon what other countries think, or want us to do. We know what we want for ourselves and we are going to do it, whatever it costs." When asked whether helping Bangladesh freedom fighters would not encourage secessionist tendencies in India, she fiercely contested the contention saying, "it is difficult for you people to understand. We do not have any divisive tendencies...." Interestingly she also asserted, "Democracy can go anywhere in the world but it will not be jeopardised in India." (GoI, 1975: 538-539, 548) This was just four years before she imposed the Emergency in 1975. Was she the same Indira Gandhi who was asserting this?

Her Press meet at the National Press Club, Washington, on 5 November 1971 was fascinating and showed how confident and articulate she was in dealing with searching and wide-ranging questions. In her opening remarks she said, "I find my relaxation and recreation when I am with people, and especially when I am with interesting people, such as in this hall today." (GoI, 1975: 549)

She was brutally frank in her interview published in *Newsweek* of January 1972. In reply to a question, 'Do you believe that normal relations can be established with Pakistan?', she said: 'I believe normal relations can come and will come if outside countries do not interfere.... I believe that Pakistan's break-up is directly due to countries that thought they were helping Pakistan; but, because they themselves were unable to assess the realities of the situation, what they considered help in fact weakened Pakistan.' In reply to a question, 'Do you feel that President Nixon genuinely misunderstood India's case?', her reply was forthright: 'It is not just a question of India's case insofar as Bangladesh is concerned. It is a question of recognising what India is, what India stands for, and what India wants to do.... Let me say there is a fantastic nonsense being talked about in America about our having received promises from the Soviet Union [to intervene in the event of either US or Chinese military action on the sub-continent]. If after all this, the US refuses to recognise what sort of person I am and what sort of country India is, then I cannot say what will happen and what sort of relationship we will have.' (GoI, 1975: 619-620) I do not think any other Indian Prime Minister had or would have spoken so bluntly.

DECISIVE VICTORY

Indira Gandhi led the country in really turbulent times. In the broadcast over All India Radio on 4 December, she announced that –

> The Pakistan Air Force suddenly struck at our airfields in Amritsar, Pathankot, Srinagar, Avantipur, Uttarlai, Jodhpur, Ambala and Agra soon after 5.30 PM on 3 December 1971. Pakistan had launched full-scale war on us.... Today the war in Bangladesh has become a war on India.... Aggression must be met, and the people of India will meet it with fortitude and determination.

Proclamation of Emergency was issued on 4 December. The Government of India recognised Bangladesh on 6 December 1971. (GoI, 1975: 590-593)

Pakistan Forces surrendered unconditionally on 16 December and India declared cease-fire on 17 December 1971.

Dhar has brought out how restrained were the reactions in India over the victory in the Bangladesh War. A deliberate effort was made not to hurt the Bengali pride and not to raise the apprehensions of India's small neighbours. An editorial in *Le Figaro*, a leading daily in France, had written: 'This is rather an amazing lesson in democracy and it is also a mystery to see the little political weight of an army which numbers more than a million men and which has won a war. India is decidedly a curious country.' A report by the British journalist Peter Hazelhurst, filed from Dacca, said it all when it concluded, '*the Indian army's performance as a temporary occupation force has surpassed its performance on the battlefield.*' *The Economist* of

London chose to call Mrs Gandhi 'the new Empress of India'. (Dhar, 2000: 185)

Writing about the Indian victory in Bangladesh, Ayub Khan, former President of Pakistan, wrote in his diary:

> Thursday December 16, 1971. The separation of Bengal, though painful, was inevitable and unavoidable...I wish our rulers had the sense to realize this in time and let the Bengalis go in a peaceful manner instead of India bringing this about in a surgical operation...I suppose the Hindu morale is now very high. *It is the first victory they have had over the Muslims for centuries. It will take us a long time to live this down.* (Devasher, 2016: 287)

Similar sentiments were expressed by a Lahore-based Urdu paper:

> ... today the entire nation weeps tears of blood. Today the Indian Army has entered Dacca. *Today for the first time in 1,000 years Hindus have won a victory over Muslims.... Today we are prostrate with dejection.*

The defeat, instead of provoking introspection reinforced the conclusion that in order to show 'Hindu India' its place, the only way out was military parity. (Devasher, 2016: 288)

SIMLA ACCORD

It is rightly said that while the armed forces of India have done their job in each of the conflicts/wars with Pakistan, it is the political executive which has failed the country and often given away what was won by the armed forces with great sacrifice. Simla Accord was no exception. The manner in which the final accord was arrived at during the last couple of hours, by Indira Gandhi and Zulfiqar Ali Bhutto discussing the matter by themselves, without any aids present, remains a mystery. "I hear a voice from the darkness", Indira Gandhi had told a reporter (Akbar, 1991: 174), just before the final conclave began.

Under the agreement of 2 July 1972, India agreed to return 5,000 square miles of territory it had captured in West Pakistan, and persuade Bangladesh to agree to the return of over 90,000 Pakistani prisoners of war who had surrendered to the joint Indo-Bangladesh command. India retained the 400 square miles of *its own territory* in POK, which it had recovered from Pakistan control during the war. A new line of control (LOC) in Jammu and Kashmir (in place of the old cease-fire line of 1949) was set up by the two sides who agreed not to upset it by the use or threat of force. Both sides also agreed to discuss a final, peaceful settlement of the Kashmir question bilaterally. (Kaul, 2000; 94)

Indira Gandhi's and Bhutto's inter-personal relationship was by no means very cordial, before the Simla encounter. Katherine Frank, in her book, *Indira – The Life of Indira Nehru Gandhi*, has brought out the relationship between Bhutto and Indira Gandhi:

> The *froideur* [coldness] that accompanied their first meeting in person was hardly surprising. Three months earlier, in an interview with the Italian journalist Oriana Fallaci, Indira had described President Bhutto as 'unbalanced'. Bhutto was so enraged by this that he summoned Fallaci to Karachi in April and denigrated those involved in the fourteen-day Indo-Pak war. Bhutto branded Mujib Rahman 'a congenital liar' with 'a sick mind'. As for Indira Gandhi, she was 'a mediocre woman with mediocre intelligence. There is nothing great about her…. It's that throne that makes her seem tall…. And also the name she bears.' Indira and Bhutto found one another repellent. (Frank, 2001: 344)

However, when Bhutto's fate hung in the balance, she addressed public meetings to focus public attention and thus stop his possible execution. Her party members staged demonstrations against such an eventuality. Later, she addressed personal communication to heads of many States – Arabs, Asians, Africans and Europeans. Their response was encouraging.... All this was being done at a time when her own future seemed bleak. (Yunus, 1980: 314)

Though Kashmir was to be the substantive issue in the discussion, as M.J. Akbar has written in his book, *Kashmir – Behind the Vale*, Karan Singh, who was Governor of J&K for eighteen years and was a member of Indira Gandhi's Cabinet at the time, was not included in the delegation, though several other Central ministers formed part of it. Since the Accord was never placed before the Cabinet for approval, at no stage Karan Singh had any opportunity to take a look at it. "Karan Singh never hid his resentment, and still believes that it was the "gang" of Kashmiri Pundits who finessed him. Dogra suspicion of the Pandit runs deep. [Maharaja] Hari Singh's advice to his son used to be to trust anyone before a Pandit." (Akbar, 1991: 179)

Much has been written about Bhutto's strategy to have his way in the talks. According to Akbar's version, Bhutto mixed emotion with extremely subtle deference and switched his pitch from give and take of politics to a higher morality. Only a person as strong and popular as Mrs Gandhi could take a generous extra step for peace; he could not return to Pakistan with the stigma of surrender, he would be destroyed politically. And so on and so forth. Bhutto told her that Pakistan was now convinced that it could never win a war with India, that Kashmir was lost. But he could not commit that on paper. "*Bharosa Keejiye,*" Bhutto pleaded; trust me. "He played this card beautifully." Indira Gandhi trusted him. (Akbar, 1991: 179)

This was totally in keeping with Haksar's logic. According to Sharada Prasad, "Haksar was one of the principal shapers of Indira Gandhi's Bangladesh policy.... In Simla, a few months later, with D.P. Dhar taking ill, the task of making assessments and advising the Prime Minister fell largely on Haksar." (Sarkar, 1989: 189) Haksar had advised the Prime Minister not to put Bhutto in a predicament of going back empty-handed or having given away too much. In this light, the outcome was a foregone conclusion and it is not surprising that Bhutto got what he wanted.

T.N. Kaul's observations in this regard are significant:

> Indira Gandhi has been criticised for not getting 'a final settlement' of the Kashmir question at Simla in 1972, when India was the victor. She tried hard but Bhutto said if he agreed to a final settlement at Simla he would be overthrown and the military would take over power and increase tension with India. *When I suggested it at the conference table, Bhutto, addressing Mrs. Gandhi, said, "Madam, I assure you that within two weeks of my return to Pakistan, I shall prepare the ground for it (a final settlement of Kashmir question)"*. After the agreement, P.N. Dhar, her Secretary, who was outside [the room] has said that there was a verbal understanding between Mrs Gandhi and Mr Bhutto, that a final settlement of the Kashmir question along the line of control (LOC) would be made. There is no record of this and when I asked Mrs Gandhi the next day, she said, "I do not trust Bhutto, but I wanted to make a gesture to the people of Pakistan with whom we have ultimately to settle this question and live peacefully together. I did not want to keep the 5,000 sq miles of West Pakistan territory. I would have antagonised the people of Pakistan and [it would have] been a millstone around our neck. Besides, we have always preached against keeping

> territory occupied in war." I believe, she was afraid of rousing criticism in her own party, and certainly in the BJP and the Opposition, if she settled on the LOC at that time, as we had been claiming the whole of J&K as Indian territory. But she could have stood firm on a final settlement along the LOC and Bhutto would have had to give in since he could not go back empty-handed to Pakistan (as his intelligence boss told an Indian friend in Simla). (Kaul, 2000: 116-117)

The apprehension about the likely opposition from BJP and other opposition parties do not seem to be justified. In a seminar organised by *Kirloskar* magazine – the oldest and widely circulated Marathi monthly – in 1990 (mimeo) L.K. Advani and Balraj Madhok had expressed disappointment that the opportunity to settle the Kashmir problem finally by converting the LOC into the international border was lost during Simla discussions. As for likely opposition from within the Congress, Indira Gandhi's position at the time was so supreme that, as brought out later, even senior leaders like Y.B. Chavan and Jagjivan Ram did not have the courage to speak out their mind during the discussion.

This whole thing thus gets curiouser and curiouser. If there was one time when this question could have been settled permanently, it was at the Simla meeting. But, Indira Gandhi's own position was far from clear, as can be seen from what she told Kaul. Personally, I believe that she was unduly influenced by Haksar's thinking and the outcome was as per Haksar's thinking. Apparently, no strategy had been worked out in advance, and the position to be taken at the talks, the fall-back position to be taken, the strong and weak points, etc, had not been discussed inter-ministerially or in the Cabinet Sub-Committee, before talks with Bhutto, except for whatever briefing Indira Gandhi had from Haksar and the two Dhars (D.P. and P.N.) This was in keeping with her style of working.

Akbar has stated that an impression was sought to be created by Government of India that the Kashmir issue had been solved. "But within weeks the External Affairs Ministry realized – although it was not yet telling – that India had been sold a pup, and a nasty little mongrel at that." However, he himself has quoted what Farooq Abdullah had told him about his visit to Pakistan after the Simla Accord. "The most significant meeting during that tour … was with Bhutto. In an interview to the author, Farooq revealed: When I went to Rawalpindi in 1974 from England, the entire bureaucracy of Pakistan and Bhutto's Secretary himself told me that a final solution has been arrived at: there can be nothing more. What we (the Pakistanis) have got (in Kashmir) we are keeping. What they have got they are keeping, and that is how it is. Bhutto confirmed this. Farooq flew to Delhi, where he briefed Mrs Gandhi in the presence of P.N. Dhar – by now the Principal Secretary." (Akbar, 1991: 180, 186)

Benazir Bhutto, in her book, *Daughter of the East – An Autobiography*, has described how tense was the Pakistan delegation and her father, in particular, during the negotiations and unsure about the final outcome:

> I was sitting on the floor of my bedroom when my father suddenly appeared in the doorway. "Don't tell anybody," he said with a new gleam in his eyes, "but I'm going to use this protocol visit to try one last time with Mrs Gandhi. I have an idea. But don't be disappointed if there are no results." And he was gone…. "If there is an agreement, we'll say a boy has been born. If there is no agreement, we'll say a girl has been born." "How chauvinistic," I commented, but no one was listening…. I was upstairs in my bedroom when '*Larka hai! Larka hai!* A boy has been born! A boy has been

> born!' rang out through the house at 12.40 AM. "How did you do it, Papa?" I asked him as the sombre silence in the house lifted to be replaced by the humming sound of one delegate passing on the news to another. "I saw that she was very tense during our visit," my father told me. "After all, failure was not only a set-back for us, but for her, too. Both our political opponents would use it against us. She kept fiddling with her handbag and gave the impression that her tongue did not relish the taste of the hot tea in her cup. So I took a deep breath and talked non-stop for half an hour...." "Did she agree?" I asked my father with mounting excitement. "She didn't disagree," he said, lighting a cigar. "She said she would consult her personal advisers and let us know at the dinner tonight."
>
> 'Mrs Gandhi agreed to return either the prisoners of war or the territory,' my father said to me when he came upstairs later. 'Why do you think I chose the territory?' 'I really don't know, Papa,' I said, quite shocked. 'The people in Pakistan would have been much happier if the prisoners had been freed.' 'And they will be freed,' he assured me. 'Prisoners are a human problem. The magnitude is increased when there are 93,000 of them. It would be inhuman for India to keep them indefinitely. And it will also be a problem to keep on feeding and housing them. Territory, on the other hand, is not a human problem. Territory can be assimilated. Prisoners cannot. The Arabs have still not succeeded in regaining the territory lost in the 1967 war. But the capturing of land doesn't cry out for international attention same way as prisoners do. (Benazir Bhutto, 1988: 64-66)

Here was a real hard-headed politician and statesman speaking. This was in sharp contrast with the idealistic advice given by Haksar to Indira Gandhi, based on the consequences of the

Versailles Treaty! There is no reference in Benazir Bhutto's account of any informal understanding on Kashmir problem arrived at between her father and Indira Gandhi. Even if there was such an understanding, Bhutto was not going to share it even with his daughter! On July 4, 1972, the Simla Agreement won the unanimous approval of the National Assembly of Pakistan; even the opposition joined in the tributes.

It may be recalled that the word Pakistan (literal meaning land of the pure), was, according to Rehmat Ali who coined it in 1933, an acronym of Punjab, Afghania (North West Frontier Province), Kashmir, Sindh and Balochistan. It was not therefore surprising that Z.A. Bhutto, in his book, *The Myth of Independence*, published from London in 1969, *well before the Simla Agreement*, had made clear his views on Kashmir and its importance for Pakistan. Bhutto had written:

> *If a Muslim majority [region] can remain a part of India, then the Raison d'être of Pakistan collapses…Pakistan is incomplete without Jammu and Kashmir both territorially and ideologically.* (Devasher, 2016: 14, 285)

Against this background, no credence should have been placed on any oral commitments made or assurances given by Bhutto.

One of Bhutto's aides, who was also very close to the Americans, fully briefed P. Sterba (the *New York Times* correspondent) on the understanding that his leader had reached with Mrs Gandhi. In his news analysis, which appeared within hours of the signing, Sterba, after referring to the inflexible positions of the two governments on the Kashmir problem, wrote: 'these positions have been drummed into the minds of the peoples of each side to the point where any compromise would be viewed largely as a "sell out" in both countries. And for years, such a sell out would have probably toppled the rulers who agreed to it.' Sterba added:

> President Bhutto, Pakistan's first civilian leader in fourteen years, came to Simla ready to compromise. According to sources close to him, he was willing to forsake the Indian held two-thirds of Kashmir that contains four-fifths of the population and the prized valley called the 'Vale', and agree that a cease-fire line to be negotiated would gradually become the border between the two countries. The key word is 'gradually'.... President Bhutto wants a softening of the ceasefire line with trade and travel across it and a secret agreement with Mrs Gandhi that a formally recognized border would emerge after a few years, during which he would condition his people to it without riots and an overthrow of his government. (Dhar, 2000: 196-197)

Dhar has stated that this was the understanding between the leaders of the two countries and this was the Simla Solution of the Kashmir problem. The agreement that was signed at Simla in the first hours of 3 July 1972 was the launching pad for an implementation of the Simla Solution. Dhar has written:

> It was in the context of an utter disregard for the Simla commitments by Pakistan that I decided to make public the substance of the Simla understanding. I did this through a two-part article which was published in *The Times of India* in April 1995. Pakistani response to this came in an avalanche of statements and comments from the government, political leaders, columnists, and editorial writers questioning the veracity of what I had said. About the only person in authority who did not react was Pakistan's Prime Minister, Benazir Bhutto ... Humayun Gauhar called it Bhutto's diplomatic artistry. Writing on this subject in the *Political and Business Weekly* of 15 May 1995, Gauhar wrote: 'If it took a private talk between Mr Bhutto and Mrs Gandhi in which he made certain commitments to her but he was clever enough not to have written [them] down in the Simla Agreement or

on a separate piece of paper, then it was diplomatic artistry of the highest order. He would have known better than anyone else that such private secret agreement, which is only verbal, was worthless. Face it Mr Dhar, even if we accept what you say, Mr Bhutto fooled your Prime Minister.' Dhar has stated that the reaction in India too was not different from what Humayun Gauhar had stated, namely, that India had lost on the negotiating table what its armed forces had gained in the battlefield. (Dhar, 2000: 198-200)

As for the Indian strategy for the Simla meeting, Dhar has confirmed that Haksar gave his soft approach a strong intellectual justification by references to comparable episodes in European history.... Haksar repeatedly referred to the baneful consequences of the harsh terms the Treaty of Versailles had imposed on the vanquished.... Haksar's intellectualism did not convince all his colleagues and some were skeptical of his approach to Bhutto.... Though Indira Gandhi had some reservations about Haksar's arguments, she went along with him. *Y.B. Chavan and Jagjivan Ram were unhappy about the return of POWs and territories to Pakistan without adequate quid pro quo, but did not, as was their wont, articulate their misgivings clearly enough*. (Dhar, 2000: 206) Dhar's assessment seems reasonable. Indira Gandhi's style of working was so authoritarian that Cabinet form of government was only on paper and mere window-dressing. All decisions were made by Prime Minister with the advice of her coterie. Therefore, it was not surprising that the two senior-most ministers – Chavan and Jagjivan Ram – did not have the courage or inclination to express their views on such a critical matter openly and clearly.

The Pakistan delegation's assessment was that though all the bargaining chips were stacked in India's favour, India's excessive anxiety to avoid the failure of the talks at any cost became its major handicap. Inevitably, the wording of the accord did not reflect Indian position on Kashmir. Bhutto is reported to have absolutely insisted on retaining as the opening commitment of the pact, "That the principles and purposes of the Charter of the United Nations shall govern the relations between the two countries". So where was the question of the issue being withdrawn from the United Nations agenda, asked Pakistan.

Pakistan also began to draw attention to the sentence in the agreement which reads: ... the representatives of the two sides will meet to discuss further the modalities and arrangements for the establishment of durable peace and normalization of relations ... (including) *a final settlement of Jammu and Kashmir*.

This is shocking, to say the least. I wonder if anyone on Indian side had even cared to read the draft agreement before it was signed. Excessively high level and high powered delegation, which must have kept out the MEA from negotiations and drafting, must have led to this kind of most awkward situation.* And still the Government of India was euphoric about the success of the negotiations and how the Kashmir problem had been solved by making it only a bilateral dispute. In fact, this is the line still being taken by India. However, since bilateral discussions have not gone anywhere during the last four decades, and, in recent years, India has refused to talk about Kashmir till the question of cross-border

---

* Akbar has written: The summit began on a note of tragedy, when D.P. Dhar had to be hospitalized with heart trouble. On a more tragicomic note, [Foreign Secretary] T.N. Kaul stomped off, possibly because of an imagined slight; he would return. (Akbar, 1991: 176-179) This conjecture was not true. Kaul has stated, "I left Simla on the evening of July 2, 1972, for Chandigarh to see off the Pak delegation next morning, because I did not think a settlement with Bhutto was likely." (Kaul, 2000: 117)

terrorism is addressed, a number of countries including the United States, China, Iran, and Turkey have started showing interest in mediating to find a solution to the Kashmir problem. As if this was not enough, some Kashmir leaders like Farooq Abdullah and his son, Hurriyat Conference and others are also suggesting that, if necessary, help of friendly countries may be taken in the matter. This shows that Simla Accord for which Indira Gandhi was being given credit has been a non-starter. To put it bluntly, in fact, Bhutto managed to fool India (India is Indira?).

In 1974, Z.A. Bhutto made Pakistan Occupied Kashmir (POK) constitutionally a province of Pakistan *without much protest from India*. (Dhar, 2000: 196) Was it because this was in keeping with India's thinking of converting the LOC into an international border?

Reference must also be made to paragraph 5 of the agreement which stated: "This Agreement will be subject to the ratification by both countries in accordance with their respective constitutional procedures…." (Kaul, 2000: 222) In India such agreements do not have to be approved by Parliament but this is not so in Pakistan. It was clear that final settlement of the Kashmir question in Simla Agreement would not have been approved by Pakistan Parliament.

The Simla Agreement was discussed in Parliament and the impression one gets is that all political parties except Jan Sangh supported it. Indira Gandhi replied to the debate in Lok Sabha on 31 July 1972 and in Rajya Sabha on 2 August 1972. Her reply in both Houses was rambling, in the style of her father Jawaharlal Nehru. Her whole emphasis was on peace having been established as a result of the agreement. She made no mention of any understanding arrived at with Bhutto on Kashmir, or why the territory won in the war was given back, without getting anything in return. The Pakistani prisoners of war were released later in consultation with Bangladesh. (GoI, 1975: 652-667)

C.S. Pandit has written:

> On the international plane, Indira's main worry was the complete standstill obtaining on the implementation of the Simla Agreement. Ever since India had withdrawn its troops from the occupied Pakistani territory, Pakistan seemed to have lost all interest in any further implementation of the Accord. Bhutto was only using the POWs hold (sic) in India as a big stick to beat India with in international forums.... Despite all this, Indira herself wrote to Bhutto on 24 January offering further steps towards normalization of relations under the Simla Agreement. He rejected the offer in his reply sent late in February, saying that any steps towards restoring normal relations between India and Pakistan must wait until the POWs returned home. (Pandit, 1977: 130)

Attention may be invited to how efforts made during the Janata regime to bring out the truth on the so-called secret understanding reached during the Simla discussions proved futile due to the inexplicable ruling given by the Lok Sabha Speaker. The Leader of Opposition gave a notice of an adjournment motion to discuss the "conduct of the Minister for External Affairs [Atal Bihari Vajpayee] in violating the oath of secrecy by his announcement at two public meetings alleging a secret understanding between Mr Bhutto and the former Prime Minister and claiming in his speech in the House on April 18 that this information was from official documents he came into contact with (sic) in his capacity as the minister." Giving his ruling, the Speaker declared that the oath of secrecy was not a blanket one. The oath of secrecy provided in the Constitution forbade a minister from disclosing information made available to him or which became known to him, except as might be required for due discharge of his duties as such minister.... The question whether a particular disclosure made by a minister was required for the discharge of his duties as such minister, was a very difficult question to decide. On this matter there could always be difference of opinion. More importantly, the Speaker observed that though the question raised was no doubt a matter of public importance, *he was unable to hold that it was a matter of such urgent public importance as to warrant disrupting the listed business of the House.* (Kashyap, 1997: 396-397) Excellent opportunity was thus lost to give out the full details of the matter once and for all. After this ruling, the Janata Party could have asked one of its MPs to ask for a discussion on the subject in Parliament. In fact, I have not been able to understand why Indira Gandhi and later governments should have kept this information secret, once it was clear that Bhutto had gone back on his assurances.

AGREEMENT WITH SHEIKH ABDULLAH

The totally indefensible chapter of high-handed detention of Sheikh Abdullah, was brought to a close with the release of Sheikh Abdullah. According to Dulat, who headed R&AW for a number of years, after Pakistan's defeat in 1971 War and creation of Bangladesh, Sheikh Abdullah realized that "Pakistan was no match for India. For Kashmiris, the 1971 War had a huge impact." (Dulat, 2015: 312)

Perhaps, the only gain of Simla Accord was the successful negotiations held by Indian government with Sheikh Abdullah in which agreement was arrived at on the following points:

- Article 370 would continue;
- Residuary powers would remain with J&K Assembly. Delhi would retain control of any legislation dealing with the sovereignty of India;

- Kashmir could alter or modify any future provisions, but only with the consent of the President of India;
- The State could review legislation after 1953 on the Concurrent List, and President's assent "would be sympathetically considered";
- Article 356 and the powers of the Election Commission would remain as they were;
- "No agreement was possible" on the question of the nomenclature of the Governor and the Chief Minister; Abdullah wanted a return to Sadar-i-Riyasat and Wazir-i-Azam.

Importantly, after this accord, the Plebiscite Front, which was in existence for twenty-five years, was wound up.

Frank's assessment is quite interesting. She has stated:

> Bhutto called the Kashmir Accord a 'sell-out' and maintained that it violated the 1972 Simla Accord. From Indira's point of view, the agreement with Abdullah had laid to rest the idea of plebiscite; it confirmed the irrevocable accession of the State to India and thereby put halt to the movement for Kashmiri self-determination. In his autobiography, Sheikh Abdullah explained that he had only agreed to co-operate in order to regain power, 'but soon had to regret my decision'. (Frank, 2001: 366-367)

It is important to note that Article 370, which the BJP is keen on repealing, was reconfirmed. I have often written that the demand for repealing Article 370 is a very ill-conceived move. In spite of this article, through a series of constitutional and statutory steps taken over the years, J&K has been fully integrated with India, like any other former Princely State, except for a few vestiges of the past. Article 370 continues to be an emotional link of Kashmiris with the past and it is best to leave it untouched. Dulat too has rightly stated: "Article 370 is by now merely symbolic. It is a fig leaf for Kashmir – so why would anyone want to take that away from them? Perhaps if Sheikh Abdullah had not been arrested in 1953, we would not have (sic) been having this debate in 2014." (Dulat, 2015: 314)

Particular attention may be invited to the assertion by Sheikh Mohammad Abdullah in his letter to the Prime Minister dated 11 February 1975 that "*the accession of the State of Jammu and Kashmir to India is not in issue. It has been my firm belief that the future of Jammu and Kashmir lies with India* because of the common ideals that we share." (Noorani, 2011: 413) But now this itself is being disputed by some political parties in J&K, with the active support from Pakistan. It is not just back to square one, but minus one!

4

The Emergency – Legalising Constitutional Dictatorship

INTRODUCTION

M.C. Chagla,[1] speaking at the All India Civil Liberties Conference in Ahmadabad on 12 October 1975, had stated: "*There is no worse form of dictatorship than what is known as constitutional dictatorship.* If behind the facade of the Constitution, technically observing the rules that the Constitution lays down and violating its spirit, you build up a dictatorship, then you have a constitutional dictatorship. I would rather have the Constitution abrogated." (Selbourne, 1997: 399) M.C. Setalvad, while speaking in Madras during the Emergency, had also used the term 'constitutional dictatorship'. (Godbole, 2008: 309) This is an unbelievable chapter in India's post-independence history which should never be forgotten.

12 JUNE 1975 – THE FATEFUL DAY

Indira Gandhi had to face one bad news after another on this day – death of her trusted colleague D.P. Dhar, defeat of the

---

1 Chief Justice of the Bombay High Court from 1947 to 1958, Indian ambassador to USA, High Commissioner in UK and later Minister for External Affairs and Education.

Congress Party in Gujarat Assembly elections, and the dreaded Allahabad High Court decision in her election case in which she was unseated and debarred from holding elective office for six years. *The Times* in London thought, "It was like dismissing a Prime Minister for a traffic offence." (Frank, 2001: 372) This was too flippant an assessment and I do not quite look at it that way, though a lesser punishment would have been more appropriate and would have served the purpose of sending a correct message in this country with rampant electoral malpractices, particularly by those occupying powerful positions.

One of the charges against IndiraGandhi was that she had used Yashpal Kapur, her Private Secretary, for electioneering when he still held a government post. Raj Thapar has written that

> Indira Gandhi tried hard to persuade Haksar to put in a backdated letter in the file dismissing (sic) Yashpal which Haksar naturally refused. She herself had to face the court and ended by making contradictory statements. (Thapar, 1991: 397)

On 24 June, the Supreme Court vacation Judge V.R. Krishna Iyer gave a conditional stay to the High Court decision and ruled that pending the final decision of the court, she would not have the right to speak or vote in Parliament. An orchestrated campaign was launched by the Congress party, spearheaded by Sanjay Gandhi, to create the illusion of public uproar that she should not resign pending final decision on her appeal.

MISUSE OF EMERGENCY PROVISIONS

When the Constitution was drafted, India was going through the unthinkable – partition of the country and the terrible holocaust which was its aftermath. It was not therefore surprising that the Constitution provided for a separate chapter XVIII titled "Emergency Provisions". During the Constituent Assembly debates it was made clear by B.R. Ambedkar, Chairman of the Drafting Committee, that these provisions would be used most sparingly, and only in extraordinary situations. The very first article in this chapter, Article 352, pertains to Proclamation of Emergency. The very first sentence thereof reads: "*If the President is satisfied that a grave emergency exists whereby the security of India or of any part of the territory thereof is threatened*, whether by war or external aggression or armed rebellion, he may, by a proclamation, make a declaration to that effect...." No one had imagined that this provision would be so blatantly and arbitrarily misused and legal luminaries like S.S. Ray and Rajani Patel would be seriously advising Indira Gandhi to take recourse to it. Even if what Ray had told the Shah Commission (that Indira Gandhi was keen on giving a 'shock treatment' to the country) was true, this was clearly a fraud on the Constitution. As can be seen from the following discussion, it was a straight and simple coup hatched in the 'palace' by none other than the 'Empress of India', Indira Gandhi.

As was to be expected, people were not wanting who acclaimed Indira Gandhi's action to save the country, by declaration of Emergency. During Emergency, M.F. Husain, an acclaimed modern Indian artist, painted a huge triptych of Indira Gandhi as Goddess Durga, riding through fire on a tiger and vanquishing her foes.

Austin, well-known American political scientist whose book has even been quoted by the Supreme Court in its judgments, in his book *Working a Democratic Constitution – The Indian Experience*, has exposed some startling details on the basis of interviews with a number of persons who were directly involved. He has written:

> Although it seems clear that imposition of Emergency of some kind had been decided for some time, the evil of secrecy does not permit us to know when the stratagem … emerged…. But the idea had been 'mooted' in January 1975 by S.S. Ray, and according to A.G. Noorani, Ray had discussed with P.N. Dhar in 1973 the idea of declaring an Economic Emergency. D.P. Dhar appears to have suggested an Emergency directly to the Prime Minister once and possibly twice between January and June [1975]. D.P. Dhar wrote to Mrs Gandhi from Moscow in January 1975 saying that he had heard that the Allahabad decision might go against her, and she should assemble a team of Haksar, S.S. Ray, and Barooah, who was personally close to Dhar, to decide what to do before and after the Allahabad decision. During his visit to Delhi in May…. Dhar visited the Prime Minister and probably recommended imposition of an Emergency or its equivalent. In a conversation at the time with the well-known editor, Nikhil Chakravarty, [D.P.] Dhar said that 'Indira is facing a crisis in the election case because her chances are only fifty-fifty. *The President can suspend the Constitution and set it aside.*' Chakravarty responded, 'That means martial law. Don't import the practice of Jammu and Kashmir' – where Dhar had been the State's Home Minister in the mid-sixties. *Dhar then said, 'After the Constitution is suspended, a new Constitution can be imposed by turning Parliament into a Constituent Assembly.'* (This was based on Chakravarty's interview with Austin.) Dhar's advice to Mrs Gandhi 'well before the Emergency' was to change the Constitution and 'even declare an Emergency to do it', a journalist close to the CPI told Austin. (Austin, 1999: 304 and footnote 27)

This is simply shocking. All this planning was merely to see that Indira Gandhi can be retained in power. With such 'committed' advisors, India is lucky to have got off with just the Emergency! It could have been much worse.

Indira Gandhi had told the President of India that the situation in the country was so alarming that it was necessary to declare Emergency. However, the Shah Commission has observed that on the economic front, there was nothing alarming. The fortnightly reports regarding law and order showed that the situation was under complete control all over the country. No reports were received by the Home Ministry from State Governments indicating any deterioration in the law and order situation in the period immediately preceding the Proclamation of Emergency. No plans were prepared by the Home Ministry prior to June 25, 1975 with regard to the imposition of Internal Emergency. The IB had not submitted any report suggesting that the internal situation in the country warranted imposition of Internal Emergency. The Home Ministry did not submit any report to the Prime Minister expressing its concern or anxiety about the internal situation in the country. Senior officers like the Home Secretary, the Cabinet Secretary and the Secretary to Prime Minister had not been taken into confidence about the intended Proclamation of Emergency. Only R.K. Dhawan, the then additional Private Secretary to Prime Minister, had been associated with the preparations for the declaration of Emergency right from the early stages. The Shah Commission has concluded:

> *The circumstances leading to the declaration of Emergency ... leave little room for doubt that the decision to impose Emergency was exclusively the decision of the Prime Minister.... In the absence of any explanation which would warrant the declaration of an Emergency, the inference is inevitable that a political decision was taken by an interested Prime Minister in a desperate endeavour to save herself from the legitimate compulsion of a judicial verdict against her.*

The Commission has also categorically stated:

> The Constitution, in the opinion of the Commission, does not contemplate the Proclamation of Emergency upon an Emergency already existing, nor prevents the courts from entertaining any challenge to the declaration of this additional Emergency. But the provisions of the Constitution were amended by the 39th Amendment of the Constitution, which prevented a challenge being raised.

The Commission has stated that this [imposition of Emergency] was more in the nature of a shock treatment, than a legally permissible Emergency, which could be declared according to the law then in force. (Sezhiyan, 2010: 236, 253)

What then was the real reason for declaration of Emergency? It is still shrouded in mystery and can only be inferred from the then prevailing circumstances. Clearly, one reason was the situation which arose after the judgment of the Allahabad High Court holding Indira Gandhi's election void and debarring her from contesting election for six years. Looking to the facts of the case, I am of the view that the punishment imposed on Indira Gandhi could not be justified and was excessive. Palkhivala, who was to represent her in this case and decided not to do so after the declaration of Emergency, wrote to her on 9 November 1975 to say: "There has never been any doubt in my mind that the judgment of the Allahabad High Court was erroneous on facts and in law and you deserved to succeed [in the Supreme Court] on every count – regardless of the subsequent amendments to the Constitution and to the Representation of the People Act." (Kamath, 2007: 190)

Another reason adduced by some serious commentators, such as Arun Shourie, is the doings of Sanjay Gandhi's Maruti business. Shourie has written:

> Justice Gupta's report on Maruti affairs has just been released. It documents the worst misuse of office and the State apparatus in independent India's history for satisfying the greed of a single household. That is a strong sentence but, I am afraid, it is the literal truth. I can think of only one another misuse of the State apparatus for personal ends which was worse than what Justice Gupta has documented, and that was the imposition of the Emergency itself. But then the two things – Maruti and Emergency – are inter-twined, they are one of a piece. By early 1975 the criminalities of Maruti had begun surfacing. It is my view that these criminalities did much more to compel Mrs Gandhi to impose the Emergency than the immediate inconvenience of Justice Sinha's judgment in June 1975. Similarly, nothing stimulated Maruti's business prospects more than the imposition of the Emergency. (Shourie, 1980: 145)

As brought out later, similar view was expressed by some prominent national dailies, after the Gupta Commission of Inquiry Report on Maruti was released. But, to me, this sounds somewhat far-fetched.

Indira Gandhi was not prepared to resign and await the decision on her appeal to the Supreme Court, as some of her well-wishers had suggested. This would have been an honourable course of action and I am sure she would have come back to power with a strong mandate.

M.O. Mathai has written about what Indira Gandhi had told David Frost, the journalist and broadcaster, after her defeat in 1977 elections: "*I felt utter, utter relief when ousted from power…. When I got the news of my personal defeat, I had a surge of relief as if a tremendous rock had been lifted from my shoulders.*" I don't think she herself believes in the statement she made to Frost … she could have [done that] by casting off the "tremendous rock" herself, when the Allahabad judgment came. (Mathai, 1978: 253) I entirely agree with Mathai, at least so far as this statement is concerned. How hypocritical can one be!

S. Mulgaonkar and B.G. Varghese wrote powerful editorials in *The Times of India* and the *Hindustan Times* respectively under the identical title "Time to Go". Tables were turned on them and they were made to realize that it was their turn to go. (Mathai, 1978: 252)

In retrospect, it is interesting to see the position of political parties and their affiliate organisations on Emergency. The CPI was, of course, fully supportive of Indira Gandhi's actions and policies. In fact, they believed that their ideology could be implemented only by supporting Indira Gandhi, as there was no chance of their coming to power at the Centre on their own. The stand of several other political parties and organisations was often self-serving and hardly principled or consistent. It also varied according to local conditions and the treatment meted out to the detainees. I have referred elsewhere to how harshly the detainees, including the top leaders of various political parties, were treated. The Shah Commission has brought out how arbitrarily detention orders were issued by district magistrates and other authorised officers, often at the behest of persons close to the centres of power. Under the circumstances, it was a game of survival for all political parties and organisations opposed to the government.

COMMISSIONS OF INQUIRY – FAR FROM A WITCH-HUNT

When the Janata government came to power in 1977, it was literally at wit's end how to fix responsibility on Indira Gandhi for all her misdeeds. Indira Gandhi being a much more astute politician than her rivals in the Janata Party, had raised a bogey of her victimisation by the government to create a sympathy for her throughout the country. The Janata government, according to me, took the very proper course of appointing judicial commissions of inquiry headed by serving and retired Supreme Court judges – Justice J.C. Shah Commission to inquire into Emergency excesses; Justice A.C. Gupta Commission to inquire into the affairs of Maruti; Justice P. Jaganmohan Reddy Commission to inquire into the circumstances leading to the death of Nagarwala involved in "fraudulent" withdrawal of cash from State Bank of India (SBI); Justice Vimadalal Commission to inquire into allegations of corruption against the then Chief Minister Vengal Rao and other ministers of Andhra Pradesh (AP); Justice A.N. Grover Commission to inquire into allegations of corruption against the then Chief Minister Devraj Urs and other ministers of Karnataka; Justice P. Jaganmohan Commission to inquire into allegations of corruption against Bansi Lal, former Chief Minister of Haryana and Minister of Defence; and Justice C.A. Vaidialingam Commission to inquire into allegations against the family members of Morarji Desai and Charan Singh. (Limaye, 1994: 480-482) It can be seen that in none of these cases, the appointment of commission of inquiry was unjustified or unwarranted. Even allegations against family members of Morarji Desai and Charan Singh were to be inquired into. How can this be called a witch-hunt?

Further, under the Commissions of Inquiry Act, 1952, the Commission is expected to conduct an open inquiry with a view to arrive at the truth.[2] Full opportunity is to be given

2 The Shah Commission had also made it clear at the inception itself that "the proceedings before the Commission are not of an adversary character. It is the duty of the Commission appointed for that purpose to make an inquiry into the subject matter of the inquiry if the subject matter is of definite public importance."

to the person against whom the inquiry is to be held. The Commission has no powers to punish anyone. It can only make recommendations to the government. There could not have been a more fair, judicious and transparent manner of fixing responsibility on a public servant. But apart from Indira Gandhi and her coterie who were highly critical of this move, even some of the senior-most civil servants like B.G. Deshmukh and P.C. Alexander, who had held responsible positions, were unhappy with the move. I find this most difficult to understand, unless public accountability is not considered relevant or important for top political executive.

Madhu Limaye has rightly brought out how, unfortunately, the entire exercise of appointment of the commissions of inquiry served no purpose as there was no coordination between the Home Minister, Law Minister and Prime Minister for taking expeditious follow-up action:

> *After the fiasco of Indira Gandhi's arrest in October 1977, on issues not investigated by the Shah Commission or Maruti Commission, the bureaucracy and police became even more un-cooperative*.... The action taken report presented to Parliament was absolutely inane. Its 67 pages consisted of the summary of the Commission's findings. On the last page the government said it accepted the findings, observations and recommendations of the Commission.... But about bringing the offenders to book it had only this milk and water stuff to offer: On a number of matters the findings disclose grounds for initiating legal action where offences appear to be made out, departmental action where irregular or improper conduct of public servants has attracted the critical attention of the Commission, and remedial or other consequential administrative action. Government has decided to initiate

> all such action in accordance with the law, rules, and administrative processes, after careful examination of each individual case. (Limaye, 1994: 495-496)

This is a classic bureaucratic mumbo-jumbo which means nothing, a clear effort to show action where there was none and not likely in the future, either.

As Limaye has regretfully noted,

> the whole gigantic effort made by the Janata government to investigate the dark areas of corruption, nepotism, abuse of power and negligence of duty on the part of those in authority, in the end, produced no positive results.... When Indira Gandhi returned to power, her government decided to bury hastily all the reports. (Limaye, 1994: 509)

SHAH COMMISSION ON EMERGENCY EXCESSES

Indira Gandhi and her battery of legal advisors raised a number of points against the working of the Shah Commission. The only purpose they served was to provide an excuse for Indira Gandhi not to appear before the Commission and give her statement on oath. I have mentioned in Annexure 5, the two main contentions raised by Indira Gandhi. The first was the preposterous claim that her decision to impose Emergency could not be questioned before anyone and that she alone was competent to take such a decision under the Constitution. If benefit of doubt is to be given to her, clearly, her legal advisors had misguided her. The wording of the opening sentence of Article 352 talks about the President's satisfaction. Same is the wording of Article 356 pertaining to imposition of President's rule in a State. The Supreme Court has declared that the court has powers to look into the material on the basis of which the President is supposed to have been satisfied and the court can also look into whether the President had applied his mind to the subject. On both these criteria, the requirements of the article had not been satisfied. Indira Gandhi knew this very well and therefore took recourse to taking a totally untenable position that her decision could not be challenged.

The second argument put forth by her was based on the oath of secrecy which she had taken while assuming office and her inability to divulge anything in contravention of the Official Secrets Act. This too did not hold water. The Commission of Inquiry appointed under an Act of Parliament had every right to ask for all relevant information. The Prime Minister of a country, claiming to be the largest democracy in the world, taking such a ludicrous stand did not make any sense.[3] But there were a number of highly placed persons who supported her stand.

Even more obnoxious than these objections was her conduct before the Commission when she had the temerity to question Justice Shah and his brother judges who had given the judgment against the government in the bank nationalisation case. She imputed motives to them alleging that they were share holders in the concerned banks and therefore had vested interest in deciding the way they did. Justice Shah had to naturally clarify that he did not have any shares in any of the banks. However, Indira Gandhi's intemperate action was lauded by her supporters and admirers for having put Shah on the defensive!!

On one point, however, her position was correct. She had stated that Justice Shah had expressed himself against Emergency even before being appointed on the Commission

---

3 In her Press conference in Madras (now Chennai) on 31 October 1977, Indira Gandhi said, "the sum total of the Emergency was one of good to the country.... The Emergency was good "as a shock treatment and self-discipline...." When her attention was drawn to the sufferings the Press had to undergo, Mrs Gandhi said she had no knowledge about how to deal with the Press. (*IE*, 31 October 2017, "Forty Years Ago", p 10)

and therefore he should not have been appointed. I find that Justice Shah had expressed his apprehensions as early as 1971 about (i) the Presidential power to declare an Emergency against the spirit of the Constitution and (ii) committed judges being appointed and their working under the political control of the ruling party. These two became the worst realities in 1975 and 1973 respectively. After his retirement from the court, Justice Shah occasionally addressed meetings organised by the civil liberties organisations such as the Citizens for Democracy founded by Jayaprakash Narayan (J.P.) or Peoples Union for Civil Liberties (PUCL) which was initiated by J.P. and of which Era Sezhiyan was one of the conveners. He was also Chairman of Statesman Limited from 1975 to 1991.[4] In 1975, he joined M.C. Chagla, N.P. Nathwani, V.M. Tarkunde and other former judges and leading advocates to address meetings against unwarranted and undemocratic imposition of Internal Emergency. These meetings attracted large audience. (Sezhiyan, 2010: 49-50)

It is interesting to note the observations of Mohammad Yunus, close confidant of Indira Gandhi. What he has written about Justice Shah shows how Indira Gandhi despised him:

> Justice Shah had come in for a great deal of criticism in 1976 over his controversial judgment in the bank nationalisation case. Many members of the then Parliament had sought to impeach him. It had been Mrs Gandhi who had been anxious to uphold the dignity of the Supreme Court, and got the move squashed. And yet he had harboured a grouse against her. Ignoring the precept of law and justice, Shah took up the role of a cheap politician.... The judge was also the prosecutor. He allowed no defence to those accused. (Yunus, 1980: 279)

---

4 *The Statesman* newspaper was known for its staunch anti-Emergency stand.

Against this background, I feel that Justice Shah should not have been appointed on the Commission. But, having gone through the reports of the Commission carefully, I find that Shah has been scrupulously fair and correct in dealing with matters which came before the Commission. If at all, I often found that his observations were far too mild when more severe strictures were warranted. However, looking to the sensitivity of the case, and the known trait of Indira Gandhi to make a political capital of every opportunity to gain sympathy and to blame the government for her alleged victimisation, it would have been best if someone else had been selected to head the Commission.

Shah Commission must be complimented for having dealt with the huge canvas of inquiry thoroughly, dispassionately, and expeditiously. The Commission held over 100 sessions, working 6 hours a day, and examined about 890 witnesses whose evidence was included in 1,191 paragraphs of the report. The Commission submitted Interim Report I on 11 March 1978, Interim Report II on 26 April 1978, and the third and final report on 6 August 1978. The full report comprised 532 double-demi size pages. Thus the inquiry was completed in record period of just over a year after its appointment on 28 May 1977. Justice Shah took remuneration of only ₹1 per month. The report was translated into eleven regional languages and was priced nominally for its wider dissemination. The Commission had hoped: "If the Commission's observations generate a public debate on some of the vital issues focused by the Commission with the object of devising corrective machinery and remedial action, the Commission's labour will be amply rewarded." But, this is precisely what Indira Gandhi did not want and, as soon as she came back to power in 1980, she had the report withdrawn and copies destroyed. As a result, not a single copy was available in India, except perhaps with a member of Parliament, Era Sezhiyan, who preserved it and then got it reprinted.

It is important to note that when Indira Gandhi was arrested on the orders of Home Minister Charan Singh while the inquiry was in progress, Shah was shocked and suspended the hearings of the Commission and went back to Bombay (now Mumbai). It was only when Prime Minister Morarji Desai apologised and assured him that this would not happen again that he returned to Delhi and continued the proceedings of the Commission.

Era Sezhiyan, who had distinguished himself as an erudite scholar and an articulate parliamentarian, has rendered a great public service by bringing out the full report of the Commission under the appropriate title, *Shah Commission Report: Lost, and Regained*. I have relied on it for writing this book.

The Janata government appointed a Committee under the Chairmanship of L.P. Singh, former Home Secretary, to suggest follow up action thereon. However, this Committee was disbanded when Indira Gandhi came back to power and the cases instituted in the courts and follow-up actions on the basis of Shah Commission reports were eventually given up. As stated earlier, the report was withdrawn and copies destroyed. The websites of the National Library of Australia and the School of Oriental and African Studies, University of London, however, showed the availability of the report with them. The Commission had mentioned in its report that it "had taped all proceedings of the public hearings in 234 tapes." However, none of these tapes are now available.

Why was Indira Gandhi so keen on destroying the report? Because, it would have brought out her true legacy? The report had authoritatively, objectively, and starkly documented the authentic record of the Emergency period:

- 1,10,806 persons arrested, tortured and detained without trial under draconian laws;
- Harsh censorship imposed on the Press and severe harassment of journalists;
- 25,962 employees of the State and Central Government prematurely retired;
- 1,50,105 slums (*jhuggi-jhonpadees*) in Delhi alone bulldozed and their residents left without any alternate housing;
- Indiscriminate compulsory sterilisation of 81,32,209 persons under Sanjay Gandhi's Five-Point Programme in 1976-77 against 26,24,755 sterilisations under the normal family planning programme in the previous year. (Sezhiyan, 2010: 8)

In its first interim report submitted on 11 March 1978, the Commission has dealt with 19 cases, which include, among others: reversion of Justice Aggarwal of Delhi High Court, refusal of Indira Gandhi to extend the term of Justice U.R. Lalit of the Bombay High Court, appointment of K.R. Puri as Governor, Reserve Bank of India, appointment of T.R. Vardachary as Chairman, State Bank of India, appointment of T.R. Tuli as Chairman and Managing Director of Punjab National Bank (PNB), misuse of powers and institution of false cases against four officers of Ministry of Industry (see Annexure 5), concessions by PNB in favour of Maruti Limited, detention of Gayatri Devi and Lt. Col. Bhawani Singh under COFEPOSA [Conservation of Foreign Exchange and Prevention of Smuggling Act], detention of Bhim Sen Sachar and seven others, and search and seizure operations under the Income Tax Act of two trade union leaders.

Interim Report II, submitted on 26 April 1978, dealt with misuse of media, cases of misuse of authority in the Income Tax

Department, import of aircraft by Dhirendra Brahmachari, arrests and detentions in Delhi, specific cases of misuse of authority, demolitions in Delhi, Turkman Gate firing, pressurising magistrates to sign and pre-date the firing order, and general observations.

The Third and Final Report, presented on 6 August 1978, discussed: wrongful confinement and torture of Lawrence Fernandes – brother of George Fernandes – by the police and his mistreatment in jail, cases from Haryana State, abuse of authority in service matters, arrests and detentions – general and Statewise report, conditions in jails – Statewise report, implementation of family planning – general and Statewise, demolitions – general and Statewise, complaints and manner of their disposal, and general observations.

I must confess that I find the reports of the Shah Commission disappointing, and far too mild considering the enormity of the crimes, blatant atrocities committed and the utter disregard for the rule of law. All institutions of governance were totally compromised, subverted and irrevocably damaged. But, in several cases the language used by the Commission is far too insipid. In most cases, the description of the events which had agitated the affected people so much due to the injustice done and the high-handedness which was evident, is far too mild and colourless. In most cases, there is no clear indictment or judgment fixing responsibility. However, note must be taken of the very difficult and stressful circumstances in which the Commission had to function and the very unco-operative stand taken by Indira Gandhi, her son Sanjay and some of her 'loyal and trusted' colleagues. It would have been much more dignified and befitting if Indira Gandhi had graciously submitted her defence to the Commission. This would have been in the best traditions of a democratic country. This would have enhanced her image world-wide. But it was not to be.

TREATMENT OF DETAINEES

Detention on political grounds is itself abhorrent. And it is unforgivable to treat political detainees like common criminals. But this is what Indira Gandhi government at the Centre and, under its directions, the State Governments did. The manner in which several detainees were treated was shocking. Jayaprakash Narayan was kept in solitary confinement. I have brought out later in this chapter the privations which Gayatri Devi had to undergo. Rajmata of Gwalior, Vijaya Raje Scindia, was kept in a solitary confinement and later on she asked to be shifted to a regular jail. She was then sent to Tihar jail in Delhi. Mrinal Gore, a leading activist and a socialist MLA in Maharashtra, was kept in a jail with women prisoners of disrepute.

George Fernandes, for whom Indira Gandhi had particular dislike, to put it mildly, has described how he was treated during his detention:

> I was brought to Delhi and driven straight to the Red Fort, where I was put in a dungeon. The first thing they did was to strip me of all my clothes. I had nothing to wear, and they gave me a blanket on which to sleep. It was June 1976, the height of summer in Delhi; and in that dungeon, there was no question of fans or any kind of comforts. A coarse blanket was spread out, and I was asked to lie on that. For part of the day, I used to be taken into a small cubicle, where one knew there were a number of eyes that were watching you from somewhere beyond. You were sitting on a stool, and there were a couple of officials who kept asking questions, who threatened to beat but never beat me. Their fight against me was more psychological, the way they interrogated me. (Tully, 1988: 120)

May be Fernandes was particularly harshly treated because he had advocated violent resistance and was alleged to have been involved in Baroda dynamite case, but his brother Lawrence too was very harshly treated and tormented. His case was looked into by Shah Commission and it has commented on it. But several others too were as badly treated during detention. I have separately discussed at length the detention of Gayatri Devi, queen-mother of Jaipur.

Jayaprakash Narayan in his letter, written from the jail, has stated: My life under detention at Chandigarh is a long story. I would like to say only this much now that during the 130 odd days of detention I remained completely isolated (solitary confinement). The total isolation was painful to me.... Both my kidneys have been damaged and there is no possibility of their being restored to normal functioning. Now I am being kept alive with the aid of dialysis and I have to live the rest of my days like this. (Narasimhan, 1977: 116-117)

But, in such a shocking situation, even the Supreme Court seemed to have shut its eyes. In the notorious *ADM Jabalpur (Habeas Corpus) case*, decided by a five-member bench, the majority of four judges not only declined to intervene in cases of detention, but, in their separate judgments went on to justify the Emergency and actions taken by the authorities. Justice Bhagwati stated, 'We must also disabuse our mind of any notion that the Emergency ... is not genuine.' Justice Chandrachud spoke of the 'cobwebs of suspicion' and warned the judges against substituting their 'personal opinions' and 'pre-dispositions'.... He said that such [alleged] misdeeds had not tarnished the record of India and that he has a "diamond-bright, diamond-hard hope that such things will never come to pass." (Godbole, 2008: 61) Only Justice H.R. Khanna gave a dissenting judgment, which cost him his elevation as the Chief Justice of India.

Against this background, it was shocking to see that B.K. Nehru, India's High Commissioner in London, wrote a letter to the *Times* in London that the care bestowed on the detainees was almost maternal. (Kapoor, 2015: 259)

MISUSE OF MASS MEDIA

The misuse of media was widespread and multi-pronged. The white paper brought out by the Janata government, *Misuse of mass media during the Internal Emergency*, in 1977 had classified the complaints received in the following broad categories: misuse of censorship provisions, harassment of journalists, allegations in regard to certification of films, and manipulation of mass media. I have given in Annexure 2 the restrictions on foreign media – correspondents who were expelled, and correspondents whose entry was banned. It was a rigorous effort by Indira Gandhi to shut out the country altogether from the democratic world outside. This also brings out how Indira Gandhi was keen on safeguarding her image abroad. Significantly, Indira Gandhi herself had presided over a number of meetings in which these crucial decisions were taken. (GoI, 1977: 3-9, 85-89)

Kuldip Nayar has in his book, *The Judgement – Inside Story of the Emergency*, stated:

> A set of convenient editors prepared a code of ethics for newspapers. It was a strange code; more than 3,000-word exhortation did not once mention 'Freedom of Press'. (Nayar, 1977: 109)

Among other major actions were the dissolution of the ten year old Press Council of India meant to protect freedom of Press; withdrawal of government and public sector advertisements; withdrawal of immunity given to journalists to report parliamentary proceedings; merger of two English news agencies and two Hindi news agencies, and so on. (Nayar, 1977: 110-111)

Zareer Masani has written in his book, *Indira Gandhi – A Biography*, about how the British edition of his biography of Indira Gandhi was not permitted to be released in India in 1975 and the kinds of problems he had to face, as the book contained some critical references to Indira Gandhi. For example, Masani had commented on "variations in her style of dressing – notably the contrast between the Khadi-clad austerity she cultivated in India and the sumptuous elegance she projected on her foreign tours.... I was solemnly informed, however, that my impressions were unfounded. *The Prime Minister desired me to know that her costumes varied only according to the season – she wore cottons in the summer and silks in the winter. There was no question of playing to the gallery*." He was also advised to either revise or delete the last chapter, which dealt with her politics, from the Indian edition. (Masani, 1975: xiii-xiv)

INDIRA GANDHI EVADED TAKING RESPONSIBILITY

Public accountability and transparency are the two main tenets of good governance which are accepted world over. In a number of countries, Prime Ministers and Presidents have had to face inquiries for their misdeeds, corruption and atrocities. In several cases, these have led to appointment of truth and reconciliation commissions. In others, they have been taken to the International Court of Justice. In some others, there have been Parliamentary Commissions. In a few, there have been Commissions of Inquiry.

Chilcot Commission of Inquiry into Iraq War

The Chilcot Commission appointed by the British government in June 2009 to look into matters pertaining to involvement of that country in the Iraq war in which 179 British service personnel were killed, tens of thousands of Iraqi civilians died and brutal sectarian war followed. After seven year study, the report was submitted in July 2016.

It is important to note that the then Prime Minister Tony Blair, or for that matter, none of his ministers and senior civil and military officers took the plea, as Indira Gandhi did in respect of the Shah Commission, that he would not be able to testify due to the restrictions of the Official Secrets Act. The Chilcot Commission had to examine top secret matters regarding the intelligence which was supplied by the government agencies, the deliberations in the Cabinet, the discussions held by the Prime Minister with the President of USA and his senior Cabinet functionaries, and so on. The Commission has given its report after fully examining all this record. The Commission came to the conclusion that Blair was not "straight with the nation" over Iraq War. It also found that Blair deliberately exaggerated the threat posed by the Iraqi regime, other options for dealing with the situation were not explored before going to war, British military was ill-equipped, and the intelligence agencies produced "flawed information". This was the most scathing official verdict on any modern British Prime Minister. Blair has defended his decisions and has taken full responsibility for them. The only defence he has taken in his comments on the Commission report is that the Commission has not ascribed any bad motives to him.

It needs to be noted that the civil servants (and not the Prime Minister or any other ministers) wanted the inquiry to be held in private but the decision was over-turned after an outcry. It is striking to see that the report of the Commission was widely read and discussed all over the country. Discussion groups were constituted by citizens to read the report publicly, with citizens taking turns to read it aloud for the benefit of the group. In a sense this was the real democracy in action. No one, at any level, tried to shirk taking responsibility for his actions or inactions.

CLAMOUR FOR PUNISHING INDIRA GANDHI

There were persistent demands for Indira Gandhi's punishment. Home Minister Charan Singh had in his statement stated:

> Perhaps those who differ from me do not realise sufficiently the intensity of the feelings among the people of our country on the government's failure to put the former Prime Minister behind bars by now. They draw all sorts of conclusions and are inclined to give credence to all kinds of stories. *They think that we, in the government, are, a pack of impotent people who cannot govern the country.* Indeed, there is even a section of our people, especially among those who had suffered grievously under her regime during the Emergency, who want Mrs Gandhi to be detained under the MISA [Maintenance of Internal Security Act], which is still on the statute book.... Many Emergency victims have come to me repeatedly and implored me that *not only should Mrs Gandhi be arrested immediately but that she should also be kept in Chandigarh in the same circumstances the Lok Nayak, Mr Jayaprakash Narayan, was kept, or in the Tihar jail in the same circumstances in which Maharani Gayatri Devi and Maharani Vijaya Raje Scindia were confined.* In his statement made in the Lok Sabha on 22 December 1978 Charan Singh had lashed out at Prime Minister Morarji Desai and Law Minister Shanti Bhushan for taking a soft line in regard to action against Indira Gandhi. (Naik, 1979: 145-146, 150-151)

In an open letter to the members of Parliament, J.B. Kripalani had strongly criticised the stand of Prime Minister Morarji Desai that she had suffered enough by her defeat in the elections. Law Minister Shanti Bhushan had also advocated a 'soft line' and thought that she had been punished by the people when they threw her out in the Lok Sabha poll:

> The approach of the government in the matter violates the deepest feelings of those who suffered during the Emergency.... Now that the government has decided to try the cases against Mrs Gandhi in the usual lengthy way, beginning with a trial at the magisterial level and ending with the Supreme Court, it is for the MPs to raise their voice against this decision.

Kripalani had also criticised the manner in which the Shah Commission reports were being processed by the government:

> The authorities gave the two interim reports ... to a panel of secretaries to find out what kind of proceedings should be initiated against Mrs Gandhi. Is this legal question to be examined by a panel of secretaries or that of eminent lawyers? (Kripalani, 1980: 207-208, 212)

But, Indira Gandhi was not prepared to take responsibility for any of her decisions.[5] In fact, her imperious stand was that no one, neither the judiciary nor the Judicial Commission of Inquiry presided over by a former Chief Justice of the Supreme Court of India, was competent to question her decision. And she called herself the leader of the largest democracy in the world!!

D.R. and Kamla Mankekar in their book, *Decline and Fall of Indira Gandhi*, have stated:

> When the atrocities committed in the name of family planning came to light and detailed reports were published in the Press, following the relaxation of censorship, Mrs Gandhi, Sanjay and other leaders blamed bureaucracy for the excesses. Thus they turned even the officialdom, of whom they sought to make scapegoats, against them. Nor

5 After the debacle in elections, Indira Gandhi sent a letter to the Congress President saying, "As one who led the government, I unreservedly own full responsibility for this defeat." This stand was at variance with the stand which she took before the Shah Commission.

> could the suffering people be hoodwinked. The villagers continued to chant: *Nasbandi ke teen dalal – Indira, Sanjay aur Bansi Lal.* [three agents of sterilization – Indira, Sanjay and Bansi Lal] (Mankekar, 1977: 159)

WHITHER RULE OF LAW

I have given other instances of her contempt for rule of law. (Annexure 5) She did not recognise the judicial commissions of inquiry set up under the enactment of Parliament. She was equally contemptuous of Privileges Committee of Parliament and had refused to take oath before the Committee. She had no respect for courts of law and made every effort to see that cases against her and her son Sanjay would be stalled indefinitely. Even the courts set up under the Special Courts Act were rendered ineffective and non-functional by the tactics employed by Indira Gandhi and those close to her – Sanjay Gandhi, Pranab Mukherjee, Bansi Lal, and Dhirendra Brahmachari – who were also prosecuted like her in the Special Courts. Arun Shourie had written a devastating piece titled "Special Courts: An Obituary" in which he has graphically brought out how it was the prosecution and not the defence which was on the run. [It had to prove that] No, the cases are not vendetta. No, the courts are not special. No, the procedures do not short-circuit anything. Yes, others too will be brought before the Special Courts.... Equality before the law, did you say? Yes, it is guaranteed by Article 14 of our Constitution just as untouchability is abolished by Article 17. (Shourie, 1983: 376-385)

In another article titled "Courts and Justice", written in April 1978, Arun Shourie has highlighted the threat to the rule of law:

> We have Mrs Gandhi and her coterie – a clear and present danger to democracy as well as the rule of law.... Consider

> first Mrs Gandhi's situation. She knows that the sort of matters Justice Shah has reported on will entail her criminal prosecution. She also knows that when all the affairs of Maruti have been uncovered she will not be able to avoid constructive and in some cases direct responsibility for the doings of her son, the political Balyogeshwar. *Therefore, her rehabilitation, her very survival, depends on destroying the rule of law itself.* That is why she today puts streets as a counter to the courts and screams that she has a higher sanction as she can bring crowds out on to the streets. She foments disorder and then presents herself as the law and order candidate. She shrieks at the judges and magistrates and has her followers smear the courts and the commissions of inquiry.

Shourie has exhaustively brought out how Justice Chawla, who was one of the judges of the Special Court, not only quashed the case against Mrs Gandhi for her refusal to take oath or make a statement before the Shah Commission, but it knocks the bottom out of the Commissions of Inquiry and provides a blanket cover for malfeasance and abuse of power.... The substance and the timing of Justice Chawla's judgement were known well enough in advance. (Shourie, 1980: 39, 44-45, 62)

Nayantara Sahgal has been equally harsh in commenting on the way in which Special Courts disposed off the cases against Indira Gandhi and her coterie:

> *A decade of political encroachment on the judicial system had severely affected the detachment and integrity of judges. Quick to respond to Mrs Gandhi's election victory in January 1980, the Special Courts declared themselves illegal soon afterward.... The Indian Express* commented editorially on this phenomenon on February 20, 1980: "The circumstances attending to the demise of the Special Courts must strike public opinion as rather odd. It took Justice Jain six

> months and Justice Joshi a month longer to come to the realization of their lack of jurisdiction on an obscure technicality. It is not the Act creating the Special Courts that the two judges have found ultra virus. What invalidates the Special Courts, in their opinion, is that the Ministries of home and law which purported to exercise the powers under the Special Courts Act were not specifically allocated these functions under the rules of business." (Sahgal, 1983: 200-201)

Since Indira Gandhi was back in power, there was no question of filing an appeal against these shocking decisions. It is interesting to note against this background that the Supreme Court is considering setting up of Special Courts to try politicians involved in criminal cases! (*IE*, 2 November 2017, p 1) What would be its final outcome is anybody's guess.

N.K. Singh, an outstanding IPS officer, who was in the CBI and investigated the *Kissa Kursi Ka* case has, in his book *The Plain Truth – Memoirs of a CBI Officer*, brought out the harassment he was made to suffer for successfully investigating this case. One shudders to read the tribulations he was made to undergo, including the death of his teen-age son in an "accident". He has written:

> Even Judge O.N. Vohra, who tried the case and convicted Sanjay and [V.C.] Shukla, was not spared. After the trial of the case, he [Vohra] in his own right had become an Additional Judge of the Delhi High Court. When his turn for appointment as permanent judge came, he was unceremoniously dropped by the new [Indira Gandhi] government. In the case filed by another Judge [S.N.] Kumar, in the Supreme Court, it came to light from official records that the Law Minister had gone through the judgement in the *Kissa* case while dealing with Justice Vohra's case for confirmation as a judge of the Delhi High Court. Yet the

claim of Mrs Gandhi, applauded by many, was that she had not been vindictive. There were numerous findings in the judgment against the accused, establishing how witnesses had been influenced or bought over.... Some tension had been observed in the court premises on February 26, 1979, when the judgement was announced. On the subsequent day fixed for the announcement of the sentence, a much larger crowd had collected both inside and outside the court room. The court room was full with supporters of Sanjay Gandhi.... As soon as the judge announced the sentence, the supporters of Sanjay Gandhi raised slogans inside the court itself. One of them threw a book which fell right in front of the judge. The judge, to our dismay, observed that one accused was like his brother and the other like his son and they must appreciate that in holding them guilty and awarding them sentence, he had done his duty. Though the judge made this remark obviously to pacify them, it had just the opposite effect as they took it as a weakness of the court, which emboldened them further. Soon thereafter, the judge thought it fit to retire to his chamber. As soon as he withdrew, one of Sanjay's supporters stood on his table, held a mock hearing in which he acquitted Sanjay Gandhi. Others were raising abusive slogans directed against me by name, Morarji Desai, Kanti Desai and the CBI. In the melee one muscleman of Sanjay Gandhi, who had already taken position, gave a few blows to our lawyer S.B. Jaisinghani.... Thereafter, the unruly mob diverted its full attention on me.... Not one of the bunch, Vasant Sathe, Shyama Charan Shukla, V.C. Shukla, far less Sanjay Gandhi, tried to restrain the avenging goons. Neither the lawyers of Sanjay Gandhi nor of V.C. Shukla did anything except watching the whole fun. (Singh, 1998: 104-106)

When Sanjay's appeal came up for hearing before the Supreme Court, Indira Gandhi was in power. A.G. Noorani, a well-known jurist, has written:

> It was a piquant situation. The government prosecuting Sanjay Gandhi was headed by his mother. A conviction would have disqualified him from membership of Parliament and sent him to prison. Co-accused Shukla would have suffered equally. In India, the government controls the prosecution agency to a remarkable degree. But the matter was now at the appellate stage before the highest court in India. Yet, Noorani points out, *the highest court in India did not see fit to take notice of the new public prosecutor's handling of the case, when he disposed off a record that ran 6,500 pages, filling 20 volumes, and a 300-page judgment, in fifteen minutes.* On April 11, 1980, the Supreme Court allowed the appeal and quashed the conviction of Sanjay Gandhi and V.C. Shukla. (Sahgal, 1983: 202)

Is any comment necessary? No rule of law was left in the country.

ONLY WAY INDIRA GANDHI COULD HAVE BEEN PUNISHED

How to hold Indira Gandhi accountable for the Emergency and its terrible atrocities was the million dollar question which Janata government could not address till the very end. Nayantara Sahgal has written that "Indira Gandhi herself seemed to expect summary punishment at the hands of men she had imprisoned without trial.... The new Prime Minister, Morarji Desai, paid a courtesy call on her, and his government, which was committed to restore the rule of law, was particular to refrain from any act or suggestion of vendetta...." (Sahgal, 1983: 197)

Madhu Limaye has, in his book, *Janata Party Experiment – An Insider's Account of Opposition Politics*, written:

> There was terrific pressure from the rank and file of the Janata Party and also the CPI(M) leadership on the government that it punish the guilty. J.B. Kripalani was

> one of them. The pressure became almost a clamour. Although the RSS chief Balasaheb Deoras talked of 'forget and forgive' the talk was hypocritical, for the Jan Sangh and RSS workers asked for strong action. *Charan Singh sometimes regretted that our law and Constitution did not permit Nuremberg type trial.*

In his letter to Morarji Desai on 4 April 1977, Limaye wrote: "While we can forget much and forgive much, everything can neither be forgotten nor forgiven." (Limaye, 1994: 476-477)

As reported in the *Hindustan Times* of 10 October 1977, Acharya Kripalani told a Calcutta audience: In any other country, Mrs Gandhi would have been imprisoned without trial, or hanged. (Austin, 1999: 453)

Indira Gandhi and her coterie sabotaged all court proceedings. As if this was not enough, the Janata government was dysfunctional and could not even take any decisions on the reports of the Commissions of Inquiry. The usual ploy of referring the findings of the reports to the Committee of Secretaries was the surest way of shelving any action. With a thoroughly politicised, demoralised and terrorised civil service, and the clear prospects of Indira Gandhi coming back to power with the disintegration of the Janata Party, any action against Indira Gandhi was impossible. At the same time, there was persistent demand in the country that Indira Gandhi must be punished.

Series of actions taken by Indira Gandhi government during Emergency – making Parliament irrelevant, restrictions on publication of discussions and debates in Parliament, arrest of prominent members of Parliament, radical changes in the Constitution to change even its basic structure – showed her scant regard for democracy. Against this background, I firmly believe that it would have been fully justified to severe her ties with elections and to deny her the legitimacy of being a representative of the people. In no other case such a punishment could have been considered more justified.

Reference may be invited in this context to the disfranchisement of Bal Thackeray, ordered by the Supreme Court, in an election petition for indulging in corrupt electoral practice by making communal and inflammatory speeches. The final orders debarring him from contesting or voting in elections for a period of six years from 11 December 1995 to 10 December 2001 were accordingly issued. The conduct of Indira Gandhi was much worse than that of Bal Thackeray. According to me, she should have been debarred for a period of 12 years by passing a special legislation for the purpose. Even her strong supporters would have found it difficult to oppose such a legislation. But this was never done by the God-fearing Janata Party.

Any action against her was criticised as political victimisation. As a result, as stated in Annexure 5, the only punishment she received was imprisonment for a few days imposed on her by Parliament, and not by any court of law. And when she came back to power in 1980, she had that resolution rescinded by Parliament and she and her minions were declared innocent! All slogans such as “howsoever high you may be, the law is above you” or “the law will take its own course” were meaningless.

PRANAB KUMAR MUKHERJEE AND EMERGENCY

Very few persons, who were ‘mentioned in dispatches’ in the Shah Commission report, are alive now or have occupied high public offices till recently. One of them is Pranab Kumar Mukherjee, who was then the Minister of State in the Ministry of Finance, and was Central minister for decades during Congress regime and later held the highest office of the President of India till 25 July 2017. His active involvement in two of the most shocking cases were documented by the Shah Commission.[6]

Detention of Gayatri Devi and Lt. Col. Bhavani Singh

Swatantra Party member of Parliament, Gayatri Devi, widow of late His Highness Maharaja Mansingh of Jaipur, and Lt. Col. Bhavani Singh, full time officer of the Indian Army, who was awarded Mahavir Chakra for gallantry in the 1971 War with Pakistan and had taken voluntarily retirement in November 1974 on personal grounds, were detained under the Conservation of Foreign Exchange and Preservation of Smuggling Act (COFEPOSA) and were lodged in Delhi's Tihar jail on 30 July 1975. The entire account of their detention given in the Shah Commission Report (First Interim Report, Para 7.204-7.231) is shocking.

Parliament had amended the COFEPOSA Act on 5 August (replacing an ordinance of July) with brazen language providing that a detention was not void even if the grounds for it were 'vague', 'non-existent' or 'not relevant', or 'invalid for any other reason whatsoever'. Further, by the amendment made in 1976, detention was permitted for two years, as against one year earlier. (Austin, 1999: 310)

The Reserve Bank of India (RBI), in its two letters dated 6 March and 5 July 1975, had clearly informed the government that the Bank was aware of the foreign holdings of the trusts and other holdings of the Maharaja of Jaipur family abroad and had referred the matter to the Ministry of Finance way back in 1969. There was thus no concealment. All that was required

6 To make life easier, Sanjay had evolved an ingenious method of influencing government decisions. In the three important ministries of his interest, that is, Home, Finance and Industry, he got appointed Om Mehta, Pranab Mukherjee and A.P. Sharma as Ministers of State.... They were all beholden to him and did what he wanted. (Gill, 1996: 289)

under the rules was to keep the government informed, which was done in this case.

Mukherjee seems to have decided on the detention of these two persons in advance, as stated by the then Joint Secretary C.T.A. Pillai. Though there was no evidence to support any allegations, Mukherjee passed an order on the file saying: "I am satisfied that Smt. Gayatri Devi should be detained as proposed. Ordered accordingly. *Declaration may also issue*." As regards the declaration mentioned in the order of Minister Mukherjee, it needs to be noted that "the adverse effect to which a person is subjected to on account of issue of declaration under Section 12A(2) is that it no longer remains necessary to disclose to the person the grounds on which the orders have been made and to refer such cases to the Advisory Board, which at the relevant time comprised three High Court judges. In the case of these two persons, no grounds were indicated as to why declarations under Section 12A(2) were necessary."

Earlier, Mukherjee had also explored the possibility of arrest of these persons under the Customs and Gold Control Acts but it was found that no case could be made out under these Acts. Shah Commission Report brings out the active interest of Mukherjee in the case and this was so evident to the officers that the case was not even referred to the Screening Committee. When asked by the Commission why this was not done, Joint Secretary Pillai had said, "*Since the Minister had already made up his mind, there was no need of Screening Committee's opinion*". *The case was also not put up to the Advisory Committee as, according to the Joint Secretary, "the decision to detain these two persons was taken by the minister"*.

The Commission has noted the urgency with which the whole matter was processed in the course of one day – i e 24 July 1975 itself. What exactly transpired on 24 July 1975 which necessitated such expeditious action for issue of orders relating to arrest remains unexplained because Mukherjee did not come before the Commission to give evidence. *At one stage, when a request for parole was made, Mukherjee recorded a note on September 7, 1975 which read: "May be released on parole as proposed. However, PM may kindly like to see." The Commission has noted: "What decision was taken by the Prime Minister in the matter is not indicated in the file, but it has been noticed that Shri Pranab Kumar Mukherjee pasted his earlier note dated September 7, 1975 recommending release on parole. If the note sheet page is put against bright light, the noting of Shri Pranab Kumar Mukherjee reproduced earlier can be easily read.... After pasting his earlier note, Shri Mukherjee recorded another note on September 12, 1975 wherein he ordered the rejection of the request."*

The Commission has rightly inferred that the rejection of the request must have been "on the advice of the PM". The Commission has also stated more than once that since Mukherjee did not appear before the Commission to explain the case, there was no way of knowing what actually transpired.

Jad Adams has mentioned in his book, *The Dynasty – The Nehru-Gandhi Story*, of an episode which perhaps shows Indira Gandhi's antagonism to Gayatri Devi: "At a meeting in Jaipur she was faced with Swatantra adherents, supporters of the Maharani who was a rival candidate, trying to break up the meeting.[7] She lost her temper to electrifying effect: 'I am not going to be cowed down. I know who is behind these demonstrations, and I know how to make myself heard. I am going to do some plain speaking today. Go and ask the Maharajas how many wells they dug for their people in their states when they ruled them, how many roads they constructed,

7 According to another version, Indira Gandhi was heckled by large crowd sympathetic to the Maharani of Jaipur.... Indira Gandhi did not especially like the Maharani. (Gupte, 2009: 328 and footnote 6)

what they did to fight the slavery of the British while they lived in luxury at the cost of the people.' (Adams, 1997: 211) In spite of this lambasting, Gayatri Devi won the election with a very large margin. It was known that Indira Gandhi had a long memory of an elephant and could be vindictive. Did she carry this grudge? But, it is difficult to believe that she would have gone to the extent of imprisoning Gayatri Devi. But who knows?

Later, Gayatri Devi was released on parole 9 January 1976. Before her release, she had written a letter to the Prime Minister on 11 December 1975 from jail in which she had written:

> As the International Women's Year is coming to an end, may I take this opportunity to assure you, Madam, all my support to you in person and your programme in the interest and betterment of the country. May I also add that I have decided to give up politics ever since Rajaji's demise and will not take any further interest in politics as the Swatantra Party has already (sic) defunct and I have decided not to join any political party.
>
> In view of what I have stated above, as well as my deteriorating health, in spite of the medical facilities allowed and provided to me, may I request you for gracious considerations that I may be released. If there are any conditions which you want to impose, I will try to abide by.

The letter was forwarded to the Prime Minister through Jail Superintendent and District Magistrate. It was not known what orders were passed thereon.

Before her release on parole, Ministry of Finance had insisted that Gayatri Devi should withdraw her writ petition filed in the Delhi High Court. The matter relating to the revocation of the detention order finally came before the

Review Committee on 14 March 1977. The Committee "felt that a view could be taken for revocation of both the detention orders but left the matter for decision of the minister for revenue and banking. Shri Pranab Kumar Mukherjee thereafter passed the following order on 19 March 1977: "Initially Col. Bhavani Singh may be released and his activities kept under close watch and the case of Smt. Gayatri Devi may be decided after some time." *Order of release of Gayatri Devi was passed by the Delhi Administration on 22 March 1977 after the revocation of the Proclamation of Emergency.*

The Commission has observed:

> The manner in which Gayatri Devi was treated in jail makes a very poignant reading.... She was not at all well when she was taken to the jail and was under medical treatment at the time of her arrest. According to her, the conditions in Tihar jail were absolutely appalling; there was complete lack of sanitation, no running water, the public latrines had failed and therefore all the people who were in the prison had to use the drain to ease themselves. Rajmata Vijaya Raje Scindia of Gwalior was also brought to Tihar jail and was kept in a 'Phasi Kothi' (cell for condemned prisoners).... She [Gayatri Devi] had lost 10 kgs in weight and her blood pressure was very low.

Mukherjee was issued a notice under rule 5(2)(a) of the Commissions of Inquiry Rules. He declined to file a statement as required by the rules. He was also served with summons under Section 8B of the Commissions of Inquiry Act. He refused to give evidence on oath in pursuance of the summons issued.

The Shah Commission has held as under: "*It is thus clear on the basis of evidence that has been brought on record that Mr Pranab Kumar Mukherjee, the then Minister of Revenue and Banking, has misused his position and abused his authority in ordering the detention of Smt. Gayatri Devi and Col. Bhavani Singh on wholly insufficient grounds. It is a clear case of subversion of lawful processes and of administrative procedures."*

It can be seen that this is a shocking case showing utter contempt for rule of law. It also shows what a "committed" bureaucracy, which Indira Gandhi wanted, can do to a citizen. Once the minister had indicated his mind to detain Gayatri Devi, the procedures laid down to avoid misuse of law, such as submission of the case to the Screening Committee and the Advisory Committee were not followed. The minister's directive that a declaration be issued so that no reasons for detention need be conveyed to the detenues, was meekly followed. Mukherjee was clearly acting under the instructions of Indira Gandhi. There was so much vendetta against Gayatri Devi that her request for parole was rejected at the instance of Indira Gandhi and she was not released till the Emergency was lifted. The letter written by Gayatri Devi, the supplicant, to Indira Gandhi, 'the Empress of India', did not evoke any response, least of all any mercy.

Mukherjee refused to appear before the Shah Commission and to make a statement on oath. When cases were filed against Indira Gandhi, Pranab Kumar Mukherjee, Sanjay Gandhi and some others for refusing to testify before the Commission, efforts were made by them to have the cases adjourned for one reason or the other, interminably. Shourie has written, "Pranab Mukherji's case has gone along lines similar to Indira Gandhi's case." (Shourie, 1980: 61) Ultimately, all these cases were dismissed! With such a former Prime Minister and former President of India, it will be a travesty to call ourselves a democracy wedded to the rule of law.

It will be pertinent to take a look at what Gayatri Devi had to say in her book, *A Princess Remembers: The Memoirs of the Maharani of Jaipur*. She has stated:

The country was disillusioned with Mrs Gandhi's leadership. Failing to recognise the grass root support of these protest movements, she interpreted them as a 'Get Indira' campaign. She retaliated and sought to divert public attention by ordering a series of raids on business houses and on members of the Opposition.... *The former royal families of Gwalior and Jaipur were singled out for these raids* because the Rajmata of Gwalior and I were members of the Opposition in Parliament ... February 11, 1975 is a day I shall never forget.... "No one can leave the premises," they said. While the search was going on in Moti Doongri [palace], I received a phone call from Pat. He told me that every single house and office of ours had been raided – the City Palace, which is the official home of our family and houses the museum, the Rambagh Palace Hotel, Bubble's home, Rajmahal, Pat and Joe's houses and my parliamentary house in Delhi. Two days later Jaigarh Fort was also raided. When Income Tax officers arrived at Jaigarh, the Meena tribals who guard the fort told the Income Tax officers that they could only enter the fort over their dead bodies! Ever since Maharaja Jai Singh build (sic) Jaigarh nobody dared entered (sic) the premises except the succeeding maharajas and their trusted officials. We remained calm throughout this exercise which went on for weeks.... The roof of the Kapatdwara treasury in the City Palace had needed repairs, so many years before Jai had all the contents moved to a specially built strong room in Moti Doongri. He had planned to have display vases made so that the visitors to the City Palace could see the Jaipur crown jewels. When the tax collectors came across these treasures they were wonderstruck.... This gold was mentioned in the last budget of Jaipur State and every single piece was accounted for.... The next day I was shocked to read in the papers that my passport had been

> confiscated because of anti-national activities. I was beside myself with rage. It angered me to think that, the government would go to such lengths, to such extremes to malign me. Later during the Shah Commission inquiry, I realised how low Mrs Gandhi government could stoop. *Her officials alleged that I planned to go to Patna, then on to Nepal from where I would catch a plane and flee the country. To this day, I have never been to Patna;* there was no truth in these allegations but the incident illustrated how far the government of Mrs Gandhi would go to harass a citizen. (Gayatri Devi, 1995: 367-368, 384)

Coomi Kapoor, in her book, *The Emergency – A Personal History*, has stated: Indira Gandhi "chose with care the politicians she thought were especially vulnerable, and two of her first targets were the charismatic *rajmatas* (queen mothers) of Jaipur and Gwalior ... *Indira Gandhi displayed the level of vindictiveness to which she could stoop.*" (Kapoor, 2015: 255)

There are several intriguing features of this case. Important questions remain unanswered. Gayatri Devi has clearly mentioned in her memoirs, *A Princess Remembers*, that there were Income Tax raids on all her premises and the underground vaults in the main palace in Rajgarh fort were also opened. There is a mention of gold coins which were found at one location but which had been declared by her family to the government earlier. **First**, was army deployed in these raids, as is still talked about in Jaipur? If so under what rules was army called in? Or was it para-military force? I am not aware of any rules under which this can be done. **Second**, Pranab Mukherjee had told his officers that Gayatri Devi was in Patna and therefore needed to be arrested and detained immediately. Gayatri Devi has mentioned that she was never in Patna and had not been there at any time in her life. **Third**, why was there no mention of Income Tax raids in the documentation prepared by Income Tax department? **Fourth**, why the Income Tax raids did not figure in the examination of the Shah Commission. **Fifth**, more than thirty-three MPs were detained during the Emergency. From Gayatri Devi's own political party, three other MPs were detained – Bhagirath Bhanwar, Janeshwar Mishra and Piloo Mody. (Henderson, 1977: 237-238) Why such special efforts were made to build up a case that Gayatri Devi was arrested and detained under COFEPOSA? She could easily have been detained under MISA, like the other MPs. Was it to bring her down in public estimation? **Sixth**, and most important, the atrocious and high-handed action taken against Gayatri Devi was clearly at the behest of Indira Gandhi, Pranab Mukherjee being a mere instrumentality. What were the reasons for Indira Gandhi's personal animosity? I have not been able to assess the reasons which were responsible for Indira Gandhi's animosity and hatred for Gayatri Devi, which was so evident. I could not find any answer for it in Gayatri Devi's memoirs. Was Indira Gandhi jealous of her? Did she want to show that Gayatri Devi may have been the Maharani of Jaipur but she was the Empress of India?

Baroda Rayon Corporation – Search and Seizure under the Income Tax Act, 1961

The Shah Commission inquiries showed that the search and seizure operation for alleged large-scale tax evasion in this case was done at the instance of Pranab Kumar Mukherjee, Minister of State in Finance Ministry. (Second Interim Report, Paras 9.1-9.27) Apparently, some information was to be collected about the donations given to the Congress Party, though this purpose was never disclosed. S.R. Mehta, Chairman, Central Board of Direct Taxes (CBDT), told the Commission that he had a quick look at the papers which were seized and he took them to Mukherjee. *This was done because information regarding concealment of income had been given to him by the Minister himself. The Minister too, it is stated, was very busy and asked Mehta to leave the papers on his desk and promised to return them after "going through them". Mehta never got them back from Minister Mukherjee.*

The investigation carried out pursuant to the search and seizure operations did not reveal any concealment of income. The Commission also noted that Mehta had directed that the residential premises of V.K. Shah, Managing Director of Baroda Rayon Corporation, and Fateh Singh Gaekawad, Chairman of the company, should not be searched. When asked why this was so, the Commission was told that there was no specific information regarding concealment in relation to these two persons. The officers going on search were specifically directed by Mehta to bring for his scrutiny certain papers.

The Commission has expressed:

> its concern at the arbitrary and high-handed manner in which the executive authority was misused in this case for a collateral purpose. The extraordinary power of search and seizure under Section 132 is intended to protect the interests of revenue against the tax evader. By the exercise of the power a serious invasion is made upon the rights, privacy and freedom of the tax-payer. The power must be exercised strictly in accordance with the law, which provides the necessary safeguards; and only for the purpose for which law authorises it to be exercised. It is distressing that, in spite of a wealth of judicial pronouncements and departmental instructions emphasising the need for utmost restraint and strict compliance with the law, the then Chairman CBDT, Shri S.R. Mehta, was himself instrumental in unleashing this dangerous weapon which could unjustly and irretrievably damage the business reputation and standing of the parties affected.

V.U. Eradi, former member of CBDT, who had worked on the staff of the Shah Commission, has written:

> Three files containing the vital information V.K. Shah, the Managing Director of the company, so helpfully placed in his briefcase were 'seized' from him and through the chain of command reached the present Finance Minister [P.K. Mukherjee] who quite legitimately forgot almost immediately what he did with them. It used to be said those days by persons close to the then important hangers-on that the party High Command was keen on verifying details of large sums of money apparently handed over to the then charismatic party leader allegedly to persuade some legislator to act in a particular manner. V.K. Shah only requested that the papers be seized from him rather than he hand them over and thus betray his Guru [Rajani Patel, President of Bombay Pradesh Congress Committee]. (*The Hindu,* 11 March 2011, p 9)

Pranab Mukherjee, the then Union Finance Minister, while replying to the budget debate had stated in Parliament on 9 March 2011 that, during the Emergency, he had, due to his deep concern for black money, ordered raids on a "very important family" that he did not want to identify. He is reported to have added, "it was not a fruitless raid. One tonne of primary gold with Swiss marks was discovered. Later on with the change of government, I was accused of causing Emergency excesses and was put in the dock before the Shah Commission." Eradi, who was the officer concerned dealing with tax matters in the Shah Commission, has in his OP-ED article titled "Put in the dock by Shah Commission – Pranab Mukherjee should specify in which case he was 'put in the dock by the Shah Commission'. History and propriety demand an honest answer", in *The Hindu* (11 March 2011, p 9), contested this. Eradi has stated that in none of the five cases pertaining to the Income Tax department, over which the present Finance Minister presided as Minister of State for Finance (Revenue), in which raids were carried out, any gold was found. There was no rejoinder by Mukherjee.

SANJAY – THE UNCONSTITUTIONAL CENTRE OF POWER[8]

Demolitions in Delhi

It was widely known that, during the Emergency, large scale demolitions were done at the instance of and under orders of Sanjay Gandhi with a view to beautify Delhi.[9] The Shah Commission has noted:

> An impression had been created that Shri Sanjay Gandhi was actively associated with the demolition programmes in Delhi.... The affected people went in deputations to Sanjay Gandhi to seek his assistance in several cases. Shri Sanjay Gandhi used to meet these deputationists and deal with them in his own peculiar way.
>
> **Demolitions in Kapas Hera village:** Demolitions carried out in this village allegedly at the instance of Sanjay Gandhi were unauthorised and procedures prescribed by law were not followed either by the Delhi Development Authority (DDA) or by the Municipal Corporation of Delhi (MCD). This was not a development area under the DDA and the

8 As Shah Commission described him (p 252).

9 Same was the position in a number of other places. "Sanjay wants the city made beautiful", Pupul Jayakar was told by the Divisional Commissioner during her visit to Benaras, at the instance of Indira Gandhi. "A Revenue Commissioner working under a state government complying with illegal oral orders of Sanjay Gandhi conveyed through some underling! Mrs Jayakar was then taken to see the 'beautification' work done on Kamacha road. It "looked as if a bomb had fallen on it." She reported the situation to Indira and showed her the photographs.... She hit the ceiling...." (Gill, 1996: 283)

DDA had no legal authority to demolish any structures here. However, witnesses stated that it was the DDA which had demolished the structures. The action of demolishing the house of Lt. Col. Ram Singh Yadav, a retired Army officer in this village, was as per B.R. Tamta [Municipal Commissioner of Delhi] taken on the orders of Sanjay Gandhi. He had also to take disciplinary action against his own officers as he was pressurised by Sanjay Gandhi. Sanjay Gandhi was responsible for initiating the entire demolition operations in this village and in so far as demolitions were illegal, he has to take his share of the responsibility for the same.

Demolitions in Karol Bagh were done at the instance of Sanjay Gandhi. Among other considerations the political affiliation of the shopkeepers to the party opposed to the Congress was one of the deciding factors which impelled Sanjay Gandhi to order the demolition of the structures in Karol Bagh. The responsibility for these demolitions must rest entirely with Sanjay Gandhi and B.R. Tamta.

Demolitions in Andheria Mor: The procedure laid down in Delhi Municipal Corporation Act was not followed. The demolition operations which took place in Andheria Mor were carried out at the instance and under the direction of Sanjay Gandhi and he was responsible for ordering the properties of the villagers to be demolished and the order was without any authority of law.

In so far as Sanjay Gandhi's role is concerned, the Commission has concluded that

(i) Though Lt. Governor of Delhi was the head of the administration and was also the Chairman of DDA, he appears to have been completely ignored by the functionaries who, for all their actions, took orders directly from Sanjay Gandhi. The demolitions of places of worship specifically required the prior orders of the Lt. Governor. The requirement was completely ignored when the DDA demolished the Arya Samaj temple. *The lament of the Lt. Governor that nobody consulted him or listened to him and that they used to take orders directly from Sanjay Gandhi has been heard by the Commission with a feeling of disgust, for he admitted that he turned a deaf ear, and a blind eye to every conceivable piece of illegality and impropriety.*

(ii) B.R. Tamta, Commissioner of MCD, had the honesty to admit that he had done wrong things because of compulsions, particularly the pressure on him of Sanjay Gandhi.

(iii) Jagmohan, Chairman of DDA, grossly misused his position and abused his authority. He, during the Emergency, became a law unto himself and went about doing the bidding of Sanjay Gandhi without care or concern for the miseries of the people affected thereby.

(iv) Sanjay Gandhi has actually aided and abetted the illegal demolitions undertaken by the DDA and the MCD and the evidence on record goes to show that *he was the prime mover in majority of the illegal operations that took place in Delhi*.

(v) In view of the Commission, the manner in which Sanjay Gandhi functioned in the public affairs of Delhi in particular is the single greatest act of excess committed during the period of Emergency for which there is no parallel nor any justification for such assumption of authority or power in the history of independent India. While the other acts of the excesses may have been in the nature of acts committed by functionaries having some shadow of

> authority acting in excess of their powers, *here was a case of an individual wielding unlimited powers in a dictatorial manner without even the slightest right to it. If this country has to be rendered safe for the future generations, the people owe it to themselves to ensure that an irresponsible and unconstitutional centre of power like the one which revolved round Sanjay Gandhi (sic) during the Emergency is not allowed to come up ever again in any form or shape or under any guise.* (Sezhiyan, 2010: 249-252)

Turkman Gate Firing

The Shah Commission has stated that though the family planning programme may have contributed to the build up of tension among the residents of the area, the firing was a direct and immediate sequel to the decisions of the authorities to proceed with the demolitions regardless of the resistance of the people and the consequences.... *The predated firing order was got signed by sub-divisional magistrate N.C. Ray due to the pressure put on him by Sanjay Gandhi.* He said though he did not know who had actually fired as "it was the Emergency period and he had apprehension about himself and the future of his service. He also feared that he might be arrested under MISA or otherwise harassed. He admitted that he was fabricating a document which was part of the public record." P.S. Bhinder, Deputy Inspector General (DIG) of police, pressurised the magistrates for doing wholly improper acts and he got the firing order signed and anti-dated through the intervention of Sanjay Gandhi. Sanjay Gandhi intervened on behalf of Bhinder and pressured the District Magistrate and his colleagues and a junior magistrate to sign and pre-date the firing order. The Commission has concluded that "*It was highly improper and unwarranted interference on the part of Sanjay Gandhi to have called the magistrates to his residence and ordered them to do a wholly improper and illegal act.*" (Sezhiyan, 2010: 138, 253)

Harassment of M/s Pandit Brothers

Partners of this firm were close relatives of P.N. Haksar, the enormously powerful former Principal Secretary to Prime Minister Indira Gandhi, who was summarily banished to the Planning Commission, after he tried to warn Indira Gandhi about the doings of Sanjay. Sanjay Gandhi wanted to teach a lesson to Haksar, and anyone else who would dare to speak against him to his mother.[10] I.G. Patel has written in his book *Glimpses of Indian Economic Policy – An Insider's View*:

> What is not in doubt is that Haksar managed to concentrate enormous powers in the PM's secretariat and that his intellect contributed much to Mrs Gandhi's tactics and strategies. He was accepted as Mrs Gandhi's alter ego, and by most as Mrs Gandhi's tutor, mentor, and sole confidant – a reputation that cost him dear in the days of Emergency. Both he and Sanjay could not be powers behind the thrown; and his allergy to Sanjay meant that he had to be humbled and ousted. (Patel, 2002: 132)

The Shah Commission has stated:

> On the basis of the evidence, there can be no doubt that the series of harassments against the firm, including the arrests of the manager and the two partners were initiated at the instance of Sanjay Gandhi.... There are certain

---

10 Contrary to some reports, it seems that PN Haksar's name was not on the arrest list, although Sanjay Gandhi considered him an enemy. But Sanjay Gandhi shortly remedied the omission by arresting Haksar's uncle in a publicly humiliating manner. (Austin, 1999: 309, footnote 41) According to Yunus, the reason for Haksar's antagonism to Sanjay was that Haksar's land in Gurgaon was acquired for Maruti project. (Yunus, 1980: 265)

striking features in this case. The partners and manager had to undergo great hardships before they were released on bail.... The use of police force in large numbers for price tag checking is also unusual.... The procedure adopted by the Income Tax authorities in dealing with the assessment case must also cause concern.... The Income Tax officer has explained that he was called by the Commissioner and repeatedly told orally to dispose of this case after making vigorous inquiries. The association of Commissioner of Income Tax with the case following his visit to R.K. Dhawan in the Prime Minister's House is also disconcerting.

It appeared to Lt. Governor Krishan Chand that Indira Gandhi knew her son was behind this. According to the Lt. Governor, the decision to launch the Sales Tax and price tag raids was a sequel to the orders that emanated from Sanjay Gandhi. In the absence of any relevant information or explanation furnished by Sanjay Gandhi, the Commission has stated: "Sanjay Gandhi who wielded such enormous power during the Emergency did not confine his activities only to the operation of demolition of houses, shops and industrial buildings. *He took a hand in getting some persons whom either he did not like or who had thwarted him, arrested and detained.* In the present case the evidence brought on record clearly points to him as the source and the motivator of all the harassments that followed the action against Pandit Brothers. On the direct responsibility of Sanjay Gandhi for the harassment that was meted out to Pandit Brothers, the Commission feels no doubt. It has, however, not been possible to establish the exact motive which prompted him to indulge in these grossly unwarranted and unlawful actions, because Sanjay Gandhi has on the pretence of claiming legal and constitutional protection of his rights, chosen not even to attempt to explain the evidence against him. (Sezhiyan, 2010: 71-76)

Justice A.C. Gupta Commission Report on Maruti Affairs

Janata government appointed on 30 May 1977 a Commission of Inquiry under the Chairmanship of Justice A.C. Gupta, a serving judge of the Supreme Court, to examine the affairs of Sanjay Gandhi's three concerns – Maruti Ltd., Maruti Heavy Vehicles (Private) Ltd., and Maruti Technical Services (Private) Ltd. The Commission examined 712 affidavits and almost 2,000 files of the Union and State Governments, statutory bodies, etc. It held 111 public sittings, and examined 268 witnesses. The Commission submitted its report on 31 May 1979.

The Commission's conclusions are worth noting:

> The affairs of the Maruti concerns ... appear to have brought about a decline in the integrity of public life and sullied the purity of administration. Legal and other requirements were brushed aside, and accepted norms of behaviour were forgotten on many occasions when the interest of a Maruti company was involved. This was due to, as witness after witness repeated, an atmosphere of fear then prevailing ... and the fear was real. Threats of detention under MISA or a CBI inquiry or other forms of harassment made it hazardous for the officers to insist on the rules or the dealers and depositors to insist on their rights. Persons in public life were in danger of having their political careers ruined. That it was not an idle threat is proved by instances of persons in whose case the threat was carried out.... From the interest taken in Maruti's progress by men from Prime Minister's Secretariat and the way even matters connected with the country's defence were subordinated to the interests of Maruti Ltd., and the prevailing sense of fear that prompted implicit obedience,

> one is left in no doubt as to the origin of the power that made such a state of affairs possible. Shri Sanjay Gandhi exercised only a derivative power, its source was the authority of the Prime Minister.

Justice Gupta has also brought out:

> the presence of unaccounted money.... What is revealed in such examination, as the Commission has been able to do, suggests that if a joint or co-ordinated examination of the records of the Maruti companies is done by the Departments of Revenue and Company Affairs, and their books of account are audited by a special team, many more irregularities are likely to come to light.

Of course, this was not possible after Indira Gandhi came back to power. In fact, to cover up the matters, the companies were nationalised! Madhu Dandavate rightly called it "nationalisation of corruption".

Gupta Commission has also documented how rules and procedures were deliberately over-looked to give series of concessions, exemptions, licences and permits to the company. The reactions in the Press, given below, to these disclosures were not surprising:

- ... as with Shah Commission report, the cumulative effect, as classified and evaluated by a fine judicial mind, comes with an impact which is *not merely horrifying, but disgusting*. (*The Statesman*, 9 September 1979)
- *... the finds have been ... certainly sufficient, under conditions of genuine parliamentary democracy, to keep son and mother out of public affairs for life.* (*The Hindu*, 12 September 1979)
- The Roman hand of Mrs Gandhi can be seen at every stage in the process by which land was acquired and enormous loans given to Maruti by banks whose

> officials were under threat or were promoted with a view to securing favoured treatment ... *it would seem that, even more than the Allahabad judgment in her election case, it was Sanjay's megalomaniac plans regarding Maruti which compelled her to declare the second Emergency in June 1975 so that the Maruti scandals could be hushed up.* (*Deccan Herald*, 11 September 1979)

However, Indira Gandhi's reaction was shockingly flippant. At her Shivaji Park meeting in Mumbai in September 1979, Indira Gandhi declared she had no time to read 'trash' published by the Commissions of Inquiry, and referred in her speech to the 'petty judge' who had dared unseat the Prime Minister. "I am unconcerned about the disclosures about Maruti", she told reporters when asked for her comment [on Gupta Commission Report]. (Sahgal, 1983: 217-225)

But, Indira Gandhi was seriously worried about the inquisition in Parliament on Maruti affairs. Madhu Limaye has written:

> *False and untruthful answers were given to our questions in the Lok Sabha.* It was established by the [Gupta] Commission that all answers by Ministers to questions touching on Maruti Limited had to be approved by Indira Gandhi. *These questions were generally converted into unstarred questions to avoid answering probing supplimentaries on the floor of the House. Sometimes the wording was changed to render them meaningless....* Mantosh Sondhi, Secretary of the Heavy Industries Ministry, helped the Maruti project up to a point. But this was not considered adequate. He and his family were harassed and a CBI case was registered against him.... The report [of the Commission] was released on 7 September 1979 by the caretaker government of Charan Singh. *The new government headed by Indira Gandhi stated that 'some of the statements made before the Commission were*

> *made under pressure.'* In the event no action was taken. (Limaye, 1994: 500-503)

No wonder, people began referring to Maruti as *ma ruti* (mother in crisis). (Nayar, 1977: 203)

When the Janata government started preparing to file criminal cases arising out of the findings of the Gupta Commission Report, Sanjay Gandhi took personal interest in the strategy which led to Charan Singh's defection and fall of Janata government.

Janardan Thakur in his book, *Indira Gandhi and Her Power Game*, has brought out the drama surrounding the withdrawal of support by Congress(I) to Charan Singh. He has written:

> The *casus belli* was Charan Singh's refusal to bail out Sanjay Gandhi from his immediate legal problems. A couple of days before Charan Singh was scheduled to seek a vote of confidence, Sanjay Gandhi warned Raj Narain that if he wanted the Charan Singh government to continue, he must get his demands accepted.... There they called an important member of the Congress(I) for consultations. The talks merely confirmed the position: either Sanjay Gandhi's demands were met or the Congress(I) support would go.... Charan Singh said he would prefer to resign rather than give in to the blackmail of Sanjay Gandhi. An angry Raj Narain stalked out of the room, saying, "This Jat will never understand anything!" (Thakur, 1979: 150-151)

SANJAY EMERGES AS HEIR-APPARENT

There can be two views on whether Nehru wanted Indira Gandhi to succeed him but there was no doubt whatsoever that Indira Gandhi wanted Sanjay to be her successor. And he was acknowledged as such. For example, Tavleen Singh has written in her book, *Kashmir – A Tragedy of Errors*, "Five years earlier, when Mrs Gandhi was temporarily out of power, the *durbar*, with Sanjay Gandhi as heir-apparent, was already in existence." (Singh, 1996: 44)

I had written in my memoirs, *Unfinished Inning: Recollections and Reflections of a Civil Servant:*

> The Emergency saw the rise of Sanjay Gandhi as a force to reckon with. He was certainly the most important extra-constitutional centre of power. Soon after the Emergency was declared, it became incumbent on Chief Ministers visiting Delhi to call on Sanjay before meeting the Prime Minister. In fact, an appointment with the Prime Minister would not come through unless the Chief Minister had met Sanjay. I used to organise Chief Minister's programme [as Secretary to Chief Minister] for visits to Delhi and invariably accompanied him on these visits. When I was told by the PMO that the Chief Minister should first meet Sanjay, I spoke to Shankarrao [Chavan]. He did not seem to like the idea and in fact resisted it. Twice the Chief Minister had to return to Bombay without getting an appointment with the Prime Minister, ostensibly on the ground that she was very busy. By then S.B. Chavan had got the message. Thereafter, even before leaving for Delhi, he would ask me to fix an appointment with Sanjay Gandhi. Yet another Chief Minister had been disciplined by the Emergency! (Godbole, 1996: 105-106)

After Indira Gandhi's return to power in 1980, Sanjay was unofficially anointed as Indira Gandhi's successor. The Chief Ministers were advised to meet Sanjay and brief him about their problems and seek his advice before calling on Indira Gandhi. This led to even senior leaders of the Congress party vying with each other to praise Sanjay. As M.O. Mathai has written, "UP Chief Minister Tiwari committed blasphemy by hailing Sanjay as Lord Krishna!" (Mathai, 1978: 252) When

Sanjay was launched as the youth leader at the Guwahati session of the Congress party, D.K. Barooah wanted youth to take over the party and compared Sanjay to Shankaracharya, Vivekananda and Akbar…. During Sanjay's visits to States, the entire Cabinet used to receive him at the airport and the Chief Ministers awaited his commands. Huge public meetings were arranged for him and glowing reports of his mass appeal sent to his mother. (Gill, 1996: 286-287) S.B. Chavan, the then Chief Minister of Maharashtra, was so profuse in his praise of Sanjay that he said. "He is not only the youth leader. He is the leader of the nation". (Yunus, 1980: 267) Chief Minister Joshi of Rajasthan had offered his shoulders to Sanjay to place his feet on while dismounting an elephant. Another Chief Minister had picked up Sanjay's *chappals* and jokes like 'who said Japan was the only land of the rising son' circulated wildly. (Thapar, 1991: 420)

Khushwant Singh was an enthusiastic supporter of Emergency. Sanjay appeared on the cover of the independence day issue of *Illustrated Weekly*, of which Khushwant Singh was the editor. Frank has written:

> Despite its banality, Khushwant Singh's interview with Sanjay reflected the growing media cult that had grown up round him. Soon other large-circulation English-language weeklies such as *Blitz* and *Current* also ran Sanjay cover stories. Of the five national English language newspapers, only *The Indian Express* criticized Sanjay, the government and the Emergency. *The Times of India*, in contrast, was soon referred to as 'The Times of Indira' … [V.C.] Shukla's Ministry [of Information and Broadcasting] was responsible, for example, for the fact that in the first two weeks of January 1976 no less than 192 news items were broadcast about Sanjay as main news bulletins on the State-owned all India Radio. (Frank, 2001: 408-409)

Sanjay was not taken in by the Leftist ideology. His views were often contrary to the ideology professed by Indira Gandhi during the first phase of her tenure prior to 1977. His interview to Uma Vasudev, which was published in *Surge* created a great deal of uproar, particularly in the left lobby, as Sanjay was critical of the working of the CPI and the undue promotion of the public sector. Personally, I did not find anything objectionable in it. But, it was finally withdrawn and the Press was advised not to give publicity to it. To counter the influence of the Congress Forum for Socialist Action, Sanjay associated himself with the Nehru Study Forum. After some time Indira Gandhi found it inconvenient to have these two forums exerting pressures and counter-pressures and asked them to be abolished.

B.K. Nehru has stated:

> I told Baboo Haksar, who by then had been shunted off as deputy Chairman of the Planning Commission, that I was going to talk to Indira about what Sanjay was doing. He said to me that it would be the greatest mistake for me to say anything critical in the slightest degree about Sanjay. *She was absolutely blind as far as that boy was concerned; she regarded him as perfect, he could do no wrong. The slightest expression of doubt about Sanjay was resented.* (Baboobhai could speak with experience because the only reason for his dismissal from the seat of power was that he had pointed out from time to time that some of the things Sanjay was doing would harm his mother....) If I ever said anything which implied any criticism of Sanjay, the immediate effect would be that access would be denied. I would never be able to meet her again. (Nehru, 1997: 560)

However, in her letter to her friend Dorothy Norman on 3 August 1980, Indira Gandhi wrote:

> Seldom has any person had to brave such hardship and such a sustained campaign of calumny. It is to Sanjay's credit that he retained his dignity and calmness of spirit and to the end was a help and a joy to be around the house. (Norman, 1985: 152)

Sanjay's accidental death affected Indira Gandhi deeply though she hardly ever gave a public demonstration of it. But in her letter to her friend Norman on 21 February 1981 she had written:

> Sanjay's going has affected me profoundly. As a Bulgarian girl said this morning, "You do not weep outside but deep within." Yet isn't this very selfish? Basically we do not weep for those who have gone but for ourselves. (Norman, 1985: 155)

The letter which Indira Gandhi wrote to Nambiar on 7 July 1980, after Sanjay's death, shows what a special place Sanjay had in his mother's heart and how much she valued his work and support. (Annexure 1)

The situation after Sanjay's tragic death has been brought out by B.K. Nehru. It shows the special place he enjoyed in Indira Gandhi household. Nehru has written:

> *It was decided that the cremation would take place in Shantivan near the spot where his grandfather was cremated.* Rajiv voiced the objection felt by many others to this course on the ground that, Sanjay, having no official position, should not be given the honour of cremation on this hallowed ground. Shantivan was not the private family cremation vault. However, the end result was that except for lying in state at Teen Murti House and the use of a gun-carriage, the ritual of the funeral was almost identical to that followed in the case of Jawaharlal, Indira and Rajiv. (Nehru, 1997: 582)

WHY EMERGENCY WAS LIFTED?

There are various conjectures as to why Indira Gandhi decided to lift the Emergency suddenly, without any formal consultations even within her own party. This will remain a mystery for ever because Indira Gandhi never divulged her mind on the subject. One of the factors which may have influenced the decision is the sharp reactions abroad. She, like Jawaharlal Nehru, was very sensitive to her image in the western world.

T.N. Kaul has stated:

> Some of us who were well-wishers of Indira Gandhi but did not agree with Sanjay's dictatorial methods – B.K. Nehru, Pupul Jayakar, G. Parthasarathy and I agreed to advise Mrs Gandhi individually to scrap the Emergency after it had already been in existence for six months, assuming dictatorial proportions. She seemed to agree and promised she would consider holding the general elections in early 1976; but Sanjay and some of her Cabinet colleagues advised her to continue the Emergency and even increase the tenure as MPs by one year. Unfortunately, she agreed with them. (Kaul, 2000: 113)

Pupul Jayakar has written that she expected Emergency to be lifted on 15 August [1975] and went to the Red Fort to hear her speak. But just before she appeared on the ramparts she received news of the assassination of [Mujibur] Rehman and his family, including his very young son. All her dormant fears and anxieties were awakened. She was certain that the murders were part of a major plot to destabilise the subcontinent and that she, her sons and her grandchildren were the next target. The Emergency continued with traumatic results for both ruler and ruled. (Jayakar, 1986: 341)

Jayakar has written extensively about Indira Gandhi's interactions with J. Krishnamurti,[11] a revered philosopher, and how she was provided solace and inner peace by him. Krishnamurti was abroad when Emergency was declared and was greatly perturbed when he heard in America that "India had become a totalitarian State", where thousands were being put in prison, and freedom of speech and freedom of Press was almost gagged. *In fact, Krishnamurti was worried whether he too will be arrested if he retuned to India. Jayakar had to assure him that he could never be jailed in India.* "By August 20, I received a second letter. His extreme concern was evident, and introduced a new question: "What is the purpose, the value, and the benefit of my coming to India?..." I was overwhelmed by the letter. To me, at that time, it seemed evident that Krishnaji [Krishnamurti] had rejected India and the people who had been his companions for many years. (Jayakar, 1986: 341-342)

Jayakar's following account is particularly significant:

> Years later, after her son Sanjay's death, I asked Indira whether she cried easily. She thought for a while then said, "No, sorrow does not bring tears." She said she had cried when she met Kamakoti Sankaracharya of Kancheepuram[12] and

---

11 Acclaimed as one of the greatest spiritual teachers of our times, in 1909, when he was just fourteen, Krishnamurti was proclaimed the world teacher-to-be in whom Maitreya, the Bodhisattva of compassion, would manifest. The proclamation was made by Annie Besant, then President of the Theosophical Society, a movement that combined western occult philosophy with Buddhist and Hindu teachings. Besant trained Krishnamurti in his role as the chosen one but twenty years later he chose to disband the order he was head of and set out alone on his endless journey. (Jacket of Jayakar's book, 1986)

12 The Kamakoti Sankaracharya of Kancheepuram is in the direct line of successive teachers or preceptors going back to Adi Sankara, the first Sankaracharya, who taught in about the eighth century AD.

> that she had wept copiously when she came to see Krishnaji [Krishnamurti] at 1 King George's Avenue in November 1976. "I sobbed and could not stop my tears. I have not cried like that for years." She also told me something of what happened during the conversation. Krishnaji and she had spoken of the events in India over the last few months, and *Indira had said, "I am riding the back of a tiger, but I do not know how to get off its back."* Krishnaji replied, "If you are more intelligent than the tiger, you will know how to deal with the tiger." She had asked him what she should do. He refused to tell her, but said she should look at the conflicts, the actions, the wrongs as one problem, and act without motive. He said he did not know the facts, but that *she should act rightly, without fear of consequences.* In later years *she told me that it was on October 28, 1976, the day she met Krishnaji for the second time, a frail movement had awakened in her, suggesting an end to Emergency, whatever the consequences.* She had mulled over this feeling, talked to a few people close to her, and finally took the decision to call for elections.... The day before he [Krishnamurti] was to leave [for Europe], he asked me to keep him informed about Indira. Then suddenly he asked, "What happens if she loses?" (Jayakar, 1986: 345-346)

This interaction with Krishnamurti may have been one of the triggers which led to the lifting of the Emergency but her letter quoted hereafter raises some doubts.

It may be appropriate in this context to refer to what Indira Gandhi thought of Krishnamurti. In her letter dated 23 March 1984 to Nambiar, Indira Gandhi had, inter alia, written:

> My friend Pupul Jayakar is a great admirer of J. Krishnamurthi (sic). He usually stays with her in Delhi and Bombay and she invites me over for a talk and a meal with him. There is something about him which is attractive. He is serious and has deep insight. But he lives in a world of his own – financially

> secure, well looked after and with a well ordered life in his various centres. The summer is divided between England and the USA in beautiful peaceful sylvan surroundings. Our short winter he spends in India – Delhi, Madras, Bombay – and visiting his schools. There is one in Benaras and one in Andhra. It is indeed difficult to understand him. I have been listening to one of the tapes of his conversation with Pupul and *must confess that some concepts are difficult to comprehend or attempt to live up to*. He seems to be very fit, goes for a daily fast walk, lectures in various places and meets people. (Balachandran, 2016: 323)

To me, these impressions of Indira Gandhi come as a surprise and do not show that Krishnamurti had any special influence on her and she considered him to be her preceptor. It is unlikely that he would have been instrumental in her decision to withdraw the Emergency.

Dorothy Norman, Indira Gandhi's friend since 1950, had stopped corresponding with her after the declaration of Emergency. Norman has written:

> Those of us in New York who had been staunch advocates of a free India asked ourselves whether conditions there were, in fact, so distressing that abrogation of civil rights had to be as extreme as the Press reported. Was it necessary to postpone, then cancel, general elections? Why were leading critics of the government arrested and imprisoned without specific charges being made against them and without their having the right of habeas corpus? Why was the Press under strict government control?.... We issued a statement that expressed our concern.... It read, in part: 'We are Americans concerned with maintaining and furthering human rights, and our concern extends to all people throughout the world. Consequently, we are distressed by the loss of fundamental human rights in India following the proclamation of a

> national Emergency there on June 25, 1975. We deplore the events.... We call for the restoration of these rights in India.' It was signed by eighty widely known and respected persons and was given wide publicity.[13] (Norman, 1985: 148-149)

When Dorothy Norman directly sent a copy of the petition to Indira Gandhi, in reply she merely received a gift accompanied by a short note saying, "If you can bear to accept a gift from 'Great Dictator', here is something ... for you ... from Bhutan." (Frank, 2001: 385)

The Secretary of the Lok Sangharsha Samiti (People's Struggle Committee), of which Morarji Desai was the Chairman and Asoka Mehta the treasurer, had written a letter to Indira Gandhi on 9 January 1976. It stated: The *satyagraha* undertaken in various States had been going on since 14 November and nearly 90,000 *satyagrahis* had been arrested during the previous seven weeks. *Satyagrahas* had been offered in nearly 3,000 places. All these had been totally peaceful. In spite of this action had been taken against the *satyagrahis*. The letter requested that atrocities against the prisoners should be stopped forthwith. (Selbourne, 1997: 400)

She must have seen similar highly critical reactions from a number of countries, including intellectuals in India, and these may have influenced her decision to lift the Emergency. But the reasons which led her to take the decision and the timing of it continue to be a mystery.

TO SUM UP

Indira Gandhi had expressed shock and surprise at the total lack of resistance among the people to the Emergency. She

13 They included Ved Mehta, Noam Chomsky, Arthur Ashe, Allen Ginsberg, Lewis Mumford, Linus Pauling, Benjamin Spock and John Updike. (Frank, 2001: 385)

particularly mentioned ... that she was more amazed at the lack of reaction among the intelligentsia. When times are bad, this category – the intelligentsia – is the most despicable in all countries. It is the intelligentsia that has both the capacity and the inclination to rationalize tyranny. And so it was in India. Fali Nariman has rightly stated: One of the lessons of Emergency was not to rely on constitutional functionaries. These functionaries failed us – ministers, MPs, judges of the Supreme Court, even President of India. (Nariman, 2010: 163, 176) If democracy is to be safeguarded in this country, lessons of Emergency should never be forgotten. The memory of Emergency must be kept alive by including, among other steps, essays thereon in the curricula of schools and colleges. Strengthening institutions of democracy must receive our closest attention.

5

Ugly Face of Majoritarianism

INTRODUCTION

India's experience of majoritarianism is most disconcerting, to put it mildly. As I had discussed in my book, *The Judiciary and Governance in India* (2008), it all began, in the very first year after the adoption of the Constitution, by introducing therein the ninth schedule. More surprising was that it was during the enlightened leadership of Jawaharlal Nehru. I would like to give Nehru and Law Minister B.R. Ambedkar the benefit of doubt. I am sure they did not foresee the extent to which the succeeding governments would misuse it. But, majoritarianism was also evident in the passage of the Fourth Amendment of the Constitution during the tenure of Jawaharlal Nehru which violated the conscious provision for judicial review, once again. A series of Constitutional Amendments made by Indira Gandhi made a mockery of the basic precepts embodied in the Constitution, with the brute majority she enjoyed.

FIRST AMENDMENT OF THE CONSTITUTION

Ninth Schedule: Article 31B, which is the gross abuse of the power of amendment of the Constitution by Parliament and makes a mockery of the protection of fundamental rights guaranteed by the Constitution, reads as follows:

> Without prejudice to the generality of the provisions contained in Article 31A, none of the Acts and Regulations specified in the Ninth Schedule nor any of the provisions thereof shall be deemed to be void, or ever to have become void, on the ground that such Act, Regulation or provision is inconsistent with, or takes away or abridges any of the rights conferred by, any provisions of this Part, and notwithstanding any judgment, decree or order of any court or tribunal to the contrary, each of the said Acts and Regulations shall, subject to the power of any competent Legislature to repeal or amend it, continue in force.

The acquiescence in this grossly arbitrary provision, which was destructive of the rule of law, for years together by the Supreme Court is difficult to fathom. It is shocking to see that the inclusion of nearly 300 Acts in the Ninth Schedule did not surprise anyone! Justice Hidayatullah, former Chief Justice of India, has commented that "then this process stopped because the Ninth Schedule threatened to become longer than the Constitution." (Hidayatullah, 1983: 158).

It is difficult to believe that this monstrosity commenced from 1951, the very first year following the adoption of the Constitution. (Provisional Parliament Debates, 16-18 May 1951, cols. 8814-9089).

Baldev Singh has rightly pointed out that Articles 13 and 31-B in Part III of the Constitution may appear to be paradoxical to any student of Indian Constitutional law. The former forbids the State to make any law which takes away the rights of the individuals and declares that any law in contravention of this clause shall, to the extent of contravention, be void. In contrast, Article 31-B says that none of the Acts and Regulations specified in the Ninth Schedule nor any of the provisions thereof shall be deemed to be void, or ever to have become void, on the ground that such Act,

Regulation or provision is inconsistent with, or takes away or abridges any of the rights conferred by any provisions of this Part. (Singh, 1995: 457-475)

Jawaharlal Nehru, while moving this unusual provision as a part of the very First Amendment of the Constitution, had stated in the Provisional Parliament, "This Bill is not a very complicated one; nor is it a big one. Nevertheless, I need hardly point out that it is of intrinsic and great importance." The Schedule, at the time of its incorporation in the Constitution, comprised only 13 Acts, mostly agrarian. Nehru had assured that "every single measure included in this schedule was carefully considered by our President and certified by him." Nehru had further stated, "Some Hon members have given notice of amendments to add other laws to the Ninth Schedule. I would beg of them not to press this matter. It is not with any great satisfaction or pleasure that we have produced this *long* schedule. We do not wish to add to it for two reasons. One is that the Schedule consists of a particular type of legislation generally speaking and another type should not come in. Secondly, every single measure was carefully considered...." The amendment was not passed in a hurry. It was deliberated in the Select Committee. The debate in the House had lasted for 6-7 days. The Bill met with stiff opposition from the very thin ranks of the Opposition parties in the House and was passed with 238 *ayes* and 7 *noes*. In retrospect, it is difficult to find any merit in the arguments put forth by Dr Ambedkar to support the amendment. He had said, "Sentimentally, there might be objection, but from the practical point of view there should not be any objection to declare such laws as valid [because the Acts included in the Schedule were not *ultra virus*]."

The 'devise' of Ninth Schedule, described as such in the Objects and Reasons to the 39th Amendment Act, was meant to meet the political urgency of abolition of *zamindari* but the medicine turned out to be worse than the disease. Initially, only tenancy laws and *zamindari* abolition laws were expected to be put in this Schedule but later, not only other laws but even Acts which had been struck down by the courts as invalid were included in the Schedule. Highly controversial and draconian laws such as the Maintenance of Internal Security Act, National Security Act, Prevention of Publication of Objectionable Matter Act, Urban Land (Ceiling and Regulation) Act, amendment of the Representation of People Act, Insurance Act, reservation laws of some States, and so on were given protection against legal challenge by including them in the Ninth Schedule. Over the years, as many as 284 Acts were included in the Ninth Schedule.

Justice Mehr Chand Mahajan has stated,

> What seemed to some of us a dangerous precedent lay rather in the fact that the First Amendment protected certain specified statutes passed by various State Legislatures against attack for unconstitutionality before the court. Of course Indian Parliament has not gone – thanks to the Constitution itself – to the lengths to which the US Congress had once proceeded when it had taken a case already before the court away from it! As the protected statutes mostly concerned existing rights in land which government was modifying and in some States even extinguishing, this provision seemed to some of us to be a sad failure on the part of the legislative draftsmen in clothing the intentions of the legislature in proper statutory form! (Mahajan, 1963: 200)

However, as the later experience showed, initial intentions were quickly thrown over-board and this constitutional monstrosity became uglier and uglier as the years passed. It was as far back as 1972 that Justice J.C. Shah had stated, "It is no secret that before the

> Constitution (Seventeenth Amendment) was moved in the Parliament, there was a clamour from the States to include in the Ninth Schedule a large number of Acts – literally hundreds of Acts ... Enactment of Article 31B and the Ninth Schedule constitutes a serious encroachment upon the Rule of Law. (Shah, 1972: 52-53)

Justice Hidayatullah has stated,

> Article 31(C) which schedules certain Acts of legislatures to protect them against the Constitution, is not a valid exercise of the power to amend the Constitution. *Such a power is not an amendment of the Constitution but a 'frustration' of the Constitution.* Next, that a Constitution cannot be amended retrospectively, except to correct a slip. Each Parliament speaks for itself, and while it is in office, the Constitution stands as made by it. A new Parliament can change the Constitution but cannot sit in the seat of the other Parliament and change the Constitution from a date when it was not in the saddle. We have attempted to change the Constitution from 26th January 1950, as if the Parliament making the change was sitting in the Constituent Assembly. In *Golaknath* case, I had summed this up by saying: *Constitution is not a sonnet written on water.* A Constitution continues unimpaired till it is changed, but it is changed only from the date when the change takes place and not earlier. In America, prohibition was once introduced and then later withdrawn; but both the Articles are found in the Constitution. Our Parliament would have erased the earlier Article as if it was never enacted.... *I had accepted the First Amendment because it was acquiesced in for a long time and had become a part of our Constitution.* (Hidayatullah, 1979: viii, 11)

It is surprising to see that, in spite of the overwhelming view as above of a number of legal luminaries, the amendment was held to be valid time and again by the Supreme Court. This was clearly the accommodation phase of the history of the Apex Court. In *Shankari Prasad* case (AIR 1951 SC 458), Justice Patanjali Sastri, speaking on behalf of the court, held that Article 31-B and the Ninth Schedule will not affect the powers of the courts to issue writs or entertain appeals. They will remain just the same and only a certain class of cases had been excluded from the purview of Part III and the courts. The court further said that the provisions were essentially amendments of the Constitution and Parliament alone had the power to do so. The constitutionality was again challenged in *Sajjan Singh* case (AIR 1965 SC 845). In the majority judgment delivered by Gajendragadkar, CJ, reliance was placed on pith and substance and it was stated that the amendment was meant to further agrarian reforms and not meant to affect the powers of the court. However, Mudholkar, J, in his minority judgment had raised a question mark on the amendment. In the *Golaknath* case (AIR 1967 SC 1643), Subba Rao, CJ, held that Parliament was incompetent to take away or abridge any of the fundamental rights and the previous amendments, namely, *First, Fourth and Seventeenth Amendments relating to the Ninth Schedule would have been unconstitutional and void but for the doctrine of prospective overruling.* In the *Kesavananda Bharati* case (AIR 1973, SC 1461), again, the court was unanimous that the Ninth Schedule device was valid. The court felt it too late to question the validity of the Schedule. It further held that in view of the doctrine of basic structure propounded by it, laws added to the Ninth Schedule after this decision will be subject to the basic structure of the Constitution. In other words, the courts were granted power to test the validity of future laws in the Schedule. For example, in *I.R. Coelho v. State of Tamil Nadu and Others*, Civil Appeal Nos 1344-45 of 1976, decided on 11 January 2007, the court held,

> A law that abrogates rights guaranteed by Part III of the Constitution, whether by amendment of any Article of Part

> III or by insertion in the Ninth Schedule, if it violates the basic structure, such law will have to be invalidated in exercise of judicial review by the court. All amendments to the Constitution made on or after 1973 by which the Ninth Schedule is amended by inclusion of various laws therein shall have to be tested on the touchstone of the basic features of the Constitution.

The entire issue came up before a nine-judge Constitution Bench of the Supreme Court in October-November 2006. It was interesting to see that apart from the Attorney General who appeared for the Central Government, senior advocates Soli Sorabjee, T.R. Andhyarujina and Ram Jethmalani (all for Tamil Nadu) defended the laws in the Schedule for protecting them from judicial scrutiny! (*IE*, 4.11.2006) It is important to note that this review arose out of a reference made by a five-judge Bench in 1999. Even on such an important matter, it took seven years for the reference to be listed before a nine-judge Bench. It is shocking to see that even after lapse of decades and so much past experience of how the Schedule was thoroughly misused by the government, making a mockery of the tenet of judicial review which is a part of the basic structure of the Constitution, the stand of the Central Government had not changed one bit. The affidavit filed by the Central Government argued that Article 31-B was a protective umbrella which cured the vice or defect of unconstitutionality of the legislation on the ground of infringement of fundamental rights. The Centre also asserted that the Parliament had the power to include in the Ninth Schedule a law which was struck down on the ground of violation of fundamental rights!

By its decision dated 11 January 2007, the court has laid down a dual test to examine the validity of a Ninth Schedule law: whether it violates any fundamental right and if so, whether it also violated the basic structure of the Constitution. If answer to both the tests was affirmative, then only a law placed in the Ninth Schedule could be declared unconstitutional. This declaration would lead to a legal challenge to a number of enactments. In the future, greater care will have to be taken by the government in sponsoring new legislation and proposing its inclusion in the Ninth Schedule since this process will not be automatic any longer. (Godbole, 2008: 64-69)

THE CONSTITUTION (FOURTH) AMENDMENT

Reference must also be made to the Constitution (Fourth Amendment) Act 1955 by which the State's power to compulsorily acquire private property and of providing State monopoly in certain trades etc, was reasserted. *It was laid down that adequacy of compensation could also not to be questioned in the courts.* This was also an unjustified curtailment of the powers of the courts and was not in keeping with the letter and spirit of the Constitution. This was just to get over the difficulty of the government in paying true or adequate compensation. In a way this was dilution of the right to property which was then a fundamental right. This was carried forward later to its logical conclusion by the Constitution (Twenty-fifth Amendment) Act, 1971 by which Articles 31 and 31C were amended by substituting the word 'amount' in place of 'compensation' in the light of judicial interpretation of the word 'compensation' meaning 'adequate compensation'. The next step, on which practically all political parties, except the then Jan Sangh and the Swatantra parties, agreed was to abolish right to property as a fundamental right.

It was disappointing that both these amendments were made when Nehru was the Prime Minister. In the real sense, this was India's first tryst with majoritarianism. It was only due to Nehru's stature and innate confidence in his respect for the dignity, respect and independence of the judiciary that these amendments were not resisted by the judiciary. Looking back on them now, I feel that they ought to have been questioned at that time itself to nip the tendency in the bud.

ORIGIN OF CONFRONTATION WITH JUDICIARY

The decisions of the Supreme Court in three major cases were responsible for leading to the confrontation of the Indira Gandhi government with the judiciary. As can be seen from the discussion below, in all these cases, the position taken by the Supreme Court was strictly according to the tenets of the Constitution. Judicial review of legislation is an important duty cast on the judiciary by the Constitution. It was an institutional issue but was given the colour as if judiciary was opposed to the programmes and policies of Indira Gandhi.

Golaknath and Kesavananda Bharati Cases

A bench of 11 judges, constituted for the first time, heard the *Golaknath* case. By a narrow majority judgment (6 : 5) delivered in February 1967, the court held that Parliament could not take away or abridge any of the fundamental rights in exercise of its power to amend the Constitution under Article 368. Indira Gandhi had made this a major issue in the elections in 1970 and after her massive victory brought in the 24th Amendment of the Constitution to reassert the right of Parliament to amend any part of the Constitution. By 25th Amendment, it had curtailed the Supreme Court's jurisdiction.

Six years later, in 1973, a larger bench of 13 judges constituted to decide the validity of 24th, 25th and 29th Amendments of the Constitution (Kesavananda Bharati case), held by a narrow majority (7 : 6) that although no part of the Constitution, including fundamental rights, was beyond the amending power of the Constitution, the basic structure of the

Constitution could not be abrogated. This case is also known as the fundamental rights case. This case, which severely curtailed the amending powers of Parliament, became the main bone of contention and Indira Gandhi attacked the judiciary for putting hurdles in her socio-economic programme.[1]

Abolition of Privy Purses and Privileges

This was one of the least justified decisions of Indira Gandhi's regime disregarding the constitutional guarantees given to the rulers of the Princely States when they voluntarily agreed to merge their States in the Indian Union. Out of the 554 States that surrendered to the Indian Union, over 450 had annual revenues of less than ₹5 lakh. The privy purse of Nizam of Hyderabad, amounting to ₹50 lakh annually, was no more than 2 per cent of the State's revenue. It must be noted that the Nizam was made to surrender his personal estate yielding an annual revenue of ₹1.24 crore in return for a compensation of ₹25 lakh per annum. The original agreement had laid down that the privy purses should be reduced with each new succession to the title. As a result, by 1967, the list of beneficiaries had been reduced from the original 600 to 200. Similarly, the amount given to them had come down from Pounds 2.3 million a year in 1948 to a third of that figure. (Kamath, 2007: 143)

Speaking in the Rajya Sabha on 31 July 1967, M.C. Setalvad, a leading constitutional expert, had emphasised that the privy purse settlements were in the nature of consideration for the surrender by the Rulers of their ruling power and also for the dissolution of their States as separate units. It was

1 Granville Austin has observed that Golaknath decision was delivered just before the Congress lost its 'brute majority' in the 1967 general elections. Some have speculated that, had Congress losses been known, the court might have ruled differently. (Austin, 1999: 200, footnote 8)

historically untrue that these were ex-gratia payments. Concluding his speech, Setalvad had said, "We are spending hundreds and thousands of crores for various purposes. Is five crores an amount which will bring us to ruin?" (Godbole, 2008: 222)

Originally, it was contemplated that only privileges like duty-free imports, immunity from civil proceedings and special number plates for cars would be abolished. But at the last minute, Mohan Dharia, one of the prominent Young Turks forced a resolution in the AICC asking for abolition of both the privy purses and privileges. Jawaharlal Nehru had, from the beginning opposed giving privy purses and privileges and called them 'anachronisms'. While moving the Constitution (Twenty-fourth Amendment) Bill in the Lok Sabha on 1 September 1970, Indira Gandhi had said: "The continuance of hereditary titles, customary rights, special privileges and privy purses without any relatable functions and responsibilities is incompatible with our democratic Constitution, the spirit of the times and the demand of changed circumstances." She made no reference to the constitutional guarantees given to the princes when they offered to merge their States in the Indian Union. Speaking in the Rajya Sabha on 5 September 1970 on Raj Narain's amendment that no compensation should be paid to the princes on abolition of the privy purses, Prime Minister said,

> It is our opinion and the legal opinion also that the privy purse is not a property and thus there was no question whatsoever of paying any compensation.[2] However, there is the human aspect. I do not think it would be fair to put an abrupt end to the payment of privy purses without providing some means for the families and dependents of these former rulers to adjust to this new situation. (GoI, 1975: 63, 74)

---

2 The Supreme Court, however, held that privy purse was property.

However, in her anxiety to hasten the abolition of privy purses, Indira Gandhi disregarded even the constitutional proprieties and when the Constitution Amendment Bill was rejected by Rajya Sabha by a fraction of a vote, instead of following the correct parliamentary procedure of bringing the matter once again before Parliament, insisted on issuing an ordinance. The President also did not consider it fit to question this move and literally signed on the dotted line, as he did later while approving the imposition of Emergency in June 1975. This is how crucial constitutional office-holders, President of India and the judges of the Supreme Court, let down the country again and again during Indira Gandhi regime.

The case was heard by an 11 member bench presided over by Chief Justice M. Hidayatullah. Legal luminaries such as Nani Palkhivala, M.C. Setalvad, and M.C. Chagla appeared for the rulers. The case was heard for 21 days. Finally, on 15 December 1970, the Supreme Court, by a majority decision, struck down the President's order derecognising the princes and restored their privy purses and privileges. Only Justice A.N. Ray upheld the action of the government. It was not surprising that later he was appointed as the Chief Justice of India by superseding Justice Shelat who was among the judges who had decided the matter against the government.

Just twelve days later, Indira Gandhi announced on 27 December 1971 the dissolution of Lok Sabha and sought fresh mandate to pursue 'her march towards Socialism'. Inder Malhotra, in his biography of Indira Gandhi has written: "The judgment coming on top of the earlier ones throwing out succession of laws concerning bank nationalisation, became the proverbial last straw on the backs of a large number of Indira's radical supporters who had been clamouring that the higher judiciary, 'determined to protect private property and vested interests', had become an 'obstacle to social justice' and therefore something 'had to be done about it'. In the circumstances, the 1971 parliamentary poll turned into a referendum on Indira Gandhi's leadership. When *Newsweek* asked her what the main issues in the elections were, her reply was short and to the point. She said: "I am the issue." (Kamath, 2007: 229)

After she came back with a massive mandate, the government brought in the Constitution (Twenty-sixth Amendment) Bill, 1971, to over-rule the Supreme Court decision and to finally abolish the privy purses and privileges.

The extent to which Indira Gandhi government went to influence the Supreme Court in its decision on *Kesavananda Bharati* case has been brought out by Justice P. Jaganmohan Reddy in his book *The Judiciary I Served*. Reddy has written:

> There was one occasion [during the hearing of the case] when J. Dwivedi made a startling proposal to Palkhivala. He said that if Palkhivala agreed to property rights being taken away, he (Dwivedi) would get Parliament to declare that other fundamental rights would not be taken away. Palkhivala replied: "Have I referred so far at any time to property rights? I was dealing with the implied limitations and natural rights, etc." How a judge could give such an assurance as Dwivedi offered and what authority he had to do so passed everyone's comprehension. Dwivedi rang me up at about 9.30 PM and said he had been indiscreet and ought not to have made that remark. (Kamath, 2007: 184)

Indira Gandhi government made a futile effort to have the decision in *Kesavananda* case reversed but this move failed miserably when opposed vehemently not only by Palkhivala but also some State Governments. The Chief Justice had no option but to order on 12 November 1975 the dissolution of the bench constituted for the purpose.

Bank Nationalisation Case

A bench presided over by Justice J.C. Shah, who later headed the Commission of Inquiry on Emergency, heard the case. By its judgment delivered on 10 February 1970, the Supreme Court, by a majority of ten to one, struck down the Banking Companies (Acquisition and Transfer of Undertakings) Act, 1969. The court held that the Act was within the legislative competence of Parliament, but it held the Act unconstitutional as it violated Article 14 of the Constitution. It was also held to be in violation of Article 19(1)(f) and (g) of the Constitution. Most importantly, the court held that the Act contravened Article 31(2) of the Constitution, as it then stood. The principles on which the compensation was paid were not considered relevant and the amount arrived at, by the methods prescribed, could not be regarded as 'compensation'. (Kamath, 2007: 201-204) However, particularly the last point was highlighted by Indira Gandhi and her supporters saying that the Supreme Court was forcing the government to pay much higher compensation. Kumaramangalam has alleged, "So, we, again in a docile way, followed in the footsteps of the judges, reframed the Bank Nationalisation Act taking into account the new view, as it were, of the Supreme Court. *I think it cost the country quite a number of crores more.*" (Nayar, 1973: 80)

Justice P. Jaganmohan Reddy, who sat on the bench which decided this case, has in his book, *The Judiciary I Served*, contested this. He has written:

> There are ways in which the banks could have been acquired for much less. The act could have specified the amount of compensation in respect of each bank and if it did, that could not have been questioned [in the court]; or alternatively the shares of each bank could have been acquired and this could not have been challenged, as earlier the Life Insurance Corporation, the Imperial Bank

of India, State Bank of Hyderabad, etc, were acquired by this method, or it could have set out principles computing the amount of compensation which were relevant (as stated in the majority [judgment]). The Act did none of these.

When the Attorney General submitted that the compensation calculated according to the method provided in Schedule II exceeded the total market value of the shares, I asked him why the government had not acquired the shares. His answer was: 'Then people would have blamed the government for taking them for a song.' I responded that if these banks could be taken over virtually validly under the law for a song, would not paying a higher price by another method, be contrary to social justice according to which the property which is to be expropriated should be bought for as little as possible, to serve the poor? In any case, the taxpayer's money was involved and consequently, we, as tax payers, would be less affected if smaller amount was paid as compensation. *What I asked the Attorney General, his reply, and mine to him, were not recorded. Therefore, people do not know even today that this could have been done but was not done, because the media did not report it;* nor was there any inclination at that time to show that the government could have done better than what it did to save the taxpayer a lot of money.... *The criticism against the court that because of its judgment the taxpayer had to pay a fabulous sum to the nationalised banks has no justification whatever.* (Reddy, 1991: 178-179, 181)

SWARAN SINGH COMMITTEE REPORT

Following the uproar on *Kesavananda* case, the Congress President D.K. Barooah appointed a Committee to "study the questions of amendment of the Constitution ... in the light of experience." On 26 February 1976, a 12-member Committee under the Chairmanship of Sardar Swaran Singh was formed, which submitted its 'tentative proposals' to the Congress President in April 1976. There was a chorus of Indira Gandhi's coterie comprising Vasant Sathe, Minister for I&B, A.R. Antulay, a prominent Muslim leader from Maharashtra and others arguing for major constitutional changes. Swaran Singh himself is supposed to have said: "We cannot shirk that responsibility. We should not at all be apologetic about changing the Constitution." The Committee worked at great speed and, according to *The Pioneer*, "consulted party MPs, party Chief Ministers, and Pradesh Congress chiefs and came up with a horrendous list of amendments to cripple the judiciary, destroy the federal character of the Constitution and to give Parliament untrammelled power to alter the document." Not everyone was happy with the Committee's recommendations. In a letter to Indira Gandhi, Justice P.B. Gajendragadkar, who was still the Chairman of the Law Commission, reiterated his views that the amendments to the fundamental law of the land should not have been left to a party committee and the modality could, advisedly, have been a committee of experts to hear all parties and persons. He further said that the Committee appointed by Congress President Barooah had "worked in a hurry, discussed issues in a casual manner and based its recommendations mainly on political considerations." The Committee, after laying down its proposals, held discussions with members of the Congress party in Parliament from 10 to 14 May 1976. It also met representatives of the Supreme Court Bar, All-India Bar and the Bar Council of India. But, it stuck to its views.

Palkhivala said that, at least in three respects, the Swaran Singh Committee's conclusions aimed at altering or destroying the basic structure of the Constitution:

- First, they proposed to overthrow the supremacy of the Constitution and install Parliament as the supreme authority to which the Constitution would be subservient. The instrument would become the master, and the master the instrument.
- Secondly, the proposals sought to enact that the eternal values enshrined as fundamental rights in the Constitution would no longer be justiciable or operate as brakes on legislative and executive action, in most fields.
- Thirdly, they would result in the enforcement of laws which are held unconstitutional by the Supreme Court or the High Court. (Kamath, 2007: 302, 306)

TAILOR-MADE LAWS AND CONSTITUTION AMENDMENTS

The Election Laws (Amendment) Bill, 1975

This Bill was introduced in the Lok Sabha on 4 August 1975. *It was unbelievably tailor-made to validate Indira Gandhi's election.* The Bill provided, *with retrospective effect*: (i) the date of commencement of a person's candidature for purposes of election expenses and other purposes should not, as laid down in the Representation of People Act (RPA) 1951, be that when, 'with the election in prospect, he began to hold himself out as a prospective candidate', but that of his nomination; (ii) *that no election symbol allotted by the Election Commission should be considered a religious or national symbol;* (iii) that the section of the RPA forbidding candidates to obtain assistance from government officers for the furtherance of their election prospects should not apply to any act done by a government officer in the discharge or purported discharge of his official duty; and (iv) that publication in the official gazette was conclusive proof of the appointment, resignation, termination of service or removal of any servant of the Union or a State Government and of the date of taking effect thereof.

The Bill was passed by the Lok Sabha very next day on 5 August with the amendment providing that the case of every person found guilty of corrupt election practices by the courts should be submitted to the President, who, after obtaining the opinion of the Election Commission, would decide whether he should be disqualified and if so for what period (up to six years) and that any person already disqualified might petition the President for the removal of his disqualification. *The only opposition to the Bill came from Mohan Dharia, who commented that the government was obviously 'steamrolling' the amendments through to solve Indira Gandhi's legal problems. The Bill was passed by the Rajya Sabha the very next day, i e 6 August in an hour without anyone speaking against it, and received the President's assent on the same day.* (Kashyap, 1997: 61-62) Who can complain of the inordinate delays in passing of laws by Parliament? To propose such amendments to serve the Prime Minister's own interests was simply shameless, to put it mildly. And the expedition with which the Bill was passed by both Houses of Parliament and assented to by the President *showed the extent to which the entire system had become sub-servient to the dictates of Indira Gandhi.*

Leaders of non-CPI opposition parties wrote a letter to the President of India on 4 August 1975 with a request not to give assent to the Bill for the following reasons: *The whole purpose of the Bill is to prevent the Supreme Court from deciding the Prime Minister's appeal in the pending election appeal according to the prevailing law.* The change of law during the pendency of the appeal is obviously for the purpose of helping the Prime Minister to succeed in the appeal. Such a Bill, if passed, is bound to destroy whatever faith the people have in the rule of law. Moreover, clause 2 and 4B of the Bill, if passed, are bound to make fair elections virtually impossible ... because *the party in power will be able to secure both official assistance as well as government machinery for its electoral success.* (Selbourne, 1997: 396) Of course, it did not serve any purpose and the President assented to the Bill as soon as it was passed.

The Constitution (Thirty-ninth Amendment) Act 1975

The Bill provided that all matters pertaining to the election of the President, Vice-President, Prime Minister and Speaker of the Lok Sabha should be referred to new authority to be set up by Parliament; that the law setting up this authority might not be called into question in any court; and that all pending proceedings in any court under the existing laws were null and void.

Article 71 of the Constitution, as it stood originally, provided that disputes arising out of the election of the President or the Vice-President would be decided by the Supreme Court and their election would be regulated by a parliamentary law. So far as the Prime Minister and the Speaker were concerned, matters pertaining to their election were regulated by the provisions of the Representation of People Act (RPA), 1951. Under the Act, the High Court had jurisdiction to try an election petition presented against either of them. It was felt by the government that the President, the Vice-President, the Prime Minister and the Speaker were holders of high offices, so matters relating to their election should not be brought before a court of law but should be entrusted to a forum other than a court.

It is interesting to note that the real objective of this Bill was to take Indira Gandhi's election cases out of the courts and to entrust them to a special forum. The President, the Vice-President and the Speaker were tagged on to hide the real purpose. Further, to divert the attention of the people from this main part of the Bill, a number of laws, including MISA, were proposed for inclusion in the ninth schedule of the Constitution to give them protection from scrutiny by the courts. The amended RPA, referred to earlier, meant for safeguarding Indira Gandhi's election, was also one of them!

As was to be expected, *the Bill was passed by Lok Sabha unopposed on 7 August 1975. It was considered and passed by the Rajya Sabha the very next day on 8 August, and after being ratified by a sufficient number of State Assemblies, received President's assent on 10 August 1975, the day before the Supreme Court was due to hear the Prime Minister's appeal* against the High Court judgment declaring her election null and void. This once again showed how powerful was Indira Gandhi. Nothing, and no one, could stop her, once she had made up her mind about anything! What else was it than a constitutional dictatorship?

At the Supreme Court hearing on Indira Gandhi's election appeal, Raj Narain's attorney, Shanti Bhushan, attacked the retrospective character of the Constitution Amendment Act and the Election Laws Amendment Act as violating the basic structure doctrine. Asoke Sen, who was the Law Minister in Nehru's Cabinet and who appeared for Indira Gandhi, argued that there was no case to try, given the revised election laws. The 5:4 majority decision validated Mrs Gandhi's election but it struck down part of the Thirty-ninth Amendment. The court accepted that the laws could be changed with retrospective effect and therefore she had not violated any law. Austin has written:

> At least three of the judges must have swallowed hard to do this. Justice Mathew said to Shanti Bhushan during the hearing, 'There is no doubt of the unfairness of retrospective laws about corrupt practices, but can you cite some legal authorities to impugn their validity?' Justice Khanna also said during the hearing that 'all retrospective legislation is repressive.' 'We disliked retrospective effect',

> recalled Justice Chandrachud. 'It is an absurd, loathsome, and dangerous precedent in Constitutional law'. (Austin, 1999: 323-324)

But all this did not make any difference to the outcome of Indira Gandhi's appeal. She got what she wanted.

The Janata government took action to restore to the Supreme Court the power to decide disputes about validity of Presidential and Vice-Presidential elections by bringing forward a Bill for the purpose, which was readily passed.

The Constitution (Forty-first Amendment) Bill 1975

It was introduced in the Rajya Sabha on 9 August 1975. It sought to amend Article 361 of the Constitution. According to the objects of the Bill, the Prime Minister, like the President of India and Governors of States would have enjoyed legal immunity for the exercise and performance of powers and duties of his/her office and for acts done or purported to be done thereby. Also it would have extended the duration or protection to all of them even after they demit office, with retrospective effect.

The Bill was passed by the Rajya Sabha on the same day with a formal amendment changing its short title to "The Constitution (Fortieth Amendment) Bill 1975". The Bill as passed by the Rajya Sabha was laid on the table of the Lok Sabha on 5 January 1976 but it could not be taken up for consideration by the Lok Sabha and lapsed on the dissolution of the fifth Lok Sabha. (Kashyap, 1997: 104-105) It was on 18 January 1977 that Indira Gandhi made an unscheduled broadcast over the All India Radio to announce the government's decision to go to polls. The fifth Lok Sabha was dissolved on that day.

This was yet another scandalous effort on the part of Indira Gandhi to save herself from any legal action. But, if she wanted, she could have easily got the Bill passed by the Lok Sabha the same day on which it was sent to it by the Rajya Sabha. The President's assent could also have been obtained the same day. This was already done in a number of other cases discussed in this chapter.

The only explanation for this inexplicable (and inexcusable?) slip up by the highly motivated and committed managers of PMO may have been that they had not visualised the lifting of the Emergency so suddenly. As discussed in the previous chapter, what made Indira Gandhi lift the Emergency is still a mystery. But, whatever may have been the reasons, India should consider itself lucky that the Bill lapsed. If it had been passed as a Constitution Amendment, all discussion, after the Janata government came to power, about fixing responsibility on her for the Emergency excesses would have been redundant, as in any case it turned out to be, as shown in chapter 4.

CONSTITUTION AMENDMENTS GALORE

During the period of the fifth Lok Sabha (1971-1977), as many as nineteen Constitution Amendment Bills were passed. This was by far the largest number of such Bills passed by any Lok Sabha. Some of these amendments were most controversial and struck at the very basic features of the Constitution. But, with the huge majority of the Indira Congress, and the support of the so-called progressive, Leftist political parties, there was practically no opposition to these measures. Indira Gandhi's word was the last word! I have selected for discussion hereafter only those amendments which were highly controversial and were vigorously contested in the Supreme Court.

The Constitution (Twenty-fourth Amendment) Act 1971

The Bill was introduced in the Lok Sabha on 28 July 1971, was considered on 3 and 4 August and passed on 4 August. It was considered by Rajya Sabha on 10 and 11 August and passed on 11 August. It was assented to by the President on 5 November 1971.

The Bill sought to amend Articles 13 and 368 to reassert the powers of Parliament to amend any part of the Constitution, and thus to overrule the decision of the Supreme Court in *Golaknath case*. Referring to the fears expressed that interests of minorities may be adversely affected by Parliament taking to itself unbridled powers to amend the Constitution, Indira Gandhi had said while intervening in the debate that *protection to minorities can be guaranteed only by this Parliament. Mere constitutional devices cannot give this guarantee.* History is replete with examples of constitutions being overthrown or thwarted. Therefore, wider and deeper democracy, a wider and deeper commitment to secularism is a more durable guarantee of the rights of minorities. She assured that her commitment to upholding in every possible way the fundamental rights of our citizens remains absolute.

The Bill was passed with Ayes 384 and Noes 23. The amendment had thus large measure of support in Lok Sabha.

The Constitution (Twenty-fifth Amendment) Act 1971

The Bill was introduced in the Lok Sabha on 28 July 1971 and sought to amend Article 31 as well as insert a new Article 31C in the Constitution. The new article provided that a law giving effect to the directive principles specified in Article 39(b) and (c) will not be void on the ground of contravention of Articles 14, 19 and 31 and that a law containing a declaration that it was for giving effect to these directive principles would not be open to judicial scrutiny on the ground that it did not give effect to those directive principles. The proposed amendment was necessitated by the judgment of the Supreme Court in the *bank nationalisation case*, in which it had held that, even if all the requirements of

Article 31 were satisfied, it must also be tested on the anvil of Article 19 to find out whether a particular legislation imposed a reasonable restriction or not. The amendment also substituted the word 'amount' for 'compensation' in Article 31 and provided that this amount may be fixed by law or might be determined in accordance with such principles and given in such a manner as might be specified in the law.

In her intervention, Indira Gandhi asserted:

> We do not want to weaken the judiciary. What we are saying is only this: let the judiciary not try to take over the powers of Parliament.... Parliament is a repository of hopes and aspirations of the people.

The Bill was passed by the Lok Sabha on 1 December 1971 and by the Rajya Sabha on 8 December. The President gave assent to the Bill on 20 April 1972 *after* ratification by 19 States. (Kashyap, 1997: 68)

Arguing in the Supreme Court in the *Kesavananda Bharati* case, Nani Palkhivala called it "*a monumental outrage on the Constitution*." By this amendment, Article 31C had been inserted in the Constitution which, said Nani, "is a vast octopus, a new monster that can entangle and devour property in all forms, in addition to land." Article 31C virtually abrogated Article 31(1), which laid down that no person could be deprived of his property save by authority of law. Under the new amendment, said Nani, the executive had been clothed with power to take away any property in whatever form it may be and from whomsoever may possess it. In other words, cent per cent confiscation would be protected by Article 31(C). It gave a "licence to any legislature to run amuck". (Kamath, 2007: 180)

S.L. Shakdhar, former Secretary-General of Lok Sabha, in his book, *The Constitution and the Parliament of India: The 25 Years of the Republic*, has stated:

> India is also a land of many religions. *Unless the right to freely profess, practice and propagate one's religion is guaranteed in the Constitution, the fanatical religious zeal of the majority may make a short work of the liberty of conscience, belief, faith and religion of the minorities*.... It is said that fundamental rights stand in the way of the directive principles of State policy. But only through the freedom for the individual citizen can directive principles be fulfilled in the true nature and spirit. Slaves cannot fulfil the requirements of the directive principles.

Shakdhar concluded with regret:

> *After the passing of the 24th and 25th Amendments of our Constitution, we have, as it were, lost the essence of our freedom.* This is what every free citizen of India has to think about. After all, we are living under a democracy. *By tampering with the fundamental rights, we have injured our democracy through our thoughtlessness*. (Shakdhar, 1976: 89-91)

The Constitution (Twenty-sixth Amendment) Act 1971

Indira Gandhi introduced the Bill in the Lok Sabha on 9 August 1971 to (i) omit Articles 291 and 362 relating to the privy purses of the former princes; (ii) insert a new Article 363A; and (iii) amend Article 366. The Bill was considered by the Lok Sabha on 1 and 2 December 1971. Prime Minister recalled that "the principle underlying the Bill had already been accepted by the last Lok Sabha with an overwhelming majority.... It had however failed to secure the requisite special majority by a fraction of a vote in the Rajya Sabha. *But that was a mere technical failure. The House of People was not in doubt.*" This was a very unfortunate way of dealing with the defeat of the Bill and implied lowering the image of the Rajya Sabha, recognised as a house of the States and representing the elders. Indira Gandhi had also said in Lok Sabha, "*A great community of equals is being created in our country, and I would invite the princes and princesses to join this community unencumbered by a sense of past authority.*" How meaningless was such a talk!

The Bill was passed by the Lok Sabha on 2 December by 381 to 6 votes. It was passed by the Rajya Sabha on 9 December and received the President's assent on 28 December 1971.

The Constitution (Forty-second Amendment) Act, 1976

It was the Swaran Singh Committee Report which led to enactment of this highly controversial and ill-conceived Bill. *Comprising 59 articles, it was the single largest Constitution Amendment, or rather Constitution re-writing, Bill* ever introduced in Parliament. Speaking on the Bill in the Lok Sabha on 27 October 1976, Indira Gandhi said that the purpose of the Bill was to 'remedy the *anomalies* that have long been noticed, and to overcome *obstacles put up by economic and political vested interests* and that the Bill was responsive to the aspirations of the people and reflects the realities of the present time and the future'. This was a clear reference to the series of judgments of the Supreme Court which had over-turned some of the major initiatives of the government.

Some of the important changes made by the amendment were the following:

- In the Preamble to the Constitution, the words 'sovereign democratic' were substituted by the words 'sovereign *socialist secular* democratic' and the words 'unity of the nation' by 'unity and *integrity* of the nation'.
- Special protection was given to laws for prevention or prohibition of anti-national activities, and prevention of formation of or prohibition of anti-national associations, even if they are inconsistent with or take away or abridge rights conferred by Articles 14, 19 and 31 of the Constitution.

- To make directive principles more comprehensive and giving them precedence over fundamental rights.
- Constitutional validity of State laws not to be considered in proceedings under Article 32A.
- Fundamental duties of every citizen were listed in a new Article 51A.
- In Article 74, the advice tendered by the Council of Ministers to the President is to be binding on him.
- Rules of business are not to be called for presentation by a court.
- Duration of the houses of Parliament increased from five to six years.
- Quorum requirements for transaction of business in houses were deleted.
- Procedure for inquiry regarding disqualification of a person for indulging in corrupt practice changed.
- Important changes were made pertaining to powers of the High Courts and the Supreme Court. Exclusive jurisdiction was conferred on the Supreme Court in regard to questions as to constitutional validity of Central laws.
- For disposing questions relating to constitutional validity of laws, special provisions were made, namely, minimum number of judges on the bench, and majority of not less than two-thirds.
- Power of the High Courts to issue certain writs were reviewed and curtailed. Constitutional validity of Central laws is not to be considered by High Courts in proceedings under Article 226.
- High Courts were debarred from declaring any Central law to be constitutionally invalid.

- Government of India was empowered to deploy any armed force of the Union or any other force subject to the control of the Union for dealing with any grave situation of law and order in any State. The force was to act according to the directions of the Central Government.
- Article 311 was amended to curtail the opportunity given to a public servant to represent against the penalty proposed to be awarded to him.
- Creation of All India Judicial Service was approved under Article 312.
- Setting up of new tribunals was approved.
- Certain changes were made in the article pertaining to declaration of Emergency.
- President was given powers to make any modifications or changes to remove difficulties during the transition period of change-over to the new provisions.

The discussion continued for three days in which as many as 95 members participated with as many as 67 participating on the third day. Responding to the discussion on 27 October 1976, Prime Minister Indira Gandhi emphasised that the Bill was 'responsive to the aspirations of the people' and reflected the 'realities of the present time and the future'. Denying that the amendments in the Bill were being rushed through, she said,

> It is not hastily conceived, it is drawn up with care and deliberation. Many of the changes were in fact suggested by the Committee set up by Jawaharlal Nehru in 1954. So, in a sense, the discussion has been going on for twenty whole years. This certainly cannot be called rushing or stampeding. (Kashyap, 1997: 93-94)

The Bill was passed in the Lok Sabha with 4 votes against it and 366 in favour. All but 8 of over 600 amendments had been dropped or defeated. The Rajya Sabha passed it by 190 votes in its favour and none against. With 13 of the 22 State Legislatures ratifying it, the President gave his assent to it on 18 December 1976.

Austin has done some research as to who were the authors of this highly controversial Bill. According to him, the drafters (sic) of the Bill were worked out (sic) at two levels: the Prime Minister; several individuals around her established the policy content. S.S. Ray was the hub of the process. He, Rajani Patel and D.K. Barooah were some times referred to as the 'three musketeers'. H.R. Gokhale as Law Minister, contributing less to substance, led the team of drafters. Austin has quoted from the diary of B.N. Tandon who was Joint Secretary in Prime Minister's Office. The diary was published later and has been listed in the bibliography as *PMO Diary*. At the time of the drafting of the Forty-second Amendment of the Constitution, Gokhale told Tandon of his fears during the Emergency, which otherwise were widely spoken of among India's judicial community. Asked by Tandon why "he did not opt out of the government," given his strong dislike of much that was happening, "Gokhale admitted that he was scared to resign during the Emergency. He firmly believed that if he did so, the Prime Minister would send him to jail." "Bhishan [Tandon], you might consider it my weakness or anything else, the fact is that I did not want to go to jail." Gokhale was a 'frightened man', according to another official, and was made miserable by his 'judicial conscience'. (Austin, 1999: 375)

As Palkhivala rightly wrote:

> Every constitutional change represents a mood [as seen from the figures of voting]. Today, the mood of the nation which is searching for its identity is hardly conducive to a proper evaluation of the long-term, mind-boggling consequences of the proposed amendments. The Bill

merely seeks to provide the exigencies of the moment, forgetting that the Constitution is meant to endure through generations to come. (Kamath, 2007: 309)

Special attention may be invited to Section 4 pertaining to Article 31C which provides that no law giving effect to a directive principle of State policy shall be deemed to be void on the ground that it violates Article 14 or 19 of the Constitution. Palkhivala has convincingly argued that this is the very quintessence of authoritarianism. Articles 14 and 19 embody human rights, which are expressly recognised as essential to a free democracy. Article 31C recognizes that the destruction of those rights is necessary in order to replace a free democracy by an authoritarian State. Palkhivala had argued:

1. Article 31C makes the Constitution stand on its head. The fundamental rights which are enforceable against the government are rendered unenforceable by Article 31C, while the directive principles of State policy which are unenforceable are virtually rendered enforceable against the citizen when they are pursued in violation of his fundamental rights.
2. The contrary constitutional scheme of subordinating the fundamental rights to the directive principles, which the Constituent Assembly was specifically asked by B.N. Rao [Constitutional Advisor] to accept and which it deliberately rejected, is revived.
3. The creative balance between the fundamental rights and the directive principles is destroyed.
4. The balance between the judiciary on the one hand, and the executive and the legislature on the other, is disturbed. The guarantee of enforcement of fundamental rights by the Supreme Court contained in Article 32 is rendered meaningless as regards Articles 14 and 19.

5. To limit the scope of Article 31C to the directive principles is really to impose no limit at all. The directive principles have an all-embracing sweep and a practically unlimited range; they comprise almost the entire gamut of constitutionally relevant legislative and government activity. Therefore the position of supremacy accorded to them destroys the fundamental rights in almost all cases. Besides, any law made by Parliament or a State Legislature would always profess to be for the welfare of the citizens falling under one or the other of the directive principles. In that event such a law can never be challenged. Thus the fundamental rights cease to be fundamental, and even cease to be rights. Only their corpses remain embalmed in Articles 14 and 19.
6. Article 31C gives to each State the power to take away the right of equality granted by Article 14 and the seven freedoms granted by Article 19. Hence, there could be pockets of dictatorship and free democracy within India. It is impossible to imagine India remaining one under such conditions.

In sum, freedom and Article 31C cannot coexist. While the basic structure of the Constitution is that of marble, Article 31C substitutes it with a framework of red bricks. Fortunately, in the *Minerva Mills* case, in a momentous decision on 9 May 1980, the Supreme Court set aside the amendments made in Article 31C on the ground that the changes violated its judgment in the *Kesavananda Bharati* case. (Kamath, 2007: 212-213, 215-16)

INDIRA GANDHI DID NOT ACT ON THE FOLLOWING

It is important to note that Indira Gandhi was reluctant to act on the following *five* important matters which could have made a significant difference to the public life in the country. This was so even after she came back to power in 1980. What Palkhivala has written is quite true:

> Providence has granted Mrs Gandhi a marvellous, exceptional opportunity to build a strong India by taking a U-turn in fiscal and other economic policies [and also equally importantly, in political matters], an opportunity as rare as rain in Iquique [a coastal city in northern Chile]. *She has massive public support. She has an over-whelming majority in Parliament. The party is solidly, in fact supinely, behind her. More than three-fourths of the States are ruled by Congress(I) ministries which are more docile towards the [Congress] High Command than the native States were in the days of paramountcy of the British Crown.* (Palkhivala, 1994: 169)

Unfortunately for India, these years too were wasted in so far as the following important public policy issues were concerned.

Electoral Reforms

Electoral reforms has been a bone of contention among political parties right since independence. One concern has been the influence of foreign funding on elections. It was not therefore surprising that Jyoti Basu cited "*A Dangerous Place* by Daniel Patrick Moynihan, the former US ambassador to India, which claims the Congress was twice given money by the CIA, both times to avert a possible Communist victory, once in Kerala and the other time in West Bengal. The second time the money was given to Mrs Gandhi herself who was then 'a party official', he says in the book." Basu has added, 'In any case, she never herself raised any objection to Moynihan's statements in his book nor did anyone else take exception to it on her behalf.' (Banerjee, 1997: 145, 245) Misuse of government machinery, religious propaganda, incitement to communal passions, excessive use of money and muscle power were some of the other points.

In his address to the two Houses of Parliament at the opening of the budget session on 17 February 1975, President Fakhruddin Ali Ahmed had made an appeal to all sections of the people to co-operate with the government in evolving national solutions to problems like corruption and electoral reforms. He had also given an *assurance that the government "would discuss shortly, with the leaders of other political parties, proposals for changes in the electoral laws."*

Replying to the debate on the motion of thanks on the President's address on 27 February, Indira Gandhi had welcomed the suggestion from Shyama Nandan Mishra (the Opposition Congress leader) for consultation between the Prime Minister and opposition leaders on all major national issues and said that *she was prepared, immediately to have a round-table conference on electoral reforms.* Talks between the government and opposition leaders on this issue took place on 22 and 29 April 1975.

In spite of the unambiguous statements as above by the President of India and herself, she never pursued the matter further. Jayaprakash Narayan and leaders of the non-Communist opposition parties led a huge demonstration which marched through Delhi on 6 March to present a charter of demands to the presiding officers of the two houses of Parliament. One of the demands in the charter was for electoral reforms, including the introduction of the right of electors to recall their representatives. A number of prominent Congress party MPs including Mohan Dharia, Chandra Shekhar and Krishna Kant, openly advocated that Indira Gandhi should enter into a dialogue with Jayaprakash Narayan. However, she rejected the suggestion. (Kashyap, 1997: 30-31)

As brought out in the earlier discussion in this chapter, the only changes in the electoral laws which were carried out by her were unashamedly meant to safeguard her own interests! With her tall leadership and over-whelming popular mandate for most of her term, she could have pushed through significant electoral reforms which would have made a difference to the public life of the country. Unfortunately, she was least interested.

Anti-Defection Legislation

Crossing of floor by legislators had assumed alarming proportions during the life of the fourth Lok Sabha (1967-1970). As Kashyap has stated:

> The general elections held in 1967 constituted a watershed in the political history of independent India. The electoral verdict led to the formation of coalition governments in several States. Change of political parties by legislators quite often affected the fate of ministries and the course of politics. Many of the legislators changed their political labels more than once and some of them as many as four or five times in a year. This subject came up for discussion in the Lok Sabha on a private member's resolution by P. Venkatasubbaiah on 11 August 1967. He said that there were hundred defections from the Congress to the opposition parties and sixty-four from the opposition to the Congress. Majority of Congress deserters had found place in opposition governments. This was a betrayal of faith reposed by people in their representatives. Members who took part in the discussion unanimously emphasised the need to arrest the menace of floor-crossing, but they differed as regards methods for doing it. Intervening in the debate, Home Minister Y.B. Chavan expressed grave concern on the way government after government had fallen due to defections. This problem was threatening to disrupt the democratic way of life. Replying to the debate P. Venkatasubbaiah called upon the Congress party, being the biggest party in the country, to take a lead by initiating a

> move to cleanse the political life in the country. (Kashyap, 1996: 285-286)

But it was clear from Chavan's intervention that the government was not keen on addressing the issues and there the matter rested for full six years till 1973.

Finally, the Constitution (Thirty-second Amendment) Bill 1973 was introduced in the Lok Sabha by the then Union Home Minister, Uma Shankar Dikshit, on 16 May 1973 with a view to (a) disqualifying a political defector from his continued membership of the legislature, and (b) to provide that the Prime Minister and the Chief Ministers shall be members of the Lok Sabha and Vidhan Sabha [lower house] respectively. The Bill was referred to a Joint Committee of the two houses. The Committee was asked to submit a report to the Lok Sabha by the last day of the first week of the tenth session. Later, four extensions were given. On 30 August 1976 again the Lok Sabha extended the time up to the last day of the session. The Joint Committee, however, could not submit its report and the Bill lapsed on the dissolution of the fifth Lok Sabha. (Kashyap, 1997: 104)

It is evident that Indira Gandhi was not keen on persuing this matter. Otherwise, someone like her who was able to push through so many other much more controversial Constitutional Amendments, would not have permitted the Joint Committee of Parliament to drag its feet for so long.

Not only was she reluctant to act on discouraging defections from one political party to another, Indira Gandhi encouraged defections. The most striking case mentioned by Zail Singh in his memoirs is that of Haryana Assembly where thirty-eight members led by Bhajan Lal crossed over from Janata Party to Congress(I) on 22 January 1980, thus averting the need for its dismissal. (Zail Singh, 1997: 151)

Austin has noted that defections and floor-crossings in State Legislatures had become a 'chronic disease', according to party President S. Nijalingappa. He attacked Mrs Gandhi for her alleged contribution to these, for attempting to undermine 'the foundations of democratic life in this country'. (Austin, 1999: 568-569)

Farooq Abdullah had incurred the wrath of Indira Gandhi and she had made up her mind to oust him from the Chief Ministership of J&K, in 1984. For this purpose, she had even engineered the split in Abdullah's party. As has been brought out in chapter 6, Congress Party even sent money through the Intelligence Bureau pouches, as recounted by the then Governor of J&K B.K. Nehru.

It was only by the Constitution (Ninety-first) Amendment Act, 2004 that the loopholes in the anti-defection provisions in the tenth schedule of the Constitution enacted in 1985 by Rajiv Gandhi government were bridged by taking away the protection from defectors on grounds of splits in the parties and to make defectors disqualified from membership and ineligible for ministership and other remunerative political posts till re-election. (Kashyap, 2009: 420) The country paid a heavy price for Indira Gandhi's inexcusable neglect of this major malady in public life.

Black Money

B.G. Verghese in his book, *Tomorrow's India – Another Tryst with Destiny*, has highlighted the menace of black money which was no less during Indira Gandhi's regime, as it is today. In fact, Indira Gandhi's Leftist policies, institutionalization of Licence-Permit Raj, and excessively high Income Tax rates of over 97.5 per cent contributed to creation of black money. Verghese has stated that since the 1970s, the black economy has been the single biggest cause of all the macro and micro problems the economy has confronted. (Verghese, 2006: 97, 101) The National Institute of Public Finance and Policy in its report, *Aspects of Black Money in India,* had estimated the black income generation at 18 to 21 per cent of the gross domestic product (at factor cost) for the year 1983-84.

In the middle of 1971, the Direct Taxes Enquiry Committee, popularly known as the Wanchoo Committee, submitted an interim report in which, *inter alia*, it recommended the demonetization of high value currency notes. As soon as the report was received, it was discussed in a series of meetings in the Finance Minister Y.B. Chavan's room. I was working as the Private Secretary to Finance Minister at the time. After detailed discussion, it was decided to undertake a series of steps, including demonetization, as recommended by the Committee. In view of the sensitive nature of the subject and the need for maintaining utmost secrecy, it was decided that the Finance Minister should speak to the Prime Minister and obtain her approval to the proposed course of action before further steps were initiated. Accordingly, the Finance Minister spoke to Prime Minister. As he told me on his return from the meeting, the conversation was very brief and crisp. When Chavan told her about the proposal for demonetization and his view that it should be accepted and implemented forthwith, she asked Chavan only one question: "Chavanji, are no more elections to be fought by the Congress party?" Chavan got the message and the recommendation was shelved. (Godbole, 1996: 87-88)

I have referred in chapter 4 to the raid by Income Tax authorities on Baroda Rayon and how that raid was merely to get the list of large donations made by the company to Congress party and how the file confiscated by the Income Tax authorities from the Managing Director of the company which was handed over to Pranab Kumar Mukherjee, the then Minister of State for Finance, was never returned by him to the revenue department. This was only a tip of the iceberg. I have brought out in this book how political corruption was institutionalized during this period.

Selbourne, in his book, *An Eye to India – The unmasking of a Tyranny*, has highlighted that the Wanchoo Committee on direct taxes had brought out the scale of parallel economy. It estimated that the money value of deals involving black money may not be less than 70,000 million rupees (pounds 4,000 million) for 1968-69, and with commensurately colossal evasion of taxation. But, by 1975, both the Planning Commission and the executive of the Congress party had received an estimate of 'rolling black money' amounting to 200,000 million rupees (or about pounds 11,000 million), and so inextricably interwoven into the fabric of the economy, 'black' with 'white', that the figure was itself without meaning. (Selbourne, 1997: 202)

When the Janata government came to power, the government took action in 1978 to demonetise bank notes of the denominational value of ₹ 1,000, ₹ 5,000, and ₹ 10,000. While moving the Bill for replacement of the ordinance, Union Finance Minister, H.M. Patel, told Lok Sabha that high denomination bank notes were being used extensively for illicit transfer of money for financing transactions which were harmful to national economy. Replying to the *brief discussion*, *Patel stated that in India the purpose of demonetisation was to ascertain whether the money was legally held and liability of Income Tax discharged on it.* (Kashyap, 1997: 349) This reply is particularly relevant in the context of the controversy over the demonetisation effected by Modi government and the impact thereof on the black money.

Appointment of Lokpal

The first official Lokpal and Lokayuktas Bill was introduced in the Lok Sabha on 9 May 1968. It sought to give effect to the recommendations of the Administrative Reforms Commission (ARC) to set up institutions of Lokpal and Lokayuktas to look into the complaints and grievances regarding the work done by ministers and secretaries and other government officials. Prime Minister was excluded from the Bill on the ground that if a minister resigned on an adverse finding against him, he merely demitted his office; but when a Prime Minister did so, the entire government went out of office. The government argued that this was a political process which was the exclusive right of Lok Sabha. Giving this power to any other functionary, however high it might be, would not be proper. There was animated discussion in which a number of members demanded that the Prime Minister should also be brought in the jurisdiction of the Lokpal. The government, however, rejected the demand for inclusion of Prime Minister and Governors in the purview of the Bill. Speaking during the clause-by-clause consideration of the Bill on 18 August 1969, Home Minister Y.B. Chavan reiterated government's stand and said that the Prime Minister was the "key-stone of the entire government structure" and if he were to resign on the basis of a recommendation of the Lokpal, the entire government would fall. He said that the agency to bring about the fall of the government could not be any other than Parliament and the Lokpal was not even the agent of Parliament. After extensive discussion the Bill was passed. But due to the dissolution of the Lok Sabha, the Bill lapsed while it was pending in the Rajya Sabha. (Kashyap, 1996: 231-234)

After elections and massive mandate received by Indira Gandhi, the Bill was reintroduced in the Lok Sabha in 1971 but clearly she was not interested in the subject and it languished for full six years and lapsed when the fifth Lok Sabha was dissolved on 18 January 1977! After she came back to power in 1980, no effort was made by her to enact a law on the subject.

Separation of Religion from Politics

After the cataclysmic Punjab agitation culminating in Operation Blue Star, one would have expected Indira Gandhi to take the bull by the horn and address the basic malady which had given rise to it, namely, inter-mixing of religion and politics. In one of her meetings during Punjab agitation, Indira Gandhi had told the Akalis that they should not mix religion with politics; the two were separate and should remain so. The Akalis argued that religion could be used for the good of politics. They pointed out how Mahatma Gandhi used '*dharma*' to articulate India's demand for independence and got the support of the masses for the national movement. (Nayar and Khushwant Singh, 1984: 44) This is the usual self-serving argument put up by communal parties to evade the important issue which has continued to plague India. Mahatma Gandhi's use of *dharma* was meant to infuse values in politics and to bridge the gap between the Muslims and Hindus and forge a united front against the British. It was a counter to the British policy of divide and rule.

After Blue Star, the public mood in the country was such that move to separate religion from politics would have been widely welcomed by large cross-sections of the people. There was widespread revulsion with the misuse of religion in politics in Punjab and particularly the misuse of religious places by the terrorists. K.P.S. Gill has written:

> Sikh politics had inexorably been thrown into the mould of competitive communalism ever since the constitution of the Shiromani Gurdwara Parbandhak Committee (SGPC), the elected body responsible for the management of Gurudwaras in Punjab in 1925. The SGPC today administers well over 700 Sikh shrines … and has often been described as a 'State within a State'. (Gill, 1997: 37)

It would be recalled that after the demolition of Babri Masjid in December 1992, Narasimha Rao at least made such an effort by bringing forth a Constitution Amendment Bill, and a Bill for amendment of the Representation of the People Act, 1951, for the purpose. But, since he could not mobilise support in Parliament, the Bills had to be shelved. Also, he did not enjoy a massive majority in Parliament, as Indira Gandhi did.

It is important to note that the founding fathers of the Constitution had fully realised the importance of separation of religion from politics. Ananthasayanam Ayyangar had moved a resolution for the purpose in the Constituent Assembly (Legislative) on April 3, 1948:

> Whereas it is essential for the proper functioning of democracy and the growth of national unity and solidarity *that communalism should be eliminated from Indian life*, this Assembly is of opinion that no communal organisation which by its Constitution or by the exercise of discretionary power vested in any of its officers or organs, admits to or excludes from its membership persons on grounds of religion, race and caste, or any of them, should be permitted to engage in any activities other than those essential for the *bona fide* religious and cultural needs of the community, and that *all steps, legislative and administrative, necessary to prevent such activities should be taken*.

Nehru had welcomed the resolution and assured that the government:

> wished to do everything in their power to achieve the objective which lies behind this resolution... The only alternative is civil conflict. *We have seen as a matter of fact how far communalism in politics has led us*; all of us remember the grave dangers through which we have passed and the terrible consequences we have seen...Resolution mentions

> administrative and legislative measures to be taken to give effect to it. Exactly what those administrative and legislative measures might be, it is impossible to say straight off; it will require the closest scrutiny, certainly the legislative part of it… I should like to make it perfectly clear again that as far as the implementation of it is concerned, more especially in regard to the legislative aspect of it, it will have to be very carefully considered and will ultimately have to come before this House…. I have no objection on behalf of the government to accept the addition of the words 'social and educational' which are mentioned in one of the amendments to this resolution. It would read: "… should be permitted to engage in any activities other than those essential for the *bona fide* religious, cultural, social and educational needs of the community…."

The resolution, as amended, was passed by the Constituent Assembly (Legislative) on April 3, 1948. (GoI, 1949: 47-51)

Nehru's assessment that the legislative aspects of the resolution will require closest scrutiny and approval of Parliament has been fully borne out by the experience of the Constitution (Eightieth) Amendment Bill 1993.

It may be recalled that the question of communal riots was discussed at great length at the Jabalpur session of the AICC on October 29, 1967. Attention may be invited to the demand made by several members to ban communal parties. Syed Mir Quasim had strongly urged to ban communal parties which were out to destroy India's nationhood, democracy and secularism. Ahmed Baksh Sindhi supported this demand and also demanded action against newspapers which propagated communal views. The demand for a ban on all communal parties was also supported by Sheel Bhadra Yajee and others. K.L. Nagappa Alva moved an amendment for a ban on communal parties. S.K. Patil, who had moved the political resolution and was a prominent member of the Congress party, however, rejected the amendment for banning communal parties and said that it was a delicate problem in as much as it would be difficult to decide whether a party was communal or not. (Godbole, 2016: 219-221)

Indira Gandhi always used to claim that the split in the Congress party in 1969 was on ideological grounds and not for strengthening her position in the party. As can be seen, if it was the old guard in the party, represented by S.K. Patil, which had taken such a retrograde view on separation of religion from politics, Indira Gandhi could have shown that she stood apart from them by taking a principled stand on the subject. On the contrary, it is shocking to see that in the Electoral Laws Amendment Act passed in 1975 (discussed earlier in this chapter) to protect her election case, a provision was made that *no election symbol allotted by the Election Commission should be considered a religious or national symbol.* This shows that she had no real commitment to secularism. Tandon has written:

> PM has never been guided by any principles or rules. She has but one objective – to win the elections somehow. She is not averse to any alliance if it will help her win – she has tied up with Muslim League in Kerala, the Shiv Sena in Bombay and the Akalis in Punjab at different times. But for public consumption she has always maintained that she is opposed to narrow communal parties. (Tandon, 2003: 325)

She had clear 2/3rd majority in Parliament and could have easily got a Constitution Amendment for separation of religion from politics passed not only in Parliament but also by the requisite number of State Legislatures. But, it is India's misfortune that like her father Nehru earlier and her son Rajiv later, she did not want to act on the subject. A golden opportunity was thus lost, for ever.

JANATA PARTY'S ELECTION MANIFESTO

The Janata Party had given commitment to give a three-fold charter to the people: political charter, economic charter and social charter. In the political charter were included the following, among other, promises: to repeal the MISA, release all political prisoners, and review all other unjust laws; enact laws to ensure that no political or social organization is banned without independent judicial enquiry; to rescind the 42nd Amendment; to amend Article 352 [Proclamation of Emergency] to prevent its abuse in the interest of an individual or a group; to amend Article 356 to ensure that the power to impose President's Rule in the States is not misused to benefit the ruling party or any favoured faction within it; to introduce electoral reforms; to re-establish rule of law; to restore the authority of the judiciary and safeguard the independence and integrity of the Bar; to ensure that all individuals, including those who hold high office, are equal before law; and *to delete property from the list of fundamental rights* and instead affirm the right to work. (Diwan, 1978: Preface)

There were no major differences between the Congress and Janata Party on economic and social issues. Even on the crucial right to property, there was agreement that it should cease to be a fundamental right. But, so far as political charter was concerned, the Janata Party's commitments reflected what the people were pining for. Unfortunately, the Janata government did not last long enough to fulfil *all* of them.

MAJORITARIANISM WAS BAD – WHETHER OF CONGRESS OR JANATA PARTY

In pursuance of the above promises, the Janata government passed the Constitution (Forty-fourth Amendment) Act 1978 by which several very objectionable features of the 42nd

Amendment were done away with. These included: 'armed rebellion' and not 'merely internal disturbance' was made a necessary ground for Proclamation of Emergency; preventive detention was not to be authorised beyond two months without the decision of the Advisory Board, and a host of other amendments which could have stifled democracy permanently.

However, I should also mention the two most objectionable amendments. The first was the omission of right to property as a fundamental right. This was highly short-sighted. As if practically all law-givers had been brain-washed with socialist ideology. To put it in the post-2014 idiom, not to be a socialist was anti-national, unpatriotic!

The second was the doing away with the provision pertaining to powers given to the Central Government by the 42nd Amendment for deployment of Central forces in States in cases of extreme law and order situations and such forces taking orders from the Centre and not the State Governments. This was the case of throwing the baby with the bath water, as the saying goes. Grave national calamities such as the demolition of the Babri Masjid in 1992 and the massacre in Godhra riots in 2002 could have been avoided, if such powers were available with the Centre, and, equally importantly, the Central Government at the time, Congress and NDA respectively, had mustered the political will to use them!

TO SUM UP

The above broad brush survey of the wide-ranging amendments carried out by Indira Gandhi government are breath-taking in their range, and disastrous in their consequences. I have serious doubts if she ever realised their consequences. If benefit of doubt is to be given to her, it will have to be said that her constitutional and legal advisors, failed to explain their implications to her fully. Or, her advisors had their own agenda which they wanted to pursue. But if neither of this is true and she decided to go ahead with these constitutional atrocities consciously, even after being advised to the contrary, we must blame ourselves for having elected her with such a large majority and given her such untrammelled powers. Giving two-thirds majority to a leader who is unable to grasp the consequences of her actions can be a real nightmare. Let us hope those days will not return, ever again.

6

Devaluing the Institutions

INTRODUCTION

Indira Gandhi regime was a watershed in which several major institutions of governance received body-blows leading to their perceptible weakening. The judiciary and the bureaucracy were not just the two institutions which were debilitated. The very survival of several other institutions was in grave danger.

COMMITTED JUDICIARY

Higher judiciary was a favourite whipping horse of Indira Gandhi. The confrontation between the executive and judiciary reached its peak during her regime. Judicial review is an important duty cast on the judiciary by the Constitution but this became the main bone of contention. Decisions of the Supreme Court in important cases which went against the government were considered as personal affronts by Indira Gandhi. "The argument of fear", as it came to be known, was instrumental in the court curtailing the powers of Parliament by enunciating the basic structure doctrine and drawing a "*Laxman Rekha*" which could not be crossed by Parliament while amending the Constitution. Subba Rao, former Chief Justice of India, had felt that many of the freedoms in the fundamental rights had been taken away or abridged since

1950. He characterized the continuance in force of the national Emergency of 1962 – with its suspension of fundamental rights Articles 14, 19, 21 and 22 – as constitutional despotism. (Austin, 1999: 199-200) It is my firm view that if Indira Gandhi had not adopted such strident position against the judiciary, Indian Constitution today would have been quite different. For example, in appointment of judges of the High Courts and the Supreme Court, the court would not have taken over the powers of selection and appointment to itself, to the exclusion of the government. The doctrine of basic structure of the Constitution may not have been enunciated if the court (and the country at large) had not been worried about the intentions of Constitution demolition squad in the Congress party, strongly supported by the Leftist parties. (Godbole, 2008: 2)

A significant point to note was that Indira Gandhi's close advisors on the subject were Law Minister H.R. Gokhale, former judge of Bombay High Court, and leading Leftist advocate of the Supreme Court, and Minister for Steel and Mines, S. Mohan Kumaramangalam. The supersession of judges by Indira Gandhi while making appointment of the Chief Justice of India led to total shock and disbelief. Jayaprakash Narayan wrote a letter to Indira Gandhi on 16 May 1973 expressing his misgivings. In her reply dated 9 June, Indira Gandhi dismissed the dismal conclusions drawn by Jayaprakash Narayan as unwarranted. She stated, "Frequent reversals of stand, not always in more liberal, more humane direction, were the main difficulty with our judicial decisions in the last decade or so. There was obvious need for greater continuity of ideas and vision.... In the appointment of the new Chief Justice, we have only freed ourselves of a convention [of seniority] which had the sanction neither of the Constitution nor of rationality. It would be atrocious to think that the independence of the judiciary is thereby affected. The outcry and controversy which have attended the appointment seem to me to be wholly misplaced." In a rejoinder dated 27 June 1973, Jayaprakash Narayan had expressed his disappointment at her response. (Nayar, 1973: 73-77)

It is pertinent to note that the question whether the appointment of the Chief Justice of India should be made solely on the basis of seniority arose in 1951 itself. At that time the Supreme Court comprised seven judges. Gadbois has stated,

> Upon Chief Justice Kania's sudden death, Prime Minister Nehru considered naming as the new Chief Justice either B.K. Mukherjea (third in seniority on the court), or M.C. Chagla, the then Chief Justice of the Bombay High Court. Upon learning that M.P. Sastri, their senior-most colleague, might not be named Chief Justice, *all the Supreme Court judges, including Mukherjea who had reason to believe that he was Nehru's choice, threatened to resign if seniority did not govern the choice of Kania's successor. Nehru bowed to this demonstration of solidarity and Sastri was confirmed as Chief Justice.* (Godbole, 2008: 513)

Reference must also be made to another case which has left its mark. F.S. Nariman has written:

> B.K. Mukherjea also established a glorious tradition of independence by refusing Pandit Nehru's offer that he become Chief Justice before his time, superseding Mehr Chand Mahajan: 'I'd rather resign', he said, 'than accept your offer.' And Mahajan was duly appointed Chief Justice in January 1954. It was only on his retirement in December of that year, that Mukherjea assumed the highest office in the land. What an admirable example, when contrasted with the sordid events of 25th April 1973 – on that day the fourth puisne judge (A.N. Ray) accepted government's

offer of Chief Justiceship over his senior colleagues on the bench. (Nariman, 2000: 21-22)

When Chief Justice M. Hidayatullah was approaching retirement age in late 1970, there was a rumour that the next-in-line in seniority, J.C. Shah, may not be promoted, and an outsider, ex-Communist Mohan Kumaramangalam, may be appointed the Chief Justice. According to Hidayatullah's account, all but one of the eleven judges said they would resign if Shah was not promoted. At that time, Indira Gandhi was not politically strong enough to force the issue and Justice Shah was appointed to succeed Chief Justice Hidayatullah.

Significantly, when the three senior-most judges of the Supreme Court were superseded in 1973 for the post of the Chief Justice of India, only they resigned and none of their colleagues had the courage to take a stand in the matter. Same thing was repeated in 1977 when the then senior-most judge, Justice H.R. Khanna, was superseded. Only he resigned. The collegial spirit in the premier institution of the country had become a thing of the past and each was only interested in looking after his own career prospects. Each was a planet spinning on itself.

Same thing happened when two judges of the Delhi High Court, S.I. Rangarajan and R.N. Aggarwal were 'punished', the former by transfer to the High Court of Assam, and the latter by being demoted as a district judge. Their only offence was that they formed the bench which had ruled against the government in the *Kuldip Nayar* case. The move launched by some judges of the Delhi High Court to give mass resignations of all judges fizzled out as only two or three judges signed the joint letter. (Nariman, 2010: 186-187) Loss of *esprit de Corps* was the most serious casualty in superior judiciary, as it has been in the civil services. It is no wonder that the political executive exploited the situation fully.

Indira Gandhi's legacy has taken a firm foothold. As was to be expected, the attempts at tampering with the institutional integrity continued even after Indira Gandhi. According to Janak Raj Jai,

> efforts were again made in 1996 to supersede Justice J.S. Verma. The Supreme Court Bar stood like a rock behind Justice J.S. Verma and saw to it that he was not superseded. (Jai, 1997: ix)

When the term of Justice Verma was to expire in January 1998, a controversy arose about whether Justice Madan Mohan Punchhi, who was the seniormost, should succeed him as Chief Justice. With the Committee on Judicial Accountability (COJA) making certain allegations against Justice Punchhi, it was a headline grabbing unsavoury controversy which the judiciary could have done without. Jai has charged that

> the COJA's proximity to certain elements in the judiciary is not-so-open secret. And it is clear to those who keep an ear to the ground that the anti-Punchhi campaign is not entirely innocent of the politics of the judiciary.... The tone, timing and setting of the anti-Punchhi campaign leave no manner of doubt that it is more personal than institutional in nature, more political than moral, more no cent (sic) than innocent. (Jai, 1997: X-XI)

But, let me revert to Indira Gandhi period. Kumaramangalam, in his piece "Chief Justice of India: Criteria of Choice", has stated:

> Let us not forget the last six years of background of what can only be described as a confrontation between Parliament and the government on the one hand and the [Supreme] Court on the other. I do not think we should forget that fact.... There has been an atmosphere in which the court looked at things in one way and we in another way. (Nayar, 1973: 79)

According to Indira Gandhi government, for bringing about social revolution and socialistic pattern of society, Constitution had to be changed completely. In the process, directive principles of State policy would have to take precedence over even the fundamental rights. Right to property which was recognised as a fundamental right had to be abolished and made into only a legal right. The powers of the High Courts and the Supreme Court had to be curtailed and their powers of judicial review had to be circumscribed. Where was all this going to stop?

The judgment of the Allahabad High Court in the election petition had angered Indira Gandhi. Her being unseated from Parliament was taken as a personal affront by her. As seen in chapter 5, a series of Constitutional Amendments were made and laws passed to put her own position beyond any challenge in the future. She even wanted to give herself immunity for life against any prosecution. In no other democracy, not even in a Princely State, laws would have been 'bent like Beckham' to suit the ruler's personal interest. It was a constitutional dictatorship at work, with full force of majoritarian politics.

But changing the Constitution in this manner could serve the purpose only up to a point. Unless the judiciary became 'Her Majesty's Voice', in every sense of the term, the objective could not be served. This meant appointment in the higher judiciary of persons aligned with the thinking and policies of the government. For the first time, blatantly, the principle of seniority which had been well accepted in the past for promotion as Chief Justice of India, was jettisoned and successively senior-most judges were superseded who had decided matters against the government. Chief Justice Sikri retired the day after delivering the judgment in the *Kesavananda* case. Indira Gandhi disregarded the seniority of three judges – J.M. Shelat, K.S. Hegde and A.N. Grover and named Justice

A.N. Ray to the post. Austin has written that Justice Hegde attributed his supersession for the Chief Justiceship in part to the ruling of the three judge bench in the Indira Gandhi appeal, which he had delivered on 15 March 1972, upholding Raj Narain's appeal about introduction of certain evidence in the Allahabad High Court case. (Austin, 1999: 315, footnote 3) Kumaramangalam has contested this by ridiculing that it was a decision in

> a small interlocutory matter in an election petition, not an election petition, let us be clear.... Justice Hegde should not judge the Prime Minister by that standard. The Prime Minister does not take a like or dislike to a judge on the basis of what the judge decides.... It is unfortunate that he should have descended to that level. (Nayar, 1973: 88)

Law Minister H.R. Gokhale's defence of government decision was lacklustre, in comparison with that of Kumaramangalam, cited above. Several opposition members charged that Kumaramangalam was specially put up to make an exposition of government's policy. Gokhale assured the House that there was no difference of opinion between him and Kumaramangalam. He assured Parliament that "We are in no way interested in having a pliable or weak court...." (Nayar, 1973: 112)

M.C. Chagla made a spirited attack on the government's decision to supersede the three judges. He charged that "we will no longer have an impartial and independent judiciary in this country.... *Henceforth there will be a competition among the judges as to who is more forward-looking and who has better imbibed the gospel of the ruling party.* I am told on reliable sources that this has already started. Junior judges of High Courts have started making speeches and writing articles *giving expression to ultra-socialistic views so as to catch the eye and the ear of the authority that will ultimately select a Chief Justice when a vacancy arises.*" Chagla said that he was a member of the Law

Commission which had made recommendations regarding the selection of the Chief Justice. The report was 'lying in archives' for fifteen years and had been retrieved only to justify the government's action, for wrong reasons. He felt that "there is greater safety in invariably appointing the seniormost judge as Chief Justice.... *Our government is becoming more and more monolithic. It cannot brook any opposition, it resents any criticism.* The only institution that has so far had the courage to thwart the intention of the government to override the fundamental rights of citizens has been the judiciary. If that goes, the lights of democracy will go out and we will lapse into the darkness of a totally and completely authoritarian regime." (Nayar, 1973: 115-116, 119)

N.A. Palkhivala has been equally hard-hitting in his essay titled "Judiciary Made to Measure". He recalled that during the hearing of the *Kesavananda Bharati* case, Attorney General had expressly referred in open court, both orally and in writing, to the alternative of "political action", if the Supreme Court's ruling did not find favour with the government. Palkhivala was also a member of the Law Commission on whose report the government had ostensibly relied while taking a decision on the new Chief Justice. Palkhivala said that on the basis of the criterion of "efficiency and capacity", the three superseded judges were fully qualified to fill the post of Chief Justice. Referring to Kumaramangalam's assertion that government wants judges "who can effectively work and help us in the Supreme Court", Palkhivala apprehended that this will eventually convert the Supreme Court into a subservient appendage to the executive. He further aptly said, "*While it is desirable to inject justice into politics, it is disastrous to inject politics into justice*". Palkhivala also contested the statement of Kumaramangalam that the Chief Justice should be one who "is able to recognise that Parliament is supreme". Palkhivala has repeated his famous argument that "the Constitution is supreme over Parliament; and not Parliament over the Constitution". (Nayar, 1973: 120-121, 125-127)

In an interview, former Chief Justice S.M. Sikri said that the superseded judges interpreted the Constitution, in some respects, differently from the government. He seriously contested a number of statements of Kumaramangalam, referred to earlier. He said, "*When a judge takes office he does not take an oath to uphold the philosophy of the government*.... If the statement of Mr Kumaramangalam is analysed and carried to its logical conclusion, *it would make a mockery of the concept of the rule of law*.... Instead we will have the rule of the philosophy of the government." *In reply to another question, Justice Sikri said, "it was reported to me that the drafts of the judgments [in Kesavananda case] had been sent [by some judge(s)] to the government.* I do not know if it is correct or not. I had no means or desire to find out." Sikri confirmed that *a complaint had been made to him by some judges that even what they were discussing informally among themselves was being reported to the government.* In reply to a question, Sikri said that he had recommended the name of Justice Shelat to succeed him. In reply to another question Sikri said,

> if I was offered a Chief Justiceship in supersession of senior colleagues, against whom there was nothing except their judicial opinions, I would decline the offer, for if I accepted it, I would be impliedly undertaking to carry out the philosophy of the government.... If I accepted the offer, I would lose the respect of my brother judges, the Bar and the public. (Nayar, 1973: 130-136)

I have brought out earlier how attempts in 1951 and 1954 for supersession of Supreme Court judges did not succeed because of resistance by the judges, including those who were to be promoted out-of-turn. Clearly, the e*sprit the corps* has vanished in higher judiciary, as in bureaucracy, due to the short-sighted policy of promoting committed judiciary and committed bureaucracy. There was no protest by any of the sitting judges of the Supreme Court when their brother judges were superseded, though the supersession revoked sharp reactions from bar associations from across the country. In Bombay, nearly 7,000 lawyers boycotted the High Court and other courts in the city and suburbs to express their resentment.

In spite of such sharp reactions, however, later, Justice H.R. Khanna was also superseded in 1977 for having decided important cases against the government. In his memoirs, Justice Khanna has written:

> From the way my other colleagues on the bench made remarks or kept silent [in *ADM Jabalpur vs Shrikant Shukla*, also known as *Habeas Corpus* case, referred to earlier in chapter 4] I became convinced that the way I was thinking, I would be the solitary judge to decide against the State.... *Article 21, in my opinion, was not the sole repository of the right to life and personal liberty. Those rights had existed even prior to the framing of the Constitution*.... It was plain that if I gave the judgment as I was contemplating, I would have to lose the office of the Chief Justice of India, as the then incumbent of office was due to retire in some months' time and I was next in seniority. I could not entertain any illusion in this respect as there had already been a precedent in 1973, when three senior judges had been superseded.... As expected, mine was the solitary dissent [in the judgment]. In the course of my judgment I observed: The cases before us raise questions of utmost importance and gravity, questions which impinge not only upon the scope of the different constitutional provisions, but have impact upon the basic values affecting life, liberty and the rule of law. More is at stake in these cases than the liberty of a few individuals or the correct

> construction of the wording of an order. *What is at stake is the rule of law.* (Godbole, 2008: 62-63)

The New York Times wrote, "if India ever finds its way back to freedom and democracy, the proud hallmark of its first eighteen years, someone will surely erect a monument to Justice H.R. Khanna of the Supreme Court." As far as I am aware, no such statue has been erected for Justice Khanna but, as my modest tribute, I had dedicated my book, *The Judiciary and Governance in India* (2008) to the four Supreme Court judges who were high-handedly superseded for the post of Chief Justice of India, and the sixteen High Court judges who were punitively transferred or whose confirmation as permanent judges was capriciously withheld for their audacity of upholding the Constitution and being the torch-bearers of the highest principles of judicial independence, integrity, objectivity, fairness and fearlessness.

Kumaramangalam Doctrine

Being a Steel Minister Mohan Kumaramangalam should not have been concerned about the appointment of Chief Justice of India (CJI) but, clearly he had a major say in the decision on the subject. As a result, effectively, he became the main spokesman of the government and was in the forefront in the interventions in Parliament. Intervening in a five-hour inconclusive debate in Parliament, Kumaramangalam contended that seniority should not be considered as the only criterion for appointments to the judiciary, and further stated that there was no constitutional requirement that the Chief Justice should be consulted in the appointment of his successor. Kumaramangalam said that the Supreme Court had looked at matters like bank nationalisation and privy purses from a different angle than the government, and this had introduced an element of uncertainty in the working of the

Constitution. Since decisions on major economic issues had been struck down by the Supreme Court, the government had thought it fit to end this uncertainty and bring about a more stable relationship between the government and the judiciary.

Kumaramangalam was blunt and he did not mince words when he said, "When we try to think *what consideration should move us in appointing a person to the high and exalted office of the Chief Justice of India, I think, we have to take into consideration – and we should not run away from that fact – his basic outlook, his attitude to life, his politics – not the party to which he belongs but what it is that makes the man – through which spectacles he looks at the problems of India.... We do want judges who are able to understand what is happening in our country; the wind of change that is blowing across our country; who is able to recognise that Parliament is sovereign.* Concluding his long speech, Kumaramangalam summarised his views by saying: **Firstly**, it is not an essential pre-condition ... that the Chief Justice must be appointed on the basis of seniority.... **Secondly**, it is not an essential pre-condition ... that a judge prior to appointment should be innocent of political views or convictions.... **Thirdly**, some knowledge of public affairs, of the larger things that move the minds and passions of millions, is an important qualification for appointment.... **Fourthly**, it is entirely within the discretion of the government of the day to appoint the person considered in its eyes as the most suitable, as having the most suitable philosophy or outlook, to occupy the highest judicial office in the country. **Fifthly**, the most important feature of the functioning of a court is its certainty and stability in relation to the major and vital questions of law. (Nayar, 1973: 79-81, 85, 91) Can there be any doubt about the kind of judiciary which Indira Gandhi wanted? Whether you call it committed or not, it would have to conform to the views and philosophy of the ruling party!

A.R. Antulay, a prominent Congressman, was a strong supporter of the supersession of the judges and had flippantly argued,

> As understood in the context of the Supreme Court, seniority is purely accidental.... Is the common man interested in this *game of musical chairs*? Should this chair be occupied by one who at the given point of time happens to be seniormost?... Why are these eminent persons so much exercised over this *trivial matter*?... *These ex-Chief Justices should feel flattered that the government found them suitable in spite of their decisions against the government.* (Antulay, 1973: vii-ix, 57)

Palkhivala ridiculed the idea of committed judiciary and said a 'committed judge' was a contradiction in terms. "It is like boiling ice cream. Either a man is committed or he is a judge in the true sense of the term. He cannot be both." (Kamath, 2007: 329)

Reign over Judges

On 18 March 1981, Law Minister Shiv Shankar, issued a circular letter to State Chief Ministers in which he had requested them: (a) to obtain from all the additional judges of the High Court in the State their consent to be appointed as permanent judges in any other High Court in the country, and (b) to obtain similar consent from those persons who had been, or in the future are to be, proposed for appointment as judges. The written consent of the additional judges and the proposed appointees had to be sent to the Union Law Minister within a fortnight of the receipt of the letter. The High Court judges were thus sought to be treated like transferable government servants.

It was shocking to see that additional High Court judges who had shown courage in deciding cases against the government were reverted from High Court to lower judiciary, or not confirmed as High Court judges or transferred to another High Court. This led to petitions by the members of the bar to the Supreme Court for intervention against such arbitrary actions. The successive decisions in the *Judges case,* over a period of years, resulted in the Supreme Court asserting its independence in matters pertaining to the appointments and transfers of High Court judges and appointments of Supreme Court judges. The Constitution would not have been rewritten in this manner if Indira Gandhi government had not been so excessively high-handed and over-bearing in dealing with the higher judiciary.

In sharp contrast, when the Janata government under Morarji Desai came to power, it appointed, Justice Y.V. Chandrachud, who had upheld the draconian law suspending fundamental rights during the Emergency in the notorious *Habeas Corpus* case[1], as the next Chief Justice of India when Justice Beg retired in July 1978.

Reference must be made in this context to what Justice P. Jaganmohan Reddy, who sat on the full bench of the Supreme Court on *Kesavananda Bharati* case, has written in his book *The Judiciary I Served*:

> Once or twice, the Attorney General [Niren De], who was most arrogant and rude, suggested, though not in so many

1 On 28 April 1976, the Supreme Court, by a majority decision of 4:1, overruled the decisions of nine High Courts and held that no person has any locus to move any writ petition under Article 226 before a High Court to challenge the legality of an order of detention. The lone dissenting judge was Justice H.R. Khanna who paid the price by being superseded for the post of Chief Justice. The four judges who gave the decision in favour of government were Chief Justice A.N. Ray, and Justices M.H. Beg, Y.V. Chandrachud and P.N. Bhagawati. After retirement, Justice Chandrachud publicly apologised for his stand in the case.

> words, that the court's future was at stake. He said at one stage that the consequences have to be borne if the decision went against the government. This, I felt, was an attempt to browbeat us. The impression that one gathered during the argument can never be conveyed by the words used because of the manner of saying it, the tone adopted, the emphasis placed and the menacing nature of the insinuations hurled at the bench. Some of the senior judges reacted by conveying their displeasure...." (Kamath, 2007: 182)

Surely, the Attorney General was not conveying his own feelings. The government must have wanted him to give the message to the court.

Justice Reddy has written:

> Ever since the bank nationalisation judgment and the judgment in the Princes' [privy purses] case, Indira Gandhi had on the advice of the famous triumvirate H.R. Gokhale, Law Minister, Siddhartha Shankar Ray, Chief Minister of Bengal, and Mohan Kumaramangalam, Minister for Steel, begun to choose judges likely to support her and her government. Subimal [Chander Roy][2] was invited to meet the triumvirate, followed by dinner at Gokhale's place, when Sikri, Chief Justice, was also invited. When Subimal went back to Calcutta the next day, his wife asked him, "Well, has the bridegroom been approved?..." (Reddy, 1991: 219)

Justice Reddy has also written in the above book that:

> [Justice S.N.] Dwivedi's daughter was married to the son of Bahuguna, Central Minister for Communication. His

2 He was the nephew of S.S. Ray, who had suggested his name. He was the second person, after Sikri, to be appointed from the Bar.

> appointment was insisted upon by the government as a political manoeuvre. Chief Justice Sikri told me a few days after he retired that he had opposed Dwivedi's appointment because he was at one time said to be a card-carrying member of the Communist Party, that he was a comparatively junior judge in the Allahabad High Court and had not made any mark. (Kamath, 2007: 184-185)

Reference may be made to a letter written by Chief Justice Sikri to Prime Minister on 3 December 1971 protesting about the severe criticism made by some of her senior Cabinet colleagues regarding the Supreme Court and its judgments. In her reply dated 18 December 1971, she gave an impression as if there was nothing objectionable in it: "Our country is going through profound social, political and economic transformation ... there are bound to be moments of conflict between Parliament and judiciary or judiciary and the executive. These are inherent in any living and evolving society." Justice Reddy has said, the readers may decide "whether subsequent actions were in conformity or otherwise with the protestations conveyed by the letter." (Reddy, 1991: 220-222)

Judge O.N. Vohra, who tried the *Kissa Kursi Ka* (KKK) case and convicted Sanjay and [V.C.] Shukla, was not spared. After the trial of the case, he, in his own right, had become an additional judge of the Delhi High Court. When his turn for appointment as permanent judge came, he was unceremoniously dropped by Indira Gandhi government. As stated earlier, in the case filed by another judge, Kumar, in the Supreme Court, it came to light from official records that the Law Minister had gone through the judgment in the KKK case while dealing with Justice Vohra's case. (Singh, 1996: 104)

B.N. Tandon, in his book *PMO Diary*, has cited a number of instances where appointments in higher judiciary were made by Indira Gandhi in an arbitrary manner and against the recommendation of the Chief Justice of India. Against this background, it is not surprising that the Supreme Court has rewritten the Constitution by taking to itself all powers of selection of judges for the High Courts and the Supreme Court, as also their promotions and transfers. One would only ask for a little more transparency in all these decisions.

COMMITTED BUREAUCRACY

At its independence, India consciously adopted the pattern of British civil service which would be apolitical and free to give fearless and objective advice to the political executive. It was expected that the civil service would have commitment to the rule of law and the precepts laid down by the Constitution. In his speeches in the Constituent Assembly, Vallabhbhai Patel had made this abundantly clear. Though several provincial governments were opposed to this concept, Patel prevailed on the Constituent Assembly to accept this far-reaching principle. India was the only developing country at the time which had accepted common All India Services – Indian Administrative Service (IAS) and the Indian Police Service (IPS) – for the Central Government and the provinces. The pattern of civil service adopted by India has been recognised as one of the strengths of Indian democracy, in spite of serious erosion of its values and weakened structure due to political in-roads.

The Commission on Centre-State Relations (Sarkaria Commission)[3] had emphasised that one of the objectives of setting up of All India Services was to ensure that political considerations either in recruitment or in discipline and control are reduced to the minimum, if not eliminated altogether. The Commission had recommended that "The All India Services are as much necessary today as they were

---

3 Comprising Justice R.S. Sarkaria as Chairman and B. Sivraman and S.R. Sen as members.

when the Constitution was framed and continue to be one of the premier institutions for maintaining the unity of the country." (GoI, 1988: 228-229) The concept of a 'committed bureaucracy' needs to be examined in this context.

C.D. Deshmukh, former ICS officer, Governor RBI and Union Finance Minister has, in his memoirs, *The Course of My Life*, bluntly stated, "the latest cult of committed civil servant is the result of complete misunderstanding of the legitimate duty of a bureaucrat…. The less committed he is, the more competent he is likely to prove." (Deshmukh, 1974: 104)

The greatest harm to the civil services was undoubtedly caused by Indira Gandhi with her concept of committed civil services. V. Subramaniam, a former civil servant and later Indira Congress minister in Maharashtra, has written:

> Her assumption of leadership happened after a strong undercurrent of national frustration developed after the 1962 border debacle, along with dissatisfaction with the then manipulative Congress syndicate leadership and her own perception of threats from all sides, including colleagues. The result was that she wanted total personal loyalty from her immediate political and bureaucratic colleagues and 'commitment' from the civil service. Her visible success in controlling the kitchen Cabinet, her thumping success in creating Bangladesh and her return to power, after Janata interlude, more or less established the 'legitimacy' of this *idea of 'commitment' as against 'neutrality'*. There is nothing in law or in civil service regulations on commitment and Desai as Prime Minister condemned it but the idea has stayed on…. *The civil service neutrality is at best indefinable now or at worst non-existent*. (Chaturvedi, 1997: 271)

In my essay titled "Bureaucracy at Cross-Roads", written for the above special issue in 1997, I had underlined the continuous down-hill journey of India's bureaucracy since independence.

> In any dispensation which was in power, questions have been raised about the imperviousness, wooden-headedness, obstructiveness, rigidity, and rule-and-procedure bound attitude of the bureaucracy.... Indian bureaucracy is perceived as incapable of giving its best in any situation in which it is asked to function.... *The watershed in this process has undeniably been the regime of Indira Gandhi*.... She made no secret of her contempt for the civil services and took every opportunity to run them down. *The concept of 'committed' services did a permanent damage to the fabric of the services. The ambitious and up-worldly mobile civil servants quickly took the hint. A new breed of civil servants was born who were prepared to crawl when asked to bend and prepared to do the bidding of the political masters, often anticipating their wishes.* The Prime Minister's 'household' and her private office started exerting considerable influence in the postings and transfers of officers.... It is often forgotten that good governance is basic to any other reform.... Everything else can be purchased for a price but not people-friendly, socially conscious and clean administration deeply committed not to any political ideology but to the basic values of rule of law, respect for secularism, human rights and the welfare of the weaker sections of society. This is the charter for the civil services. (Chaturvedi, 1997: 560-561, 566)

Marina R. Pinto, in her essay titled "Civil Service Neutrality in India – The Career of a Concept", written for the above volume, has stated:

> Civil service neutrality was blamed for non-performance and inability of government to deliver the goods. *Neutral bureaucrats were viewed as 'stumbling blocks' on the road to progress and development.* They had to be 'committed' to the ruling party's ideology, policies and programmes.... Indira Gandhi voiced this sentiment and Congress leader Jagjivan

> Ram was of the opinion that 'the theory of a neutral bureaucracy is hardly relevant to Indian conditions.' Commitment that was sought meant politicization of a high order.... India soon evolved her own special brand of the 'Yes Minister' or 'service politicians' syndrome.... *The unmistakable message was that to survive, one must be compliant and supplicant and hardly ever defiant.* (Chaturvedi, 1997: 604-605, 610)

While there is no authentic record of who advised Indira Gandhi to adopt such a perilous course for the governance of the country, it is believed that her Principal Secretary P.N. Haksar was largely responsible for it. H.Y. Sharada Prasad, Information Advisor to Prime Minister for a long time, was an admirer of Haksar. He has written:

> Haksar is not a 'regular recruit' and so an outsider. Again he does not share their [Administrative Services'] neutrality in regard to the purposes of the State. He is a Nehruite whereas most officials are Patelites. This is what explains the outcry that broke out when Haksar spoke of commitment on the part of officialdom. It was interpreted as an apologia for a bureaucracy suborned and subservient to the party. (Sarkar, 1989: 185)

It is difficult to agree with Sharada Prasad's position. Haksar had no background or experience of Indian administration and was least qualified to advise on such a critical subject. But, Indira Gandhi became a strong advocate of the concept.[4] Over the years, all political parties found it a convenient tool to wield

4 The results of committed bureaucracy are brought out by the following: the day after the declaration of Emergency, Prime Minister expounded to a meeting of some thirty top officials (Secretaries to government) her reasons for imposing Emergency. Her request for questions elicited one. Otherwise, there was pin-drop silence.... More were frightened by penalties expected from dissent. (Austin, 1999: 307, footnote 33)

the instruments of power. As a result, one now sees senior civil servants strongly aligned to the political ideology of the ruling party and swearing personal loyalty to one political leader or the other. This half-way house between the British and American style of management of civil services has become the bane of the system. To this highly complex phenomenon is added the innovation of lateral entrants in the civil services who have a firm commitment to the political party whose government is instrumental for their induction in the civil services. Political parties can never be expected to take any corrective actions in these matters as it would be a self-goal. Though over the years, the Supreme Court has dealt with a number of issues raised before it by way of public interest litigation, in spite of repeated efforts, the court has been reluctant to address the issues which pertain to the very survival of civil services. For example, the public interest litigation filed by me in the Supreme Court in 2004 was not even admitted by the court. (Godbole, 2004: 14-16)

The conduct of civil services during the Emergency is fully documented by the Shah Commission. Rule of law was given total burial. The entire bureaucracy became totally subservient not only to Indira Gandhi, but also to the PMO presided over by Sanjay Gandhi, her henchmen, kitchen Cabinet and her minions. Shah Commission has brought out only a few of the cases of gross abuse of power. In reality, the misuse of power was much more rampant. After coming back to power in 1980, since Indira Gandhi took the most unusual step of withdrawing all copies of the report and destroying them, no action was taken against any of the officers who took law into their own hands to implement the orders given by Indira Gandhi, her son Sanjay and her/his minions. As if this was not enough, after returning to power, she blatantly supported these officers by showering favours on them. She also consciously took action against those officers who, during the Janata government, had to take action against her and her son. This is borne out by what Raman has stated:

> *Indira Gandhi's return to power was followed by a witch-hunt* of serving and retired officers of different departments, who were associated with the various investigations against her by the CBI and the various enquiries against her on charges of excesses during the Emergency, conducted by the Justice Shah Commission and the L.P. Singh Committee. The IB played an objectionable role in helping her and her aides from her party *to identify and prepare a black list of serving officers involved in these investigations and enquiries. Her first few months in office were spent in settling scores with those whom she thought had betrayed her when she was out of power*.... While Suntook [a senior officer in R&AW] himself escaped any negative consequences to himself with the support of Kao, neither he nor Kao could protect four senior IPS officers of the R&AW ... from being humiliated by her. On the basis of unsubstantiated tales carried to her and her aides that these officers had played a very active role in the investigations and enquiries against her, she had them thrown out of the organization and ordered their reversion back to their respective States. (Raman, 2007: 72)

The fear of the unknown which prevailed in the civil services during Indira Gandhi regime and its disastrous consequences for the rule of law can be seen from the shocking manner in which the case pertaining to the alleged burial of money and documents by Indira Gandhi in her farm house on the out-skirts of Delhi was handled by the top civil servants. Even at this length of time, Arun Shourie needs to be complimented for authentically documenting the happenings on a day to day basis. (Annexure 3) In view of the importance of the case and its long term implications for the future of the civil service, I have fully reproduced the article published by Shourie in *The Indian Express* in 1979. What is important is that at least four persons who were directly involved in it – Cabinet Secretary Nirmal Mukerjee, Home Secretary T.C.A. Srinivasavaradan, Director CBI C.V. Narasimhan, and Joint Director of Intelligence Bureau V. Nagarkar – were persons of highest integrity and unblemished record. Nagarkar was apparently pressing for expeditious action to raid the farm house but the others dithered for months together. Even Prime Minister Morarji Desai asking explanation of Home Secretary for inexcusable laxity shown in the case did not have any effect. This is simply shocking. The only reason I can think of is the mortal fear these officers must have had of Indira Gandhi coming back to power and going after them and their families, as had happened in several cases during the Emergency. And their fears turned out to be true. Zail Singh, who was Home Minister in 1980, has written in his memoirs that T.C.A. Srinivasavaradan, though very competent, was shifted from Home Ministry as he was responsible for taking "stern measures" against her when Janata government was in power. (Zail Singh, 1997: 147) The travails of N.K. Singh, and some others, narrated hereafter, bring out how justified were these fears.

N.K. Singh, an upright Indian police service officer known for his integrity, had the 'misfortune' to work in CBI and to investigate jeeps purchase and *Kissa Kursi Ka (KKK)* cases in which Indira Gandhi and Sanjay Gandhi, respectively, were involved.[5] Singh has described in his book *The Plain Truth:*

5 Raj Thaper has written about her impressions after watching this film: The men and women on the screen were dressed in strange costumes but there was something about the dialogue that caught and captured us that evening, and our groans gradually became silent as the story unfolded, and by the time it ended we were strapped to our seats with an unknowing fear, an extension, a heightening of my own personal mood. It was, I thought, our first political film, but a horror film, somehow laying bear the political

(*Contd.*)

Memoirs of a CBI Officer (1996), how he was harassed, even to the extent of being arrested by the Haryana police on charges of conspiracy and wrongful confinement of a witness in the *KKK* case. It was reported in *The Indian Express* that on May 26, 1977, the nephew of Ram Chandra, the Maruti company driver, went to Gurgaon police station accompanied by Sanjay Gandhi and filed a complaint that he feared his uncle had been abducted from Gurgaon by two CBI inspectors at the behest of Singh. Ram Chandra was a prosecution witness in the KKK case. (pp 313-315) Singh was given death threats. (p 312) On the first day of the hearing of the appeal in the Supreme Court in the KKK case, "Bhandari, son-in-law of the Law Minister of Emergency days Gokhale, whose wife was advocate on record of Sanjay Gandhi, came to me and while wishing a happy new year, *also wished a 'safe year' for me*. I was a bit startled but kept quiet." (p 117) His teen-age son, who was not only talented and good in studies but was a good sportsman and a debater and had even qualified for the IIT [Indian Institute of Technology] test, met with a motor accident on 13 May 1978 while trying to cross the road to catch a bus for coming home. *He was knocked down by a very fast-moving jeep coming from the right side. After the accident, the jeep had sped away,* leaving him on the road. "*Because of the background and certain past incidents, there were many who were highly suspicious. Quite a few made no secret of it and were somewhat vocal*". In spite of the best possible treatment, he died in the ICU of Safdarjung Hospital. "*The government that day faced a stormy Parliament when the members from the ruling [Janata] party in particular gave expression*

---

state of the nation and pointing definitely to sure disaster. We did not know then that we would be the only people who would ever get to see 'Kissa Kursi Ka' with its grotesque images all true to life at the time. We literally tottered home and I couldn't sleep that night because we hadn't as yet nailed down why it had us so affected. (Thapar, 1991: 394) *to their apprehension and wanted the government to unearth the whole truth.* The Prime Minister [Morarji Desai] personally assured the House that everything possible to save the life of the boy had been done and all possible efforts were being made to nab the culprit." (pp 90-94) As was to be expected, the driver of the jeep or the real culprit were never found! And finally, Singh was repatriated to Orissa and 'put on the shelf' by giving him the inconsequential post of Deputy Inspector General, Orissa Police Computer Centre. A loud and clear message was sent to all officers what to expect if their commitment was to the Constitution and the rule of law, and not to the party in power and its supreme leader and her household.

All I can say is that if this could happen to some of the best known officers of the so-called "steel frame of the country", what remains of the steel frame now is hardly anything to be proud of. As I can see, this legacy of Indira Gandhi will not be erased any time in the future and may eventually lead to abolition of the British pattern of civil service in India, which has now remained only in name.

Reference must be made to the shocking case of withdrawal of ₹ 60 lakh by Rustam Sohrab Nagarwala from the State Bank of India, Parliament Street Branch, Delhi, by impersonating that he was speaking from the Prime Minister's house. Intervening in a debate in the Lok Sabha, and replying to a sarcastic question by Piloo Mody, Finance Minister Y.B. Chavan said, "I entirely agree that it is fantastic and unbelievable that an officer of long standing, with more than twenty years of experience, should act in such a stupid manner. If I may say so, it was something more than that. But I do not want to express an opinion at this stage." Madhu Limaye has written: "The mystery of the Nagarwala case could not be cleared up even by the Reddy Commission. Further, *Justice Reddy was not able to solve the riddle of the death of Assistant Superintendent of Police Kashyap,* who had been put in charge of the Nagarwala investigation *nor of Nagarwala's own death in jail after his conviction [prior to the day on which he was to make some public revelations]*.... The police investigation of the case, as the Commission itself confessed, had only deepened the enigma wrapped up in the heart of a mystery." (Limaye, 1994: 505) No one was prepared to believe the government or police version that it was a case of impersonation and cheating. People believed that the head cashier had dealings with the Prime Minister's house and was trying to hide something. In both Houses of Parliament, fears were expressed that the government was trying to shield Ved Prakash Malhotra [chief cashier] and to hush up the case. These doubts have persisted over the years. Inder Malhotra describes the Nagarwala case as "bizarre". Khushwant Singh underlined [in his article "Nagarwala in Fiction", in *Sunday*, 5-11 May 1991, p 19] that, "*Nagarwala was arrested the same evening [when the episode happened]. He confessed to his 'crime'. In the record time of three days, he was tried, convicted and sentenced to four years in jail. He died in March the following year. Six months later, the police officer who had investigated the Nagarwala case was run over by a police car and killed.* (Godbole, 1996: 86)

As I have mentioned in my memoirs, *Unfinished Innings – Recollections and Reflections of a Civil Servant,* it was widely known that Indira Gandhi had dossiers compiled on various State and Central ministers. One day Y.B. Chavan[6] [with

6 Chavan with his solid political base, extensive grass-root support, a clean image and sophistication was highly regarded nationally and internationally as an eventual candidate for Prime Ministership. Wellef Hangen in his book *After Nehru Who?* had this to say about Chavan: "Chavan has a more balanced combination of political attributes than any other Indian leader I have met except Nehru. All things being equal – which they rarely are in politics – I think Chavan has better chance than any other politician now in the running to become durable distinguished Prime Minister of India." (Quoted in *The Week*, 7 July 1991)

whom I worked as Private Secretary during the time] came to know from very reliable sources that a dossier was kept on him as well and that a close watch was also being kept on his activities.[7] He was upset and angry. I had never seen him so upset at any other time. He felt it was wrong to treat one's colleagues in this manner. He finally decided to go and confront Indira Gandhi about this personally. I tried to dissuade him from doing so but he was firm. This was when he had moved over to the Finance Ministry. He asked the Prime Minister if this was true. She denied all knowledge of it and said she had not given any such instructions to anyone. When Yeshwantrao looked unconvinced, she swore in the name of Sanjay and Rajiv and said this was not true. After Yeshwantrao came back, I was anxious to know what had transpired as this could have led to a total break in their already fragile relationship. He told me what had happened, but he did not believe that she was telling the truth. (Godbole, 1996: 91)

Misuse of Intelligence Bureau is seen from the shocking disclosure made by B.K. Nehru, for the period when he was Governor J&K and dismissal of Farooq Abdullah was being pursued by PMO.

> For arranging defections of MLAs, the funds were provided by my friend Tirth Ram Amla, a staunch and tried Congress worker, and were supplied to him in cash from the Congress party money in Delhi, ***transported** in the mail pouches of the Intelligence Bureau. The use of official machinery for party purposes had by then become so commonplace that it did not call for any eyebrows to be even slightly raised.* (Nehru, 1997: 627)

It is important to take note of another development. All senior appointments in Central Government and public sector

---

7 Shah Commission had commented on how watch was being kept by IB on Jagjivan Ram, Minister for Defence.

undertakings have to be approved by the Appointments Committee of Cabinet (ACC). As I had written in my memoirs, during Indira Gandhi's regime, the ACC consisted of the Prime Minister, Home Minister and minister of the concerned ministry. Chavan continued to be the member of the ACC even after he moved to finance, replacing the Home Minister. There were a number of cases in which he was overruled by the Prime Minister. This had rarely happened earlier. As a result, he was so exasperated that on some ACC files, very uncharacteristically, he recorded strongly worded notes. Later, he stopped taking interest in ACC matters. This suited the PMO for they now had an ACC with only the Prime Minister as an effective member. (Godbole, 1996: 93)

Misuse of Bureaucracy – Observations of Shah Commission

The Shah Commission Report is a case study of the perils of committed bureaucracy. The Commission, in its interim report II has, inter alia, stated:

- With the Press gagged and a resultant blackout of authentic information … effective dissent was smothered…. Desire for self-preservation as admitted by a number of public servants at various levels became the sole motivation for their official actions and behaviour. Anxiety to survive at any cost formed the key-note of approach of the problems that came before many of them. The fear generated by the mere threat of and without even the actual use of the weapon of detention under MISA became so pervasive that *the general run of public servants acted as willing tools of tyranny.*
- *A calculated effort was made to place persons in vital positions who were willing to further the interests of the centre of power in gross violation of the established administrative norms and practices.*

- In the final analysis, this country will be governed well or ill by the competence and character of the government officers. If they are content to be mere tools and willing to lend themselves to questionable objectives, there will never be a dearth of unscrupulous operators. There is no substitute for a vigilant, enquiring and enlightened public opinion which keeps a close watch on the doings of the public servants.

The Shah Commission, in its final report, has made some important observations:

- A large number of officers – District Magistrates and Commissioners of Police, who exercised the powers of District Magistrates ex-officio, obediently carried out the instructions emanating from politicians and administrative heads issued on personal or political considerations.
- *The political system that our Constitution has given to our country is such that it contemplates parties with different ideologies administering the affairs of the Centre and State Governments.* It is necessary in the interest of the territorial, political and economic integrity of the nation to ensure that the factors which contribute to such integrity are for ever and continuously strengthened and not impaired ... it appears that unscrupulous and over-ambitious officers were prepared to curry favour with the seats of power and position by doing what they thought the people in authority desired.
- *Unless the services work for and establish a reputation of political neutrality, the citizens will have no confidence in the impartiality and fairness of the services.*

The Shah Commission also took the trouble to peruse the findings of several Commissions of Inquiry appointed by the

State Governments and the Centre earlier. The Commission came to the conclusion that hardly any effective action had been taken to address the maladies identified by several Commissions. (Godbole, 2014: 70-72) Unfortunately since the Shah Commission Report was withdrawn and destroyed by the government after Indira Gandhi came to power in 1980, these issues did not receive any public attention. This was precisely what she wanted!

MISUSE OF ARTICLE 356

Several members of the Constituent Assembly had serious reservations about making a provision for imposition of the President's Rule in the provinces (as the States were known then). In fact, the provision was an exact copy of the provision for Governor's Rule – Section 93 of Government of India Act, 1935, – which the Congress party had severely criticised during the freedom struggle. B.R. Ambedkar, Law Minister and Chairman of the Drafting Committee, pleaded with members saying: "If at all they [Emergency provisions] are brought into operation, I hope the President, who is endowed with these powers, will take proper precautions before actually suspending the administration of these provinces. I hope the first thing he would do is to issue a warning to the province that had erred, that the things are not happening in the way in which they were intended to happen in the Constitution. If that warning fails, the second thing for him to do will be to order an election allowing the people of the province to settle matters by themselves. It is only when these two remedies fail that he would resort to this article." (Pandya, 2001: 791, footnote 1) Like in the case of the ruling of the Supreme Court in respect of the office of Governor, discussed later in this chapter, the hopes expressed by Ambedkar had remained on paper. As seen from the following discussion, Article 356 was being grossly misused.

Indira Gandhi had the distinction of dismissing maximum number of State Governments during her term as Prime Minister. Since she did not believe in inner party democracy, selection of Chief Ministers and their removal was her feudal prerogative. Chief Ministers were literally at her beck and call.

Coomi Kapoor has written how the dismissal of Karunanidhi government in Tamil Nadu was stage-managed by Indira Gandhi, and Governor K.K. Shah was made to sign on the report drafted in Delhi recommending imposition of President's Rule in the State. (Kapoor, 2015: 261)

When Indira Gandhi came back to power in 1980, she dismissed nine State Governments, just as the Janata government had done in 1977. Unfortunately, the Supreme Court had upheld the arbitrary action of the Central Government in 1977, which was yet another self-inflicted wound by the Supreme Court which undermined the public respect for it. Zail Singh has written: "I told Mrs Gandhi that personally I was not in favour of dissolving the non-Congress(I) State Assemblies.... In the emergency meeting of the Cabinet on 17 February 1980, it was decided to recommend the dissolution of nine State Assemblies.... The Secretary in the Home Ministry, T.C.A. Srinivasa Raghavan (sic) used almost the same wording in the note, as was done at the time of the Janata regime taking similar action. (Zail Singh, 1997: 150) Accordingly Zail Singh moved a resolution in the Lok Sabha on 25 March 1980 for approval to the proclamation of President's rule in Bihar, Gujarat, Madhya Pradesh, Maharashtra, Orissa, Punjab, Rajasthan, Tamil Nadu and Uttar Pradesh. It was argued by the Central Government that the ruling parties in various States had only a small portion of votes cast: Bihar 23.5 per cent, Gujarat 36.85 per cent, Madhya Pradesh 31 per cent, Maharashtra 32 per cent, Orissa 19 per cent, and Punjab 23 per cent. (Kashyap, 1998: 57-58) Haryana was spared only because Bhajan Lal, the then Chief Minister, walked over with all 38 MLAs of the Janata Party to Congress(I).

Indira Gandhi had taken an intense dislike for N.T. Rama Rao (NTR), Chief Minister of Andhra Pradesh (AP), who had taken an initiative to bring all non-Congress Chief Ministers under one forum. Indira Gandhi was upset when NTR raised in the National Development Council (NDC) the issue of dismissal of Farooq Abdullah as Chief Minister of J&K. This led to the walk-out of the non-Congress Chief Ministers from the Council.

After a few months, Ram Lal, Governor of AP, peremptorily sacked NTR and installed N. Bhaskar Rao as Chief Minister. But, soon it was found that he did not have the support and NTR had to be reinstalled as Chief Minister. Indira Gandhi disclaimed all knowledge of it. No one believed her. But later, P.C. Alexander confirmed her contention. It transpired that Arun Nehru, Minister of State in the Home Ministry, had telephoned to Ram Lal to do the dirty trick.

Farooq Abdullah, who had succeeded his father Sheikh Abdullah as Chief Minister, had fallen foul with Indira Gandhi as he was considered close to NTR and the non-Congress Chief Ministers conclave. Indira Gandhi had made up her mind to remove him from the post. Tavleen Singh, in her book, *Kashmir – A Tragedy of Errors*, has written about how Farooq Abdullah reacted angrily when she asked him to respond to charges that his election had been rigged and unfair. 'My God, Mrs Gandhi's elections have been more unfair than what they consider my elections to be. What about Assam? Do they call those fair? Just because they won there it is fair and just because Farooq Abdullah won here by fair means it becomes unfair.[8] It is unfair because Congress did not win.' Even more

8 The illegitimacy of elections in Assam, in the midst of widespread violence, has been briefly discussed in chapter 8.

ominously, he suggested in the interview that *if there was to be a repoll then it should be held under the supervision of the United Nations as he could no longer trust the Election Commission. 'I have no faith in the Election Commission of India as it stands today because of the way they conducted themselves here....'* The writing was on the wall. Even a political novice should have been able to see what was likely to happen in Kashmir if Farooq was toppled.... *This was the time before Operation Blue Star when she believed that she could play with fire without getting burned.* (Tavleen Singh, 1996: 44, 48)

Dulat, who was closely associated with the Kashmir imbroglio, has asked a question: "What if Farooq Abdullah had not been dismissed in 1984 at the behest of Prime Minister Indira Gandhi? It was a terrible mistake, and the only reason Jagmohan came to J&K as Governor was to dismiss Farooq.... Farooq's dismissal suddenly woke up Kashmiri regional sentiment. A Kashmiri think-tank came together with an idea from the *Aftab* editor-in-chief, Khwaja Sanalluah Bhat, that the Kashmiris had to get together to resist the Delhi onslaught. That they had to build a counter to it. (Dulat, 2015: 314)

As brought out later, two different versions of the events leading to Farooq Abdullah's dismissal, are given by the two successive Governors of J&K, B.K. Nehru and Jagmohan.

Austin has rightly commented that the established pattern of 'federal' relationships ... were increasingly centralised.... Mrs Gandhi's election victories of 1971 and 1972 and her skills at manoeuvre concentrated in her hands authority in the Congress, in the Central Government, and the Centre-State relations.... Even Chief Ministers were appointed by the Centre. No one with a mass base was allowed to come up. The States have become virtually the *Zamindaris* of the Centre, and the Centre too has become the hand-maid of the Prime Minister.... As a Congress General Secretary of the time, A.R.

Antulay, put it, 'the Chief Ministers became *subedars* of the Centre, whether they were members of the Congress or opposition parties. While she ruled largely outside the Constitution, altering the text of the Constitution's Centre-State relations provisions proved to be another matter.' President's rule was proclaimed 22 times during the years 1967-73. Four instances involved non-Congress State Governments. Several other instances involved States in which the Congress was part of coalition governments ... Mrs Gandhi's return to office in 1980 ... saw relations between the Centre and the State Governments at their most tormented since independence – a condition that would endure into the 1990s. In general, her policies worsened instead of calming the difficult situations in Punjab, Kashmir, and the north-east. (Austin, 1999: 568-571)

It is important to note that there seems to be an unholy alliance between the Congress and the Opposition parties on the use of Article 356. This was evident from the imposition of President's Rule in Tamil Nadu in January 1991 by the then Chandra Shekhar government, when even Governor S.S. Barnala had resigned in protest. The Forty-second Amendment of the Constitution had extended the maximum length for a period of President's Rule from six months to twelve months and provided that any law made during the period would remain in force until repealed. Previously, such laws would expire automatically one year after the period of President's Rule had ended. The Forty-fourth Amendment restored the six month period, but the Janata government left the rest of the earlier amendment intact.

The recommendation of the Commission on Centre-State Relations (Sarkaria Commission) that Article 356 be "used very sparingly, in extreme cases, as a measure of last resort, when all available alternatives fail to prevent or rectify a breakdown of constitutional machinery in the State", made in 1988, has fallen on deaf ears. (GoI, 1988: 179) If the Supreme Court had not intervened so unambiguously, the article would have continued to be misused, whichever political party was in power.

Fortunately, the Supreme Court has put a stop to the gross misuse of this article by its judgment in *Bommai* case[9] in which a question was raised whether the validity of the proclamation issued under Article 356 could be challenged even after it was approved by Parliament. Earlier, in the *State of Rajasthan* case, the court had held that if the satisfaction [of the President] was malafide or was based on wholly extraneous and irrelevant grounds, the court would have jurisdiction to examine it. The scope of judicial review has been further expanded in *S.R. Bommai* case. The court has held: There is no reason to make a distinction between the proclamation as approved and a legislation enacted by Parliament. If the proclamation is invalid, it does not stand validated merely because it is approved by Parliament. The nine-judge bench has unanimously held the Presidential power under Article 356 to be amenable to judicial review. The court also laid down that the power, though based on subjective satisfaction, is only conditional and not absolute. The President can be satisfied only when a situation as laid down in the article exists. The President was under an obligation to consider the advisability and necessity of the action. This has more or less completely stopped the misuse of this article. In that sense, the Supreme Court has effectively rewritten the Constitution in respect of yet another provision of the Constitution. A clear majority of six judges in the nine member bench has also ruled that the material submitted by the government to the President can be called for and examined by the court. Any claim to privilege will

---

9 S.R. Bommai *vs* Union of India (1994) 3 SCC 1.

also be decided by the court. As Noorani has rightly stated, 'Once the doors to judicial review are thrown open, everything will be exposed to the scrutiny of the courts and the glare of public opinion. No government of India can act as arbitrarily as was the case with governments in the past. (Noorani, 2000: 271) Thus the intentions of the founding fathers of the Constitution have now been restored.

INSTITUTION OF GOVERNOR – DEFILED

There was considerable debate in the Constituent Assembly on whether the institution of Governor was necessary to provide in the Constitution. Several members felt that it was a vestige of the British raj and should have no place in independent India's democratic republic. But, the mindset of the Congress elite was to perpetuate the British institutions and procedures, as has been seen by the incorporation of several important provisions of the Government of India Act, 1935, in the Constitution. Even during the reign of Jawaharlal Nehru, the institution of Governor had become controversial. But, Indira Gandhi brought it into total disrepute.

This was evident from the fact that a motion seeking to discuss and disapprove the role of certain Governors was moved by Nath Pai, one of the most respected, balanced and articulate MPs, during the November-December 1967 winter session. The motion read as follows: "*This House disapproves the action of the Central Government in using the institution of the Governors of States not as instruments for proper functioning of the Constitution but as agent of the party in power at the Centre*, as exemplified by current developments in Bihar and West Bengal." (Kashyap, 1996: 295-296) As is the general end-result in such cases, it was talked out.

There was considerable controversy about the role of Governors in Bihar, Madhya Pradesh, Uttar Pradesh and West

Bengal during 1968-1970. One of the issues was about whom the Governor should call to form a government, if there is no clear majority for any one party or a coalition of parties. An expert committee was formed and its recommendations were discussed in two meetings of leaders of political parties but no consensus could be reached.

L.P. Singh and Govind Narain, former Union Home Secretaries and Governors, have quoted the five-member Constitution Bench decision of the Supreme Court (AIR 1979, SC 709) delivered on 4 May 1979 to underline that Governor was not to function as an agent of the Central Government:

> It is no doubt true that the Governor is appointed by the President which means in effect and substance the Government of India, but that is only a mode of appointment and it does not make the Governor an employee or servant of the Government of India. Every person appointed by the President is not necessarily an employee of the Government of India. So also it is not material that the Governor hold office during the pleasure of the President. It is a constitutional provision for determination of the term of office of the Governor and it does not make the Government of India the employer of the Governor. His office is not subordinate or subservient to the Government of India. He is not amenable to the direction of the Government of India, nor is he accountable to them for the manner in which he carries out his functions and duties. His is an independent constitutional office which is not subject to the control of the Government of India. He is constitutionally the head of the State in whom is vested the executive power of the State and without whose assent there can be no legislation in exercise of the legislative power of the State. (The Governor, 1985: 44, 58)

No other ruling of the Supreme Court has been so far removed from the reality! Dharma Vira, who was Cabinet Secretary and later Governor of West Bengal and Karnataka, has raised a question:

> How do we create an atmosphere in which the Governor can operate independently and with objectivity?… At present, the normal tenure of a Governor is five years, but he holds his office only at the pleasure of the President. The President, however, is guided in all matters by the advice of his ministers. Thus, in actual fact, Governors hold office at the pleasure of the ministry in power at the Centre. Such a situation leaves the Governor completely at the mercy of the Centre, and in most cases this tends to obstruct his independence and objectivity – particularly when quite a few Governors have been appointed as a consequence of political patronage. It is therefore necessary to evolve some system of selecting Governors with great care. The practice of consulting the State Chief Ministers prior to appointing Governors in their respective areas has more or less been reduced to nullity; the practice should immediately be revived. There should also be a greater security of tenure for Governors. The Constitution should ensure that a Governor cannot be removed except through processes which have to be observed in the case of judges of the Supreme Court. (The Governor, 1985: 88)

In a hard-hitting essay titled "A Spoke in the Federal Wheel", E.M.S. Namboodiripad, former Chief Minister of Kerala and a prominent Marxist leader, invited attention to how, in Indira Gandhi's second tenure (particularly in 1984), the occupants of the gubernatorial office in Sikkim and Andhra Pradesh, were active Congressmen sent as Governors to create trouble for the elected ministries, while in the third – J&K – the job was done by a civilian who had earned notoriety for his high-handedness during the Emergency. All of them obviously were persons who would do anything to please their bosses in Delhi. (The Governor, 1985: 97-98)

P. Upendra, a former Central minister and Telugu Desam Party leader, has in his essay titled "The Ramlal Episode: A Breach of Democracy" described how scandalous was the dismissal of N.T. Rama Rao (NTR), as Chief Minister of Andhra Pradesh by Ram Lal, Governor, at the behest of the Central Government:

The N. Bhaskar Rao government installed by Ram Lal had to go in a few days as he did not enjoy the support of his party. *Perhaps, this was the first occasion when legislators were paraded before the President of India.* NTR was reinstalled as the Chief Minister. Governor Ram Lal resigned 'to uphold the dignity of the high office he held'.

Upendra has made a number of suggestions to curtail the powers of the Governor for such arbitrary actions. He has rightly concluded, "whatever the future may hold, it is necessary to avoid more Ram Lals if Indian democracy is to survive." (The Governor, 1985: 106, 130)

The title of the article written by Palkhivala in *The Times of India* on 30 August 1984, "Ram Lal – The Shameless Governor" could not have been more explicit. (Palkhivala, 1994: 56)

The dismissal of four Governors in 1980 was the fourth instance when a government at the Centre decided to curtail the tenure of Governors by withdrawing the President's pleasure. However, it is the first time when a "mass dismissal" of Governors had taken place. In October 1980, Tamil Nadu Governor, Prabhudas Patwari, an appointee of the Janata government, was dismissed by Indira Gandhi. She did not give Patwari, known as a Gandhian in the Raj Bhavan, the option to resign. The dismissal of Patwari without any valid reason was an instance of political abuse of Article 156(1) of the

Constitution, which states that a Governor "shall hold office during the pleasure of the President". Palkhivala has written:

> Personalities apart, the dismissal of Patwari raises two crucial issues. It was constitutionally unauthorized, and *the manner of dismissal was not only uncivil but uncivilized*.... Governor Patwari was dismissed at a late hour Sunday evening and the next incumbent was sworn in within an hour.... Even a subordinate deserves to be treated with more courtesy. (Palkhivala, 1994: 61)

In August 1981, Rajasthan Governor Raghukul Tilak was removed from office under similar circumstances. Tilak challenged his dismissal in the Rajasthan High Court. The High Court rejected his petition, saying the pleasure of the President was not justiciable.

Equally sordid was the story of dismissal of Farooq Abdullah at the insistence of Indira Gandhi in 1984. As mentioned earlier, Tavleen Singh, a seasoned journalist, in her essay titled "A Tale of Two Governors" has brought out the full details of the events leading to Abdullah's ouster. Abdullah later wrote in his book *My Dismissal*, that Jagmohan was appointed as Governor 'with the sole intention of having a convenient and pliable being, who was to carry out orders from Delhi faithfully'. Tavleen Singh has rightly stated, 'although there can be two views on whether Dr Farooq Abdullah was a competent Chief Minister or not, it is difficult to think of any viewpoint that could condone the manner of his dismissal.' (The Governor, 1985: 131, 143)

Jagmohan, in his book, *My Frozen Turbulence in Kashmir*, has given his own version of the goings on in Kashmir and how the position had become untenable for Farooq Abdullah and why he could not continue as Chief Minister. When Jagmohan called on Prime Minister before taking over as Governor, she said:

> there were strong forces both within and outside the country, which were bent upon 'encircling' India and creating permanent headache for her in Punjab, Kashmir, North-East and Tamil Nadu.... She thought that B.K. Nehru had become rather old[10], and certain forces of destabilisation were taking full advantage of the fact. About Dr Farooq Abdullah, she was both bitter and light-hearted. She talked of his boyish, inconsistent and erratic ways. She thought that he was under the influence of some crafty men and, whenever it suited him, he would whip up communal and parochial emotions and promote 'hate-Centre' feelings. She was particularly worried about his extraordinary friendship with Sikh fundamentalists in Punjab.[11] (Jagmohan, 1991: 267)

Reading the full account of events given by Jagmohan, the reader is left in no doubt that Jagmohan's objective was to remove Farooq Abdullah from Chief Ministership, as soon as possible. But, one is not clear why he was so keen on imposing Governor's rule in the State, without calling a Legislative Assembly session and giving an opportunity to Abdullah to prove his majority. May be this was not the mandate given to him by Indira Gandhi!

There is no end to the antics of Governors who were prepared to do the bidding of the Central Government, setting aside all constitutional proprieties. Sunanda K. Datta-Ray has written a devastating piece titled "Himalayan Caprice" in which he has minced no words when he wrote:

> It was the Governor who attracted universal condemnation by arbitrarily dismissing an elected Chief Minister and trying to prop up a substitute who did not enjoy public or

---

10 If this was Indira Gandhi's feeling, I wonder why he was sent as Governor of Gujarat.

11 This comes as a surprise. I have referred in chapter 2 to the efforts made by Abdullah for an amicable resolution of the Punjab agitation.

> legislative approval. When the gamble failed, [Governor] Taleyarkhan invoked Article 356 rather than admit his blunder or allow MLAs to exercise their constitutional right to choose the majority leader.... As Nar Bahadur Bhandari told *The Indian Express* in 1983, *'The people of Sikkim removed the Chogyal; now they have got a mini-Chogyal'*. (The Governor, 1985: 152-153)

B.K. Nehru, who worked as Governor in three States (J&K, Gujarat and Assam) was very disillusioned by the manner in which the Governors were being treated and how some Governors had played politics. He has stated:

> The fact is that the concept of what a Governor was and what he was supposed to do was in the process of change. Today that change is complete.... The erosion of the original concept commenced fairly early after independence. It started with *Governors being 'transferred' from State to State during their five year term of office, a practice totally alien to the letter and spirit of the Constitution*. The Governor's position now is very clearly that he is not an independent official, that he is under the orders of the Central Government and, more often than not, *he is an agent and an active member of the party in power at the Centre*.... Some Governors had already accepted it. Homi Taleyarkhan, then Governor of Sikkim, proudly announced to me that he had taken action in Sikkim which would ensure that the Congress party would always remain in power in that State. He hoped that I was doing the same in J&K. (Nehru, 1997: 618)

In a sense, with different political parties in power in States, inevitably the role of Governors has become suspect and controversial. Even Governors, who came from civil service, could not remain away from controversy. Thus, Dharma Vira, who had a distinguished career in the civil service and had retired as a Cabinet Secretary, had a difficult time as Governor in West Bengal.[12] Jyoti Basu, who was perhaps the longest serving Chief Minister in that State later, has alleged that Dharm Vira's dissolution of the United Front ministry was "not only unethical but unlawful as well". (Banerjee, 1997: 125)

Against this murky background, the recommendations of the Centre-State Relations Commission (Sarkaria Commission) regarding the criteria for selection of Governor appear to be eminently justified:

(i) He should be eminent in some walk of life.

(ii) He should be a person from outside the State.

(iii) He should be a detached figure and not too intimately connected with the local politics of the State, and

(iv) He should be a person who has not taken too great a part in politics generally and particularly in the recent past. (GoI, 1988: 122)

Unfortunately, none of these recommendations has been acted upon by the government so far. The legacy of Indira Gandhi continues to cast its long shadow. Politically convenient arrangements, which undermine the role and prestige of office, are impossible to get rid off. Though almost all political parties have been in power at the Centre during the three decades since the departure of Indira Gandhi from the scene, the role of Governor continues to be as controversial.

CENTRE-STATE RELATIONS UNDER SEVERE STRAIN

Centre-State relations came under considerable strain in 1968-70 on issues such as non-implementation by State

---

12 The situation has not changed over the years. P Sathasivam, Governor of Kerala, who was former Chief Justice of India, came in for criticism by the CPM government for deleting some references critical to the centre and the BJP from the text of the Governor's address approved by the Cabinet. (*IE*, 24 January 2018, p 10)

Governments of orders banning the strike in Central Government establishments, deployment of Central forces in the States, etc. The Central Reserve Police Force had to be deployed by the Centre in States like Kerala, Assam and West Bengal to guard Central Government establishments as the States were reluctant to oppose the Central Government servants' strike. The Chief Ministers of AP, Kerala and Orissa had expressed general dissatisfaction with the state of Centre-State relations.

The Chief Minister of Kerala wrote a letter in 1969 to the Prime Minister and the Home Minister suggesting the setting up of an Inter-State Council under Article 263 of the Constitution. The constitutional provision envisaged establishment of a council charged with the duty of:

- inquiring into and advising upon disputes which may have arisen between States;
- investigating and discussing subjects in which some or all of the States, or the Union and one or more of the States, have a common interest; or
- making recommendations upon any such subject and, in particular, recommendations for the better co-ordination of policy and action with respect to that subject.

As can be seen, the council was envisaged as an important instrument for strengthening federal structure in the country. But, Indira Gandhi, with her emphasis on centralisation of all authority in herself, did not take any interest. This was in sharp contrast with her father Jawaharlal Nehru who, through his fortnightly letters to Chief Ministers, involved them in evolution of policies on all important matters, not just domestic but also international. During the formative years of India's independence, these letters contributed immensely to strengthening national integration and the feeling of belonging to one nation. National Development Council (NDC) and Chief Ministers conferences were the two other institutions Nehru created and used with advantage. But, Indira Gandhi did not take kindly to any dissent and therefore such forums were frowned upon by her. The Inter-State Council was finally set up only in 1990 by the V.P. Singh government. But, it was practically in disuse for several years since then due to the reluctance of the successive Prime Ministers to take Chief Ministers on board. The NDA government under Narendra Modi has, however, revived the Council by convening its meetings. The successful conclusion of the very complex negotiations with States on evolving and launching the Goods and Services Tax (GST) from July 2017 is a pointer to what can be achieved in co-operative federalism. A number of complex issues involving the need for Constitutional Amendments need to be similarly addressed. But this will call for statesmanship both at the Centre and the States.

Replying to the discussion on the Cossipore firing and the strike in West Bengal, Home Minister Y.B. Chavan had underlined in Lok Sabha on 24 April 1969:

> We do accept the position that in this country it is quite possible – and we see it now as a matter of reality – that there will be State Governments of different complexions and there will be a Central Government of different complexion. This is a reality. We do not want to underestimate things. We have to live with it.... These two Articles [Article 256 pertaining to obligations of States and the Union, and Article 257 regarding control of the Union over States in certain cases] embody the spirit of co-operative federalism ... namely, in what manner State executive power should be employed or exercised. It should be so exercised that the executive power of the Centre is not obstructed.

The situation came to such a stage where the Home Minister Y.B. Chavan, had to say in Lok Sabha on 26 March 1969: "*The time has come, if we want to save this country, that we should have all-party government in the States and a national government at the Centre. We will sooner or later have to do this.*"

There were newspaper reports that the former Speaker of the then Madras Assembly, S.B. Adityan, had been openly demanding the secession of Tamil Nadu from the Union. There were heated discussions in the Lok Sabha on 20 August 1970 regarding the demand of Chief Minister of Tamil Nadu for a separate flag. (Godbole, 1996: 81-83) Forty-seven years later, in 2017, Karnataka has made the same demand. More the things change, more they remain the same!

The Government of Tamil Nadu had appointed, on 22 September 1969, a Committee comprising P.V. Rajamannar as Chairman, and A. Lakshmanswami Mudaliar and P. Chandra Reddy as members, on Centre-State relations. The Committee in its report submitted in 1981 made sweeping recommendations which included, in so far as the subject matter of this book is concerned, the following:

- The Governor should be appointed always in consultation with the State Cabinet. The other alternative will be to make the appointment in consultation with a high power body especially constituted for the purpose. The Governor should be rendered ineligible for a second term of office as Governor or any other office under the government. He should not be liable to removal except for proved misbehaviour or incapacity after inquiry by the Supreme Court.
- A specific provision should be inserted in the Constitution enabling the President to issue instrument of instructions to the Governors.

- The provision in the Constitution laying down that the ministry holds office during the pleasure of the Governor should be deleted.
- It should be made clear that Article 163(1) confers powers on the Governor to exercise discretion only in relation to matters in respect of which the Constitution makes express provision.
- Articles 356 (provision in case of failure of constitutional machinery in State) and 357 (exercise of legislative powers under proclamation issued under Article 356) may be totally omitted. In the alternative, sufficient safeguards should be provided in the Constitution itself to secure the interests of the States against the arbitrary and unilateral action of the ruling party at the Centre. The Committee had suggested specific safeguards for the purpose.
- Article 365 (effect of failure to comply with, or give effect to, directions given by the Union) should be omitted.
- National Emergency: Articles 352 (Proclamation of Emergency), 354 (applications of provisions relating to distribution of revenues while a Proclamation of Emergency is in operation) etc. – These drastic provisions ... should not be put into operation, unless there is war or aggression by a foreign power. The expression 'internal disturbance' occurring in Article 352 should be interpreted to mean that it must be comparable in gravity to the repelling of external aggression.
- Article 353(a): No direction under the article should be issued except after consulting, and with the approval of, the Inter-State Council.
- Article 360 pertaining to Financial Emergency should be omitted.

- All India Services – Recruitment to these services should either be by transfer of members of the existing gazetted services under the control of the States or by direct recruitment or by a combination of both these methods, if need be by holding an examination confined to each State under the supervision of the Union Public Service Commission, if deemed necessary or expedient. Article 312 should be amended to omit the provision for the creation of any new All India Services in future. Preferably, English may be the medium of examination for All India Services, although recruitment may be on a Statewise basis.
- It should be expressly provided in the Constitution itself that the territorial integrity of a State should not be interfered with in any manner, except in accordance with any one of the following three alternatives: The consent of the State; the issue should be referred to and decided by a high level judicial tribunal to be constituted; and the opinion of the people of the area or areas concerned ascertained by holding a special poll. (Government of Tamil Nadu, 1971: 221-224)

The confrontation between the States and the Centre gained momentum after non-Congress governments came to power in a number of States. Culmination was the Srinagar conference of 17 opposition parties in October 1983.[13] In the note circulated by CPI(M) at the conference, the strained relations between the States and the Centre were analysed and it was underlined that the party which was in power at the Centre was not the ruling party in several States. The note underlined that for resolution of the problem, 'a drastic cut in the dictatorial power of the

13 Farooq Abdullah, Chief Minister of J&K at the time, had taken the initiative in organising the conference. This had incensed Indira Gandhi and finally this led to his ouster from the office.

ruling party' will be necessary. The note suggested a number of important amendments of the Constitution: deletion of Articles 200 and 201 regarding reservation of Bills for consideration of the President, Article 356 for dealing with the failure of the constitutional machinery of the State and imposition of President's Rule, Article 357 regarding exercise of legislative power when the State is under President's Rule, and Article 360 providing for dealing with Financial Emergency. The note also suggested abolition of the office of Governor. (The Governor, 1985: 102-105)

It can be seen how strong was the feeling against the Centre and its arbitrary actions. The distrust created in Centre-State relations since the time of Indira Gandhi has continued to this day. Clearly, the legacy of Indira Gandhi is not easy to shed!

DEBASING PARLIAMENT

Subhash Kashyap, the then Secretary-General of Lok Sabha has, in the *History of the Parliament of India*, bemoaned:

> The fourth Lok Sabha (1967-1970) had to bid goodbye to the artificial plane of political stability, democratic maturity and parliamentary sophistication at which Indian polity thus far had appeared to operate. *One could see a trend towards devaluation of values and a general deinstitutionalization of established institutions. All respect for cleanliness of means and values of service, sacrifice and the like in public life were getting eroded and politics was being transformed gradually into a naked struggle for power. Legislators were being freely sold and purchased for a price like cattle. Even otherwise, the fourth Lok Sabha period was a crucial testing time for parliamentary democracy in India.... The fourth Lok Sabha will be remembered for the fundamental changes in the idiom, the style and the culture of parliamentary politics. Hereafter it was politics in the raw with much of the masks and gloves off. These developments had a lasting*

and rather irreversible impact on the entire political process and all political parties." (Kashyap, 1996: 376, 378)

This was Indira Gandhi's way to begin her innings in parliamentary democracy of which the foundation was laid by her father, Jawaharlal Nehru, with such meticulous care and abiding commitment. Instances have been brought out elsewhere in this book to show how the functioning of Parliament during Indira Gandhi's term reduced its credibility and public respect.

The Public Accounts Committee (PAC) is considered the most important Committee of Parliament. In his observations in Lok Sabha on 22 August 1966 while permitting a discussion on PAC report, *the Speaker had emphasised that the PAC is a House in miniature.* Its decisions should be respected and its dignity enhanced. There all parties work together in team spirit and no note of dissent is appended nor allowed. They work in the interest of the nation and of the House on behalf of the House. (Kashyap, 1996: 115)

These hallowed traditions were trampled during Indira Gandhi's time in a case involving import of crude oil. Kuo oil deal entered into on the directive of P.C. Sethi, the then Minister for Petroleum, resulted in a loss of about ₹9 crore to ₹12.5 crore. This matter was first raised in the PAC on 20 February 1982 when the then Chairman Indian Oil Corporation (IOC) was being examined. He had said that he would rather not answer any questions on the deal as the IOC had not been consulted in the matter, as the government had in writing directed the IOC to enter into the contract on terms that the government itself had decreed. He had said that the questions should be directed to the government. (Shourie, 1983: 176-77) In spite of this clear position, the government stone-walled any questions. At one stage the PAC was told that the file was with PMO. Thereafter it was stated that it was missing. Unfortunately, the rulings of the presiding officers of the two Houses were also inexplicable. I had discussed this case fully in my book, *India's Parliamentary Democracy on Trial.* (Godbole, 2011: 42, 131-132,332) This was a sad chapter in the history of Parliament.

INSTITUTIONALISATION OF CORRUPTION

It can be said without any contradiction that political corruption was legitimised by Indira Gandhi. Her public pronouncement that corruption is a universal phenomenon conveyed her thinking unmistakably.

I.G. Patel has written how he came under pressure to do irregular things during Indira Gandhi regime.

> The pressure came from L.N. Mishra who was Congress Treasurer, but everyone knew that PM was backing him.[14] The pressure took the shape of many files coming to me for clearance; to favour some firm or another for obvious *quid pro quo*. I was called on the phone at work or home, and his subordinates made imperious demands. I had no such experience before, and I was not going to begin a new and unfamiliar and unpalatable chapter in my life. My refusal to toe the line even brought some verbal hectoring from Mishra himself. (Patel, 2002: 147)

Patel has described how Y.B. Chavan, who was Finance Minister at the time, supported him strongly and said he should send such inconvenient files to him with his informal

---

14 Mohan Dharia, the Young Turk, who was in the forefront of the leftist group in the Congress party, has in his Marathi book *Sangharshamaya Safar* (Utkarsha, Pune, 2010, pp 371-372) written how he had urged Indira Gandhi not to induct L.N. Mishra in the Council of Ministers due to his reputation for corruption but Indira Gandhi brought back Mishra in the Cabinet once again as Railway Minister on 11 October 1974.

advice and he would pass orders thereon himself. Chavan also suggested to him that Patel could lock up such files in his cupboard till elections are over and that no one would ask for the files thereafter! How many ministers would be prepared to take such a position even today.

On this background, it is shocking to read how contemptuous Haksar was of Chavan. Patel has written:

> Haksar once told me disdainfully: "Chavan will do anything to remain in power. He likes to eat a chicken at every meal. Who is going to provide him that when he is not in power?" Such is the dynamics of power. Its fuel is cynicism. (Patel, 2002: 148)

Perhaps, Haksar was reflecting Indira Gandhi's contempt for Chavan. It also shows how over-bearing were the persons close to Indira Gandhi. I.G. Patel's woes continued even after Indira Gandhi came back to power.

> Some of the baggage she acquired after the Congress split and the Emergency was, to say the least, drawn from the bottom of the political drawer; and being asked to facilitate various shady deals, some of them were not averse to coming up with a few of their own. (Patel, 2002: 174)

C.S. Pandit has in his book, *End of an Era – The Rise and Fall of Indira Gandhi,* stated:

> A lot of information, not yet substantiated, has been coming out since the defeat of Indira Gandhi at the hustings. Much of it concerned corrupt and unethical practices indulged in by people close to Indira Gandhi during the 19 months of national Emergency. In some cases even her personal collusion is alleged. (Pandit, 1977: ix)

Gill's narration of his first-hand knowledge of how corruption evolved during Indira Gandhi's regime is striking. What is more shocking is the brazenness of it all:

> The next stage in corruption was reached with the decision to stop running after Indian 'donors', and arrange kickbacks in foreign contracts. I was myself a witness to one of the earlier deals during my stint as Joint Secretary, Ministry of Shipping. My Minister of State finalized the purchase of a ship from Singapore for the Shipping Corporation of India. Later, S.M. Nanda, Chairman of the Corporation, obtained a substantial reduction in the agreed price. The minister was furious and threatened to teach Nanda a lesson. The Admiral, a Bangladesh War hero, met Mrs Gandhi and explained that he had acted wholly in the interest of the country. *The PM admired his devotion to duty but advised that if after his best efforts the party is able to get some donation from the suppliers, he need not bother.* (Gill, 1996: 367)

This is confirmed by the following account of my own experience. The Italian connections had started working during the period and were quite evident in the award of contracts for the fertiliser projects. I saw this at close quarters in respect of Thal Vaishet project of Rashtriya Chemicals and Fertilisers (RCF), a public sector undertaking. I was Joint Secretary, Economic Affairs, in Finance Ministry at the time and was handling the IMF/World Bank desk. The World Bank had sanctioned a loan of $250 million. Under the loan agreement, the criteria for short-listing of consultants, as also the procedure for their selection, had been agreed upon with the Bank. One of the conditions for the effectiveness of the loan agreement with the World Bank was the appointment of consultant for the ammonia plant. However, the selection of consultant ran into trouble as it was not in keeping with the guidelines of the World Bank. After prolonged consultations, the Bank was of the view that any further examination of the matter was likely to raise awkward and embarrassing questions and the GoI should seriously consider whether it would like to continue the dialogue on the subject with the Bank. During my discussions, *the Bank officers regretfully suggested that earlier they had considered that India stood apart from other developing countries, but now political corruption seemed to be taking its toll and India was joining the same league as some of the South-East Asian, African and West Asian countries. Though I protested against these suggestions vehemently, I knew that we had lost our face internationally and not just a loan for a fertiliser project.* At this stage, I left the Ministry of Finance and went on deputation to the Asian Development Bank in Manila.

The loan agreement stood terminated on 31 December 1980. However, the government politically created the impression that India was being penalised for exercising its freedom to select a consultant, and was praised for its stand in the Lok Sabha by Congress(I) members. They said it did not matter even if the cost of the project went up further due to delays in tying up foreign exchange funding from other sources. The government also refused to be drawn into the discussion on whether the selected technology was costly. Repeated questions raised by Madhu Dandavate in the Lok Sabha were stonewalled (Lok Sabha Debates, 17 February 1981). The government also refused to discuss the objections raised by the World Bank. In reply to Rajya Sabha starred question No. 110 by Bhupesh Gupta, the government said, "it is not in the public interest to disclose the details". A discussion on the issue was raised in the Lok Sabha on 23 December 1980 by K.P. Unnikrishnan who placed certain documents in regard to this matter before the House. Transparency in public dealings was of no relevance. In fact, it was considered to be in public interest not to furnish information on such "sensitive" matters. What else was the Official Secrets Act for? (Godbole, 1996: 159-162)

Award of contracts for urea and ammonia plant of the Trombay V expansion programme of the Fertiliser Corporation of India was similarly based on considerations other than merit. The proposal was strongly opposed by the Ministry of Finance but was finally approved by Indira Gandhi. This case was examined at length by the Shah Commission secretariat but could not be considered by the Commission for want of time.

Licence-Permit Raj came very handy in mobilisation of funds. This was the beginning of institutionalisation of corruption. Gill has noted: several ministers and Indira aides became fund raisers 'for the party'. Quotas were fixed for various Chief Ministers before every election. There is little doubt that these worthies did not pass on all the money they collected to the party treasurer. (Gill, 1996: 366)

B.N. Tandon, who was Joint Secretary in the PMO, has written in *PMO Diary I: Prelude to the Emergency*, that Orissa government wanted to prosecute Hare Krushna Mehtab on the basis of a CBI enquiry. However, Indira Gandhi was reluctant in view of its effect on the Congress party. Tandon has rightly stated:

> Politics should have no place in tackling corruption but these days decisions are being taken mainly on the basis whether a decision will harm the Congress party, particularly the supporters of the PM. I have seen this in countless instances. (Tandon, 2003: 151)

Tandon has also mentioned that strict instructions had been issued to all concerned that in any matters pertaining to Sanjay Gandhi's Maruti project, the drafts had to be got approved by the Prime Minister. Madhu Limaye, a prominent, fire-brand MP, had written to the RBI seeking some information. The Prime Minister wanted to see the draft of RBI's reply. Though it was to the effect that Maruti had not infringed any rules, she was delaying her approval and was 'furious' that Maruti was being unnecessarily harassed. (Tandon, 2003: 151)

Romesh Thapar had become scandalised by stories of corruption in PMO. Raj Thapar has written in her memoir:

> Yashpal Kapur, that oily cupbearer, was growing in stature by the minute and his corruption was becoming legend, and his ability to get Indira to sign on the dotted line became the bazaar gossip. We did not know how much to believe but Romesh felt duty-bound to tell her. He sought an appointment, went to the office, gave her a run down of what an average person was thinking, of how the PM's office now harboured a nest of corrupt people led by the favoured Yashpal. She was furious. "You know I would never touch a penny." "May be. But *you are seen as the queen bee. The others do the collecting*." This made her fume even more. "It's people like you who create this mood of gloom and doom," she said. At that remark Romesh rose from his chair and said, "if that's what you think, I'd better leave. There is no point in continuing this conversation." She was quick to react, jumped up from her chair and said, "No, no. Don't be silly. I didn't mean it like that." But he knew that a part of her did mean it because she was not given to making statements like that for nothing. Which meant, of course, that another part of their relationship, of their understanding, was over....[15] An unending string of stories were current about Yashpal's power, how he was sought after by the high and mighty, how he was well in with Sanjay who was beginning, bit by bit, to tamper with the administration in his favour. Yashpal was of course no longer in PM's office. His place had been taken by his nephew, R.K. Dhawan, who was rapidly to assume vaster powers than his erstwhile uncle and together they were to manipulate patronage in this vast country. (Thapar, 1991: 337-338)

---

15 Romesh Thapar closed down his influential monthly *Seminar* when served with a pre-censorship order.

Meghanad Desai has, in his book, *The Rediscovery of India*, stated:

> Corruption now became second nature to Congress leaders. It was deeply entrenched and institutionalised, P.N. Haksar told her [Raj Thapar] and, indeed, it became necessary to bolster party coffers. (Desai, 2009: 355)

Nayantara Sahgal's observation too is significant:

> The impression grew that there were key figures in her confidence whose services could not be easily replaced. Her patronage of them made them flashpoints of a rising resentment. While L.N. Mishra, associated with fund raising for the party, remained in the background, Bansi Lal, a crusader and more colourful political figure, was involved in open controversy, and known to have the Prime Minister's special protection in return for his staunch support and some 300 acres of requisitioned land provided for her son's car factory in his State. (Sahgal, 1978: 99)

Inder Malhotra has written about Antulay's clever ploy to collect huge funds by setting up a series of trusts, one of them named after Indira Gandhi. He has stated:

> Indira Gandhi's instinct was to shield Antulay and to reject the demand for his ouster, which had turned into a nation-wide roar. Rajiv, on the other hand, put his foot down and insisted that Antulay must go. (Malhotra, 1991: 32)

There is no better way to end this section than to refer to what B.K. Nehru has written:

> The day after the funeral [of Sanjay], I asked Rajiv whether the money Sanjay had collected allegedly for the Congress was safe. He said all they found in the almirahs of the Congress office was ₹20 lakh. I asked how much Sanjay had. He held his head in his hands and said, "crores and uncounted crores." (Nehru, 1997: 582)

In this regard, the observation of Katherine Frank is quite pertinent:

> It seems unlikely that Sanjay would have kept very much of the money he had amassed during the Emergency in his mother's house. Sanjay had friends both in India and abroad who could safeguard money for him. (Frank, 2001: 530, footnote 4)

This is a highly depressing account of Indira Gandhi's tumultuous regime. In the ultimate analysis, strength of democracy lies in its institutions. When these come under such intense attack, the very survival of democracy comes in peril.

7

Mirage of Socialism – Lost Opportunities

INTRODUCTION

The first phase of Indira Gandhi's regime was marked by 'one slogan a day'. It was a march towards Socialism with the nationalisation of banks, a spate of Leftist and socialist policies, nationalisation of general insurance and nationalisation of a number of other industries. In fact, most of what is being dismantled since 1991 was erected during this period. And it has been an uphill task, with ideological baggage of a number of political parties and vested interests coming in the way.

ECONOMIC COMPULSIONS FACING INDIA

The first years, after Indira Gandhi took over as Prime Minister, were marked by acute agricultural distress. The *Economic Survey 1966-67* has stated that during 1966-67, food grains output was only around 76 million tonnes as compared to 72 million tonnes in 1965-66 and 89 million tonnes in 1964-65. Crop failures were particularly serious in parts of Bihar, UP, MP, Rajasthan and Gujarat. Consecutive failure of rains led to severe drought and imports of food grains were increased substantially – from 6.7 million tonnes in 1964-65 to 8 million tonnes in 1965-66 and 10.4 million tonnes in 1966-67. Imports of food grains were 9 million tonnes during 1967.

The good harvest of 1967-68 brought a measure of relief to the economy from the strains under which it was operating in the previous two and a half years. But 1971-72 was again one of the most difficult years India had faced due to influx of nearly ten million refugees, and the outbreak of hostilities in December 1971.

One of the very first decisions Indira Gandhi had to take on assuming charge as Prime Minister was that of devaluation. Even the tallest of leaders found it difficult to take such a decision due to its political fall-out. Least of all, a newly installed Prime Minister, who did not have much support within her own party and had several contenders for the post. But, with the over-valued rupee and the pressure of donors, including the World Bank and the IMF, there was hardly any option. Finally, she bit the bullet and the rupee was devalued in 1966 by 66 per cent – from ₹4.76 to a US dollar to ₹7.5 to a US dollar. The decision was severely criticised at home. Kamraj, who had supported her election as Prime Minister, was particularly upset and she seriously thought of going back on the decision but the die had been cast and it was not possible to go back. The difficulties were compounded when international aid did not materialise, as expected. Exports also did not increase as was expected. In fact, export earnings for 1966-67 declined by 8 per cent. In 1968-69, they were mere 4 per cent above the level of 1964-65. Without reasonable prospects of aid forthcoming on the scale contemplated, the finalization of the Fourth Plan had to be postponed till 1969. The interval was popularly called 'Plan holiday' which covered a period of three annual plans. This was a wrong footing on which to start one's innings but, it was to her credit that she was able to surmount it. The Fourth Plan too ran into difficulty due to the Bangladesh crisis with the influx of ten million refugees.

The *Economic Survey 1971-72* has brought out that the industrial licensing policy was modified in January 1972 by which industrial units were permitted to utilise the licensed capacity fully. But these relaxations were not to apply to the production of goods reserved exclusively for the small sector. Nor were they to apply automatically to the companies in which foreigners owned a majority of the equity or to those belonging to the large industrial houses. Companies belonging to these categories were to apply for being allowed to increase production. I have given this example just to illustrate how self-defeating were the policies designed purely in pursuance of the Leftist ideology.

SOCIALISM – THE DRIVING FORCE

Socialism, which was the single most brandied about word during Indira Gandhi regime, more than even Nehru's, was more a window-dressing for her pursuit of power, than anything else. Not many people were taken in by it. J.B. Kripalani, a former Congress President and himself a socialist, had written: "The word 'socialism' does not appear to be as innocent as it looks on the surface. It may be likened to Hinduism or Christianity. There are so many varieties of 'socialism' both in India and the world." He had pleaded that the word 'socialist' included in the preamble to the Constitution by the 42nd Amendment should be deleted. (Kripalani, 1980: 193-195)

Palkhivala, in *We, The Nation – The Lost Decade*, has rightly stated:

> The concept of 'Socialism' did not figure anywhere in the Constitution as originally enacted. On the contrary, the Constitution provided in the directive principles of State policy that the State shall endeavour to secure that "the ownership and the control of the material resources of the community are so distributed as best to subserve the common good" and that the "operation of the economic system does not result in the concentration of wealth and

> means of production to the common detriment". These words rule out State ownership – the monolithic State – which is the hallmark of communism, euphemistically called socialism.... *The Economist* rightly remarked in January 1987 that Socialism as practised in India has been a fraud. (Palkhivala, 1994: 5-6)

Piloo Mody, MP, who was known for his sarcasm and humour in Parliament, had said:

> The entire economic programme of this government has been based on 'some stray thoughts, rather hurriedly dictated', which miraculously transformed themselves into an economic programme which is supposed to herald the Great Socialist Dawn.... The one thing in the [Five Year] Plan which is typical, which truly describes the planning process in India today, is what can aptly be termed 'Maruti Socialism'.... There are five things which are common to all socialist countries without exception. They are high taxes, high prices, shortages and queues for everything, black markets and the brain drain.

Piloo Mody also ridiculed Indira Gandhi's frequent allegations of CIA's interference in India, by going to Lok Sabha with a prominent pendant, round his neck, proclaiming "I am a CIA agent". (Mody, year of publication not given: 84, 95, 167)

But, there was some truth in Indira Gandhi's allegations about CIA. German historian and political scientist Kiessling has written:

> The CIA and the ISI also cooperated in working against Indira Gandhi government after she signed an agreement with Moscow on 7 August 1971 confirming peace, friendship and cooperation between India and the Soviet Union.... Only after the murder of Prime Minister Indira Gandhi in 1984 did the CIA-ISI campaigns come to an end. (Kiessling, 2016: 28)

This is also borne out by what Raman, who worked in R&AW for a number of years, has stated:

> Her fears were not totally imaginary. Between 1971 and her assassination in October 1984, the PSYWAR division of the CIA mounted a vicious disinformation campaign against her projecting her as a Soviet surrogate. All sorts of false stories against her were disseminated through compliant foreign journalists.... The CIA's disinformation campaign against Indira Gandhi was at its height between 1971 and 1977. It was discontinued between 1977 and 1980.... After Indira Gandhi returned to power in 1980, the disinformation campaign against her was revived ... the post-1980 disinformation campaign was caused by what the US perceived as the Indian support to Moscow on the Afghanistan issue and by US suspicion that the R&AW was collaborating with Khad, the Afghan intelligence agency, and the KGB against US interests. (Raman, 2007: 40)

On one Question Day of Prime Minister in Parliament, Piloo Mody asked Indira Gandhi, "Can the Prime Minister explain why Indians seem to thrive economically under every government in the world except hers?" (Zakaria, 2003: 53)

Deng Xiaoping had said, "The West builds capitalism for capitalism. We build capitalism to build Socialism." This wisdom was the anti-thesis of mindless pursuit of Socialism by Indira Gandhi.

Zareer Masani states:

> Questions of political ideology find Indira Gandhi's thought at its weakest. Socialism is a word she uses often.... But she has yet to supply coherent definition of the theoretical and practical content of her Socialism. 'I don't think my Socialism is of a very dogmatic kind,' she has told the author. "I have never thought we should

nationalise everything or do many of the things that go with the ... official view of Socialism. But I have always felt very strongly about equality ... economically and also socially...." Asked to clarify whether her Socialism was closer to Marxism or to the social democracy of the welfare State, she replied, "I would not put a label on it at all...." As a political theory, Mrs Gandhi's Socialism raises more questions than it answers.... Indira Gandhi's brand of Socialism is a mixture of vague populism and pragmatism which can scarcely be called a political ideology. (Masani, 1975: 280-281, 286)

This is corroborated by what her one time Information Advisor, George Verghese, once remarked, "She has no consistent vision; everything is tactics." A wag said that Indira was 'left of self-interest'. (Gill, 1996: 369)

Though so many years have elapsed since Socialism, whether Nehruvian or Indiraian variety, became a part of India's political rhetoric as also the preamble of the Constitution, the gap between the rich and poor shows no sign of narrowing. The richest 1 per cent in India now have claim to 60 per cent of the country's wealth, with the bottom 50 per cent having just 2 per cent. Measures like abolition of privy purses and privileges, setting up of Monopolies and Restrictive Trade Practices Commission and Urban Land Ceiling Act, to name just a few, were a mere tokenism in which the Congress party has excelled over the years!

LEFTWARD TURN OF THE CONGRESS

Zaidi in his book, *A Tryst with Destiny – A Study of Economic Policy Resolutions of Indian National Congress During the Last 100 Years*, brings out the evolution of the policies over the years. It can be seen that Indira Gandhi alone cannot be blamed for the policies which she adopted during the period. It was the AICC which too was goading her. In its resolution passed in its meeting on 23-25 June 1967, the AICC asked the government to adopt the ten point programme as follows:

Ten-Point Programme

1. Government should take steps to implement sociai control of the banking institutions.
2. Nationalise general insurance.
3. Export and import trade should be progressively undertaken through State agencies.
4. A national policy of public distribution of food grains particularly to the vulnerable sections of the community should be worked out and the Food Corporation of India (FCI) and co-operative agencies should be utilised to the maximum extent.
5. Consumer co-operatives should be organized to cover urban and rural areas for supply of the more essential commodities to the community at fair prices ... processing and manufacturing in the State and co-operative sectors should be established on an extensive scale.
6. The Working Committee of the AICC welcomes the decision of the government on the Monopolies Commission Report and hopes effective steps would be taken to curb monopolies and concentration of economic power.[1]
7. Positive steps should be taken towards the provision of minimum needs of the entire community.

---

1 It is important to note that The Monopolies Inquiry Commission was appointed by the government in April 1964 to enquire into the existence and effect of concentration of economic power in private hands. The report was received in 1965. Its implementation became a part of Indira Gandhi's leftist agenda.

8. Limitations of urban income and property.
9. Rural works programme to give employment to the landless, improved implementation of land reforms; credit against personal security of assets that are to be created to agricultural labourers; drinking water.
10. *Privileges, other than privy purses*, enjoyed by the ex-rulers are incongruous to the concept and practice of democracy. Government should examine it and take steps to remove it. (Zaidi, 1985: 223-225)

It may be noted that the resolution had called for only the social control of the banks and not their nationalisation. Further, only the privileges, and not the privy purses, of former rulers were to be abolished. But, Indira Gandhi went much beyond these suggestions, to appease the Leftist sections of the Congress party.

As can be seen, even before the split in the Congress party, the programme laid down by the AICC set the ball rolling and gave Indira Gandhi the authorisation to implement Leftist policies. These wide-ranging decisions were based on the political philosophy of the Congress party. Their economic merits and demerits were not examined before making the recommendations. Neither was there such an examination and scrutiny before they were given effect to by the government.

The AICC had expressed concern at the drought in the previous two years which had led to large imports and emphasised the importance of agricultural self-sufficiency. Towards this end, the Committee had suggested a number of steps to be initiated by the government. (Zaidi, 1985: 225-226)

After the 'stray thoughts' expressed by Indira Gandhi at the Bangalore session, the AICC passed, on 10-13 July 1969, a three page resolution, more or less, endorsing the stray thoughts, reportedly jotted down by P.N. Haksar. This was the real beginning of socialist action. It was a long list of action points, based on ideological grounds, rather than anything else, which, inter alia, contained the following: *impose ceiling on unproductive expenditure and conspicuous consumption of corporate bodies*; expeditious appointment of *Monopolies Commission*; *the consumer industries should be reserved wherever possible for development in the co-operative and small-scale sector and entry of the big business should be banned in the manufacture of these industries; foreign capital should not be allowed to enter* fields in which local technical know-how is available. Interestingly, the resolution stated:

> There is a strong feeling in the country regarding the nationalisation of private commercial banks. *We had taken a decision at an early (sic) AICC but perhaps we may review it. Either we can consider the nationalisation of the top five or six banks or* issue directions that the resources of banks should be reserved to a large extent for public purposes. (However, within a short time thereafter, fourteen large banks were nationalised.) Can we not consider the nationalisation of the import of raw materials? The policy of the distribution of import licenses should also be reviewed. We should review the licensing system so that licences are not given only to bigger houses. Shares should be distributed more equitably. Some thought should be given to profit-sharing in industrial establishments. (Zaidi, 1985: 231-234)

As can be seen, distrust of the private sector was the prime mover. Nationalisation was the only answer to all problems. There was such a tunnel-vision among practically all political parties – except for Jan Sangh and Swatantra Party, which were considered as outcasts for their capitalist ideology – that there was no opposition to this Leftist programme.

In the AICC resolution in Bombay session in 1969, the government was, inter alia, *directed to unearth black money and prevent its proliferation*. (Zaidi, 1985: 242) This is one item on which Indira Gandhi failed to take any concrete action. As brought out in chapter 5, she rejected the recommendation of Wanchoo Committee to demonetise high value notes. Excessively high Income Tax rates became incentives for tax avoidance and evasion. The Licence-Permit Raj perpetuated by her, in fact, laid firm foundations of crony capitalism in the country.

The AICC resolution in Chandigarh session on 9 and 10 October 1972, talked about *bringing "agricultural incomes within the tax net.* In this effort it may be necessary to go beyond the recommendations of the Wanchoo Committee. It is expected that the Raj Committee would provide valuable suggestions in regard to taxation of agricultural incomes. The remaining two years of the Fourth Plan must be utilised to push through the comprehensive tax reforms." (Zaidi, 1985: 275) It is important to note that *Indira Gandhi's Leftist programme did not extend to putting any curbs on or taxing the rural rich. She was pragmatic enough to know that this will destabilise the very foundations of her power.*

The Congress Working Committee resolution on 17 April 1973 welcomed the steps taken for takeover of *wholesale trade in food grains* beginning with wheat from the rabi season, and *nationalisation of coking and non-coking coal. The Bidhan Nagar session of the Congress had directed the generation of 5,00,000 job opportunities for educated unemployed. But during the entire period of Indira Gandhi's tenure this remained a distant dream.*

In her address at the Institute of Social and Economic Change, Bangalore, in 1974, Indira Gandhi had, inter alia, called for a strict fiscal and monetary discipline to be imposed both in *government and private sector*; *regulating all incomes; top accounts in all banks to be subjected to strict scrutiny.* The AICC had unreservedly supported these policy directions. (Zaidi, 1985: 323) These off-hand statements remained only on paper.

After the 'hard decisions and bold measures' taken by the government, at Komagata Maru Nagar, the Congress noted that time had now come to talk of social revolution. According to AICC resolution passed at Gauhati session on 21-22 November 1976, these gains, to a very large extent, had been made possible because of the dynamic and inspiring leadership of Indira Gandhi. It said, *'the formulation of a national policy on wages and prices ... requires government's early attention.' The AICC was also now talking about provision of fuller employment!* It reiterated that public sector should occupy the commanding heights of the economy and warned the private sector that "unjustified retrenchments, lockouts and lay offs will not be tolerated." (Zaidi, 1985: 341-343, 345) The talk of evolving a national policy on wages and prices again turned out to be mere political rhetoric and was clearly not feasible and was never talked about thereafter.

A significant development which gave a momentum to Indira Gandhi's Leftist policies was the entry of Communists and socialists in the Congress party. Frankel has observed:

> The dominant reality in the Indian situation, the Communists conceded, was the influence of the Congress among all classes of people. By December 1964, at the first post-split meeting of the party, the CPI officially recognized the vital role of the progressive forces inside the Congress as potential allies in the formation of a national democratic front. Frankel has cited the book by Satindra Singh, *Communists in Congress, Kumaramangalam's Thesis.* In it, Singh, a journalist and former member of the Communist Party, had written that he hoped its 'exposure' might "help Mrs Gandhi see light before it is too late for her as well as for democracy." (Frankel, 1978: 405 and footnote 39)

The terms 'vested interests', 'rightist and reactionary forces', 'obscurantists', etc, appear in AICC documents again and again and show the increasing influence of Communists and socialists in the deliberations of the Congress party.

Indira Gandhi was an astute politician with admirable sense of timing in taking major decisions. This was first seen when she brought about the split in the Congress party in the name of discarding the dead wood, though it was a part of the strategy to increase her hold on the party. This brought her party in minority in the Lok Sabha. She then took the help of CPI and continued not just to rule but to usher in important Leftist policies such as bank nationalisation, setting up of the Monopolies Commission, and the abolition of privy purses. Her mental make-up was such that she could not countenance the opposition of the Supreme Court. She then decided to dissolve the Lok Sabha, first time in the country, 14 months before the due date and go for a fresh mandate. Speaking in the Lok Sabha on 27 December 1970, she thundered, "These attempts to accelerate the pace of social and economic reforms have naturally roused *the opposition of vested interests. Reactionary forces have not hesitated to obstruct in every possible way*…." (GoI, 1975: 76) She had mastered the Communist jargon by now!

WHAT WAS ACHIEVED

Economic performance during Indira Gandhi's regime was hardly anything to write home about. Vijay Joshi, in his book, *India's Long Road – The Search for Prosperity*, has brought out that the decadal growth rate of GDP in 1970-71 to 1979-80, which largely comprised the aggressive socialist phase, was just 3 per cent per annum, and the per capita growth rate was just 0.7 per cent per annum. The growth rate of GDP was just 2.9 per cent per annum during 1965-66 to 1979-80. Key social indicators of China and South Korea were significantly higher than of India. (Joshi, 2016: 31-32)

Dreze and Sen have, in their book, *An Uncertain Glory – India and Its Contradictions,* highlighted that per capita growth rate of GDP at constant prices was just 1.8 per cent in 1950-51 to 1960-61, the Nehru years, 1.2 per cent in 1960-61 to 1970-71, and 1.2 per cent in 1970-71 to 1980-81. During 1970-80, the average annual growth rate of per capita GDP was just 0.9 per cent in India, while it was 2.2 in Pakistan, 2.6 in Sri Lanka, 5.4 in China, 5.5 in South Korea, 5.3 in Indonesia, and 4.6 in Thailand. (Dreze, 2013: 4, 293)

Virmani has in his book, *Propelling India from Socialist Stagnation to Global Power*, analysed the performance of Indira Gandhi years lucidly. He has stated:

> The period of 30 years from 1950-51 to 1979-80 was the phase of socialist experimentation, in which the Indian version of Socialism was developed.... In this phase, the economy averaged rate of growth of 3.5 per cent per annum and average income, measured by per capita GDP, grew at 1.3 per cent per annum. Growth during this period was fairly volatile, with a coefficient of variation of 1. (Virmani, Vol 1, 2006: 42)

He has further underlined:

> The extent and range of market distorting policies and market substituting institutions introduced between 1960 and 1980 was phenomenal for an economy that was, in essence, a market economy. The conventional wisdom in India is that the economy (GDP) grew at 'Hindu rate of growth' of 3.5 per cent per annum during the three decades till 1979 ... in reality, the outcome of the Indian version of 'State Socialism', was *disastrous fall in the growth rate to 2.9 per cent per annum during the fifteen years from 1965-66 to 1979-80. This abysmal performance, put India in the bottom quarter of developing economies....* The pre-1980 and post-1980 periods could, therefore, be characterised as the lower and

> upper portions of an Indian growth cycle. (Virmani, Vol 2, 2006: 52-53)

P.N. Dhar has quoted Sir Donald MacDougall who had examined India's balance of payments problem. MacDougall had estimated:

> An annual growth rate of 8 per cent in exports as the minimum necessary to relieve the balance of payments constraint. However, the feasibility of export growth of this order which involved what he called 'almost revolutionary change in the structure of India's export trade' depended on policy changes which were inconsistent with the opinion held in the Planning Commission and the government. Had Donald's view prevailed, India should have embarked on a bold export drive during the Third Plan period, the results of which would have been harvested for the Fourth Plan. (Dhar, 2003: 118, footnote 5)

This is yet another prognosis of missed opportunities during the crucial years.

J.B. Kripalani, a staunch socialist, has stated:

> There was a three year planning holiday. The Prime Minister Mrs Gandhi herself said in Parliament that the country had not fared worse in these three years when there was no plan. But, ideologically the authorities were so wedded to their particular type of planning, that they would not allow our economy to take its free course, confining themselves to exercising strict supervision and careful control.... How could the nation be without a plan! (Kripalani, 2004: 918)

PUBLIC SECTOR – ANOTHER BLINDSPOT

Year after year annual economic surveys had been referring to the poor performance of public sector undertakings. The *Economic Survey 1966-67* observed:

> The revenue of public sector undertakings, including the railways, were supposed to be an important source of finance for development expenditure. These resources were lower than anticipated during 1966-67. While the fall in receipts was largely due to lower levels of output, there is clearly need for increase in the returns from these undertakings, through higher levels of production, greater efficiency and adjustments in prices which may be at uneconomic levels.

This peroration was repeated year after year.

The Fourth Five Year Plan (1969-74) had stated:

> Many of the projects undertaken in the public sector represent new and complex ventures and, to an extent, initial difficulties are only to be expected. But even after allowing for this, the fact remains that the concern for speed, economy and efficiency has not been as pervasive as it ought to be. The public sector has the responsibility to set much higher standards of performance and it has yet to fulfil its role in generating adequate surpluses for investment. (GoI, 1969: 8)

Palkhivala, while speaking on 1973-74 budget had, inter alia, damned the socialist ideology of the Congress government. He said, "The Constitution of India did not make nationalization one of the directive principles of State policy, but in practice the government seems to have adopted it as an end in itself, irrespective of the results. That is presumably why", he said, "the budget speech made no mention of the 84 public sector undertakings on which over ₹5,000 crore had been invested and which had incurred a net loss of ₹18.8 crore in 1971-72. Seldom has any country laid so costly a sacrifice at the alter of ideology. To believe or say any evil of the public sector is merely to invite censure that you are not a patriot and not a true socialist."[2] (Kamath, 2007: 377)

The situation was no different several years later. The Sixth Five Year Plan (1980-85) stated:

> In so far as successive five year plans have laid emphasis on the leading role of the public sector in basic and producer goods industries, government has the responsibility of planning the requisite investments.... [It also recognised] the paramount importance of improving the efficiency of the public sector. This applies to industrial undertakings in the public sector as much as to those concerned with provision of power and transport.... The total investment in the Central Public Sector Undertakings as on March 1979, amounted to ₹ 15,600 crore of which approximately ₹ 12,800 were invested in industrial and mining undertakings. Arising from these large investments in the public sector, the share of public sector in the net domestic product in organised industry and mining has also moved up from 8 per cent in 1960-61 to 28.9 per cent in 1977-78. (GoI, 1980: 85-86, 259)

P.N. Dhar, in his book, *The Evolution of Economic Policy in India – Selected Essays*, has stated:

> The public sector was expected to generate surpluses on an increasing scale, as stated in the industrial policy resolution of 1956. In fact, *Mahalanobis, the ideologue, and member of the Planning Commission, believed that there would*

---

2 This reminds me of what is happening in India after the BJP government came to power in 2014, when saying anything against Hindu religion is considered anti-national and unpatriotic. Public sector and socialism were the symbols of Indira Gandhi's religion, till later phase of her regime, when she too turned to conventional religious rituals (Hindu and Muslim) for a solace and peace of mind.

> *be no need for additional taxation in about fifteen years time, that is by the beginning of the 1970s. After more than thirty years, that is, after more than twice the period in Mahalanobis's calculation, the expectations about the generation of surpluses by the public sector had not been realized* ... the net profit on capital employed in 221 industrial and commercial public enterprises in the Central sector worked out at the rate of mere 3.8 per cent for 1987-88, slightly above the 3.4 per cent for the previous year. *And if the profits earned by the public sector oil companies are excluded, the net profit is wiped out or becomes negative.* This meagre result is the end product of a period of good performance since 1981-82, which was preceded by four consecutive years of net losses. This is the performance of enterprises which are supposed to be in the better-managed segment of the public sector. The performance of State-level enterprises was much worse. Despite this dismal performance, the public sector continued to expand. (Dhar, 2003: 124)
>
> Public sector enterprises continued to be a major drain on the economy. Commercial losses of Central and State-owned enterprises were ₹2,400 crore in 1985-86 [just a year after Indira Gandhi's assassination] which is about 22 per cent of gross capital formation in the industrial sector (manufacturing). According to surveys carried out by RBI, the number of sick enterprises at the end of 1983 exceeded 80,000 and their outstanding credit was about ₹3,000 crore. (Dhar, 2003, 114, footnote 28)

In this context, observations of P.L. Tandon, a distinguished manager with experience of both the public and private sectors, in *Mainstream* of 3 May 1987, are worth noting: The recourse to public sector is taken because money can be spent on purchases, advertising, travelling, vehicles, guest houses, entertainment, employing staff – all of which in a government department would come under strict scrutiny, which can all be shed in a corporation in the name of autonomy. (Dhar, 2003: 127, footnote 22)

Bimal Jalan, in Kaushik Basu's *The Oxford Companion to Economics in India,* has said:

> The first period of Indira Gandhi's rule (1966-77) "was perhaps the darkest in India's history.... In order to cope with the extremely difficult economic situation, the wide-ranging government controls on the economy were further intensified and expanded to banking, insurance, real estate and several other sectors.... The second period (1980-84) was, however, remarkably different and progressive [?], as compared to the earlier period. Controls on industrial production and investment in industry were loosened; the import licensing system was liberalized; the rigidity of price and distribution controls reduced, and tax rates on personal and corporate incomes were lowered.... The growth rate of the economy increased to about 6 per cent. Growth rate of industrial production also accelerated.... *Politics was the primary driver of Indira Gandhi's economics.* To understand the economics of her time, as also the impact of her policies on India's development, it is necessary to pay attention to the conflicting pulls and pressures at different points of time in India's political evolution. (Basu, 2007: 212-214)

INDIRA GANDHI'S CHANT, *GARIBI HATAO*

With the Goebellion technique of image-building, Indira Gandhi's name, even now, is inexorably associated with *garibi hatao* (remove poverty). This was her password for sweeping polls, year after year. As S.S. Gill has aptly described,

> Indira Gandhi was one of the most successful practitioners of populist politics.... Her one sure-fire *mantra* was that

> when in trouble, talk radicalism.... Mrs Gandhi's skill lay in using variations on the same theme of poverty and social justice, year after year, election after election, with remarkable effect. And this, despite the fact that she did not implement most of the promised reforms. (Gill, 1996: 363)

As a result, the results achieved were hardly commensurate with the rhetoric. Even in 2017, over three decades after her departure from the scene, India is still struggling with its poverty. During Indira Gandhi regime, the per capita availability of food grains did not record any noticeable change. It was 449 grammes per day in 1965-66, 446 grammes in 1970-71, 434 grammes in 1975-76, 448 grammes in 1980-81, and 455 grammes in 1985-86. (Alagh, 1991: 2) The percentage of population below the poverty line was 54.9 per cent in 1973-74, 51.3 per cent in 1977-78 and 44.5 per cent in 1983. However, the number of people below poverty were 321.3 million in 1973-74, 328.9 million in 1977-78 and 322.9 million in 1983. (Kelley, 2010: 90)

The manifesto of the Congress party for 1977 elections claimed that the country had achieved tremendous success under Congress rule. But, *the problem in liquidating poverty* [the much touted *Garibi Hatao* slogan of Indira Gandhi] *was 'mainly linked with population growth'*. The manifesto stated that it would be unwise to allow our planned development efforts to be wiped out by a population explosion. After the Emergency excesses, particularly in vasectomy operations, the manifesto was cautious and assured that 'the Congress categorically states that there cannot be and will not be any compulsion in the family planning movement. It will be a voluntary movement and it will be a people's movement. The movement can succeed only by educating and persuading the people and popularising the benefits of a small family. This is the thrust behind the adoption of the National Population Policy. (Zaidi, 1985: 348-349)

Speaking about the Union Budget for 1974-75, Palkhivala said: The income per capita in real terms (ie after making allowance for the factor of inflation) rose at an annual average rate of 1.7 per cent during the 1950s; but in the 1960s the rate of growth dropped precipitously to 0.8 per cent. The painful truth is that, after 1970, there has actually been a drop in per capita income at constant prices. (Palkhivala, 1994: 144)

According to the Planning Commission, the percentage of people below the poverty line declined from 48.3 per cent in 1977-78 to 41 in 1981-82. The latter estimate has been contested by B.S. Minhas, L.R. Jain, S.M. Kansal, and M.R. Saluja, "on the choice of appropriate consumer price indices and data sets for estimating the incidence of poverty in India." (Dhar, 2003: 122, footnote 11)

Multiple Dimensions of Poverty

In looking at human development, the concept of poverty has now been refined by the UNDP into a multi-dimensional poverty index which looks at, apart from the headcount, intensity of deprivation, population at risk of multi-dimensional poverty, population with at least one severe deprivation in – education, health or living standard, and population below income poverty line – Purchasing Pcwer Parity (PPP) of $1.25 a day, and national poverty line. In 2010, based on multi-dimensional poverty, 55.4 per cent of India's population was below poverty line, with intensity of deprivation of 53.5 per cent. Based on national poverty line, however, population below income poverty line was 28.6 per cent. (UNDP, 2010: 162)

To me, the multi-dimensional approach seems much more appealing and appropriate than the simplistic criterion of per capita consumption adopted all these years.

Kaushik Basu, in his book, *The Retreat of Democracy*, has added another dimension to the study of poverty. He has stated:

> In evaluating economic well being, we should look at the per capita income of the poorest 20 per cent (quintile income); and that we should assess progress by looking at the growth rate of per capita income of the poorest 20 per cent (quintile growth). *The mitigation of inequality is important but should be considered secondary to the aim of improving the lot of the poorest*. (Basu, 2007: 98)

Both these refinements shed a new light on the gigantic problem of poverty still facing India and ought to become a part of the national policy for dealing with the problem.

WAS INDIRA GANDHI REALLY A LEFTIST?

Jawaharlal Nehru was proclaimed a socialist and often addressed his fortnightly letters to Chief Ministers as 'Dear Comrades'. But, it was his daughter who, more to retain her hold over the party and to side-line the old guard in the Congress Party, took steps to take energetic steps towards making India a socialist State. Even the Preamble to the Constitution was amended to preface the word 'socialist' before the word republic.

Someone like I.G. Patel, eminent economist who worked closely with her as Secretary, Economic Affairs, and was later Governor, RBI, should know. He has stated:

> Haksar, a very able foreign service officer, was apparently an old friend and a Leftist who was closer to Mrs Gandhi personally, if not ideologically. [But] *there was nothing basically ideological about Mrs Gandhi. Everything was as it suited her at the time.*

Patel was also of the opinion that:

> *Much of the so-called policy divide … was cosmetic and rhetorical and designed to obtain political mileage.* Neither Panditji nor Mrs Gandhi were really socialists of the Marxist or Soviet hue. And Morarji, when he became the Prime Minister in 1977, did not dismantle any of the essential features of Panditji's or Mrs Gandhi's policies. (Patel, 2002: 109-110, 193)

P.N. Dhar, who worked closely with Indira Gandhi, has, in his book, *The Emergency and Indian Democracy*, observed, "*Indira Gandhi had no ideological fixations in economic matters*." In an interview given to Dhar, before he joined on her staff, she had stated:

> In the circumstances here in India it would be difficult to change entirely and suddenly what we have been committed to. We have been committed to the concept of a mixed economy. Within that there is considerable room for movement. As far as I am concerned, and I think my party is concerned, *we believe we should remain centrists but left of Centre,* if I may put it that way. *Personally, I do not feel that the words left or right have much meaning….* I think mixed economy is a viable concept and it can be the means of attaining a socialist society. (Dhar, 2000: 114)

This was in 1970. But, later, this was far from true, as brought out in the resolutions passed by the AICC and the Congress Working Committee. A series of decisions taken by the government, including nationalisation of banks, nationalisation of coal mines, abolition of privy purses and major Constitutional Amendments clearly showed that the above averment was far from true. For retaining her hold on the party, she was prepared to go as far left as necessary.

But this phase ended when she came back to power in 1980 with a massive mandate once again. I.G. Patel has observed:

> *Mrs Gandhi's return to power in 1980 certainly injected a new life in Indian politics but not so much in Indian economic policy. My impression is that Mrs Gandhi had by then lost any revolutionary fervour* that she might have had, and *did not need any radical crutches now*. Her position was secure.... What her return did bring in ... were a new set of actors on the political scene who were all anxious to make their mark by hook or by crook. That meant more people to fend off for the Governor of the RBI. (Patel, 2002: 164)

Indira Gandhi often used to be called India's Margaret Thatcher, the tough British Prime Minister. Indira Gandhi's speech to trade union conference reminded one of Thatcher's stand on coal workers' strike in England. Indira Gandhi told the trade union conference: In a country where there are millions of unemployed and underemployed, what is needed is a fair distribution of opportunities for gainful employment. In this sense, the employed, particularly in the organised sector, who enjoy a measure of social security, should recognise that in our country to be employed is in itself a privilege. (Adams, 1997: 248) Hardly any national leader is prepared to speak so bluntly to organised labour even today.

NATIONALISATION OF BANKS

Bank nationalisation was being talked about in Congress Party forums for a long time. It was considered imperative for achieving the goal of socialistic pattern of society. But, it was formally raised in the meeting of the National Development Council for the first time in 1969. Finance Minister Morarji Desai and D.R. Gadgil, Deputy Chairman of the Planning Commission, were opposed to it and wanted a fair trial to be given to social control of banks which had been launched some time ago. I.G. Patel's observations in the matter are interesting:

> At the meeting, *Mrs Gandhi said clearly that she was not in favour of nationalisation of banks*, that we had yet to make a success of what we had already nationalised and that there was little point in taking on new responsibilities. Besides, social control must be given a fair trial. In the light of subsequent developments, *I have a suspicion that this matter was deleted from the minutes of the Planning Commission. Differences on this matter were also the source of Mrs Gandhi's abominable treatment of Gadgil in the months to come.* (Patel, 2002: 130)

Patel has recalled how in July 1969, Indira Gandhi sent for him and simply said:

> *For political reasons, it has been decided to nationalise the banks.* You have to prepare within 24 hours the Bills, a note for the Cabinet and a speech for me to make to the nation on radio tomorrow evening. Can you do it and make sure there is no leak?... *There was no pretence that this was not a political decision*.... I summoned courage, however, to make two suggestions: to leave the foreign banks alone, and nationalize only the major ones.... She immediately agreed and added that she could trust the details to me.... Fourteen banks were selected for nationalization as between them they accounted for some 85 or 90 per cent of the deposits.... On my own, I inserted a sentence in Mrs Gandhi's speech: 'This is not the first step in a new wave of nationalization. This, in fact, is the culmination of the process which began with the nationalization of life insurance and the Imperial Bank to occupy the commanding heights of finance.... Not a word of what I wrote was changed by Haksar or Mrs Gandhi next morning.... *It is remarkable how momentous decisions are made in the heat of political struggle.* After this, Mrs Gandhi was heralded as the angel of the poor and she made most of *Garibi Hatao*. (Patel, 2002: 136)

Atal Bihari Vajpayee raised a serious question of propriety in connection with the ordinance issued on nationalisation of banks. He argued that there was neither any urgency nor any Emergency and, in these circumstances, the issuing of ordinance barely forty hours before the sitting of Parliament was "undemocratic and unprecedented" and had lowered the dignity of the House. Indira Gandhi defended the government's action. I believe that looking to the nature of the case, issuing of ordinance was clearly justified.

The Bank Nationalisation Bill was introduced within three days of the beginning of the new session of the Lok Sabha. Rules of procedure requiring a notice period of seven days before a Bill could be introduced and another two days of study prior to its consideration, were suspended by the House. The speed of the legislative process was accelerated further by eliminating the normal one-day pause between amendment of the Bill and the final reading.... Indira Gandhi was criticised in Lok Sabha by Asoka Mehta, Sucheta Kripalani, and others, for being under the influence of Communists and fellow-travellers. (Frankel, 1978, 421, footnotes 75, 78)

Bhabatosh Datta, in his book, *Indian Planning at the Crossroads*, has brought out how the government gained control of over ₹3,871 crore of deposits (out of an all-bank total of ₹4,646 crore at the end of June 1969) by paying the shareholders a total compensation of only ₹84 crore. (Dutta, 1992: 114) But, as brought out in chapter 6, even for this "exorbitant" compensation, the government blamed the Supreme Court.

Patel has regretted that due to the legal challenges to nationalization (which I have discussed in chapter 5), the question of restructuring the acquired banks could not be pursued. He has written:

> I had myself prepared a note outlining such a restructuring [to make them more efficient and more responsive to social needs]. The idea was to allow only one or two major banks to remain as all-India banks, catering to the wholesale markets for credit so to speak and with a monopoly of foreign exchange business. They could then compete on equal terms with foreign banks, be sources of innovation and enable a better implementation of foreign exchange control. The rest would be re-organized, merged and re-packaged to create several entities which would work in specific regions and concentrate on agriculture, small industry and trade and hitherto credit-starved areas. There should be two or three regional banks operating in each region so that there would be some competition. At the same time, there would be greater economy as some branches could be merged and excessive expansions avoided in the future. Above all, the emphasis would be on local needs and exploiting local opportunities: two cultures living together and interacting, so to speak. But such ideas were not even discussed, so great was the anxiety to make nationalization stick legally and politically. (Patel, 2002: 136-137)

I have serious reservations on the scheme of reorganization of banks contemplated in the above note. It was a typical attempt of top-down planning, from the so-called 'commanding heights of finance', in a socialist, regimented society. But, in any case, that was the mindset at that time. Dutta has stated that the Banking Commission of 1972 had recommended a scheme of reorganization, with a few 'national' banks with countrywide operations and a large number of regional banks. The recommendation was rejected outright, when its implementation would have been easy. (Dutta, 1992: 117)

Even though nearly five decades have elapsed since then, no thought has been given to restructuring of public sector banks. In fact, whether bank nationalization was a correct step and has achieved what it had sought to, has not been critically examined, beyond the political rhetoric of bank branch expansion, mobilisation of deposits from the rural areas, catering to the needs of agriculture etc. As for the spread of rural credit, the role of rural co-operative banks has been much more significant than the public sector commercial banks. Also, the negative fall out of nationalization in terms of large-scale politicisation of bank operations, their bureaucratization, exponential growth of bad loans (euphemistically called non-performing assets), arbitrary appointments at policy-making levels, large-scale corruption which came to light in the demonetisation period, lax supervision of the RBI as evidenced time and again in bank scams, shoddy audit of banks, and so on, has been overwhelming. It may appear to be a travesty but occupying commanding heights of finance and economy, including bank nationalisation and perpetuation of license-permit raj, has led to strengthening of crony capitalism in the country. What happened during the Emergency in regard to the SBI, the Central Bank and the Punjab National Bank was only the tip of the iceberg. Dozens of scams thereafter have brought out the close nexus between the politicians, banks and even the regulatory authorities. Vijay Mallya and the large bank defaulters represent the state of decay of the banking system in India. The government-run banks have written off record amount of ₹81,683 crore bad loans in the year ending March 2017, an increase of more than 41 per cent as compared to the previous year. The loan write-offs have increased to ₹55,356 crore in the first six months of 2017-18. The editorial 'No Silver Bullet' in *IE* (28 August 2017, p 10) has stated:

> RBI's latest financial stability report shows that the gross bad loan ratio of PSU banks could be as high as 14.2 per cent by March 2018, if there is no economic rebound. The credit rating agency, Moody's, reckons that the government which has budgeted ₹10,000 crore for fiscal year 2017 for capitalizing banks will have to set aside close to ₹95,000 crore for eleven State-run banks over the next two years. In August 2017, the government has decided to set up an 'Alternative Mechanism' to expeditiously examine the proposals for merger and consolidation of the banks to create a few stronger public sector banks.

But, bad loans is not the only concern. The problems are much more deep-rooted. It is the question of governance and management of these banks, as a whole. It is not for the first time that these issues have come to the fore but, 47 years after nationalisation of banks, these issues are being spoken about at the government level. It is time a full-fledged high level expert committee is appointed to examine the real gains from bank nationalization. This can happen only now since a non-Congress government, without any political, ideological baggage, is firmly in the saddle at the Centre with a clear mandate. It is for the first time that, under public pressure, names of large loan defaulters have been made public and some action has been started to recover the large outstandings of public sector banks.

I.G. Patel, who retired as Governor, RBI, himself seemed to have reservations on the manner in which nationalized banks were functioning. He has been candid in his observations.

> By all accounts, the nationalization of banks was a great success *initially*.... The rot started with the Emergency; and what political opportunism started was compounded by the bank staff of all grades. With nationalization came the entry of national unions owing allegiance to different

> political parties, mostly the Congress and the Left. Shielded by political support, the bank staff proceeded to create for themselves a vast superstructure of perks and privileges under which they could define and limit work, enforce over-staffing and generally encourage indiscipline and incompetence without any fear of being held accountable. Merit went by the board as did customer service; and seniority and closeness to political power held the sway. Fraud could not be far behind. (Patel, 2002: 139-140)

This underlines my suggestion for a comprehensive study of what nationalization of banks has achieved.

Kuldip Nayar has, in his book, *India – The Critical Years*, mentioned some significant developments during the period:

> The government was reluctant to lay down a labour policy after the nationalisation of banks. The Fourth Plan draft contained a chapter on employment and labour which was deleted from the final document lest the stand taken should look less 'radical' than the nation's mood at that time.... When workers of LIC [Life Insurance Corporation of India] were on war path, her instructions through a noting in a file was that a 'settlement' should be found – the reason plainly being that the LIC unions were backed by the Communists, who were helping Mrs Gandhi in Parliament to stay in power. The settlement gave labour more than twice the amount they had expected to get. (Nayar, 1971: 86)

URBAN LAND CEILING

Reference must be made to the imposition of ceiling on urban property which was a part of Indira Gandhi's Leftist agenda. Though some Chief Ministers were opposed to the proposal, she pushed it through and had the urban land ceiling law enacted. Uttar Pradesh and Maharashtra legislatures had passed resolutions under Article 252 requesting the Central Government to legislate in this regard for the States. Like several other initiatives of that period, it became a source of rampant corruption. The objective of making affordable housing units available to the poor was hardly achieved. Finally, the law was repealed as a part of economic reforms.

MONOPOLIES AND RESTRICTIVE TRADE PRACTICES

The Monopolies and Restrictive Trade Practices Act passed in 1969 was yet another step taken by the government purely on ideological considerations. Fakhruddin Ali Ahmed, Minister of Industrial Development, Internal Trade and Company Affairs told Lok Sabha that the government was of the view that the incentives given for the development of the economy and for industrial production had actually benefited only a few, with the result that there was a demand for appointing a commission in regard to concentration of wealth. The Monopolies and Restrictive Trade Practices Commission was therefore given mandatory powers in respect of restrictive trade practices. The Act made provisions for exercising control over undertakings belonging to a group having total assets of the value of not less than ₹20 crore. It was ostensibly meant not to impede industrial production, and at the same time to see that such tendencies were not allowed to develop which, while permitting expansion, would result only in the concentration of wealth in a few hands to the detriment of the people at large. (Kashyap, 1996: 235)

Palkhivala made some very significant points in his observations on Union Budget 1977-78, which were highly relevant to the damaging policies pursued by Indira Gandhi over the years:

- *What we call 'big' business is in truth really small* in the context of the modern emphasis on economies of scale and technological methods of mass production. That is why Indian goods have to be subsidized in the world markets. *One unit in Taiwan produces more polyester staple fibre in a month than all the four manufacturers in India produce in a whole year.*
- Having regard to the problem of unemployment in the country, we protect our labour force against what we regarded as the ravages of automation. But it is often overlooked that such a policy is bound to have its effects on the price of the end-product. A textile mill in Hongkong producing 2 lakh metres of cloth per day would employ less than a thousand workers in the three shifts taken together, while a mill in India would need at least 5,000 workers to achieve the same production level.
- *Several industries already have their capacity 'frozen' by the existing constraints.* To take the oldest Indian industry, the textile mills produced 4,100 million metres of cloth in 1953-54, while in 1975-76 their production aggregated to no more than 3,961 million metres. In 1951-52 they had 79 per cent of the textile market; today it is 50 per cent as a result of expansion of powerlooms and handlooms.
- The government is the greatest beneficiary of the expansion of the corporate sector – way above the 'capitalist' shareholders. For every ₹ 100 earned as profits by the corporate sector, the public exchequer gains ₹ 780 in the aggregate: ₹ 527 as Excise, ₹ 135 as Sales Tax, ₹ 118 as Corporate Tax.
- Savings in private hands invariably fructify far better than public savings. (Palkhivala, 1994: 156-157)

It is difficult to disagree with these very logical arguments of Palkhivala, except in regard to adoption of labour-intensive technologies in India, not mindlessly but keeping in view the other requirement of retaining the competitive edge of the products.

CONFISCATORY TAX REGIME

Nani Palkhivala's speeches on Central budget held at the well known Brebourn cricket stadium in Mumbai each year became an universally acclaimed event. I am giving below, illustratively, his assessment pertaining to some budgets during Indira Gandhi years, which bring out how damaging were her Leftist policies.

It is interesting to note that even someone like Palkhivala, who consistently and persistently advocated lower rates of income taxation, was totally despondent about Congress party's policies regarding personal taxation. Writing about suggestions for tax reforms in his book, *The Highest Taxed Nation*, he had suggested, "the maximum marginal rate on individuals should be reduced to 72 per cent this year and to 65 per cent next year"! (Palkhivala, 1965: 77) This was in 1965. It can be seen how far we have come since then in terms of lowering of the tax rates.

Commenting on the Union Budget 1968-69, Palkhivala had stated: There are several socialist countries in the world, but India is the only country where Income Tax and Wealth Tax can together amount to more than the total income. (Palkhivala, 1994: 132)

Speaking on the Union Budget 1970-71, Palkhivala had said: It has been called an 'imaginative' budget. It is only so in the sense that it imagines certain consequences to ensure from the budget which are contrary to all known motivations of human nature and all rules of sound economics. Palkhivala further said that of 150 countries in the world, only two countries had corporate taxation as high as in India. They were Burma and Faroe Islands – the latter with a population of 34,000. It is not coincidence that of all the developing countries of Asia, the lowest rates of economic growth are in Burma and India, where the rates of corporate and individual taxation are the very highest. (Palkhivala, 1994: 136)

The Union Budget 1971-72 upped the highest individual Income Tax rate to 97.75 per cent and Wealth Tax rates going up to 8 per cent (plus 7 per cent in the case of urban property) virtually amounted to annual confiscation of income and wealth. Palkhivala had said, "More than any other budget in the last 111 years, that year's budget was in its conception ideology-oriented ... *Amiri hatao* [remove prosperity] at budget time was an excellent political substitute for *garibi hatao* [remove poverty] at election time." (Palkhivala, 1994: 137)

The Direct Taxes Enquiry Committee under Justice K.N. Wanchoo had in its report submitted in 1971 recommended reduction in the rates of taxation and had cautioned that the prevalence of high rates was the first and foremost reason for tax evasion. But it had very little effect on the thinking of the government, as can be seen from the budgets for the following years.

On the Budget for 1972-73, Palkhivala said that, in India, the burden of Income Tax and Wealth Tax combined, was the highest in the world at the time. He added sarcastically, "It is still possible to become wealthy in India, but not by mere ability, industry or enterprise, or even by a combination of all the three. The five classes of the new rich are: tax evaders, blackmarketeers, bosses of co-operatives, prosperous farmers and some successful politicians." (Palkhivala, 1994: 140)

Talking about the Budget for 1973-74, Palkhivala regretted that public authorities in India had no compunction about repudiating their solemn promises given as incentives for investment and industrialization. Citizens who bought shares in the past on the basis of exemption from Wealth Tax, have found the exemption suddenly withdrawn. Annuity policies purchased on the faith of existing law will now be disqualified for tax relief.... It will be wise to adopt in India the refreshing recommendation of Sir Richard Clarke that there should be no secrecy about budget proposals. (Palkhivala, 1994: 141-142)

In the Budget for 1974-75, the rate of personal taxation was reduced from 97.75 per cent to 77 per cent. The only two years since independence when the rates of Income Tax on individuals were so slashed – 1957 when the rate was reduced to 77 per cent and 1965 when it was dropped to 74.75 per cent. The political atmosphere in the country is so little conducive to dispassionate economic thinking that ... it is regarded as evidence of great political courage.... The rest of the budget is as pedestrian as its predecessors *in our last eight years of stagnation. Some other countries have doubled in eight years their gross national product at constant prices!* (Palkhivala, 1994: 143-144)

As for Union Budget 1975-76, Palkhivala aptly described it:

> Like the budgets of several past years, *this year's budget is again essentially a bullock cart budget.... The rate of growth in industrial production was about 9 per cent in the second and the third plans, while it has been only around 3 per cent since 1966-67. In important items of industrial production, we are behind even the third plan targets in 1965-66; in other words, we are two plans behind....* The apparent continuation of the old rates involves imposition of an additional hidden tax by inflation.... India still follows the hugger-mugger budgetary practices which are at least half a century out of date. (Palkhivala, 1994: 149-151)

In the Budget for 1976-77, the maximum marginal rate of Income Tax was reduced from 77 per cent to 66 per cent. But there were some disconcerting features as well. The new rate of Wealth Tax on the initial slab of net wealth up to ₹5 lakh was fixed at 0.5 per cent; 1.5 per cent on the slab ₹5-10 lakh; 2 per cent on the slab of ₹10-15 lakh; and 2.5 per cent for wealth of over ₹15 lakh. At the same time, the exemption limit for Wealth Tax for Hindu undivided families was reduced from ₹2 lakh to ₹1 lakh. These high rates were a powerful incentive for under-valuation of wealth. (Suri, 2009: 316-317)

Indira Gandhi returned to power as Prime Minister in 1980. I have given earlier laudatory comments of Bimal Jalan regarding this phase of Indira Gandhi's term. Palkhivala brings out the unnerving stark reality year after year. On the Union Budget 1980-81, Palkhivala has written:

> While many eminent thinkers have been repeatedly highlighting for two decades the anomaly that Income Tax is not levied on agricultural income, *the budget now proposes to abolish the existing Wealth Tax on agricultural property* on the ground that "the valuation of agricultural land posed difficulties...." If this argument is valid, most urban assets should also be given the same compassionate and sensitive consideration!... The most reprehensible part of the budget is the set of provisions which seek to give retrospective operation to various amendments. Retrospective legislation is the bureaucrat's dream but the taxpayer's nightmare.... A nation which will not let its industry to retain sufficient funds to provide for obsolescence will itself soon become obsolescent. (Palkhivala, 1994: 160, 162)

Speaking about the 1981-82 Budget, Palkhivala said:

> We do not have have the system which prevails in Denmark, the Netherlands, Canada, Australia and other countries, of automatic indexing of exemption limits and other tax reliefs by reference to the rate of inflation....

> Public amnesia is the politician's best friend. *It is commonly forgotten that the corporate surcharge was introduced in December 1971 to pay for Bangladesh War. Ten years have passed since the end of the war, but the surcharge is unending*.... The most unforgivable feature of the budget was the levy of 15 per cent customs duty on the import of newsprint. It is a tax on public information and public knowledge.... From the viewpoint of the strategy of the war on poverty and unemployment, on inflation, the black market and foreign trade deficit, the budget must be treated as a failure. (Palkhivala, 1994: 165, 166)

Palkhivala's comment on the Union Budget 1982-83 was equally devastating:

> The budget leaves untouched the major and urgent economic problems of India. In a point of approach and vision, it is the budget of a grocery store, not of a nation on the march.... *In 1980-81 the total investment in the public sector had reached ₹18,231 crore and the net profit before tax on this staggering capital investment was only 0.2 per cent; while companies in the private sector, chosen at random by the RBI showed a net profit before tax of approximately 10 per cent*.... But we still cling to our out-dated notions of Socialism and propose to invest the sale proceeds of the capital investment bonds in public sector enterprises.... *At a reasonable estimate, black money will continue to be generated at a rate approaching ₹40 crore per day.* With excessive taxation and the multiplicity of insensate controls, the termites of black money will go on sapping simultaneously both our economy and character.... Surely, the time has come for Parliament to enact some new legislation – say, Prevention of Cruelty to Taxpayers Act – which should over-ride all fiscal legislation.... *This year's budget is merely one more step in the perpetuation of our age-old poverty.* (Palkhivala, 1994: 171-173)

The Union Budget 1983-84 was the last of Indira Gandhi's term as Prime Minister. Particular attention may be invited to Palkhivala's comment on sharp decline in India's share in world exports.

> In 1955, the exports of India were larger than those of South Korea, Hong Kong, Taiwan, Indonesia and Singapore. In sharp contrast, in 1981 the exports of these far smaller countries were substantially higher than those of India. India's share dropped from 2.2 per cent of world exports in 1950 to 1.05 per cent in 1960 and to 0.4 per cent in 1981. Among the exporting countries, India ranked 16th in 1950, 21st in 1960, 31st in 1970 and by 1981 its rank dropped to 46th! Reference must also be invited to yet another significant observation of Palkhivala: The damage to the economy of our country and the welfare of our people, arising from the maddening instability of our laws, is truly incalculable. Look at the avalanche of new laws at the Union level. Between 1971 and 1982 the Centre amended the Constitution 22 times, passed 796 Acts, 161 Ordinances and 129 President's Acts for States which were under President's Rule.... (Palkhivala, 1994: 176, 178)

TO SUM UP

During these years, the finance portfolio was held by stalwarts such as Morarji Desai, Indira Gandhi, Y.B. Chavan, C. Subramanaim and R. Venkataraman, but it made no difference to the policy. Each one, including Desai, swore by Socialism and pursued policies laid down by his supreme leader! Perhaps, Chavan alone was a 'real' socialist and a [M.N.] Royist. In seventy years of India's national life since independence, sixteen long years of Indira Gandhi's term as Prime Minister are a tragic tale of lost opportunities. What a legacy!

8

An Enigma

INTRODUCTION

The analysis in the preceding chapters brings out many facets of Indira Gandhi's personality as a ruthless politician, all powerful political leader and a statesman. In a sense, this was a challenging but a somewhat straightforward task. But, when it comes to analysing and understanding her as a person, one is faced with insurmountable difficulties. An intense, deeply troubled person, she had to spend her working life among politicians and their tribe whom she detested. She was an amalgam of so many diverse personalities. Putting together a cogent picture is not easy. I have therefore decided to collate together what she herself said about herself, and what others close to her had seen and written about. I would like to leave it to the reader to put the jig-saw puzzle together, in whatever hues and colours he considers appropriate. Indira Gandhi wanted to write her side of the story, "her truth" as it were, after retiring from public life but this could not come about due to her untimely and tragic assassination. Fortunately, there are scores of letters written by her to her American friend, Dorothy Norman, from 1950 to 1984, and a few written to the family friend A.C.N. Nambiar in Switzerland. I have drawn on this treasure-trove, along with other important observations, comments and inputs for presentation in this chapter. Finally, I have discussed some of her enduring achievements, which in effect, is her undisputed, lasting legacy.

CHILDHOOD AND EARLY YEARS

Nehru had poured out his worries about Indira to his sister, Vijayalakshmi, in a letter written from prison on 6 March 1933. He worried that Indira had become self-centred and selfish and a 'languid, languishing type of girl', and he wanted her to do something practical to bring her down to earth. He worried that she had not written to him for over a year despite his regular letters. (Brown, 2003: 358, note 20)

Indira Gandhi's book, *Remembered Moments – Some Autobiographical Writings of Indira Gandhi,* sheds light on Indira Gandhi's childhood and provides some indications of how her complex personality must have been shaped. She has recounted:

> A little later took place my first encounter with conscience and duty. Being an only child, I liked playing by myself but I liked to have my mother within my range of vision and hearing. One evening she had a visitor, a relative returning from Paris who had brought an exquisite embroidered dress for me. Mummy smilingly returned it saying we now wore only hand-spun and hand-woven material. The visitor could not understand this, and glancing at my mother's clothes – the only Khadi available then was thick and rough as sacking – she could not help noticing that wherever her skin had rubbed against the sari it had become sore and red. She burst out: "I think you have all gone mad. But you are adult and if you want to be ill, I suppose that is your business; you certainly have no right to make the child suffer and it is for her that I have brought this gift." "Come here, Indu," called my mother. "Aunty has brought you a foreign frock. It is very pretty and you can wear it if you like but first think of the big fire where we burnt our foreign things. Would you like to

> wear this dainty thing when the rest of us are wearing Khadi?" The temptation was too strong – my eyes shone with desire. I stretched out a small hand to touch the dress but even before my hand reached it I found myself saying: "Take it away – I shan't ever wear it." "But why not, don't you like nice things?" the visitor teased. "I do – I do – but –" I repeated all the arguments I had overheard from the elders' talk, when she said, "All right, Miss Saint, how is it that you have a foreign doll?" It was an idle remark, thoughtlessly made. Adults so often look upon children as playthings.... The doll was my friend, my child.... For days on end ... the struggle went on between the love of the doll and pride in the ownership of such a lovely thing and, I thought, duty towards my country.... At last the decision was made and, quivering with tension, I took the doll up on the roof-terrace and set fire to her. Then the tears came as if they could never stop and for some days I was ill with a temperature. To this day I hate striking a match.
>
> Our house was beginning its new career of being a centre for political activities. There were constant meetings, big and small. My favourite game was to collect as many servants as I could, stand on table and deliver a speech – repeating disjointed phrases that I had picked up from grown-up talks. (Gandhi, 1991: 10-12)

The article written by her in *Roshni* in November 1959 titled "My Sixteenth Year" sounds so real and touching, even today:

> I had wanted to be a boy but at sixteen the delight of being a woman began to unfold itself and almost overnight the long-legged tomboy in frocks changed into a sari-clad young lady. I came to Calcutta to be with my mother and to share with her the unsatisfactory but greatly treasured *20-minute fortnightly interview with my father*. Mummy and I spent much time in the Ramakrishna Math. Sitting

> peacefully by the riverside, a new world of thought and experience opened out to me. (Gandhi, 1991: 13)

It would be pertinent to see the extracts of her interview with Madame Marianne Lohse of *Madame le Figaro* [of France] on 13 October 1981:

- I like trees, greenery, flowers but if I have to choose between trees and flowers I would have trees.... Then I like music, dancing. I like children. I like animals.
- If I have a free day and there is an exhibition, whether it is art or something I like, I go to it – no matter how much else there is to be done.
- I think everybody is alone. It has nothing to do with your family or what you are doing. Some people hide it and try to smother it either by noise or what they call having fun or something like that. *But I think everybody has a core of loneliness. I would say that I was far less lonely than most people I know because I have always got on very well with myself*, perhaps because I was the only child and quite happy inventing my games. I do not feel I needed somebody to entertain me. And in those days even toys were much less than they are now.
- No, I did have lots of cousins. *What I am trying to say is that I didn't mind being alone.*
- *You have spaces within you just as you have in the universe.* (Gandhi, 1991: 61, 66, 67)

These were thoughtful observations made during light conversation and could only be by a very sensitive and highly evolved person.

Several persons have written about Indira Gandhi's somewhat lonely childhood and her troubled marriage. Amrita Shah has written:

> Indira Gandhi's childhood had been insecure and lonely, shadowed by her mother's frail health and her father's intermittent imprisonment. She herself had suffered from tuberculosis that entailed long periods of convalescence in distant sanatoria. (Shah, 2007: 151)

Indira Gandhi's own observations about herself in her letters to Dorothy Norman bring out some interesting facets:

- I was frequently ill for three years; in 1939, I spent the entire year in a sanatorium in Switzerland, but in the winter of 1940 I returned to England in the middle of the London Blitz. (p 14)
- I have no memory of the luxurious ways in which the family had lived, but we always were comfortable.... In Lisbon, I needed money so I gave English lessons. (p 15)
- *I was imprisoned for eleven and half months* without a trial... At first, because of the spirit of the way in which we had courted imprisonment, discomfort didn't seem to bother us too much. Almost at once, though, I became ill; I ran a high temperature. (p 16) (Norman, 1985)

PRIVATE INDIVIDUAL BEHIND PUBLIC IMAGE

Norman, with whom Indira Gandhi was in correspondence from 1950-64 (with brief interludes and then a long interlude from 1976-1980), has written in the introduction to the book, *Letters to an American Friend – 1950-1984*:

- I sensed her continued loneliness and her reaching out to speak with trust and without restraint. (p xiii)
- In the midst of glamorous events which took place in Jawaharlal's honour during his visit to the USA in October 1949, retiring, reserved Indira – just over thirty

– remained largely in the background. I was touched by her modesty, dignity, quick intelligence. Intuition guided her; she was sensitive, elegant, unostentatious. (p xiv)

- When Norman stayed in Nehru home in January 1950, she has noted: Indira "was not herself drawn to power." (p xv)
- After she became Prime Minister in 1966, Mrs Gandhi was often enigmatic and controversial.... She was not cold, as often inferred, but warmly thoughtful and caring. (p xvi) (Norman, 1985)

LOVE FOR MUSIC

During Indira Gandhi's 1971 visit to New York, Norman has written:

> Indira was ever eager to hear music in New York. We attended a performance of the New York Philharmonic Orchestra, conducted by Leonard Bernstein. I bought tickets for George Balanchine's New York City Ballet. At the last moment, Indira said she could not join me. I showed my surprise; she looked unnerved and sad. I could not understand what had happened; we had spoken of how we looked forward especially to a new Stravinsky ballet. Indira commented only, "I can't go. It will be too wonderful. I won't be able to bear it." She was on the verge of tears. In the morning she had regained her equilibrium. (Norman, 1985: 135)

FEROZE AND DOMESTIC LIFE

Judith Brown, in her book *Nehru – A Political Life*, has written that Nehru "clearly felt uneasy at Indira's choice [of Feroze], for Feroze was a man who lacked the cultivated background and interests of the Nehru family, had no university education or indeed any profession." (Brown, 2003: 145)

Indira Gandhi had herself written on 31 May 1955 in her letter to Dorothy Norman:

> I have been and am deeply unhappy in my domestic life. Now, the hurt and the unpleasantness don't seem to matter so much. I am sorry, though, to have missed the most wonderful thing in life, having a complete and perfect relationship with another human being: and only thus, I feel, can one's personality fully develop and blossom. However, and perhaps, as compensation, I am more at peace with myself...I think I have come to a stage where home is wherever I go. (Norman, 1985: 29)

Amrita Shah has written:

> An impetuous marriage that might have offered some relief from her enforced state of solitude had long fallen apart. (Shah, 2007: 151)

The assessment of marriage as above is shared by Vinod Mehta:

> That the authoress [Sonia Gandhi] has a small gift for understatement is revealed when she notes: "My mother-in-law's marriage had been full of ups and downs." Nevertheless, I believe this is the first public acknowledgement by a member of the Nehru-Gandhi clan that the marriage was a farce. Rajiv, in fact, always nursed a grudge against his mother for keeping him away from his father. Even when Feroze and Indira visited Doon School on the same day, they saw their sons separately.
>
> Pupul Jayakar at least tells us that Indira's marriage was a farce, but what she omits is the impact the farce had on Indira, the human being. Was her loneliness, her cold exterior, her difficulty in making friends connected with the fact that her marriage was a disaster?... (Vinod Mehta, 1999: 116, 119)

After the death of Feroze, in her letter dated 21 September 1960 to Norman, she wrote:

> Although Feroze had been proposing to me since I was 16, it was on the steps of the Basilica of *Secre-Coeur* that I finally and definitely decided...One changes all the time, so perhaps I do more often now but up till now I had somebody to whom I could pour out my thoughts – *even if there was a lack of attention and sympathy* – and with the removal of that outlet I have to look outward. (Norman, 1985: 78)

In a further letter to Norman dated 24 September 1960 she wrote:

> We met about three months ago but I am not the same person now. Neither to look at nor deep down inside. Maybe by the time I reach NY I should feel better – less empty – but I don't think I can ever again be quite the same. Isn't it strange that when you feel full, you are also light as air but when you feel empty and hollow you feel an enormous weight crushing you down? Will I ever be free from this burden or be able to touch and see without the feeling "the heartbreak in the heart of things"? (Norman, 1985: 78-79)

She wrote to Norman on 24 September 1960:

> About the other thing [Feroze] – I'd like to talk but it is so difficult. Right now that hollow empty feeling seems surrounding me and covering me from all sides. I feel as if my luck has run out and I have no confidence in myself. Also the sixth sense or "seeing eye" (as somebody called it) is quite shut off. (Norman, 1985: 79)

Norman has written after Indira Gandhi's visit to her late in 1960:

> After we were alone, Indira spoke of Feroze's death. Tears flowed. She had loved him always, with her virginal first enchantment. She had depended on his love for her, beyond all the vicissitudes that had beset and seemingly separated them. "He really loved me, after all," she said, with a youthful wistfulness that revealed a touching vulnerability behind the disciplined 'public mask'. (Norman, 1985: 80)

FREQUENT FITS OF DEPRESSION

There are frequent references in Indira Gandhi's letters to Norman to her being depressed: I have been very depressed all this summer. (30 July 1957: p 46) Many a time I wanted to write but I was so depressed that I felt I would be bound to convey some of it in my letters! Apart from the mental depression there was a physical one too. I lost a lot of weight and have been quite shaky on my feet, fainting off a couple of times and so on. However, I am better now. (20 September 1959: p 59) If I sometimes seemed depressed, you know the cause – it certainly had nothing to do with the programme. (19 November 1960; p 82) I am feeling much better – the fits of dark dark despair and depression do come but that is something I have always had – heaven knows when one looks around the world there is plenty to be depressed about! But on the whole I have got over that awful self-pity and preoccupation with my own sorrow. (4 December 1960; p 83) I am feeling so terribly depressed that I have not felt like writing and even this brief note dictated days ago has just been lying around. (15 April 1961; p 84) I have been hesitating to write to you, waiting until I felt better. But now I really don't know if such a time will ever come. I have always thought of myself as a positive person. Now I feel terribly negative. I am not ill. I'm not well. I just don't feel alive. Nobody seems aware of the difference! Do you think I have merely exhausted the supply of "mescaline" inside me? (17 July 1961; p 85) East Africa was exciting in many ways but depressing too. Am afraid my forebodings are coming true. My own mood has changed and I am in the depths of depression, for no special reason.... Although I have been in the thick of things in India, I have a curious sense of isolation from everything – I hope I am more alive and awake by the time I get to the US (17 October 1961; p 86) Heaven alone knows how I am going to survive this trip. The tiredness seems to reach deep inside and I am so depressed. (Washington DC, 26 March 1962; p 88) ... gave a dinner at the Beverly Hilton (wonderful food) and the brothers of Loraine Cooper (wife of US Ambassador to India) sent the most fabulous bouquet – pink roses and giant-size orchids. Nothing is lacking except me – just I don't know where I am. The body is there – grinning, talking, but it's just a shell. The real me is non-existent. Is it dead or dormant? It's most depressing and I miss me, if you know what I mean. (In flight Los Angeles to Sacramento, 4 April 1962; p 89) At a time of life which is difficult in the best of circumstances, I have been under tremendous physical and emotional strain, struggling with anaemia, low blood pressure, hormone imbalance – to mention only a few of my ills. (26 September 1963; p 94) In India, I am so tensed up and even if there is time I cannot really unwind. (BOAC flight Frankfurt-Rome, 28 April 1964; p 102) (Norman, 1985)

AS SHE FELT AT TIMES

- I myself am feeling very unsettled – is it age, do you think? Ever since I was a small girl, there seemed to be some force driving me on – as if there were a debt to pay. But suddenly the debt seems to be paid – anyhow I get a tremendous urge to leave everything and retire to a far

far place in the mountains! Not caring if I ever did a stroke of work. Through the winter I felt carefree and light. Several people remarked that I looked "lit up from inside." As suddenly as it came that excellent mood has passed off. (22 December 1957) (Norman, 1985: 47)

- I have been quite out of touch with people other than politicians – can you imagine anything more dreary? (30 July 1957) (Norman, 1985: 46)
- It is quite impossible to have a real holiday in the country. Going out of the country even for a brief holiday is refreshing. (30 July 1957) (Norman, 1985: 46)
- I have been very moody these days. Except in the early years there has hardly ever been a moment free and available for introspection. To think of the usual questions "Who am I and why am I?" Always just ahead was a task to be done which brooked no delay. So it seems strange – on second thought perhaps it is natural and a part of the aging process – to sit and think of myself and of life. (3 June 1973) (Norman, 1985: 145)
- Yes, I am quieter, sadder. Yet is it hardly fair to want more? Life has given of its fullness to me, in happiness and in pain. How can one know one without the other?... [W.B.] Yeats said things fall apart, the centre does not hold. What is centre, and where? (During visit to NY after spending some time with Dorothy, 2 August 1982) (Norman, 1985: 162)

AS PEOPLE SAW HER

Nayantara Sahgal says that, as a child, Indira Gandhi had imagined herself as Joan of Arc, a liberator of her people with the forces of a foreign power ranged against her. *As an adult, she continued to see herself as a martyr.* (Sahgal, 1983: 180)

Inder Malhotra has stated:

> With the possible exception of Charles de Gaulle, no twentieth century leader had identified himself so thoroughly with his country as Indira had with hers. *In fact, she had seldom taken the trouble to hide her belief that she incarnated her country.* (Malhotra, 1991: 24)

Dorothy Norman, has written:

> Mrs Gandhi was often enigmatic and controversial ... an aristocrat of the spirit, she was as much at ease with international celebrities as with the most untutored peasants. Her responses were invariably natural, effortless, artless. Wary of flattery, she was direct, in spite of an innate shyness; ... she was unspoiled and fearless, impatient with any suggestion that she was fragile. Determination and inner stamina served her well. She had blind spots, to be sure, as do we all. (Norman, 1985: xvi)

Pupul Jayakar, who had known Indira Gandhi since 1931, has described Indira thus:

> Fragile, withdrawn, an austere young girl living in enclosed spaces of fantasy.... Indira continued to hide behind an aloof exterior; a sensitive, eager human being, she turned to the unusual, to people and to events in the outer world.... I often spoke to her of self-knowing perceptions. It was only when barriers were lifted that she began to ask me of the nature of self-knowing and of an observation that was free of the observer. She shyly spoke of her own finely honed perception. While young, she found herself watching herself speak; saw things behind her; was aware of events she could not possibly have seen; had often experienced exalted sensory perception. "You know Huxley's doorways of perception?"she said. "I saw the world with the same intensity, but hid my perceptions, as

> people laughed at me and did not understand." From childhood she felt she could "drown in colour…." When she became Prime Minister in 1966 her vulnerability lessened. (Jayakar, 1986: 338)

But, to be frank, while her vulnerability lessened, India's vulnerability increased! It is also difficult to agree with Jayakar's observation that Indira Gandhi was "fragile and living in spaces of fantasy".

Jayakar has written extensively about Indira Gandhi's association with J. Krishnamurti over the years, which had a healing influence on her mind and spirits. One such meeting was in Rishi Valley:

> In the eighteen hours she [Indira Gandhi] had been in Rishi Valley, an unwavering compassion had flowed from Krishnaji, enveloping her. I do not know if she was aware of the timeless energies that emanated from him, healing body and mind…. Indira had brought away within her the silences and the compassion of the valley. It soon became evident that her senses were quickening. A young, vulnerable look was replacing the ravaged face. Her step had grown light and her shoulders straight. (Jayakar, 1986: 356)

When in the company of Norman while on visits abroad, Indira Gandhi was a different person altogether. Norman has written:

> In New York, we went to bookstores, concerts, record shops, theatre…. I also took Indira to the Museum of Modern Art, so that she could see the Children's Carnival…. During the 1961 trip to the United States by Nehru and Indira, both Indira and Nehru were eager to go to the theatre than ever before. We saw Laurence Olivier and Anthony Quinn in Jean Anouilh's Becket…. Backstage after the performance, we congratulated the cast, and

> Nehru invited Olivier to visit him and Indira the following day at his hotel.... I took Indira to Henry Denker's *A Far Country*. Because it was about Freud's approach to psychoanalysis, I thought it might interest her; it made a vivid impression. (Norman, 1985: 80-81, 86-87)

It must be stated that throughout her career, Indira Gandhi faced the situations with exemplary courage. She was a real fighter. Adams has narrated an episode worth noting:

> A brick was thrown at her in a public meeting in Orissa which hit her face, fracturing her nose. Blood poured down her face, but she covered it with her sari and refused to leave the platform (sic), telling the crowd, "This is an insult not to myself but to the country, because as the Prime Minister of India, I represent the country." She described her appearance to Dorothy Norman: 'I looked like a boxer – I was a terrible sight in the mirror. My nose, the left side, looked completely crooked. As it was, I tried to put it right myself and heard a little "tic" sound. The left lip had swollen to the size of a big egg. Most of my face was also discoloured and I bled for quite a while through the nose.' Back in Delhi, her nose was operated on and she playfully said afterwards that the doctors had failed to take the opportunity of improving her looks by shortening her nose. In fact she was serious as she wrote to Dorothy Norman, "ever since plastic surgery was heard of, I have been wanting to get something done to my nose. I even started putting money by for it." She went on with her tour to Calcutta, though she must have been in extreme pain. (Adams, 1997: 211-212)

M.O. Mathai, who worked as Private Secretary to Jawaharlal Nehru for a long time and had become practically a part of the Nehru household, has in his book, *Reminiscences of the Nehru Age*, written a chapter titled "Indira". Reading the book as a whole, one gets an impression that Mathai was a man of great likes and dislikes and was highly self-opinionated. His criticism of Indira Gandhi cannot therefore be taken at face value but a few of his observations are worth noting. He has stated: "With Indira, conceit swelled with success.... Indira hated small cars. When Hindustan Motors put their first car on the road, Nehru asked me to get rid of his 'chariot' which was a Buick and buy a Hindustan. I promptly carried out his wishes. It was only when she saw the small Hindustan that she realized that the Buick had gone. She was livid with rage and did not talk to me for week....[1] Indira had a constant complaint against her father – that he always kept quiet at mealtimes, when they were alone, and never gave satisfactory answers to her questions.... Once she said to me, with a lump her throat and moist eyes, that while she was in England and Europe as a young girl she was kept in want (sic) and that on a few occasions she had to starve. This was also an indirect complaint against her father.... On Nehru's death Indira flagrantly flouted the wishes expressed in his will that he did not want any religious ceremonies after his death.... (Mathai, 1978: 247-248)

Y.B. Chavan once said in a Congress Party meeting that "what happens to her happens to India, and what happens to India happens to her." (Yunus, 1980: 309) In a sense, this was true. The Allahabad High Court decision brought the Emergency in the country. But, this statement reminds one of that classic pronouncement of D.K. Barooah, the then Congress President: "India is Indira, and Indira is India". This was a heady praise which would turn anyone's head. But Yunus has stated how Barooah changed his tune after she was defeated. "After March 1977 the same Barooah made fun of the same Indira. He was reported to have said during a dinner

1 This is particularly interesting because her son Sanjay wanted to mass-produce a small car and she was supporting his venture assiduously.

in February 1977: I had equated Indira with India. I never realized she was international also! He was referring to a newspaper report about some export firm called Indira International! (Yunus, 1980: 310)

Y.B. Chavan in his retirement from politics was nostalgic about the old days and had told this author: Of *bal hutta, stree hutta* and *raj hutta* (the tantrums and whims of a child, a woman and a king), even one is bad enough. You can imagine what happens when they are combined. (Godbole, 1996: 94)

Tavleen Singh has written:

> Mrs Gandhi liked men who followed orders and she also seemed to have a special weakness for people with a stenographer's approach to political decisions, people who could take orders without asking any questions.... Jagmohan appeared to fit this mould, showing an inability to see the difference between loyalty to a bad Prime Minister and real patriotism. He suited Mrs Gandhi's Kashmir policy to perfection. In fact, for what she wanted done [Farooq Abdullah's ouster], she could not have found a better man. (Tavleen Singh, 1996: 57)

Jyoti Basu, former Chief Minister of West Bengal and a prominent CPI(M) leader, had known Indira Gandhi since her young days. They were together in London. He also knew Feroze Gandhi very well. Therefore his observations on Indira Gandhi become particularly important. In his authorised biography, Basu said:

> 'In Nehru, one could sense the mind of a thoroughbred politician, but Indira had no base in politics when she became Prime Minister'. Basu interacted with Mrs Gandhi for nearly five decades. He says, she could be '*vindictive and unscrupulous*'. Once Basu asked Feroze 'how Indira had developed into such an autocratic and ruthless woman'.

> Feroze said to Basu: "If you had lived in Nehru's house you would have seen how important Congress leaders and freedom fighters behaved with her as sycophants. Any young woman's head would have been turned at such behaviour...." Beyond the political arena, Basu and Indira were on amicable terms, though, he says, she could at times be affable and abrasive in the same breath with people.... Basu thinks that *the present day disintegration of values in Indian politics started with Indira.* "It was Indira who started it. *The two major drawbacks of Indira were her political excesses and vindictiveness. The imposition of Emergency was unforgivable. She loved to settle scores with her political as well as personal adversaries."* ... *"Actually, Indira felt herself threatened all the time,"* says Basu. '*She took the government as her family property. And she never trusted anybody.*' She was always reshuffling the Cabinet. She changed the Chief Ministers too frequently and was always restructuring the Cabinet as if she was solving a jigsaw puzzle. This was her policy of preventing anyone from building a strong personal base which might pose problems for her. *And the most disgraceful was her decision to pass her mantle on to her son Sanjay*, he says feelingly.... Indira simply could not tolerate a non-Congress government anywhere in India. (Banerjee, 1997: 244-245)

This indictment from one of the most respected and admired opposition leaders sums up Indira Gandhi admirably.

Another staunch Gandhian and freedom fighter, J.B. Kripalani, is bitter when he recalls in his, *My Times – An Autobiography*, Indira Gandhi's utterances when he was fighting a bye-election from Amroha. As he has observed (which is true to this day), *in India, a man in one province can never be domiciled in another province, however long he may have lived there. A Bengali will ever remain a Bengali, however long he may have remained in another province. Jawaharlal will always be a*

Kashmiri, in spite of the length of time his ancestors lived in UP. A Kripalani is always a Sindhi, though Sind is no more a part of India.

The Congress party had put up one Hafiz as a candidate against Kripalani. He has written:

> The daughter of the Prime Minister, Mrs Indira Gandhi, came to canvass for Hafiz. She not only addressed general meetings but also especially called women's meetings. In one of her speeches, she said:
>
> > "*Who says Kripalani is a leader? He was only a clerk in the AICC office.*" She further said that when she came from England and saw Kripalani she had remarked in surprise: "Is this the General Secretary of the Congress? From that day, I never wanted to see him again."
>
> In my meetings, I replied to all these assertions of hers. I said: "Who says I am national leader? I am not even a leader in my own house (Sucheta [his wife] was then in the Congress and was a minister in UP). As for my being a clerk in the AICC office, I said, "both her grandfather Motilal and, Jawaharlal held the same position in the Congress, whether it was that of a clerk or the highest office in the organisation, next to that of the President! These 'clerks' were the members of the Working Committee, the highest executive of the Congress before they were chosen as General Secretaries." I further said that I could quite understand that, after her first look at me on her return from England, she had no desire to see me again. It was natural for Mrs Gandhi. After all, I did not wear clothes washed by a washerman! *How could a young lady fresh from England imagine a General Secretary who washed his own clothes*? (Kripalani, 2004: 822)

This shocking recollection of Kripalani shows the distance between Indira Gandhi and the Congress party, her aristocratic upbringing and her haughty temperament. There is a great deal of commonality in the assessment of Jyoti Basu and Kripalani.

Malhotra has written about 'her vice-like grip on both the government and her party':

> By the start of the eighties, her party had been reduced to a little more than a praetorian guard. It had also become an inverted pyramid, the 'supreme leader' carrying the rank and file on her shoulders rather than vice versa. The government was no more than an extension of the Prime Minister and a handful of trusted advisers and aides among whom one or the other son occupied pride of place. (Malhotra, 1991: 25)

This aspect of Indira Gandhi's working has also been brought out sharply by Madhu Limaye:

> Between 1972 and 1977, Bihar saw three Chief Ministers in quick succession: Kedar Pande, Abdul Gafoor and Jagannath Mishra. Madhya Pradesh had P.C. Sethi and Shyama Charan Shukla. Maharashtra's relatively efficient administration was dealt a blow by the game of musical chairs. Between 1972 and 1977, the State had V.P. Naik, S.B. Chavan and Vasant Dada Patil as Chief Ministers. In Uttar Pradesh, we had during this period Kamalapati Tripathi, H.N. Bahuguna and N.D. Tiwari. (Limaye, 1992: 26)

HER POLITICS

It is interesting to know, first hand, how Indira Gandhi looked at her political struggle within the Congress party. In her letter to Norman on 4 September 1969, she wrote:

> Unfortunately *the institution of bossism* created a clash between the [Congress] party and the people as a whole.

> Each State boss came to believe that he *was* the State. This is what I have tried to break through. Perhaps because I have tried to be accommodating, they all thought I was weak. These last two years have been of tremendous pressure and difficulty. If it had been a question of myself or my position, it would not have mattered but *the manner in which I was being pushed around, with a view to finally pushing me out of office, would certainly have not only split the Congress but weakened it all along the line*. The Communists have been able to come to power in West Bengal and Kerala, because of the split in the State Congress. In both cases this was avoidable and I had pleaded with the then Congress President, but *the opinion of the local (or State) Boss prevailed.* (Norman 1985: 122-123)

She recalled in her letter dated 23 April 1971 to Norman:

> In the forty-three days at my disposal [before the 1971 elections], I travelled over thirty-six thousand miles, addressed over three hundred meetings. The official estimate is that about thirteen million people attended my meetings and another seven million lined the roads. (Norman, 1985: 132)

Her persecution complex is seen again and again. For example, In her letter dated 19 October 1972 to Norman she wrote:

> Parliament will be sitting November-December. The opposition – all parties, extreme Left and extreme Right included – are said to have finally decided to concentrate on *a vilification campaign. As I wrote earlier, Jayaprakash Narayan is a party to all this.* (Norman, 1985: 141)

A SPLIT PERSONALITY

The Cambridge dictionary describes a person with a split personality as one who behaves so differently at different times that he seems to have more than one character. *Such a person also has a persecution complex and feels that other people are trying to harm him.*

In her letter to Dorothy Norman on 20 September 1959, Indira Gandhi herself had written:

> *Are most people not just a split personality but several personalities? I feel I am and have learnt to make all the separate personalities quite friendly with each other.* But, I still don't know how to present them to the world. Different people see different mes! (Norman, 1985: 59)

Indira Gandhi's split personality is likely to have been caused by many factors including emotional abuse, severe childhood trauma, and continuous feeling of insecurity. As for her childhood, I have referred to the situations which may have left a permanent scar on her mind and psyche. But, equally important was the feeling of insecurity in her political career which continued, for example, even when she was at the peak of her power in 1971. In her letter to Nambiar, based then in Switzerland, she had written on 15 September 1984, just a few months before her death:

> The opposition, the Press and the self-styled liberals, seem to have a new yardstick to measure democracy, and that is 'Anything said or done against Indira Gandhi and the Congress is right'. (Balachandran, 2016: 328)

In some ways, she comes across as a simple, loving, caring woman like any other person next door. She is as doting and protective of her son Sanjay as any other mother, who had been separated from her husband and had to bring up her children on her own. Her letters to her friend Dorothy Norman and also her caring correspondence with A.C.N. Nambiar, a close family friend, brought out later, show Indira Gandhi in a new light altogether. Same is true when it came to her interactions with

Pupul Jayakar and J. Krishnamurti. But as a politician, leader of her party and the Prime Minister, she was an altogether different person – ruthless, inscrutable, unscrupulous, harsh, a person without any scruples, without any values and prepared to do anything to protect her position. This stark contrast is so striking that one is left with no other choice but to describe it as a split personality.

A.C.N. Nambiar, who worked closely with Subhas Chandra Bose and Jawaharlal Nehru from abroad during the freedom movement, became a close family friend of Nehru family. In fact, he was treated as a member of the family by both Nehru and Indira Gandhi. Balachandran has done commendable research and published, for the first time, in his book, *A Life in Shadow – The Secret Story of A.C.N. Nambiar: A Forgotten Anti-Colonial Warrior*, 14 unpublished letters written by Nehru and Indira Gandhi to Nambiar over the years. Indira Gandhi used to address him as 'Nanu' and sign off the letters as from 'Indu'. Only in a couple of letters, I have referred to earlier, had she written about the political situation in the country. In others, she has made loving enquiries about Nambiar's health, and urged him to come back to India. On his return, she suggested, on 17 April 1984, that if he was feeling lonely, he could stay in India International Centre in Delhi where he would be able to meet interesting people. In her letter dated 22 October 1984 written in hand, she had said, "It is nice to have you back in India. But please don't think it as an imposition for you to drop in at mealtimes when you feel like it, or at any other time. If you let me know as to what times you have your meals, we can send something." (Balachandran, 2016: 324, 329)

In yet another letter dated 30 April 1984, she wrote:

> My grandson Feroze Varun is not allowed to see me. I saw him for just a minute or so by chance at a function. The

> next day was his birthday and we very much wanted him to come here but he was not sent in spite of telephone calls, sending a person etc. Since we had some gifts for him, Sonia went to his school to give those. She also saw him only for a few moments, as someone was sent to fetch him home. And the next day we were horrified to see in the newspapers that Sonia had been accused of attempting to kidnap the little boy. He has now been moved to another school. We do not know which one it is and we have no opportunity of meeting him. (Balachandran, 2016:325)

Reading these letters, who would associate Indira Gandhi with the atrocities in Emergency or scores of unreasonable and unjust decisions during her regime? And yet, she had written in her letter to her friend Norman on 14 September 1980: "You know me well enough to appreciate that *I am neither authoritarian nor cold*. But I am not effusive, and perhaps this is misunderstood." (Norman, 1985: 154)

T.N. Kaul, the then Foreign Secretary, her close confidant and one of the *panch* [five] *Pandavas*, has written:

> Even after her convincing leadership which resulted in the defeat of Pakistan, her popularity did not last long. Some of the opposition leaders ganged up against her and created crisis situations, especially in 1974.... *Indira Gandhi seemed to have lost her self-confidence and developed a sense of insecurity.* She had few colleagues whom she trusted. (Kaul, 2000: 111)

Indira Gandhi's total insensitivity in some situations was simply shocking. Arun Shourie has written at length how she unrelentlessly pushed through the elections in Assam in the face of strong opposition.

> By March 1982, Mrs Gandhi's efforts to install a Congress(I) government in Assam had finally fallen through.... The

> Congress High Command ... came to the conclusion that election was the only way out. "Elections, yes; but elections at all cost without revising the rolls...." The stage for a total breakdown, for a war of all against all, began to be set the moment it became clear that Mrs Gandhi had set her mind on elections.... On the police's own count, between 7 January, the day to hold elections was announced, and 21 February, the day the polling was finished, police opened fire on 202 occasions, killing (once again according to the count of the police itself) 126 and injuring 162. Like the massacres, most of the firings were bunched around the days of polling.... So complete was the breakdown that by early February, K.P.S. Gill, IGP, literally visited seven to eight district headquarters every day, not to prevent the carnage but ... just to hold forces from complete collapse.... In the forenoon of 18 February, 1,383 men, women and children were butchered in and around Nellie.... The killings took place not in one isolated village but in ten.... In a sense, the Assam elections constitute a vindication of Mrs Gandhi's divide-and-win electoral strategy.... But, while Mrs Gandhi has won a major victory, the democratic process has suffered a terrible blow. Never since independence – indeed, never since elections as we know them were introduced in India – have laws been perverted the way they were in Assam.... The electoral rolls that were used were grossly and admittedly defective; the perquisites for a free and fair poll were totally absent; the actual polling was a farce. (Shourie, 1987: 217, 225-226, 232-233, 255)

However, reference must be made to Indira Gandhi's own defence for holding these elections. In her letter to her friend Norman dated 10 February 1983, Indira Gandhi wrote:

> Our Constitution compels us to hold elections every five years. We can postpone them by Constitutional Amendment. But

> when this idea was put to the Opposition parties, they did not agree to support us and our strength in the Upper House is not sufficient to act by ourselves. Now that the elections have been announced and the process is taking its inevitable course, some of the Opposition parties are pressing for postponement. (Norman, 1985: 170)

I.G. Patel, who worked with her closely for several years, has written: There was always this 'love and hate' or 'pull and push' between her and experts or persons supposed to be more knowledgeable. She wanted to be known that she liked them; but she did not quite trust them. *She was more at home with creative persons like writers, artists and craftsmen, and made it a point to meet whenever she could.* (Patel, 2002: 109)

Turn of events in life, particularly major set-backs such as humiliating defeat in elections in 1977 followed by Shah Commission of Inquiry, criminal cases, howsoever brave face she might have put up publicly, and finally the tragic death of her wayward son in an air accident, must have led to her thinking afresh about her life and what she had been able to achieve. Back in 1971, she had said in a television interview in Britain that she did not believe in God. But in the 1980, she had become highly religious.

> Before she moved into the official residence as Prime Minister in early February 1980, priests from Varanasi conducted eight-day religious rites. During the first thirty-eight days in office, she worshipped at about a dozen shrines from Jammu in the north to Tamil Nadu in the south. There were series of news items about her visiting well-known shrines, temples and Dargahs all over the country. For example, in January 1980, it was Padmanabha Swamy Temple in Guruvayoor, in February, it was Lord Venkateswara Temple in Tirumala, in March, it was Vaishno Devi Temple in Jammu, and Amba Mata Temple

> in Gujarat, and the tomb of Khwaja Moinuddin Chisti, in April, Lord Vishwanath Temple in Varanasi, and temples of Annapurna, Sankatamochan and Vindhyavashini, and Kamala Nath Temple, and a number of other temples in Madhya Pradesh. (Sahgal, 1983: 227-228)

The only other VVIP that I can think of, who visited as many or more temples by Indian Air Force special plane, was President Shankar Dayal Sharma!

HER ENTOURAGE

It is rightly said that the man/woman is known by the company he/she keeps. In no other case it is more true than in the case of Indira Gandhi. Janardan Thakur, in his book, *All the Prime Minister's Men*, has given striking chapter-headings, some of which are: Bansi Lal: The Jat Bully; V.C. Shukla: The Playboy Goebbels; D.K. Barooah: The Sly Jester; Yashpal and Dhawan: The Factotums; Dhirendra Brahmachari: Indira's Rasputin; and Khidmatgars and Cronies. (Thakur, 1977: Contents page)

Writing about the persons at the decision-making level in Delhi at the time when the plans for dismissal of Chief Minister Farooq Abdullah were being hatched in PMO, B.K. Nehru has written, "P.C. Sethi, the Home Minister, was simply unaware of what was going on. *The appointment of Sethi as Home Minister was not quite explicable. It was well known that he was not quite right in the head.* His position in regard to Kashmir was simply that he was neither informed nor consulted though he was sometimes made to sign a letter of which the draft was put up to him by other people." (Nehru, 1997: 624)

The persons in Prime Minister's Office who were close to her have been described by various names: B.N. Tandon calls them 'palace guards', while Romesh Thapar calls them 'small people'. The people in her close circle, on whom he and her son relied, were also commented upon harshly and severely by people like M.O. Mathai and Mohammad Yunus, leave aside political commentators.[2] It was like a typical case of palace intrigues. Om Mehta, though only a Minister of State for Home Affairs, was virtually running the ministry, with the Home Minister having been side-lined. As in the case of Mathai, I am inclined to overlook some observations of Yunus on a number of persons. But, in some cases, they seem credible. For example, Yunus has written: "The case of Om Mehta comes to mind. Here was another sub-mediocre candidate for the trust reposed in him to be a minister. He did not deserve to be associated with her name in any situation." He has also referred to "Dinesh Singh and what was known as her Kitchen Cabinet. They strutted about the stage for a while. A 'Kashmiri Ensemble', with the shadow of the powerful Steel Minister, Mohan Kumaramangalam, hovering over them, ruled the roost for nearly three years.... This Kashmiri group was succeeded by a political trio. It consisted of D.K. Barooah, S.S. Ray and Rajani Patel." Yunus has also written: "I came to know later how each Chief Minister – Ray in Bengal, Shukla in MP, Nandini Satpathy in Orissa, and Hardeo Joshi in Rajasthan were grabbing innocent people. They would get away by saying that they were doing it "on instructions from the Prime Minister...." The differences between Ray, the Chief Minister and the two Central ministers – Chattopadhya and Pranab Mukherjee – made it difficult to apportion blame or catch the

2 How close Yunus was to Indira Gandhi can be gauged from the letter which she wrote to Yunus from Tihar jail on 20 December 1978 in which she had written: "Keep well and cheerful and do keep an eye on my household, especially Sanjay. (Sanjay had undergone a major operation at the All India Medical Institute at that time.) Going to court will be a big strain, physical and mental, at a time when he should have had complete rest. Rajiv and Sonia have been very helpful and sweet. God bless them all and you." The letter was signed off Indu. (Yunus, 1980: 315)

culprit. It made confusion worse confounded in West Bengal." (Yunus, 1980: 256, footnote 1, 285-286)

HER SENSE OF HUMOUR

I.G. Patel has recalled that soon after taking over as Information and Broadcasting Minister, Indira Gandhi had called a meeting of the so-called 'intellectuals' in which he was also included. Much was said by those present. When Patel's turn came, he simply said he had nothing to say as he knew nothing of information and broadcasting. She laughed and said rather sarcastically: "Obviously you and I are the only ones who do not know anything about I&B." (Patel, 2002: 109)

Sheila Dhar, wife of P.N. Dhar and a noted classical singer, saw a different side of the Prime Minister. According to her, Indira Gandhi 'had a puckish sense of humour which her own life wasn't very hospitable to.... There was definitely a sporting and fun-loving person in her that did not often get a chance to emerge.' (Austin, 1999: 572, footnote 51)

After her return to power in 1980, the Lok Sabha was dealing with the issue of freedom fighters' pension during the Question Hour. Madhu Dandavate asked a question, "what about the benefits to those who participated in the second battle of freedom against the national Emergency promulgated in 1975?" Pat came the reply from Gandhi: "I thought they were amply rewarded. It is a different story, they threw away the reward...." Madhu Dandavate, himself known for parliamentary wit and humour, was to admit that on this occasion, he 'was caught on a wrong foot'. (Kashyap, 1997: 441)

NOTABLE TRAITS AND STYLE OF FUNCTIONING

Though acclaimed as the only leader with all India outlook and credentials with no regional biases, her close official advisors and confidants were all Kashmiri Brahmins – P.N. Haksar, her Principal Secretary; D.P. Dhar, ambassador to USSR, and later Deputy Chairman, Planning Commission; P.N. Dhar, Secretary to Prime Minister; R.N. Kao, Secretary, R&AW and later Senior Security Advisor; and T.N. Kaul, Foreign Secretary. I.G. Patel calls the first three 'Kashmiri Pundit triptych' [an alter piece with a central panel and two flanking panels half its size that fold over it]. (Patel, 2002: 132) Others have called it 'Kashmiri mafia' and '*panch* [five] *Pandavas*'.

Mohammad Yunus, who called himself the uncle of the family, had a strong contempt for 'the gang' as he calls them.[3] He has written:

> Haksar, who was made much of by Mrs Gandhi, had no inhibitions about wielding prestigious and powerful jobs under her. He was pleased to get extensions. He did not consider resigning as long as she was in power. He never showed any resentment at what was later termed as Mrs Gandhi's authoritative (sic) ways. He and his Sancho Panza – P.N. Dhar – stuck to the prestige she gave them as long as it was feasible.... Once she was out, they did not have the basic decency to own her (sic) or maintain any links. They had clung to power and later fell off like rotten fruit. Except for T.N. Kaul, the rest of the gang got its reward from those who replaced her in March 1977. *Kao was the first to alert the Janata leaders about Mrs Gandhi's plans to escape,* and thus to get her passport impounded along with her family's, mine and others close to her. (Yunus, 1980: 287)

The statement about Kao certainly does not appear to be correct as he was appointed as Senior Security Advisor when

---

3 Yunus was also contemptuous of MO Mathai. (Yunus, 1980: 304-307)

she returned to power in 1980. This would not have happened unless she had full confidence in him.

I.G. Patel has stated: "For her, nothing was by merit and everything had to be a favour granted by her." Patel considered her shabby treatment of D.R. Gadgil, eminent economist and Deputy Chairman, Planning Commission, as

> a dark spot on Mrs Gandhi's career. In a nutshell, Gadgil was too honest a person for Mrs Gandhi's liking. He would not always suit her purpose. After Morarji's ouster, she must have decided to remove Gadgil too; and her resolve must have been strengthened by the fact that Gadgil refused to praise the nationalization of banks from the roof-tops.... Whether he was finally asked to go or whether it was made clear to him that he had outlived his welcome and forced to resign, I do not know. But I know how unhappy Gadgil was, although he never gave vent to his unhappiness.... Thus came the end in a moving train of one of India's noblest sons with no one but his wife to bid him good-bye. *Fate punishes everyone in her own way; and Mrs Gandhi had more than her share of punishment*. (Patel, 2002: 122, 141-142)

As for punishment, it must be stated that Lok Sabha would not have, for example, punished her for breach of privilege to the extent of imprisoning her and expelling her, if her conduct had not been so rude, defiant and domineering. While moving the motion on 8 December 1978 for requesting the Speaker to call her to the Bar of the House, Prime Minister Morarji Desai had, inter alia, referred to the fact that:

- She committed a further breach of privilege and contempt of the House by her refusal to take oath/ affirmation before the Committee;
- She also committed a breach of privilege and contempt by casting aspersions on the Committee in her statement

> dated 16th June 1978, and that the last two breaches of privilege have aggravated the first mentioned contempt. (Kashyap, 1997: 416)

This was in sharp contrast to the highly deferential conduct and humility of her father, Jawaharlal Nehru, when it came to dealing with Parliament. He had elevated Parliament as a 'grand inquest of the nation'.

B.G. Deshmukh, former Cabinet Secretary, was highly critical of the working of both the PMO (Prime Minister's Office/Secretariat) as also PMH (Prime Minister's House), which later became much more powerful.[4] Deshmukh has written:

> It was also a reflection of her personality. She wanted a strong body close to her *through which she could operate and even manipulate*.... Instead of using normal channels of government, Haksar bypassed or usurped them. He must have rued his role in making PM's secretariat such a very strong body when a PMH emerged and displaced it.... It is an irony of fate that *the PMH, as symbolised by Sanjay Gandhi, came to overshadow even the Prime Minister herself*, whether she was in office or out.... *When Indiraji came back to power in 1980, the PMH was completely overshadowing the government and the PMO.* After Sanjay Gandhi's death, importance of the PMH reduced considerably. But it still continued to be a force to be reckoned with.... It was a clear policy of the Janata government ... to cut down the importance of the PMO. They changed the name from Prime Minister's Secretariat to Prime Minister's Office. (Deshmukh, 1998: 28)

---

4 This assessment is fully shared by BN Tandon, who was Joint Secretary in Prime Minister's Secretariat. He has deprecatingly referred to the role of what he has called "palace guards".

P.N. Dhar, who was Secretary in PMO and later her Principal Secretary, has made some pertinent observations on her style of working:

> She had the reputation of being aloof, secretive and haughty.... One could not always depend on her undivided attention in face-to-face encounters, it was not easy to cut through preliminaries, and long hours had to be spent writing unnecessarily long notes.... She also had a disturbing habit of reading papers lying on her desk while one was talking to her. The first time this happened to me, I stopped talking; she raised her head and asked me to go on, adding that she could do several things at the same time. She practised this style sometimes even in her meetings with foreign dignitaries. I remember vividly an occasion when the Shah of Iran was talking rather earnestly to her in his Niyavaran palace in Teheran about the future prospects of the oil industry. She suddenly turned her gaze away from him towards window, from where she could hear the twittering of *bulbuls*. Sardar Swaran Singh swiftly stepped in to save the situation by appearing to hang on to every word the Shah uttered and nodded his head vigorously, while I increased the speed of my note-taking. Her mental resistance against following complicated arguments was partly responsible for this kind of reaction in her.... The longest and most tedious meetings with Indira Gandhi had to do with the preparation of her speeches. (Dhar, 2000: 120)

Dhar's some other observations are also revealing. He believed that

> Although Indira Gandhi was immensely proud of her patrimony, she believed Jawaharlal Nehru was a weak man. She suspected his weakness was rooted in his goodness. She often said, 'People call Gandhiji a saint, actually it was my father who was a saint.' *To achieve her political objectives,*

> *she did not hesitate to manipulate men and events in a manner that would have been anathema to her father. She did not have much use for what she called public school morality, and she did not mind her critics calling her amoral and ruthless....* Nehru was more genuinely liberal and open-minded, and less temperamentally authoritarian and autocratic than his daughter. On this account, Nehru's court appears in retrospect to have been less feudal than Indira Gandhi's. *In her time the feudal ethos became much more pronounced.* (Dhar, 2000: 123, 133)

P.C. Alexander, who was her Principal Secretary, has written:

> Indira Gandhi had to deal with six Presidents: Radhakrishnan, Zakir Hussain, V.V. Giri, Fakhruddin Ali Ahmed, Sanjiva Reddy and Zail Singh. Except Radhakrishnan, none of the other Presidents seriously tried to offer advice to her beyond the limits of their normal constitutional responsibilities. By and large, they chose to remain within formal constitutional responsibilities. (Alexander, 1995: 34)

Gill has written about the case of S.C. Chhabra, Chairman of New Delhi Municipal Corporation who had been falsely implicated in corruption cases as he had opposed efforts of some Congress leaders to start hutment colonies on government land. Sanjay Gandhi wanted him to be dismissed. Romesh Thapar sought C.D. Deshmukh's advice to save Chhabra. Deshmukh said, "You must approach Indira Gandhi like a supplicant. You must address her as if she were an empress." Thapar drafted an appeal accordingly, and all cases against Chhabra were dropped. (Gill, 1996: 284-285)

The Congress party lost its organisational hold and came to be micro-managed by Indira Gandhi. Any Chief Minister who had a base in the party was considered a threat and either removed or cut to size. Indira Gandhi herself decided which of the State Ministers would get party tickets. Four veteran Chief Ministers, Mohanlal Sukhadia of Rajasthan, Brahmananda Reddy of Andhra Pradesh, M.M. Chaudhury of Assam, and Shyama Charan Shukla of Madhya Pradesh, each powerfully backed in his State, were replaced by her nominees -- Barakatullah, P.V. Narasimha Rao, S.C. Singh, and P.C. Sethi, respectively. Same was the position about appointment of State Congress Committees. Even selection of candidates for State Legislatures was decided by Indira Gandhi. (Sahgal, 1978: 82)

M.O. Mathai has been blunt in his criticism of Indira Gandhi's leadership. He has written:

> Indira's tenure as PM was marked by some very unhealthy trends: (i) Her absurd advocacy of committed civil servants, committed judiciary, and committed Press; (ii) the sickeningly vulgar solidarity rallies artificially arranged in Delhi on the slightest provocation at public expense by Delhi State and the adjoining States of Haryana, Punjab, Rajasthan, Madhya Pradesh and Uttar Pradesh. A tribe of paid rally men were as readily available as instant coffee, and public transport was always there; (iii) reducing the Council of Ministers to a bunch of nonentities; (iv) befriending and making use of the Communist Party of India and ex-Communists while she was shaky and discarding them when she felt politically safe; (v) making ghost-writers out of all except chaprasis. The classic example of a committed civil servant was P.N. Haksar, who had some experience only in the Foreign Service in rather minor position, and who did not possess a modicum of discipline and detachment so essential in a civil servant. He was allowed to play party politics for which he was singularly unfit. (Mathai, 1978: 251-252)[5]

5 Mohammad Yunus calls Haksar one "who remained tied in the stable like a 'Trojan Horse' till the end." (Yunus, 1980: 267)

There can be two views only on his observation on Haksar. Haksar came with his own agenda and wielded enormous influence on Indira Gandhi. As discussed in this book, not all his advice, such as during Simla negotiations, and on committed civil service and a number of Leftist policies, was sound or well thought out. His over-bearing style of functioning did not permit any open, free and frank discussion, except in the close group of Kashmiri confidants.

Yunus has written: "Mrs Gandhi listens to her many advisers, quietly, but leaves them wondering about her reactions." (Yunus, 1980: 270) This was certainly not true so far as Haksar was concerned.

Even when she was out of power, she was her imperious self – someone born to rule. During her visit to Agra, she addressed a public meeting and was modest enough to confess: "People come to Agra to visit Taj Mahal and Agra Fort. People go to Delhi to see Qutab Minar and Indira Gandhi!"

Madhu Limaye had highlighted the extra-constitutional expansion of the Prime Minister's Secretariat which had virtually superseded the Cabinet form of government. (Limaye, 1994: 479)

Comparing Nehru with Indira Gandhi, Austin is of the view that Indira Gandhi removed collegiality from the Central Government's functioning, tamed Parliament and the Congress State Governments, and drastically weakened whatever federal structure the Congress party had – all in the name of social revolution. She over-centralized for personal survival.... Her situation made her a brilliant political tactician, but by personality she was not a nation-builder, although her longevity in office and her wide popular appeal contributed to national consolidation. (Austin, 1999: 573)

In some cases, Indira Gandhi's policy brought India in disrepute. One such case was when a secular India unnecessarily wanted to join the Muslim countries' conference at Rabat in the middle of 1969 to condemn Israel on the burning of the Al Aqsa mosque in Jerusalem. The Government of India had claimed that with its 60 million Muslim population, India had a right to be invited to the conference. Pakistan strongly objected and even threatened to walk out of the conference. As a result, the delegation led by Fakhruddin Ali Ahmed had to return ignominiously, without being permitted to attend the conference. Later, the King of Saudi Arabia sent a message to Indira Gandhi saying that it would be very difficult for the Muslim nations to keep silent if killings like at Ahmedabad continued unabated; at least some action should have been taken so that Muslims all over the world would know that the Government of India was doing its best to punish the guilty. It was thus a slap in the face of New Delhi. (Nayar, 1971: 213-215)

In his authorised biography, Jyoti Basu, has stated that he met Indira Gandhi with a deputation on 31 January 1972 to appraise her of the situation in West Bengal. To his utter astonishment, Indira Gandhi said all Basu's reports were unfounded and denied the charge that the Congress was behind the mayhem in the State. "I have come to Indira Gandhi, the Prime Minister, not Indira Gandhi, the Congress leader, for redressal," said Basu. "On the contrary, it is the Communists who have created this panic in the State," she alleged. "In that case, you have to prove this, where is the concrete proof?" demanded Basu. Indira could not answer Basu's question and left the meeting in a huff. (Banerjee, 1997: 149-150)

HER PRESS CONFERENCES

Though denigrated as a *gungi gudiya* (dumb doll) when she took over, within a few years, Indira Gandhi emerged as the tallest leader in India. A Prime Minister's mettle is tested in Press conferences. I, as Union Home Secretary, had sat through hours of briefing sessions for Prime Minister P.V. Narasimha Rao before his Press conferences which invariably turned out to be colourless and ineffective. Nehru held a number of Press conferences but often his replies to questions were far too rambling. After Nehru, Indira Gandhi must have held the record of addressing the largest number of Press conferences in India and abroad. We have seen how several Prime Ministers have been reluctant to face Press conferences, thereafter. She personified supreme self-confidence and presence of mind. Her replies were crisp and to the point. At times she was blunt and even ticked off the questioner. This added spice to the event. Her performance in the Press conferences abroad was particularly impressive. The questions covered a very broad canvas and the replies showed how the Prime Minister was firmly in the saddle. No one could have been in any doubt as to who was in charge in India. Replies to tricky questions were diplomatically handled with a great deal of finesse.

In the Press meet at the National Press Club, Washington, on 5 November 1971, her opening remarks made her position clear. She had said, "I should like to plead with the world not to press me for a solution [to the East Pakistan question] which leaves out the people of East Bengal…. The process of democracy admits no geographical disqualification. If democracy is good for you, it is good for us in India, and it is good for the people of East Bengal. The suppression of democracy is the original cause of all the troubles in Pakistan. She took the opportunity to explain in the context of the Indo-USSR treaty of peace and friendship that non-alignment does not mean being neutral or unconcerned, or ignoring what is happening in the world. It merely means that we do not belong to a military bloc and that we reserve the right to judge each international issue on its merits. In reply to a question, "Do you have any comments to offer on Dr Kissinger?", she said, "Well, he is a very nice man." (Laughter) A question asked was, "Do you think that you, Golda Meir and the Prime Minister of Ceylon should form a new bloc of influential lady heads of State?", Indira Gandhi quipped, "Perhaps the Women's Lib should begin a campaign for this kind of getting together of lady Prime Ministers." (Laughter) A question was asked, "What is your reaction to the defeat of the US Foreign Aid Bill?", she promptly replied, "I think it is an internal matter which affects many countries." (Laughter) A question was asked, "What advice would you give to American women who aspire to careers in politics or government?" She replied, "I think that American women are quite smart to figure this out for themselves." (Laughter and applause) Another question was, "Have you considered unleashing Krishna Menon against the Government of Pakistan?", she was quick to reply, "If this question had been asked in our Parliament, we would have said it's a suggestion for action." (Laughter) (GoI, 1971: 68-87) There were many questions on larger policy issues and world affairs. Here was an astute, articulate and highly evolved stateswoman, with a fine sense of humour and presence of mind.

In one of Indira Gandhi's Press conferences, K.R. Sunder Rajan of *The Sunday Observer* began asking his question on the credibility of the government-controlled media. Even before he had finished his question, Indira Gandhi shot back, "What is the credibility of your newspaper?" and indicated that she had nothing more to say on the subject. (Vinod Mehta, 1999: 67) This was even better than what American President Donald Trump has been doing in his Press conferences.

SPECIAL FLAIR FOR FOREIGN AFFAIRS

Inder Gujral, who was minister, and later ambassador to USSR during Indira Gandhi and Janata government regimes, has given his assessment of Indira Gandhi:

> Whatever else one may say about Mrs Gandhi's politics at home, I think in foreign affairs she was excellent. She had a very good assessment of Indo-Soviet relations. Sometimes people were uncharitable to her, as if Soviets had influence on her; but I don't believe it. Mrs Gandhi was so conscious of our national interest and the safeguarding of it that she did it with remarkable finesse. For instance, she never accepted the desirability of the Soviets entering Afghanistan. She did not come out to criticise them openly, not because she was beholden to the Soviet Union, but because of the American policy in Pakistan. I was privy to this, that Mrs Gandhi had told the Russians in categorical language that she could never approve of their entry into Afghanistan. Mrs Gandhi always held her ground on essentials; and the Soviet leaders respected her a great deal, because they knew they could not take her for granted. (Tully, 1988: 112-113)

Talbot has written about Kissinger's visit to Delhi which was meant primarily to consult with Indira Gandhi. Like many American officials during her long tenure as Prime Minister, he found her hard to take. He complained in his memoirs about "her assumption of almost hereditary moral superiority" and "a disdain for capitalism quite fashionable in developing countries…." But Kissinger also found in Mrs Gandhi a steeliness of character and hard-headedness about the way of the world with which he could relate…. Briefings that Kissinger gave to reporters who travelled with him to New Delhi suggested that he accepted, and even grudgingly admired, the way Mrs Gandhi put that theory into practice with the Buddha's smile test. (Talbot, 2004: 16)

Tully has rightly concluded that "Indira Gandhi may have lacked her father's moral or intellectual stature; but *Nehru never enjoyed the power or prestige his daughter did at the end of*

1971, crowned with such decisive electoral and military victory within the short space of a year." (Tully, 1988: 113)

Raj and Romesh Thapar were close friends of Indira Gandhi for quite some time but drifted apart after Emergency was declared and a new facet of Indira Gandhi's functioning and Sanjay's antics became evident. Referring to Indira Gandhi's visit to New York and her lecture at the Central Hall in Washington, Raj Thapar has in her book, *All These Years – A Memoir*, written:

> Apart from being terribly proud of her, we knew at once that it was any day now [India walking into Bangladesh]. She did look good standing there, even though I strongly disapproved of her change in dress style, hair style, when she stepped out of our Indian borders. It became a kind of Jekyll and Hyde business, long-sleeved khadi at home, elaborately coiffured hair abroad with changing emphasis on the white streak. I would have had her retain the simplicity but I think people generally loved to see that we could have leaders who were no different from 'royalty' abroad. (Thapar, 1991: 334)

And Thapar was not alone to think this way. There were several others. But, personally, I feel that this was doing injustice to Indira Gandhi. It cannot be denied that she looked majestic and was very impressive and articulate on visits abroad which contributed in no small measure to creating a new image of India.

Writing about her first visit to USA after taking over as Prime Minister, I.G. Patel, who had accompanied her, has perceptively written:

> In many ways, the visit was a one-sided affair. Everyone knew that Mrs Gandhi could not be rushed; that behind her docile facade, she was an imperious daughter of a proud father, she had to be humoured rather than lectured

> to.... Mrs Gandhi listened politely, even regally. There was no question of making a response. No commitments were expected or made. In many ways, it was like a royal visit. (Patel, 2002: 110)

One thing a number of persons, who saw her at close quarters, have talked about is her silences, which were most eloquent. I.G. Patel has recalled that on her way back from USA, Prime Minster Wilson was most anxious to atone for his *faux pas* in the Pakistan war and invited Mrs Gandhi to spend a day or two in London. But Mrs Gandhi would have none of it, and Wilson had to be content with calling on Mrs Gandhi at an airport hotel and giving her a lunch there. For the most part, *Mrs Gandhi listened again and confronted Wilson with her Mona Lisa smile.* (Patel, 2002: 110)

According to I.G. Patel, again, the spirit of the visit to the USSR was best exemplified as [Prime Minister] Kosygin was taking leave of Mrs Gandhi. He put his hand on her shoulder and said that he was old enough to give her some advice. He said:

> Madame Prime Minister, I know how difficult the role of a Prime Minister is; and yours is perhaps the most difficult of all. Do not neglect your health and do relax from time to time. It is necessary for your work. If you cannot get away from work in India, you come to our country even if it is for two or three days. We will leave you entirely free to rest and recuperate." This was said with the utmost affection and sincerity. (Patel, 2002: 111)

Henry Kissinger has, in his book, *World Order*, described Indira Gandhi as 'formidable'. (Kissinger, 2014: 201)

ROLLER COASTER RIDE OF PEOPLE'S MANDATE

Four Lok Sabha elections were held during the tenure of Indira Gandhi as Prime Minister. The first of these was the fourth general election held in February 1967, without the presence of Jawaharlal Nehru, and after Indira Gandhi took over as Prime Minister. In the 1967 elections, Indira Gandhi travelled over 15,000 miles and addressed 160 public meetings in two months. (Adams, 1997: 210-211) It saw the undivided Congress party getting 40.8 per cent of votes and 283 seats in the Lok Sabha, just a bear majority. Swatantra Party emerged as the largest opposition party with 8.5 per cent votes and 42 seats, Jan Sangh with 9.3 per cent votes and 35 seats, and SSP and CPI parties with 4.9 per cent votes each and 23 seats each. Of the sixteen State Assemblies for which polls were held along with those of the Lok Sabha, Congress lost absolute majority in eight and failed to form governments in seven. (Kashyap, 1996: 204-205) This was quite a set-back for the Congress party and made Indira Gandhi's position much shakier and vulnerable.

As was to be expected, in the matter of law-making, the fourth Lok Sabha (1967-1970) became notable for the stiff and boisterous opposition put up against several legislative measures proposed by the government. The opposition used every possible procedural device to thwart their progress and passage. For example, during the 31 sittings of the 1968 winter session, as many as 36 divisions were called. (Kashyap, 1996: 225)

It was in November-December 1969 session of Lok Sabha that the split – or the defection of 62 Congress members to the opposition to form the Congress(O) block – took place, reducing the Congress party to a minority. For the first time since independence, official opposition party – Congress(O) – emerged. After the set-backs to abolition of privy purses and bank nationalisation, Indira Gandhi decided to ask for a fresh mandate from the people. The House was dissolved on 27 December 1970, more than a year short of completing its five year term.

When she went to the electorate in 1971 for a fresh mandate, she won 352 seats, more than two-thirds majority. With this brute majority, she was able to carry through the radical amendments to the Constitution and enact laws which trampled on citizen's rights. J.B. Kripalani has charged:

> The elections in 1971 were rigged. Important leaders of democratic opposition parties were not only defeated, but some of them even lost their deposits. In Delhi, the stronghold of the Jan Sangh, it could not get even one seat, though it had captured all seats in the 1967 elections. Shortly after, it swept the polls in the elections to the Municipal Corporation of Delhi. (Kripalani, 2004: 945)

The next electoral encounter was in 1977. Once the elections were announced in January 1977, Indira Gandhi, was again in the fighting mood. In spite of severe pain due to the attack of herpes, she covered some 40,000 kilometres, addressed 244 election meetings and visited every State except J&K and Sikkim. But, the mood in the country was different and she could sense it.... Indira Gandhi lost by 55,000 votes, Sanjay by 75,000 votes. George Fernandes won by an astounding margin of 3,00,000 votes although he was behind bars and had not set foot in his constituency. (Kapoor, 2015: 317, 324)

The full implications of Indira Gandhi's defeat in Lok Sabha polls in 1977 are often not understood fully. If analysed regionwise, the results bring out a different perspective. It is often argued that the country had rejected Indira Gandhi altogether in 1977 Lok Sabha elections. In fact, on this reasoning, the Janata government had dismissed nine State Governments and had imposed President's rule therein. The simplistic logic of Uttar Pradesh ie India ie Bharat has been dinned in our minds for too long. The election results showed a complete divide between the north and the south, as somewhat narrowly defined. In the north comprising UP, Bihar, Punjab,

Haryana, Delhi, HP, MP and Rajasthan, out of the total 238 Lok Sabha seats, Congress won only 2 seats – one each in MP and Rajasthan. By comparison, in the four southern States – Andhra, Karnataka, Kerala, and Tamil Nadu including Union Territory of Pondicherry, out of 130 seats, Congress won as many as 92 seats – 41 out of 42 in Andhra; 26 out of 28 in Karnataka; 11 out of 20 in Kerala, and 14 out of 40 in Tamil Nadu and Pondicherry. Thus, even after all the excesses of Emergency, southern States were still supporting Indira Gandhi.

After her defeat in 1977 elections, when J. Krishnamurti had advised her to quit politics, she had said, "I have only two alternatives, to fight or to let them destroy me like a sitting duck." So, the indomitable fighter in her took over. She knew that her real battle lay in the public arena.

Madhu Limaye has written:

> The main reason was the expectation that she would be arrested. For, P.C. Sethi, Yashpal Kapoor and R.K. Dhawan ... had been rounded up on 15 August. She thought that the next blow would fall on her. It was probably in anticipation of this that she chose the Belchi issue to advertise her return to active politics with a bang. (Limaye, 1994: 515)

Her visit to Belchi, a village in Bihar, was a landmark event. Eleven Harijans had been murdered and burnt in that village. It was August and she travelled through a heavy downpour by jeep and tractor, crossed a river in spate on elephant back, and reached in the remote, Godforsaken place in the evening. She listened to the woes of the villagers, gave them solace, and it was late at night by the time she returned. (Gill, 1996: 297) She was hailed all over the country as the only saviour of the poor and destitutes. Her public image began to change.

The unthinkable happened. The infighting among the constituents of Janata Party and particularly the factional war carried out by Charan Singh and Raj Narain, with active support of Indira Gandhi and Sanjay, finally resulted in total disillusionment of the people and return to power of Indira Gandhi by massive majority in 1980. Indira Gandhi's return to power in 1980 was decisive. She won 353 seats. Of the candidates who lost their deposits, the highest number was from the Janata Party – 115, as compared to only 7 from the Congress. There was such a rout of the opposition parties that no single party or group was able to secure the minimum ten per cent of the seats in the House required for being a recognised opposition party. As Morarji Desai said, it was a personal victory of Indira Gandhi and not of the Congress(I).

The days of massive mandates ended with Indira Gandhi. Rajiv Gandhi's huge victory (415 seats) in Lok Sabha elections in 1984 was, in fact, a tribute by the electorate to the memory of Indira Gandhi who had been assassinated a few weeks earlier. It was not a mandate for the little known Rajiv Gandhi at that time. In 1989 elections fought under Rajiv Gandhi's leadership, Congress party won only 197 seats and was the single largest party. For the first time since Independence, except during the brief Janata Party spell after the Emergency, Congress party sat in the opposition. The transition from the Indira Gandhi regime was complete in every sense of the term.

NO-CONFIDENCE MOTIONS

In spite of enviable mass following, Indira Gandhi's leadership style did not win her many supporters. She did not carry the opposition parties with her. This was evident from the series of no-confidence motions she had to face in Parliament.

During the short spell of just three years of its life, the fourth Lok Sabha (1967-1970) witnessed tabling of seven no-confidence motions, of which five were admitted and discussed.

I have not discussed the fifth Lok Sabha period here as it was a negation of parliamentary democracy in every sense of the term. The series of amendments passed during this period have been discussed at length in chapter 5.

In her short second term from 1980, she faced three no confidence motions which were defeated due to the massive majority she enjoyed. The first was by George Fernandes on 8 May 1981. The stormy discussion lasted for 10 hours and 40 minutes. The second was soon thereafter by Samar Mukherjee on 17 September 1981 which was discussed for 9 hours and 47 minutes. The third was by H.N. Bahuguna on 16 August 1982 which was discussed for 10 hours and 5 minutes. (Kashyap, 1998: 51)

DID SHE WANT TO BE PRESIDENT OF INDIA?

Did she have Presidential ambitions? Several of her supporters and well-wishers such as B.K. Nehru, Vasant Sathe and A.R. Antulay had floated the idea of switching over to a Presidential form of government but she had shown her disinclination. In the public mind, such a change meant perpetuation of her rule for ever. B.K. Nehru, who was one of the strong proponents of the idea, has written in his book, *Nice Guys Finish Second*, that when he discussed it with her,

> she said she did not approve of it without really giving me any cogent reason for her disapproval. I asked her if she would have any objection to my discussing these proposals with the leaders of public opinion including her own party leaders. She said she would have no objection but told me very clearly and emphatically that in no way was I to give any impression to anybody that the plan had her approval because it did not.... I discussed the plan with the senior leaders of the Congress party – Jagjivan Ram, Swaran Singh and Y.B. Chavan – individually. The response of all three,

> though put in different words, was in essence that if the Prime Minister wanted these changes to be made, they would support them.... *What they were really interested in was to find out whether the Emperor thought it was high noon or midnight*.... The response of Zail Singh, then Chief Minister of Punjab, was that whatever 'Bibiji' wanted was alright with him. The response of Bansi Lal, then Chief Minister of Haryana, was typical of this follower of Sanjay Gandhi and illustrative of the total unsuitability of near perfect twenty-first century Constitution that India had given to itself.... He said, '*Arey Nehru Saheb, yeh sub election phelection ka jhagra khatam kariye. Main to kahta hoon ki Behenji ko President for life banadijiye baaki kucch karne ki jaroorat nahin hai* (Nehru Saheb, get rid of all this nonsense election. If you ask me, just make our sister President for life and there's no need to do anything else). (Nehru, 1997: 558-559)

G.K. Reddy wrote in *The Hindu* on 2 November 1980 that those around the Prime Minister *wanted to 'return to a pliable judiciary, a supine bureaucracy, and a conditioned public opinion'*. The CPI thought Mrs Gandhi was seeking the Presidential System to give her 'absolute power'.

It is for the first time it has become clear that she was seriously thinking along those lines of becoming the President of India. According to her Principal Secretary, P.C. Alexander, who has written in his book, *My Years with Indira Gandhi,* she asked him in May 1982:

> "Haven't I done enough for the Party and shouldn't I now hand over the burden to others?", she asked me once in great mental agony.... She said she wanted some time for rest and writing, which the Rashtrapati Bhavan could provide, and her advice to a new government would still be available in her capacity as President. I knew she was talking seriously.

> He recalled further that the mood lasted for two weeks 'as she seriously considered the pros and cons of this proposition', but then she turned her mind to whom (sic) might be a suitable candidate for the Congress(I) to nominate for the Presidency. (Austin, 1999: 493-495)

SOME ENDURING ACHIEVEMENTS

Playing politics helps one to get into power and retain it but does not help in leaving one's legacy behind, unless one has vision, foresight and statesmanship. With all her faults as a politician, Indira Gandhi clearly had no dearth of the above qualities, as can be seen from the following:

Indian Scientific Expedition in Antarctica

In a statement made in Lok Sabha on 19 February 1982, Indira Gandhi informed the House about successful landing, on 9 January 1982 at Antarctica, of the first Indian scientific expedition of 21 scientists and technicians. The main objectives of the expedition, she added, were to study the meteorological and other conditions of Antarctica which controlled the monsoons. The team also carried out observations in glaciology, geomagnetism, geology, and physical, chemical and biological oceanography. Some rock samples, which appeared to be similar to rocks found in the Deccan, were collected by the team. Detailed analysis, however, would be needed to establish whether Deccan and Antarctica were joined together at any time. The expedition team, Indira Gandhi announced, had set up an unmanned weather station to collect meteorological data in Antarctica. Power was supplied to the station by solar panels fabricated in India. The site of the station had been named "Dakshin Gangotri" and a brass plaque commemorating the expedition had been set up. With the landing of the expedition on Antarctica, India, she added, had joined a select band of countries. (Kashyap, 1998: 92-93)

This would not have been possible without active support and encouragement of the government.

Nature and Wild Life Conservation

Long before environment and nature conservation came on the agenda of international bodies, from the very beginning of her term as Prime Minister, Indira Gandhi had publicly extended her strong support for sustainable development. In her inaugural speech at the tenth General Assembly of the International Union for Conservation of Natural Resources, in New Delhi, on 24 November 1969, she had struck a personal note: "As an only child whose childhood was invaded by the turbulence of a vast national upheaval, I found companionship and an inner peace in communion with nature. I grew up with love for stones, no less than trees, and for animals of all kinds. I have always felt that closeness to nature helps to make one a more integrated personality. I say this especially because of the general lack of concern or feeling for these things now-a-days, at least in my country.... As one looks around the universe, one marvels at the order and the balance. How beautifully everything fits in. How remarkably well everything is organised. (GoI, 1975: 264-265)

In her address to the plenary session of the UN Conference on Human Environment at Stockholm, on 14 June 1972, she had underlined:

> All the 'isms' of the modern age – even those which in theory disown the private profit principle – assume that man's cardinal interest is acquisition. The profit motive, individual or collective, seems to overshadow all else. The over-riding concern with self today is the basic cause of the ecological crisis....

She had ended her speech with the hymn to earth which the sages of the *Atharva Veda* chanted:

"What of thee I dig out, let that quickly grow over,
Let me not hit thy vitals, or thy heart." (GoI, 1975: 451, 453)

Silent valley is an evergreen forest in the Palakkad district of Kerala, in which a hydro-electric project was planned but was finally shelved due to Indira Gandhi's firm stand to preserve the valley. As Jayaram Ramesh has highlighted in his book, *Indira Gandhi – A Life in Nature*, the project was to produce 240 megawatts of cheap hydel power, apart from irrigating around 10,000 hectares, and was being supported by the left parties, and the local Congress leaders in the State. In her letter to Governor of Kerala, she had emphasised that this was not a legal matter [of just the High Court vacating the stay] but "a question of the protection of the environment and the conservation of one of the only remaining tropical rain forest areas in the world. Eminent people all over the world have expressed concern over the project." (Ramesh, 2017: 269-270) She remained firm, in spite of considerable political pressure. It brings out how sustainable development can be promoted if a Prime Minister is committed to the cause.

But one is equally disappointed with her decision to permit the location of a refinery at Mathura. Taj Mahal, the world-heritage monument is located just 40 kilometres from Mathura and the Bharatpur bird sanctuary is just about 60 kilometres away. Serious doubts were expressed about the pollution likely to be caused by the location of the refinery at Mathura. However, Indira Gandhi failed to take a firm stand on the subject and herself laid the foundation stone of the project. A very uncharitable thought comes to my mind. Is it because UP was her own electoral turf while Kerala was too far away?

She personally wrote to the State Chief Ministers of J&K and Assam for early adoption of the Wildlife (Protection) Act, 1972. (Ramesh, 2017: 160, 212) Creation and preservation of tiger reserves was yet another subject close to her heart.

Peaceful Nuclear Explosion

There are various conjectures as to when Indira Gandhi decided to encourage building up of a nuclear device. Amrita Shah, in her biography of Vikram Sarabhai titled *Vikram Sarabhai – A Life*, has tried to shed some light on it. On 24 April 1968, Indira Gandhi had said in Lok Sabha: 'We think that nuclear weapons are no substitute for military preparedness involving conventional weapons.... [It] may well endanger our internal security by imposing a very heavy economic burden.' Vikram Sarabhai was not very enthusiastic about India building a nuclear device. Shah has stated:

> Raj Chengappa maintains that the seed of a schism between Indira and Vikram was laid in the late 1960s itself ... the scientists at AEC [Atomic Energy Commission], as shown time and again, considered themselves the keepers of India's security. Vikram had failed completely in his efforts to change that mindset and push nuclear defence policy where he felt it belonged, in the public arena. On the other hand, it is conceivable that Indira, with her growing tendency to play people against each other, could have given a patient ear to the scientists' anxieties. Perhaps the reservations she had expressed earlier about a weapon programme were never based on conviction. Her advisors too had changed.... *There are signs that Indira was seeking military assertion in other ways. In November 1970, she had asked the DRDO to launch a feasibility study on building a long-range ballistic missile. Two months before that she had apparently asked for a similar study on a nuclear-propelled submarine. As Chengappa observes, 'Mrs Gandhi had laid plans for India to join the big boys' club'. But, crucially, he maintains, some time in mid-1970 she had also asked Vikram to prepare for a nuclear explosion.* (Shah, 2007: 204-205)

During Indira Gandhi's visit to Trombay on 7 September 1972, she was asked by Sethna whether they could go ahead with the preparations of the bomb. She had replied, "Get it ready. I will tell you whether to do it or not." There was no going back thereafter.

George Perkovich, in his book, *India's Nuclear Bomb – The Impact on Global Proliferation*, has stated:

> The scientists involved in the eventual nuclear test of 1974 hinted that Sarabhai had been an impediment to their desire to build and detonate nuclear explosive devices.... Homi Sethna recalled in a later interview that he 'almost quit' over disagreement with Sarabhai ... and was persuaded by Indira Gandhi and her Principal Secretary P.N. Haksar, to remain. (Perkovich, 1999: 160)

No authoritative public chronology exists of Indian decision-making regarding the 1974 explosion. Indeed, according to two of the few officials who participated in the decision-making process, written records of policy deliberations were not kept. "There was not a single scrap of paper on it," said the then Chairman of AEC Homi Sethna in an interview.... Mrs Gandhi did not consult or inform the Cabinet. (Perkovich, 1999: 170, 174)

With the explosion of an underground nuclear device at Pokharan in Rajasthan on 18 May 1974, India became the world's sixth nuclear power. The project with a code name 'smiling Buddha', apostle of peace, and was scheduled on Buddha Jayanti (birthday of Buddha). The name was certainly intriguing.[6] It is

---

6 Strobe Talbot has interpreted it to mean "as though to mock the notion that India, as the birthplace of a pacific religion and of an earlier Gandhi who preached non-violence, was somehow culturally and ethically obliged to deprive itself of the most potent weaponry." (Talbot, 2004: 14) According to Raj Chengappa, it was with a reference to the encounter of Buddha with the dacoit Angulimala."Three thousand years later, the land of the Buddha and the world around India are still searching for the fundamental answers to end conflict.... Some nations now wear a necklace of nuclear bombs like the fingers around Angulimala's neck." (Chengappa, 2000: 439-440)

believed that it was the scientists who pressed the issue, though Haksar and P.N. Dhar were not keen on it. India was also driven to conduct a test after China exploded a nuclear bomb in October 1964. There was a persistent demand in Parliament that India should not waste any more time.

The American decision to send the nuclear aircraft carrier task-force to the Bay of Bengal during the Bangladesh War had a long term impact on Indian defence policy. It accelerated the Indian nuclear programme and eventually led to the testing of a nuclear device two and a half years later, in May 1974. (Dhar, 2000: 184)

As for the timing of the test, it is generally believed that Indira Gandhi's declining popularity in the country led to the decision. But I find it difficult to agree with this view. A nuclear test cannot be organised to suit such political exigencies.

Prime Minister of Pakistan Bhutto was shocked with India's nuclear explosion and in the letter to Nixon stated that "the explosion of a nuclear device developed by India is bound to have sinister global repercussions and has qualitatively changed the situation in our region for the worse." He said, "Indian protestations that the nuclear tests were for peaceful purposes would mislead no one." Bhutto warned that 'It is bound to embolden not only the presently threshold powers but also others to develop these weapons.' Indira Gandhi's efforts to alley the fears of Bhutto did not yield any results according to Perkovich. She assured in her letter to Bhutto that India remained fully committed to its traditional policy of developing nuclear energy entirely for peaceful purposes. (Shanker, 2010: 366-367)

It is significant to note that military considerations did not weigh in taking a decision on the nuclear test. In an interview with Rodney Jones in 1978, Indira Gandhi had stated: "We don't want nuclear weapons. They only bring danger where there was none before." This reflected both the Prime Minister's and the nuclear establishment's desire to exclude the military from nuclear policy. As a former AEC Chairman put it, "one thing we learned is to never allow the military or the bureaucracy to have a role in the nuclear programme. The Indian programme never took the army into confidence. We didn't discuss details with them. It wasn't a military programme." (Perkovich, 1999: 178)

But, Stephen Cohen has, in his book, *India – Emerging Power*, talked of the Indira Doctrine which represented a tough, uncompromising attitude towards neighbours, large and small. Two principles were laid down: No foreign power should be allowed to cross the crest of Himalayas, and India would consider the presence or influence of an external power in the region as adverse to its interests, unless the power recognized Indian predominance. Cohen argues that "the Indian public embraced Indira Doctrine, although there was a feeling that with Soviet support, India need not rush to strengthen its military capabilities." (Cohen, 2001: 137-138) Most of these were conjectures.

Raj Chengappa, in his book, *Weapons of Peace – The Secret Story of India's Quest to be a Nuclear Power*, has stated:

> It was in January 1981 when Ramanna met Mrs Gandhi and briefed her on the bomb issue. He told her that scientists had made a more compact version of the bulky 1974 device so that it could be delivered by a fighter aircraft. And they had mastered the technology to make a more advanced boosted fission bomb that would, for the same amount of plutonium, give four times the yield. Ramanna then asked for permission to test the two new devices as they had to be validated.... Mrs Gandhi agreed and apart from clearing the digging of two shafts wanted Ramanna to get the bomb team to keep their devices ready.... Mrs Gandhi also pushed Ramanna to get the floundering nuclear submarine project off the ground. However, the tests had to be given up as

> Americans had got to know about them. Later, when asked by General Krishna Rao as to why the tests were given up, Indira Gandhi had explained that "testing would attract undue attention" and said: "we will leave it for appropriate moment. We will develop other things and keep them ready. And meanwhile make further improvements in our designs." The 'other things' Mrs Gandhi had in mind was developing long range ballistic missiles and soon initiated a massive programme for it. How the Americans got wind of the tests still remains a mystery. A hand-written note from Mrs Gandhi to Sethna hints at the problems she was having with secrecy. 'Be careful,' she wrote, 'too many people are listening in.' (Chengappa, 2000: 246-248, 260-261)

It must be said that it was only due to the strong and far-sighted leadership of Indira Gandhi that the nuclear test could be done. Looking to the rapid rise of China as a super-power and its unceasing efforts to building up of Pakistan, the importance of nuclear deterrence cannot be over-emphasised. So far as India's national security is concerned, the contribution of Indira Gandhi has been phenomenal.

There was strident criticism of India's peaceful nuclear explosion, from some countries such as Canada. Palkhivala defended India's stand in a forthright manner in the USA when he was Indian Ambassador there. He had underlined:

> In 1970, the United States and the Soviet Union had 6,000 deliverable strategic nuclear warheads, while in 1978 they had over 14,000 – an increase of 1,000 per year.... The nuclear weapons States have the means but not the will to check vertical proliferation.... The nuclear weapon States are highly selective in their perceptions of risks, and their non-proliferation effort is almost wholly pre-occupied with horizontal proliferation. Since the Nuclear Non-proliferation Treaty of 1968 the gospel of

> non-proliferation has been preached by the nuclear weapon States amidst the din of dozens of their own explosions every year. Forty-eight such nuclear tests were recorded in 1978 – Soviet Union 27, United States 10, France 6, China 3 and Great Britain 2.

In a debate in the Harvard University on "Disarming the Unarmed", Palkhivala had assured that in India, the role of the atom is that of worker, and not of a soldier. India uses its nuclear capability entirely for peaceful purposes and primarily for the generation of electricity. (Palkhivala, 1994: 325-326, 328)

It must be noted that though Indira Gandhi had agreed to further tests being conducted, they had to be given up as Americans had come to know of them. But, she did not agree to the development of an hydrogen bomb. India had become a member of the super-select nuclear club. Indira Gandhi had once again established her capability to take bold decisions where national interest was involved.

Space Programme

U.R. Rao has written about how Indira Gandhi had enthusiastically supported the space programme. When M.G.K. Menon called on Indira Gandhi and told her about the on-going discussions on Indo-Soviet co-operation in space in February 1972, she was very supportive and wanted to know how much it would cost, before giving her final approval. After consulting his colleagues, Rao told her that it would cost ₹ 3 crore, including ₹ 1 crore in foreign exchange! She immediately gave a go ahead and permitted agreement to be signed. When the first Indian satellite was due to be launched in March 1975, three names were recommended to Indira Gandhi – 'Aryabhata', 'Jawahar', and 'Maitri'. She promptly chose the name 'Aryabhata'. The government also decided to release a special postage stamp coinciding with the launch.

The first offer to fly an Indian astronaut on the Soyuz/Salyut mission was made by President Brezhnev in 1978 when Morarji Desai was the Prime Minister. Desai was not, however, enthusiastic about it. Fortunately, when Indira Gandhi came back to power in 1980, President Brezhnev renewed the earlier offer of a joint manned mission. It was readily accepted by Indira Gandhi and squadron leader Rakesh Sharma became the first Indian astronaut to go into space. As the space programme developed, Indira Gandhi asked the space department to provide complete assistance to the armed forces. (Rao, 2014: 33, 41, 86)

TO CONCLUDE

The above account vividly brings out the complexity of the wide and varied canvas on which Indira Gandhi functioned in her own inimitable style. Here was a towering leader genuinely interested in music, art, culture, literature, poetry, and nature. She played a number of roles – a doting and protective mother, a mother-in-law, a caring house-wife, a loving friend, an astute stateswoman, a national figure with a foresight and courage to take bold and difficult decisions where national interest demanded, and most importantly, a ruthless, unscrupulous politician who excelled in the cut-throat world of politics. Which of these was the real Indira Gandhi? What legacy has she left behind? I hope this book will provide some answers.

Annexure 1

Letter to A.C.N. Nambiar After Sanjay Gandhi's Death

978
प्रधान मंत्री भवन
Prime Minister's House
New Delhi
July 7, 1980

Oh Nanu! What can I write? Other deaths in the family have followed grave illnesses. But Sanjay was so vitally, so vibrantly healthy, of such a resplendent personality. You cannot imagine how much he had developed even in the last months. So much and so many depended on him. He did not interfere in government but he was good in Parliament, he had inspired the young to constructive purposes.

Sanjay faced all the calumny, the false propaganda and the hardship of the last years with remarkable dignity and maturity. To me he gave the sort of support that comes not from a son but from an older brother.

In the last month's elections he attracted larger crowds than I did. And today, the peoples' grief is such as has not been witnessed since my father's death. The poor, especially the women and young people who are thronging my compound do not commiserate with me but ask – "what is going to happen to us?"

What is worse is that some (sic) those who had, and have, no foothold are now trying to stage a come-back.

(signed) Indu

Mr A.C.N. Nambiar
11, Splegellase 6,
Zurich (Switzerland)

Source: Balachandran, Vappala, *A Life In Shadow – The Secret Story of A.C.N. Nambiar: A Forgotten Anti-Colonial Warrior*, New Delhi, Roli Books, 2016, p 314.

Annexure 2

Restrictions on Foreign Media during Emergency

Correspondents Expelled

1. Mr Lewis M. Simmons, *Washington Post*
2. Mr Peter George Gill, *Daily Telegraph*
3. Mr Peter Bruce Hazelhurst, *The Times*, London
4. Mr Loren Bernard Jenkins, *Newsweek*
5. Mr Edward John Cody *AP* (America)
6. Mr Jacque Robert Leslie, *Los Angeles Times*
7. Mr Lawrence Stephen Lifschultz, *Guardian* and *Far Eastern Economic Review*

Correspondents Whose Entry was Banned

(i) Mr Robert Kovin Rafferty, *Financial Times*
(ii) Mr Stephen Claypole, *Sydney Morning Herald*, Sydney (Australia)
(iii) Mr Martin Woollacott, *Guardian*, London
(iv) Mr Tony Clifton, *Newsweek*, New York
(v) Mr Peter Collins, *CBS News*, New York
(vi) Mr Bo Anders I Gunnarson, *Dangens Nyheter*, Stockholm
(vii) Mr Ulf Neilson, *Expressen*, Stockholm
(viii) Mr Daniel R. Southerland, *Christian Science Monitor*, Hong Kong
(ix) Mr Robert Allen Tamarkkn, *Chicago Daily News*
(x) Mr David Barrington Thomson, *Times Weekly* (USA)
(xi) Mr Karl Robert Pfeffer, Editor, *Stern Magazine*, Bimburg
(xii) Mr Mark Tully, *BBC* (Ban revoked)
(xiii) Mr Ronald Edward Moreau, *Newsweek*, New York
(xiv) Mr T.D. Allman, *National Review*, Sydney (Australia)
(xv) Mr Bruce Scott, *London Daily Telegraph*

(xvi) Mr Karel Gerardus Van Welferen, *NBC*, Handelsblad, Rotterdam, Holland
(xvii) Mr Bernerk David Nossiter, *Washington Post*
(xviii) Mr John Saarhill, *Washington Post*
(xix) Mr John D. Cahill, *Toronto Star*, Canada
(xx) Mr Marcel Hahlweg, *Der Tages Spiegel*, Berlin and Arbeiter
(xxi) Zitung of Vienna
(xxii) Mr Edward Behr, *Newsweek*, New York
(xxiii) Mr Colin Welch (also known as James Colin Ross Welch), *Daily Telegraph*, London
(xxiv) Mr Henry St. Amant Bradsher, *Washington Star*
(xxv) Mr Marr Bryan Cameron British Journalist
(xxvi) Mr Borries Paul Adolft Gard Gallasch, *Der Spiegel*, FRG
(xxvii) Mr Michael Chinoy correspondent for *Chicago Daily News*
(xxviii) 27. Mr David Leslie Iver Loshakk, *Daily Telegraph*, London
(xxix) Mr Siegfried Kogelfranz, *Der Spiegel*, FRG
(xxx) Mr Ian Jack, *Sunday Times*

Source: Government of India, *White Paper on Misuse of Mass Media During the Internal Emergency*, New Delhi, August 1977, Appendix 15 and 16, pp 63, 64.

Annexure 3

Administrators: Sloth, Lunacy or Conspiracy?

The last week of March, 1977. The Janata leaders are heady with success; *they*, not the people, have defeated the Indira regime; *their* sagacity, *their* shrewdness, *their* mass base, not the suffering, the silent anger of the people have toppled the Emergency regime.

Heady, they have begun quarrelling over the Prime Ministership, over portfolios, over which Minister is to get which of the spacious bungalows they have so recently sworn not to occupy.

Four men carry valuables in a van to Indira Gandhi's farm near Mehrauli on the outskirts of Delhi. With the help of labourers who are constructing the yet incomplete farm house of our Lady of Hope the valuables are buried at six places in the compound of the farm. In addition one large steel almirah (5 feet by 2 feet by 6 feet) is buried in a room the flooring of which has not been completed.

A female labourer makes an inconspicuous mark in the room where the almirah has been buried. She also notes the six places in the compound.

Later in the evening she visits the *pradhan* of the village (he is a BLD [Bharatiya Lok Dal] sympathiser) and gives an account of the sort of things that have been buried and the places at which they have been buried.

The *pradhan* waits for things to settle down in Delhi. In April C.V. Narasimhan replaces D. Sen as Director, CBI. The *pradhan* goes to Narasimhan in the last week of May and gives in the details that he has learnt.

Narasimhan makes perfunctory inquiries. Nothing is done.

The *pradhan* runs from pillar to post with the information. A full year and two months pass. Instead of investigating the information he is giving them, officers ascribe motives to him ... he has this bee in his *pugri*, they reassure each other; he is just trying to curry favour with the new government, they say.

June 1978. The matter reaches Morarji, who is also looking after the Home portfolio now. He asks the Intelligence Bureau to get to the bottom of the matter.

The Intelligence Bureau sets out to locate other witnesses who can corroborate what the female labourer has said. Its investigators learn that the man who had assembled the labourers to construct the farm house is dead. The labourers had come from different places and cannot now be traced. However, two had come from the neighbourhood. Efforts are made to trace them. They too have died.

The Bureau then sets out to devise a plan for actual physical verification. A way has to be found for someone who knows metal detection work to enter the compound and the house itself. To start with, the farm is put under 24-hour surveillance.

The son of a head constable in the IB is selected as he has done MSc in Physics. He is sent for training in metal detection work to the National Geo-Physical Laboratory, Hyderabad. The training takes one month. (Don't ask me why someone already familiar with metal detection work was not picked from another department such as Customs, BSF, etc.)

The young man returns from Hyderabad in early August. A compact metal detector is procured. By an ingenious plan devised with the help of a small band close to George Fernandes, the young man is able to spend two full hours inside the farm house on August 31, 1978.

The metal detector's readings are, to quote a Cabinet Minister familiar with the case, "strongly positive". (The investigation is done only inside the house so as not to alert the *mali-cum-chowkidar*).

The results are fully reported the very next day at a meeting. The meeting is attended by N. Mukerji, Cabinet Secretary, T.C.A. Srinivasavaradan, Home Secretary, V.V. Badami, Chairman, Central Board of Direct Taxes, John Lobo (who has taken over as Director, CBI, in November 1977), Raj Deo Singh (who has been appointed Special Director, CBI, in May 1978), S.N. Mathur, Director, Intelligence Bureau, and V.V. Nagarkar, Joint Director, IB.

The Intelligence Bureau officers strongly urge that a raid should be ordered forthwith. Others hedge and haw.

The matter, therefore, is left to Badami, the Chairman, Central Board of Direct Taxes, and the Inspection Directorate under him. His vigilant [*sic*] departments send their independent investigators to begin the investigation *ab initio*. Instead of winning the confidence of the witnesses, the Income Tax worthies threaten and intimidate them.

The frightened witnesses, including the village *pradhan*, rush to George Fernandes, "is this what your government does to people who risk their lives to give you information?" He summons officials from the Intelligence Bureau. These officials give him their long tale of woes, of the rebuff their efforts have met.

By now Chikmagalur is in the air. The Finance Minister rules that the raid should be postponed till after the election on the ground that the government cannot afford another abortive, infructuous sally at Mrs Gandhi. The raid is, therefore, fixed for November 6, 1978, the day after the Chikmagalur polling. It is to be organised by Raj Deo Singh, Special Director, CBI, with the assistance of the Inspection Directorate.

November 5: The raid is mysteriously deferred to December 29. Raj Deo Singh, in particular, suddenly says that he is not quite sure whether he has the authority to conduct the raid. (He arrives at these doubts after reflecting on the matter for five months.) Someone says that high-ups in the government feel that raid should be postponed as a raid so soon after what is certain to be Indira Gandhi's Chikmagalur victory will appear to be vindictive.

Intelligence Bureau officials knock their heads at other doors. Frustrated and fed up, they send a long memorandum on November 18 to the Cabinet and Home Secretaries listing the enormous amount of information they have furnished about secret accounts, about the farm and a host of other matters, none of which have been acted upon. Can something not be done, for heaven's sake?

They are mollified. After all, the raid has already been scheduled for December 29. Won't you bear with us? In fact, as plans for the raid are in the final stages, please furnish a detailed floor plan of the house and the farm with places having the buried stuff marked clearly.

But these have been furnished long ago.

Yes, I know, but please go over them once and ensure that every detail you know is incorporated.

The new maps as well as a detailed write-up are furnished to the Special Director, CBI, Raj Deo Singh, on December 21.

On December 23 the *National Herald* carries a report on its front page that officials of "Government intelligence agencies" are keeping a 24-hour watch around Mrs Gandhi's farm.

Intelligence Bureau officials rush to the Home Secretary with the news item: Her people know what is going on, we should raid immediately. No, no, we should not panic. There is no reason to advance the date of raid from December 29. But one thing we should do is to withdraw the surveillance. After all, we don't want some paper to publish photographs of your men standing around the farm.

The surveillance is thus withdrawn for a fortnight.

On December 28, the raid is once again postponed for inexplicable reasons. Not December 29, Special Director Raj Deo Singh decrees, but January 5.

January 4: Raj Deo Singh suddenly says he wants to once again meet the young man who had done the metal detection work. But you have already met him; he has already briefed you and everyone else. Yes, but I want to meet him again; there are some points I want clarified.

In the event the raid set for the next day is again postponed; this time no new date is set for the raid. Raj Deo Singh again interrogates the young man. After this session he expresses full satisfaction at the method by which the detection has been done. But he still does not set any date for the raid.

January 8: the fortnight over, IB recommences its surveillance of the farm.

Meanwhile, the *pradhan* of the village has been contacted by the Manipur Emergency Excesses Commission. He testifies before it on January 17 and blurts out what he knows about the buried items and about how the government has completely failed to act for a year and a half.

On January 18 Delhi papers report his testimony.

Intelligence Bureau officials rush to the Home Secretary. They implore him to order an immediate raid as the information is out in the public.

They are told that the matter will be considered with the urgency it deserves.

8 AM, January 19, 1979: the Director or the Joint Director, Intelligence Bureau (I have not been able to pinpoint which of the two) receives a phone call from one of the IB men at the farm. Two young men arrived in a car (DLY-1) half an hour ago, he is told. They have begun digging in the farm.

The IB officers rush to the Home Secretary and they contact Raj Deo Singh, Special Director, CBI: for heaven's sake, let us raid the damned place now, at least; Sanjay's men are digging the stuff out at this very moment. No need to panic, says the unflappable Home Secretary, at least we now know the IB information is correct. Let us all meet in my office at 11 am sharp.

The 11 o'clock meeting commences. The group that had met on September 1, 1978 is again in session, barring the Cabinet Secretary. Srinivasavaradan, Home Secretary, Badami, Chairman, Central Board of Direct Taxes, John Lobo, Director, CBI, Raj Deo Singh, Special Director, CBI, Mathur, Director, IB, Nagarkar, Joint Director, IB, are all present.

For two and a half hours this group discusses the pros and cons of now raiding the farm. It is a bizarre meeting. The surveillance men near the farm have already reported the progress of the two diggers. But the arguments flow to and fro. The last message from the surveillance men reports that the two have loaded a large steel box into DLY-1 and have sped off.

The junior men on the spot – uncertain and thrown off balance by the fact that their seniors are not passing out any order even in such a desperate situation – follow the car but do not stop or search it. (They do not stop and search the car even though the officer of the Inspection Directorate who is present knows that he has full powers under the Income Tax Act to do so.) The car reaches and enters 12 Willingdon Crescent, the residence of Mrs Gandhi, with the steel box and other items intact.

The Home Secretary's meeting disperses at 1.30PM having decided that the farm should indeed be raided.

The raid commences at 4PM. The young man who had done the metal detection work is part of the raid party. The raid party finds big pot-holes in the farm, some full of water from the rains of the preceding days. One of them has been freshly dug. Upon reaching the room where his metal detector had registered "strong positive" readings, the young man exclaims that the flooring is not what it was on August 31, 1978.

(Later inquiries are to reveal that the digging up and reflooring were done immediately after IB surveillance was lifted on December 23. The digging on the morning of January 19 took out only the last items that were left in the compound.)

January 20: The morning papers flash photographs and reports of the infructuous raid. The PM – who is still looking after the Home portfolio – is upset.

He sends a stiff note to the Home Secretary. In this he records the different stages through which, according to his information, the investigation had progressed. The last paragraph of the note is scorching: he wants, says the PM, a detailed written explanation from the Home Secretary of the reasons on account of which the raid has been postponed again and again; he wants the explanation "immediately". He with his own hand and pen underlines that last word "immediately".

The PM's note is never answered.

At a Cabinet meeting the discussion drifts to the enormous delays in filing cases against Mrs Gandhi and to the infructuous raid at her farm. Madhu Dandavate, the Railway Minister, says that, with officers like Raj Deo Singh in charge of the operation, you can expect nothing else. He says that as Railway Minister he has had ample opportunity to review Raj Deo Singh's record in the Railway Protection Force and that he knows how far Raj Deo Singh went to curry Sanjay Gandhi's favour.

At the next Cabinet meeting at someone's initiative T.C.A. Srinivasavaradan, the Home Secretary, testifies that there are no grounds for Railway Minister's apprehensions.

On April 21 newspapers carry a report that Raj Deo Singh, the Special Director, who has given such an outstanding account of himself in these proceedings, is being appointed Director, CBI.

Alarmed, three Cabinet Ministers – Madhu Dandavate, George Fernandes and Mohan Dharia – meet the PM and express their strong opposition to the proposed appointment.

On June 7 a notification announces that Raj Deo Singh, Special Director, CBI, will succeed John Lobo as Director, CBI, when the later retires on June 30, 1979.

Sloth, lunacy or conspiracy?

Infer what you will. No one cares a damn in any case.

Source: Article by Arun Shourie published in *The Indian Express* on 29 June 1979, and reproduced in Shourie, Arun, *Institutions in the Janata Phase*, Bombay, Popular Prakashan, 1980, pp 81-87.

Annexure 4

Indira Gandhi's Letters to Dorothy Norman

Prime Minister's House
New Delhi
October 13, 1963

Dorothy dear,

Your letter came yesterday. My promised letter is stuck halfway. I don't know when it can be completed.

This is purely personal. I have reached some kind of equilibrium at long last.

My need for privacy and anonymity has been growing steadily these last three years until now I feel I cannot ignore it without risking some kind of self-annihilation. Privacy, unfortunately, is not possible for me even in the remotest corner of the subcontinent. I have had people presenting their cards and their problems even at the foot of the Kolahoi glacier (16,000 ft high)! It is not just meeting people but that they come only to get or ask something. And not even a few moments are left for thinking or relaxing or just being oneself.

Last May in London, I lost my heart to a small house which was for sale. Such a wonderful location. Central, yet very quiet and next door to a park. If only I could have bought it! One room for myself and the rest (only two, I fear) rented out. Rents are so high and this would have solved the foreign exchange problem. But the major hurdle was the foreign exchange with which to buy it. I spent much time in figuring out ways and means and finally when I learnt that an acquaintance had bought it, I was terribly depressed for months. It was as if a door had been slammed in my face.

My father and sons have kept me tied to Delhi. Part of that problem is solved – Rajiv is in England and Sanjay finishes school by the end of the year. I should very much like him to go to England too. My living in London would make it easier for him to go abroad. And I would be able to see something of the boys and yet be on my own. Free to work or to rest. It doesn't sound much to ask of life yet it seems to be out of my reach. The only way out might be to get an adequate job – not under Indian government or business auspices.

Again, a couple of days ago, I spoke with Pupul. Her response was that I should talk with Krishnamurti* who is due in Delhi next month.

I am not running away from anybody or anything. I can claim to have done my duty to my country and my family all these long years. I don't for an instant regret it, because whatever I am today has been shaped by these years. But now I want another life. It may not work out. I may not like it or be good at it. But at least it deserves a trial. There is a compulsion within me which is driving me away from the old life. Is this wrong?

Love,
Indira

*Indian philosopher and author.

Prime Minister's House
New Delhi
May 8, 1964

Dorothy dear,

The whole question of my future is bothering me. I feel I must settle outside India at least for a year or so and this involves earning a living and especially foreign currency. This isn't just yet but it is a nagging worry. The desire to be out of India and the malice, jealousies and envy, with which one is surrounded, are now overwhelming. Also the fact that there isn't one single person to whom one can talk or ask advice even on the lesser matters.

Keep well.

Love,
Indira

Source: Norman, Dorothy, *Indira Gandhi: Letters to an American Friend 1950-1984*, New York, A. Helen and Kurt Wolff Book, 1985, pp 96-97, 103.

Annexure 5

Contempt for Rule of Law

The question of holding Indira Gandhi and her son Sanjay accountable for their lapses and excesses remained unanswered till the end. I am giving below a few instances of how all attempts to fix responsibility on them were frustrated by them, time and again. They clearly believed that they were above the law of the land.

The Shah Commission of Inquiry

The Commission has stated: "Smt. Indira Gandhi objected to the procedure [adopted by the Commission] and declined to file a statement pursuant to the notice under rule 5 (2) (a) and in the manner provided under rule 5(3) and to take oath or give evidence on oath; and raised a number of objections, which are broadly:-

(i) That the Commission has no power to inquire into the circumstances, which preceded the declaration of Emergency and the manner in which the advice for the declaration of Emergency was given… (*Interim Report I*, para 3.10)

… One objection, which was strenuously urged before the Commission by the counsel appearing for Smt. Indira Gandhi … was that in view of the oath of secrecy taken by a Minister entering upon his office under clause (4) of Article 75, … Smt. Indira Gandhi was unable to disclose any information relating to the matters of the State which she dealt with in the course of her functioning as the Prime Minister of India till she relegated that office….

The Commission had ruled that the oath of secrecy of office taken by a Minister of the Union does not prohibit a Minister from disclosing the information before a Commission of Inquiry especially when the Central Government has directed the holding of an inquiry for the purpose of ascertaining facts relating to matters of public interest…. In the view of the Commission, the disclosure of information before a Commission of Inquiry held in pursuance to a direction of the Central

Government after a person has ceased to be a Minister, does not amount to a breach of the oath of secrecy of the Minister concerned. (*Interim Report I*, paras 3.30-31)

As Pupul Jayakar has written, "The Janata leadership failed to realise that in their decision to force Indira to appear before the Shah Commission, they had provided Indira a stage. She was adept at political theatre and now fighting for the survival of her son and herself, she assumed the role of a Joan of Arc on trial, refusing to recant or retrace a step."(Jayakar 1988: 352)

Kissa Kursi Kaa Case

By its order dated 5 May 1978, the Supreme Court had cancelled Sanjay Gandhi's bail, "for a period of one month from today" and directed that he be taken into custody, for apprehensions that "Maruti witnesses" were likely to be won over. (N.K. Singh 1996: 311)

The appeals against the conviction of Sanjay Gandhi and V.C. Shukla filed by the State for enhancing the punishment and by the accused for setting aside their conviction were pending in the court.... Sanjay Gandhi, thereafter, visited the Supreme Court regularly for inspection of the documents kept in the room of one of the Deputy Registrars of the court. He was always accompanied by a contingent of his musclemen and followers. On October 22, 1979, when he tried to enter the court room of the Chief Justice, a CRP constable on duty, Arjun, tried to stop him. As usual, Sanjay was accompanied by about 30 of his followers. He caught hold of Arjun's collar, gave him a slap, pushed him away and walked into the court. On entering the court room, he complained to the Chief Justice that he had been punched by the constable on duty. The Chief Justice replied that he was sorry to hear this and would look into it. His goons in the meantime took charge of Arjun, dragged him to the open terrace in front of the court of the Chief Justice and assaulted him. In the process, his private part was also hurt, as a result of which he had to be hospitalised. After considerable delay, the Delhi Police registered a cognizable case about this incident against Sanjay Gandhi and others.

On October 31, 1979, Sanjay Gandhi, again accompanied by about 30 of his followers, entered the room of the Registrar for inspection of the documents. *During the inspection, some people were caught red-handed while trying to remove the original documents. This was a very serious matter. It was brought to the notice of the Registrar who rushed there. Sanjay Gandhi reportedly misbehaved with him. It was perhaps the first incident of attempt to remove original documents by the accused persons from the precincts of the Supreme Court.* After this, security measures were tightened....

On November 2, 1979 evening, a crowd of 50 to 60 supporters of Sanjay Gandhi came to the gate of the official residence of the senior counsel of this case, Ram Jethmalani, and raised vulgar slogans against him and hailed Sanjay Gandhi and Mrs Gandhi. They dispersed only after the local police belatedly arrived there. (N.K. Singh 1996: 109-110)

Indira Gandhi's Second Term

Arun Shourie has in the fascinating account of Indira Gandhi's second reign, described how the higher judiciary was sought to be brought under government control through appointment of High Court judges, not extending the term of additional High Court judges, manipulating IB reports regarding the antecedents of candidates for judgeships, making the Chief Justice of India just an advisor to the government in matters for appointment as Chief Justice of India and so on. The account also throws light on how the Special Courts Act was made into a dead letter by the tactics employed by Indira Gandhi and her followers. The original question referred to the Special Courts was about the Emergency and its excesses; that had been reduced to 21 First Information Reports; these in turn had been reduced to four cases. Now, if truth be told, the courts never really got around to examining the substance of even these paltry cases. (Shourie 1983: 243-53, 264-307, 381-386)

Institution of False Criminal Complaints Against Four Senior Officials

This case pertained to the four officers of the Ministry of Industry who had annoyed Indira Gandhi because they were collecting information for preparing a reply to a Parliament question asked by Jyotirmoy Bosu regarding import of machinery by Maruti Private Limited. The evidence before the Shah Commission clearly showed that Indira Gandhi had *personally directed* that CBI should initiate action against the four officers. T.A. Pai, Minister for Industry, who was called by Indira Gandhi, found her "completely upset and furious". In the presence of Shri Pai, Indira Gandhi called Dhawan [her Private Secretary] and directed him to contact D. Sen, Director, CBI and ask him *to start inquiries into the conduct of these officers and raid their houses.* She also asked Dhawan to send for D. Sen. Against this background, I find the observations below of Justice Shah far too mild. The Commission has noted: "In the present case there was nothing against any of the four officers.... The CBI mounted the whole series of actions in their armoury at the end of which nothing incriminating was found. But in the process the CBI had destroyed these officers socially, physically and morally. *Now that we have seen that even the man at the top of the CBI with all his seniority and status can still lend himself and his organisation to serve the purposes other than strictly legal, constitutional and moral,* it has to be ensured that in future no such individual or organisation should be capable of being rendered a helpless and unquestioning tool in the hands of the powers that be. The Commission feels that certain safeguards need to be provided by making the Director CBI accountable to an independent body. Yet another suggestion can be that the Director CBI may be statutorily rendered independent of the executive ministry and his term of office made subject to tenure." (Shah Commission, Interim Report I, paras 7.73 and 7.104)

After Janata government came to power, Parliament treated this as a major case of breach of its privileges since it was an effort to stop collection of information for replying to a Parliament question. Indira Gandhi, D. Sen and Dhawan were held guilty after detailed enquiry by the Committee on Privileges and all three were sentenced to prison term. I feel that this was over-reaction but this was the only case arising from the Emergency excesses in which Indira Gandhi was punished – not by a court of law but by Parliament for the breach of its privileges.

When Indira Gandhi came back to power in 1980, she wanted "to set the record straight", in total disregard of rule of law. At her instance, Parliament rescinded the resolution adopted by the Lok Sabha on 19 December 1978 and on 7 May 1981 passed the following resolution and declared that:

(a) the said proceedings of the Committee and the House shall not constitute a precedent in the law of parliamentary privileges;

(b) the findings of the Committee and the decision of the House are inconsistent with and violative of the well accepted principles of the law of parliamentary privilege and the basic safeguards assured to all and enshrined in the Constitution; and

(c) Indira Gandhi, R.K. Dhawan and D. Sen were *innocent of the charges* levelled against them. (Kashyap, 1998: 147-149)

The high moral ground taken in sub-paras (a) and (b) above was meant as a cover-up for the indefensible decision in sub-para (c). By no stretch of imagination were the three persons "innocent of the charges".

Bibliography

Abbas, K.A., *20th March 1977 – A Day Like Any Other Day*, New Delhi, Vikas Publishing House, 1978.

Adams, Jad and Whitehead, Phillip, *The Dynasty – The Nehru-Gandhi Story*, London, Penguin Books, 1997.

Aggarwala, Satish C. and Aggarwala, Adish C., *Legacy of Indira Gandhi*, New Delhi, Socialist Age Publications, 1985.

Ahluwalia, B.K. (Ed), *Indira Gandhi: Saviour of Democracy*, New Delhi, Newman Group of Publishers, 1977.

Akbar, M.J., *Kashmir Behind The Vale*, New Delhi, Viking, 1991.

Alagh, Yoginder K., *Indian Development Planning and Policy – An Alternative View*, New Delhi, Vikas Publishing House, 1991.

Alexander, P.C., *The Perils of Democracy*, Bombay, Somaiya Publications, 1995.

———, *India in the New Millennium*, Mumbai, Somaiya Publications, 2001.

Antulay, A.R., *Appointment of a Chief Justice*, Bombay, Popular Prakashan, 1973.

Austin, Granville, *Working a Democratic Constitution – The Indian Experience*, New Delhi, Oxford University Press, 1999.

Bakshi, P.M., *The Constitution of India with Selective Comments*, Delhi, Universal Law Publishing Co, 1998.

Balachandran, Vappala, 'Lest we revisit 1984', *The Asian Age*, New Delhi, 25 August 2005.

———, *A Life in Shadow – The Secret Story of A.C.N. Nambiar: A*

Forgotten Anti-Colonial Warrior, New Delhi, Roli Books, 2016.

Singh, Baldev, Ninth Schedule to Constitution of India: A Study, New Delhi, *Journal of Indian Law Institute*, Vol 37, 1995.

Bandyopadhyay, Tamal, "India's bad loan problem", *Mint*, Mumbai, 12 June, 2017.

Banerjee, Surabhi, *Jyoti Basu – The Authorised Biography*, New Delhi, Viking, 1997.

Baru, Sanjay, *Strategic consequences of India's economic performance*, New Delhi, Academic Foundation, 2006.

Basu, Kaushik, *The Oxford Companion to Economics in India*, New Delhi, Oxford University Press, 2007.

Basu, Kaushik, *The retreat of Democracy and Other Itinerant Essays*, Ranikhet, Permanent Black, 2007.

Bhutto, Benazir, *Daughter of the East – An Autobiography*, London, A Mandarin Paperback, 1988.

Brar, Lt. Gen. K.S., *Operation Blue Star – The True Story*, New Delhi, UBS Publishers Distributors, 1993.

Brass, Paul R., *An Indian Political Life – Charan Singh and Congress Politics 1937 to 1961*, New Delhi, Sage Publications, 2011.

Brown, Judith M., *Nehru – A Political Life*, New Delhi, Oxford University Press, 2003.

Chandra, Bipan, *In the Name of Democracy – J.P. Movement and the Emergency*, New Delhi, Penguin Books, 2003.

Chandra, Bipan, et al, *India After Independence 1947-2000*, New Delhi, Penguin Books India, 1999.

Chatterjee, P.K., Article 356 Must Be Removed, New Delhi, *Mainstream*, November 18-24, 2005.

Chaturvedi, T.N. (Ed), "Fifty Years of Indian Administration – Retrospect and Prospects", New Delhi, Special Number, *The Indian Journal of Public Administration*, July-Septemeber 1997.

Chengappa, Raj, *Weapons of Peace – The Secret Story of India's Quest to be a Nuclear Power*, New Delhi, HarperCollins Publishers India, 2000.

Cohen, Stephen P., *India-Emerging Power*, New Delhi, Oxford University Press, 2001.

Critique – Selected Works of Piloo Mody, New Delhi, Newsindia Publications, year of publication not given.

Dabholkar, Dattaprasad, *Kashmir Seminar,* Kirloskar Magazine, 1990 (Mimeo)

Das, Durga, *India From Curzon To Nehru and After*, London, Collins, 1969.

Deshmukh, B.G., *A Cabinet Secretary Thinks Aloud*, Mumbai, Bharatiya Vidya Bhavan, 1998.

Deshmukh, C.D., *The Course of my Life*, New Delhi, Orient Longman, 1974.

Desai, Meghanad, *The Rediscovery of India*, New Delhi, Allen Lane, 2009.

Devasher, Tilak, *Pakistan – Courting the Abyss*, New Delhi, HarperCollins Publishers India, 2016.

Dhar, P.N., *Indira Gandhi, the 'Emergency', and Indian Democracy*, New Delhi, Oxford University Press, 2000.

_______, *The Evolution of Economic Policy in India – Selected Essays*, New Delhi, Oxford University Press, 2003.

Diwan, Paras, *Abrogation of Forty-Second Amendment – Does Our Constitution Need a Second Look*, New Delhi, Sterling Publishers, 1978.

_______, *Indian Constitutional Amendments – From First to Forty-Fourth*, New Delhi, Oxford University Press and IBH Publishing Company, 1980.

Dreze, Jean and Sen, Amartya, *An Uncertain Glory – India and its Contradictions*, London, Allen Lane, 2013.

Dulat, A.S., *Kashmir – The Vajpayee Years*, New Delhi, HarperCollins Publishers India, 2015.

Durant, Will, *The Case for India*, Mumbai, Strand Book Stall, 2015.

Dutta, Bhabatosh, *Indian Planning at the Crossroads*, New Delhi, Oxford University Press, 1992.

Eradi, V.U., "Put in the dock by Shah Commission", *The Hindu*, 14 March 2011.

Frank, Katherine, *Indira – The Life of Indira Nehru Gandhi*, London, HarperCollins Publishers, 2001.

Frankel, Francine R., *India's Political Economy 1947-1977: The Gradual Revolution*, New Delhi, Oxford University Press, 1978.

Gadbois, Jr, G.H., The Institutionalisation of the Supreme Court of India, in John R. Schmidhauser (Ed), *Comparative Judicial Systems: Challenging Frontiers in Conceptual and Empirical Analysis*, London, Butterworth, 1987.

Gae, R.S., *The Bank Nationalisation Case and the Constitution*, Bombay, NM Tripathi Private Limited, 1971.

Gandhi, Arun, *The Morarji Papers – Fall of the Janata Government*, New Delhi, Vision Books, 1983.

Gandhi, Indira, *Peoples and Problems*, New Delhi, Hodder and Stoughton with BI Publications, 1982.

_______, *Remembered Moments – Some Autobiographical Writings of Indira Gandhi*, New Delhi, Indira Gandhi Memorial Trust, 1991.

Gayatri Devi, *A Princess Remembers – The Memoirs of the Maharani of Jaipur*, New Delhi, Rupa Publications, 1995.

Gill, K.P.S., *Punjab – The Knights of Falsehood*, New Delhi, Har-Anand Publications, 1997.

Gill, S.S., *The Dynasty – A Political Biography of the Premier Ruling Family of Modern India*, New Delhi, HarperCollins Publishers India, 1996.

Godbole, Madhav, *Unfinished Innings – Recollections and Reflections of Civil Servant*, New Delhi, Orient Longman, 1996.

_______, *The Changing Times – A Commentary on Current Affairs*, New Delhi, Orient Longman, 2000.

_______, *A Quest for Good Governance*, Pune, National Centre for Advocacy Studies, Working Paper Series No.20, 2004.

_______, *The Judiciary and Governance in India*, New Delhi, Rupa and Co, 2008.

_______, *The God Who Failed – An Assessment of Jawaharlal Nehru's Leadership*, New Delhi, Rupa and Co, 2014.

_______, *Good Governance Never On India's Radar*, New Delhi, Rupa & Co, 2014.

_______, *Secularism – India at a Crossroads*, New Delhi, Rupa and Co, 2016.

Gooptu, Nandini, and Parry, Jonathan, *Persistence of Poverty in India*, New Delhi, Social Science Press, 2014.

Gorwala, A.D., *Not In Our Stars*, Bombay, Jaico Publishing House, 1958.

Government of India, Ministry of Finance, *Economic Survey 1966-67*, New Delhi.

Government of India, Ministry of Finance, *Economic Survey 1967-68*, New Delhi, 1968.

Government of India, Planning Commission, *Annual Plan 1968-69*, New Delhi.

Government of India, Ministry of Finance, *Economic Survey 1970-71*, New Delhi

Government of India, Ministry of Finance, *Economic Survey 1971-72*, New Delhi

Government of India, Ministry of Finance, *Economic Survey 1972-73*, New Delhi

Government of India, Ministry of Finance, *Economic Survey 1975-76*, New Delhi

Government of India, Ministry of Finance, *Economic Survey 1976-77*, New Delhi

Government of India, Ministry of Finance, *Economic Survey 1977-78*, New Delhi

Government of India, Planning Commission, *Fourth Five Year Plan, 1967-1974*, New Delhi, 1969.

Government of India, Planning Commission, *Fifth Five Year Plan, 1974-79*, New Delhi, 1976.

Government of India, Planning Commission, *Sixth Five Year Plan, 1980-85*, New Delhi, year of publication not given.

Government of India, Ministry of Information and Broadcasting, Publications Division, *India Speaks – Selected Speeches of Prime Minister Indira Gandhi On Her Tour Abroad (September – November 1971)*, New Delhi, 1971.

Government of India, Ministry of Information and Broadcasting, Publications Division, *Democracy and Discipline – Speeches of Shrimati Indira Gandhi*, New Delhi, 1975.

Government of India, Ministry of Information and Broadcasting, Publications Division, *The Years of Endeavour – Selected Speeches of Indira Gandhi August 1969 – August 1972*, New Delhi, 1975.

Government of India, Ministry of Information and Broadcasting, Publications Division, *Consolidating National Gains – Speeches of*

Shrimati Indira Gandhi, New Delhi, 1976.

Government of India, Ministry of Information and Broadcasting, Publications Division, *White Paper on Misuse of Mass media During the Internal Emergency*, New Delhi, 1977.

Government of India, Ministry of Home Affairs, *P. Jaganmohan Reddy Commission of Inquiry [Regarding Shri Bansi Lal] Report (1st, 2nd, and 3rd Reports)*, New Delhi, 1977.

Government of India, Ministry of Home Affairs, *Report of the Commission of Inquiry on Maruti Affairs*, New Delhi, 1979.

Government of India, *White Paper on the Punjab Agitation*, New Delhi, July 1984.

Government of India, *Commission on Centre-State Relations Report*, Parts I and II, New Delhi, 1988.

Government of Tamil Nadu, *Report of the Centre-State Relations Inquiry Committee*, Madras, 1971.

Grover, K.L., *The Verdict – Inside Story of Shrimati Indira Gandhi's Case with Unabridged Judgment*, Allahabad, Legend Publications, 1975.

Guha, Ramachandra, *India After Gandhi – The History of the World's Largest Democracy*, London, Picador, 2007.

Gupta, Ray M.K., *Birth of a Nation*, New Delhi, Har-Anand Publications, 2016.

Gupte, Pranay, *India – The Challenge of Change*, London, Metheun-Mandarin, 1989.

_______, *Mother India – A Political Biography of Indira Gandhi*, New Delhi, Penguin/Viking, 2009.

Hart, Henry C. (Ed), *Indira Gandhi's India – A Political System Reappraised*, Boulder, Colorado, Westview Press, 1976.

Henderson, Michael, *Experiment with Untruth – India under Emergency*, New Delhi, Macmillan Company, 1977.

Hidayatullah, M., *A Judge's Miscellany*, Second Series, Bombay, NM Tripathi, 1979.

_______, *Right to Property and the Indian Constituion*, Calcutta, Arnold Heinemann, 1983.

Hutheesing, Nehru Krishna, *Dear to Behold – An Intimate Portrait of*

Indira Gandhi, London, Macmillan Company, 1969.

India and Other Essays, Hyderabad, Orient Blackswan, 2010.

Jagmohan, *My Frozen Turbulence in Kashmir*, New Delhi, Allied Publishers, 1991.

Jai, Janak Raj, *Assault on Judiciary and the Role of Parliament*, New Delhi, Associated Legal Advisors Private Limited, 1997.

Jairam, Ramesh, *Indira Gandhi – A Life in Nature*, New Delhi, Simon & Schuster, 2017.

Jayakar, Pupul, *Krishnamurti – A Biography*, Gurgaon, Penguin Books, 1986.

Jha, Prem Shankar, *India and China – The Battle Between Soft And Hard Power*, New Delhi, Penguin/ Viking, 2010.

Joshi, Vijay, *India's Long Road – The Search for Prosperity*, Gurgaon, Penguin/ Random House India, 2016.

Kagzi, M.C.J., *The Kesavananda's Case*, Delhi, Metropolitan Book Company, 1973.

Kamath, M.V., *Nani A. Palkhivala – A Life*, New Delhi, Hay House India, 2007.

Kapoor, Coomi, *The Emergency – A Personal History*, New Delhi, Penguin/Viking, 2015.

Kapur, Jagga, *What Price Perjury – Facts of the Shah Commission*, New Delhi, Arnold-Heinemann, 1978.

Kashyap, Subhash C, *History of the Parliament of India*, Vol 3, Delhi, Shipra Publications, 1996.

———, *History of the Parliament of India*, Vol 4, Delhi, Shipra Publications, 1997.

———, *History of the Parliament of India*, Vol 5, Delhi, Shipra Publications, 1998.

———, *Constitution Making Since 1950: An Overview*, Delhi, Universal Law Publishing Company, 2004.

———, *Concise Encyclopedia of Indian Constitution*, New Delhi, Vision Books, 2009

Kaul, T.N., *A Diplomat's Diary 1947-1999 – China, India and USA*, New Delhi, Macmillan India, 2000.

Kelley, Michele and D'Souza, Deepika (ed), *The World Bank in India*

– *Undermining Sovereignty, Distorting Development,* New Delhi, Orient BlackSwan, 2010.

Khasru, B.Z., *The Bangladesh Military Coup and the CIA Link*, New Delhi, Rainlight/ Rupa, 2014.

Kidwai, Rasheed, *24 Akbar Road – A Short History of the People Behind the Fall and Rise of the Congress,* New Delhi, Hachette India, 2011.

Kiessling, Hein G., *Faith, Unity, Discipline – The ISI of Pakistan*, London, Hurst & Company, 2016.

Kissinger, Henry, *World Order – Reflections on the Character of Nations and the Course of History*, London, Allen Lane, 2014.

_______, *World Order – Reflections on the Character of Nations and the Course of History*, London, Allen Lane, 2014.

Kripalani, J.B., *The Nightmare and After*, Bombay, Popular Prakashan, 1980.

_______, *My Times – An Autobiography*, New Delhi, Rupa & Co, 2004.

Lewis, Primila, *Reason Wounded – An Experience of India's Emergency*, New Delhi, Vikas Publishing House, 1978.

Limaye, Madhu, *Decline of a Political System – Indian Politics at Crossroads*, Allahabad, Wheeler Publishing, 1992.

_______, *Janata Party Experiment – An Insider's Account of Opposition Politics*, Delhi, BR Publishing Corporation, 1994.

Lok Sabha Secretariat, *Lok Sabha Debates,* Vol 6, New Delhi, 1971.

_______, *Lok Sabha Debates,* Vol 7, New Delhi, 1971.

_______, *Lok Sabha Debates,* Vol 9, New Delhi, 1971.

_______, *Lok Sabha Debates,* Vol 16, New Delhi, 1972.

_______, *Lok Sabha Debates,* Vol 18, New Delhi, 1972.

_______, *Lok Sabha Debates,* Vol 53, New Delhi, 1975.

Mahajan, Justice Mehr Chand, *Looking Back*, Bombay, Asia Publishing House, 1963.

Maheshwari, Shriram, *President's Rule in India*, New Delhi, Macmillan Company, 1977.

Malhotra, G.C., *Motions of Confidence and No-Confidence*, New Delhi, Lok Sabha Secretariat, Metropolitan, 1998.

Malhotra, Inder, *India Trapped in Uncertainty*, New Delhi, UBS Publishers' Distributors, 1991.

Malhoutra, Manmohan (Ed), *New Century: Whose Century?*, UBS Publishers' Distributors, 2001.

Mankekar, D.R. and Mankekar, Kamla, *Decline and fall of Indira Gandhi*, New Delhi, Vision Books, 1977.

Marshall, Kathryn, *Indira Gandhi – Women Achievers in Politics*, New Delhi, Orient Longman, 1997.

Marwah, Ved, *India In Turmoil: Jammu & Kashmir, the Northeast and Left Extremism*, New Delhi, Rupa & Co, 2009.

Masani, Zareer, *Indira Gandhi – A Biography*, New Delhi, Oxford University Press, 1975.

Mathai, M.O., *Reminiscences of the Nehru Age*, New Delhi, Vikas Publishing House, 1978.

Mathew, George (Ed), *George Fernandes Speaks*, Delhi, Ajanta Publications, 1991.

Mavalankar, P.G., *'No, Sir' – Being the Collection of 24 Speeches in the Lok Sabha during the Internal Emergency in India*, Ahmedabad, Sannishtha Prakashan, 1979.

Mehta, Vinod, *"Mr Editor, how close are you to the PM?"*, New Delhi, Konark Publishers, 1999.

Menon, K.P.S., *The Indo-Soviet Treaty – Setting and Sequel*, Delhi, Vikas Publishing House, 1971.

Mohan, K.T.J., *Independence To Indira and After*, New Delhi, S Chand & Company, 1977.

Mukherjee, Pranab, *The Dramatic Decade – The Indira Gandhi Years*, New Delhi, Rupa & Co, 2015.

Mukherjee, Rudrangshu (Ed), *Great Speeches of Modern India*, New Delhi, Random House India, 2007.

Naik, J.A., *From Total Revolution To Total Failure*, New Delhi, National Publishing House, 1979.

Narasimhan, V.K., *Democracy Redeemed*, New Delhi, S. Chand & Co, 1977.

Nargolkar, Vasant, *Jayaprakashji Vindicated!*, Part I, Vasant Nargolkar, 1976.

_______, *J.P. Vindicated!*, New Delhi, S. Chand & Company, 1977.

Narayan, Shriman, *Those Ten Months – President's Rule in Gujarat*, Delhi, Vikas Publishing House, 1973.

Nariman, Fali S., 'Fifty Years of the Supreme Court: A Balance Sheet of Performance', *The Indian Advocate*, Vol 29, 1999-2000.

_______, *Before Memory Fades – An Autobiography*, New Delhi, Hay House India, 2010.

Nayar, Kuldip, *India The Critical Years*, New Delhi, Vikas Publications, 1971.

_______, *Supersession of Judges*, New Delhi, Indian Book Company, 1973.

_______, *The Judgement – Inside Story of the Emergency*, New Delhi, Vikas Publishing House, 1977.

Nayar, Kuldip and Singh, Khushwant, *Tragedy of Punjab – Operation Blue Star & After*, New Delhi, Vision Books, 1984.

Nehru, B.K., *Nice Guys Finish Second*, New Delhi, Viking, 1997.

Norman, Dorothy, *Letters to an American Friend – 1950-1984*, New York, Harcourt Brace Jovanovich Publishers, 1985.

Noorani, A.G., *Constitutional Questions in India*, New Delhi, Oxford University Press, 2000.

_______, *Article 370: A Constitutional History of Jammu and Kashmir*, New Delhi, Oxford University Press, 2011.

Palkhivala, N.A., *The Highest Taxed Nation*, Bombay, PC Manaktala & Sons,1965.

_______, *We, the Nation – The Lost Decade*, Bombay, UBS Publishers' Distributors, 1994.

_______, *We, the People*, Bombay, Strand Book Stall, 1994.

Pandit, C.S., *End of an Era – The Rise and Fall of Indira Gandhi*, New Delhi, Allied Publishers, 1977.

Pandya, B.P., Article 356 and Judicial Review, *Indian Journal of Public Administration,* Vol 47, Indian Institute of Public Administration, New Delhi, 2001.

Patel, I.G., *Glimpses of Indian Economic Policy – An Insider's View*, New Delhi, Oxford University Press, 2002.

Perkovich, George, *India's Nuclear Bomb – The Impact on Global*

Proliferation, Berkeley, University of California Press, 1999.

Prime Minister Indira Gandhi Visits USSR, New Delhi, Sovietland Booklets, year of publication not given.

Provisional Parliament Debates, *The Constitution (First Amendment) Bill*, 1951, 16-18 May 1951.

Raghavan, Srinath, *1971: A Global History of the Creation of Bangladesh*, Ranikhet, Permanent Black, 2013.

Rajya Sabha Secretariat, *Rajya Sabha Debates*, Vol 77.2, 1971.

_______, *Rajya Sabha Debates*, Vol 78.2, 1971.

_______, *Rajya Sabha Debates*, Vol 80.2, 1972.

_______, *Rajya Sabha Debates*, Vol 81.2, 1972.

_______, *Rajya Sabha Debates*, Vol 93, 1975.

_______, *Rajya Sabha Debates*, Vol 98, 1976.

Rao, Amiya and Rao, B.G., *Why Emergency – Lies Unmasked*, New Delhi, Printox, 1975.

Rai, Commodore (Retd) Ranjit B., with Chacko, Joseph P., *Warring Nuclear Nations – India and Pakistan*, New Delhi, RR Consultancy, 2014.

Raman, B., *The Kaoboys of R&AW – Down Memory Lane*, New Delhi, Lancer, 2007.

Rao, U.R., *India's Rise as a Space Power*, Delhi, Foundation Books, 2014.

Rawat, Basant and Ramaseshan, Radhika, "Blemish Buried in Buried History", Calcutta, *The Telegraph*, 17 June 2011.

Ray, Lt. Col. M.K. Gupta, *Birth of a Nation*, New Delhi, Har-Anand Publications, 2016.

Reddy, Justice P. Jaganmohan, *The Judiciary I Served*, Hyderabad, Orient Longman, 1991.

Sadhana Vindicated, Abhay Prakashan, Pune, 1976.

Sahgal, Nayantara, *Indira Gandhi's Emergence and Style*, New Delhi, Vikas Publishing House, 1978.

_______, *Indira Gandhi: Her Road to Power*, London, Macdonald & Co, 1983.

Sanajaoba, Naorem (Ed), *Basic Issues on Centre State Relation*, New Delhi, Omsons Publications, 1985.

Sarkar, Bidyut (Ed), *P.N. Haksar – Our Times and The Man*, New Delhi, Allied Publishers, 1989.

Sathe, Vasant, *Towards Social Revolution – A Case for Economic Democracy*, New Delhi, Vikas Publishing House, 1984.

Selbourne, David, *An Eye To India – The Unmasking of a Tyranny*, New York, Penguin Books, 1977.

Sengupta, Barun, *Last Days of Morarji Raj*, Calcutta, Ananda Publishers, 1979.

Sezhiyan, Era, *Shah Commission Report – Lost, and Regained*, Chennai, Aazhi Publishers, 2010.

Shakdhar, S.L. (Ed), *The Constitution and the Parliament in India: The 25 Years of the Republic*, New Delhi, National Publishing House, 1976.

Shah, Justice J.C., *The Rule of Law and the Indian Constitution*, Bombay, NM Tripathi, 1972.

Shah, Amrita, *Vikram Sarabhai – A life*, New Delhi, Penguin/Viking, 2007.

Shankar, Kalyani, *Nixon, Indira And India – Politics and Beyond*, New Delhi, MacMillan Publishers India, 2010.

Shastri, Paromita, What If Indira Gandhi Hadn't been PM? *Outlook*, 23 August 2004.

Shourie, Arun, *Symtoms of Fascism*, New Delhi, Vikas Publishing House, 1978.

_______, "Sloth, Lunacy or Conspiracy?", *Indian Express,* 29 June 1979.

_______, *Institutions in the Janata Phase*, Bombay, Polpular Prakashan, 1980.

_______, *Mrs Gandhi's Second Reign*, New Delhi, Vikas Publishing House, 1983.

_______, *Religion in Politics*, New Delhi, Roli Books International, 1987.

Shourie, Arun, Roy, Prannoy, Bedi, Rahul and Gupta, Shekhar, *The Assassination and After*, New Delhi, Roli Books International, 1985.

Singh, Baldev, Ninth Schedule to Constitution of India: A Study,

Journal of Indian Law Institute, Vol 37, New Delhi, 1995.

Singh, N.K., *The Plain Truth – Memoirs of a CBI Officer*, Delhi, Konark Publishers, 1996.

Singh, Patwant, and Malik, Harji (Ed), *Punjab – The Fatal Miscalculation*, New Delhi, published by Patwant Singh, 1985.

Singh, Tavleen, *Kashmir – A Tragedy of Errors*, New Delhi, Penguin Books, 1976.

Singh, Zail, *Memoirs of Giani Zail Singh, The Seventh President of India*, New Delhi, Har-Anand Publications, 1997.

Sorabjee, Soli J. (Ed), *Law and Justice: An Anthology*, Delhi, Universal Law Publishing Company, 2003.

Sury, M.M. (Ed), *Finance Commissions of India (I to XII) 1952-57 to 2005-10*, New Delhi, Indian Tax Foudation, 2005.

——— (Ed), *Budgets and Budgetary Procedures in India 1947-48 to 2009-10*, New Delhi, New Century Publications, 2009.

Talbott, Strobe, *Engaging India – Diplomacy, Democracy and the Bomb*, New Delhi, Penguin/Viking,2004.

Tandon, B.N., *PMO Diary I: Prelude to the Emergency*, Delhi, Konark Publishers, 2003.

———, *PMO Diary II: The Emergency*, Delhi, Konark Publishers, 2006.

Thakur, Janardan, *All The Prime Minister's Men*, New Delhi, Vikas Publishing House, 1977.

———, *Indira Gandhi and Her Power Game*, Sahibabad, UP, Vikas Publishing House, 1979.

Thapar, Raj, *All These Years – A Memoir*, New Delhi, Seminar Publications, 1991.

The Governor – Sage or Saboteur, New Delhi, Roli Books International, 1985.

Tully, Mark, and Masani Zareer, *From Raj to Rajiv – 40 Years of Indian Independence*, London, BBC Books, 1988.

———, *No Full Stops in India*, New Delhi, Viking/Penguin India, 1991.

United Nations Development Programme, *Human Development Report 2010, The Real Wealth of Nations: Pathways to Human*

Development, New York, Palgrave Mcmillan, 2010.

Unnithan, Sandeep, The Untold Story – The Secret Operation Before Blue Star, New Delhi, *India Today*, 10 February 2014.

Vasudev,Uma, *Two Faces of Indira Gandhi*, New Delhi, Vikas Publishing House, 1977.

Venkataraman, Wing Commander R., *India's Higher Defence – Organisation and Management*, New Delhi, KW Publishers, 2011.

Verghese, B.G. (Ed), *Tomorrow's India – Another Tryst with Destiny*, New Delhi, Penguin/Viking, 2006.

Virmani, Arvind, *Propelling India from Socialist Stagnation to Global Power, Vol 1: Growth Process*, New Delhi, Academic Foundation, 2006.

_______, *Propelling India from Socialist Stagnation to Global Power, Vol 2: Policy Reforms*, New Delhi, Academic Foundation, 2006.

Yadav, R.K., *Mission R&AW*, New Delhi, Manas Publications, 2014.

Yunus, Mohammad, *Persons, Passions and Politics*, New Delhi, Vikas Publishing House, 1980.

Zakaria, Fareed, *The Future of Freedom – Illiberal Democracy At Home and Abroad*, New Delhi, Viking, 2003.

Zaidi, A.M. (Ed), *A Tryst with Destiny – A Study of Congress Economic Policy Resolutions Passed During the Last 100 Years*, New Delhi, Indian Institute of Applied Political Research, 1985.

Index